To Louise

Rescue Warriors

Enjoy the read,

Regards,

[illegible]

6/3/10

Also by David Helvarg

50 Ways to Save the Ocean
The Ocean and Coastal Conservation Guide
Blue Frontier
The War Against the Greens

Rescue Warriors

The U.S. Coast Guard, America's Forgotten Heroes

David Helvarg

THOMAS DUNNE BOOKS
ST. MARTIN'S GRIFFIN NEW YORK

THOMAS DUNNE BOOKS.
An imprint of St. Martin's Press.

Printed in the United States of America. For information, address St. Martin's Press,
175 Fifth Avenue, New York, N.Y. 10010.

Photographs on pages 1, 57, 77, 101, 153, 173, 225, 279, and 307 courtesy of the United States Coast Guard.
Photo credits as follows: NyxoLyno Cangemi (1); Tom Gillespie (57); Tom Sperduto (77, 173); Adam Eggers (101); Jeffrey Pollinger (153); Mark Jones (225); Mark Piber (307).
Photographs on pages 31, 127, 197, and 249 by David Helvarg. Courtesy of the author.

Design by William Ruoto

THE LIBRARY OF CONGRESS HAS CATALOGED THE HARDCOVER EDITION AS FOLLOWS:

Helvarg, David, 1951–
Rescue warriors : the U.S. Coast Guard, America's forgotten heroes / David Helvarg.—1st ed.
p. cm.
Includes bibliographical references and index.
ISBN 978-0-312-36372-7
1. United States. Coast Guard—History. 2. United States. Coast Guard—Biography. 3. Heroes—United States—Biography. 4. Rescues—United States—History. 5. Lifesaving—United States—History. I. Title.
VG53.H45 2009
363.28'60973—dc22

2008044633

ISBN 978-0-312-62814-7 (trade paperback)

First St. Martin's Griffin Edition: May 2010

10 9 8 7 6 5 4 3 2 1

To the Guardians who've crossed over the bar,
"so that others may live,"

and to my own departed, who continue to inspire me
to do good work:

Eva Lee (Helvarg)
Max Helvarg
Richard Cross
John Hoagland
Nancy Ledansky
Deborah Helvarg

CONTENTS

ACKNOWLEDGMENTS

In the wake of 2005's Hurricane Katrina, during which the Coast Guard saved over thirty-three thousand lives, *Time* magazine dubbed it "the little service that could," and I was able to convince my agent, Kevan Lyon of the Sandra Dykstra Literary Agency, that this was a story that could engage anyone who's ever walked a beach, sailed an ocean, or felt the unnerving tug of an undertow. Living by the beach in Del Mar with a daughter who surfs, she got the idea pretty quick. She also proved to be a helpful reader and critic throughout the process.

Sitting in his prow-like office in the famed Flatiron Building in New York, publisher Tom Dunne indicated that he recognizes a good story when he hears one but would rather see it written down. When family loss and work conflicts caused me to ask for a deadline delay, Tom proved both tolerant and gracious. Editor Joel Ariaratnam also proved to be an engaging and insightful reviewer and critic of my work in progress.

The Coast Guard gave me tremendous access to its people, stations, boats, cutters, and aircraft in more than a dozen states, including Alaska and Hawaii, as well as Washington, DC, Bahrain, and the North Arabian Gulf.

In addition I traveled with and spoke at some length to more than four hundred active-duty and reserve members of the service, from trainee recruits to Commandant Thad Allen. I regret I was unable to incorporate all their tales of human and physical adventure into one volume. I just didn't have the heart to kill as many trees as would be necessary to begin to tell the full story of America's Rescue Warriors.

Given the rapid change in rank and postings among this smallest of the armed services, I've chosen to identify active-duty people by their rank and location at the time I interviewed them between 2005 and 2008 rather than try to update the reader with career minutiae that could only be of interest to their parents, spouses, and service detailers. Again, my apologies to any captain who's now an admiral, E-6 who's since made chief, or retired lieutenant commander now running a dive charter in the South Pacific.

I did find the public affairs specialists of the Coast Guard, both full-timers and those for whom it's collateral duty, to be genuinely helpful and professional, unlike some other military services, companies, and agencies I've dealt with. Among those who tolerated me over time are Commander Andrea Palermo in DC and Dan Dewell in California. Also thanks to Joe Bowes and brothers Jim and Brendan McPherson at headquarters, Bill Carson in Cape May, Dave French at the academy, Jim McGranachan in New York, Dan Molthen in North Carolina, Marsha Delaney in Hawaii, Rachel Behrens in Bahrain, and Kurt Fredrickson, Richard Brahm, and Steve Bonn in Kodiak. Coast Guard historian Dr. Robert Browning and his staff at headquarters were also more than tolerant and props to Chief Kimberly Smith for helping us find our photos.

To all the mariners, watchdogs, public servants, sailors, fishermen, and other informed sources who helped provide me varied perspectives for this work, I'm sorry I can't individually acknowledge each of you for your time, knowledge, and considered opinion. Some of you are probably just as glad I can't.

While many contributed to this book, any faults, errors, and omissions are, of course, the copyeditor's. No, only kidding. They'd be mine, though hopefully they're not here. I should also demur with a quote from Richard Henry Dana Jr., who at the conclusion of his nonfiction work *Two Years Before the Mast*, published in 1840, wrote, "Whatever attention this book may gain, and whatever favor it may find, I shall owe almost entirely to that interest in the sea, and those who follow it, which is so easily excited in us all."

INTRODUCTION

You Have to Go Out

I was riding with another Coast Guard crew, this time in the air rather than on the sea, though they could be anywhere that's close to water. Our orange HH-65 Dolphin helicopter landed in the rain, and Art Vega, the mechanic and rescue hoist operator, jumped out and did his walkaround under the still-turning rotor blades. On the left side he saw the four-foot by two-and-a-half-foot engine cowling gone and the shrapnel holes it had left in the rear stabilizer and thought, "It's amazing we're still alive."

With additional nicks and scratches on the rotor blades, it was also amazing none of us had felt anything while flying over Texas from Air Station Houston to Corpus Christi at 150 knots during the Coast Guard response to Hurricane Ike. We'd done some aggressive maneuvering, banking 45 degrees in tight circles over a 25-foot boat floating upside down off the storm-battered city of Galveston and then circling to check out what looked like a body in the sand but turned out to be marine debris near a navigation buoy that had been pushed ashore.

"We were probably descending when it happened," Lt. Ed Aponte, the twenty-nine-year-old pilot and aircraft commander, speculated, staring at the damaged tail stabilizer. "We were very, very lucky. It's pure luck we didn't crash." Then he asked me to take a picture of him and his three crewmates standing by their helicopter.

Despite a bad habit of having its side door pop off in midflight, the Dolphin tends to be a very forgiving aircraft, although ten days earlier, on September 4, 2008, a crew of four had died when another Coast Guard 65 crashed during a training mission off Honolulu. I'd been on Oahu at the time and was surprised when I got back to the mainland to find little or no national coverage of the accident. I figure the least people who go into harm's way to help others deserve is that we remember their names. Their names were Thomas Nelson, forty-two, Andrew Wischmeier, forty-four, David Skimin, thirty-eight, and Joshua Nichols, twenty-seven.

In 2008, as in 2004 and 2005, the hurricane season was an active one. While I'd been in Hawaii, Gustav had threatened New Orleans with another Katrina-like disaster before weakening and making landfall west of the city.

Now Hurricane Ike had blown up into a nine-hundred-mile-wide monster threatening Texas. On Friday, September 12, I drove from my home in the San Francisco Bay Area to Air Station Sacramento, where a big four-prop C-130 Hercules was standing by to take two helicopter replacement crews from San Francisco and Humboldt Bay to Texas; Ike was expected to strike there within twelve hours. I arrived at the station gate as they were holding a memorial service for their fallen aviators in Hawaii.

A year later one of their own C-130 crews of seven, along with the two Marine aviators, would be killed when their aircraft collided off the coast of Southern California in a more widely reported incident. The Marines were on a training mission in a Cobra helicopter. The C-130 was, not surprisingly, involved in a search and rescue mission for a missing boater. The Coast Guard continued to search for the lost boater even as they sought to recover their own dead—Che Barnes, 35; Adam Bryant, 28; John Seidman, 43; Carl Grigonis, 35; Monica Beacham, 29; Jason Moletzsky, 26; and Danny Kreder, 22.

But on that day I showed up in 2008 they had little time for their memorial service. Within two hours we were airborne, landing at Air Station Corpus Christi, 180 miles south of the Galveston/Houston area, about an hour before Ike hit there as a Category 2 at 2:00 A.M.

Early Saturday morning a Falcon jet took off from Corpus, flying into 50-knot winds, to get survey video of the flooded coast. They also launched five of their small 65s on SAR—search and rescue—missions. A short time later I flew on a second Falcon to Houston. We flew over the battered and flooded coastline past Galveston. Unlike on the Mississippi coast after Katrina, most houses here and in other hard-hit areas [excepting the Bolivar Peninsula] were still standing. We passed over Galveston Bay, a few small oil slicks and a Coast Guard buoy tender heading out from its boat station, where all the cars in the parking lot were piled on top of each other like Matchbox toys. 90 percent of the navigational buoys in the Houston Ship Channel were lost to the storm and would have to be replaced in order to restore maritime commerce.

When we landed at Air Station Houston at Ellington Field, there was no power or water, and a couple of NASA hangers had collapsed. There were Coast Guard fuel trucks and cots, however, and by the end of the hot, muggy day the "Coasties" had rescued over a hundred people and a dozen pets and begun transitioning from SAR to medical evacuations and survey missions. Coast Guard small boats were also operating in flooded communities from Sabine Pass, Texas, up to Louisiana and Arkansas.

Capt. Bill Diehl, a slim guy with a gray crew cut and sharp blue eyes, was running the frontline response from Houston, where they'd suffered moderate wind damage and a citywide blackout. Earlier Saturday he'd gotten some big tugboats to help prevent a 680-foot bulk carrier that lost power from running into the 610 highway bridge. The C-130 Herc I'd come in on was now tasked to fly over the offshore oil rigs with a safety officer and look for damage. At least half a million gallons of crude oil would spill in and around the Gulf of Mexico as a result of the storm.

On Sunday I flew with them to Mobile, Alabama, to pick up a Ford Expedition, extra water, and a crew from the Gulf Coast Strike Team, one of the Coast Guard's environmental response units. Their team leader, Cdr. Virginia Kammer, told me that most of Houston's petrochemical complexes were undamaged, but a fertilizer plant had sprung a leak, and there were other reports of hazardous spills to investigate.

We flew them back to Houston, where things were now jumping. C-17 cargo planes were unloading, a bigger Coast Guard Jayhawk was on the flight line with the 65s, and TV cameras were rolling as the secretary of homeland security got off a Customs helicopter and onto his personal jet a day ahead of the president's visit. A minute later an F-16 fighter jet screamed off the runway.

Despite some fifteen deaths in the first days alone, billions of dollars in damage, and some three million people who were without power, I thought Ike was more of a mess than a national disaster, an assessment Captain Diehl agreed with. A lot of the cleanup and recovery to come would take place on barrier islands where people had built stilt houses on concrete pads on the sand and then ignored evacuation orders. Few of them died because Ike wasn't all it might have been and God loves fools.

Along with hurricane response, I've also had the chance to see the Coast Guard perform many of its other maritime missions. I've been fortunate in never having to be a "customer" of their search and rescue service, but a few of my friends have been.

"It was a bit like being in a car parked on a train track when suddenly a train piles into the side of you," Roz Savage says, recalling the moment a wave capsized her partially enclosed 23-foot rowboat 140 miles off the coast of California. "There's this huge shock wave through the boat and the boat's hitting and hitting and hitting and you are bouncing off the wall and all the objects in the cabin that aren't tied down are flying around you and you are hoping that you remembered to stow everything that's sharp! Eventually the boat comes to rest and you are lying on [strapped to] the ceiling hoping you closed all the vents and hatches and that the boat's going to come the right way up again and you hold your breath, and it seems like a long time but eventually, slowly, it starts to roll back into position and everything that was flying clockwise before is now flying counterclockwise, but of course it doesn't end up where it started out."

It would be another two days, August 23, 2007, before my environmental project was rescued by my book project. The Blue Frontier Campaign, a nonprofit group I founded based on an earlier book, works for the protection of our public seas. One of our projects was Roz's quest to become the first woman to row solo across the Pacific. She was doing this to raise awareness of our oceans at risk, though now it was the plucky, slight thirty-nine-year-old Englishwoman who was at risk. The year before, she had rowed across the Atlantic. In July '07, we'd held a launch party for her new trip by San Francisco's Golden Gate, but the onshore winds wouldn't let up for a month, and when she finally did launch from farther north, they held her close to the coastline for over a week before a storm came on her. Her rowboat, the *Brocade,* capsized a second time that Tuesday.

On Wednesday she had a new experience. "A powerful wave rear-ended my boat. I shot down my bunk, my sleeping bag tobogganing over the slippery vinyl of the mattress. I came to an abrupt halt when my skull collided with the wall at the end of the cabin. I sat up. Blood trickled down my face. I explored the damage with my fingers. It didn't seem too bad. I dabbed the blood away with a washcloth and lay back down on my bunk to try to sleep."

Unfortunately, sleep would be denied her. The boat capsized yet again after the sea anchor that kept it facing into the waves tore away. Again she banged her head. She also lost the restraining straps that kept her secured to the floor, along with her GPS and other external communications masts. When she went outside on her safety line to check on the missing sea anchor, she was inundated by a huge ice-cold wave.

She then got on her satellite phone to discuss her situation with her land crew and Hawaii-based weather guy, still convinced she could "tough it out." Someone decided to report her predicament to the Coast Guard, however.

Soon a big Coast Guard C-130 prop plane from Sacramento was flying overhead, and a 576-foot tanker, the *Overseas Long Beach,* had been diverted to her side. The ship, part of the Coast Guard–administered Amver (automated mutual-assistance vessel rescue) system, provided her some leeward shelter from the rough seas while also trying to get her a new sea anchor without coming so close as to swamp her.

Eventually they were able to toss one down to her, but it didn't work when she deployed it. Meanwhile the C-130, low on fuel, had to return to base to be replaced by a second aircraft. An 87-foot Coast Guard cutter, the *Dorado,* also set out to meet her but was forced to turn back due to worsening weather.

While she discussed her situation with the Coasties through much of Thursday, her rowboat was rapidly drifting out of the 150-mile range of their HH-65 Dolphin rescue helicopter waiting to be launched from the Humboldt Bay Air Station.

Later I spoke with Lt. Steve Baxter, the pilot who eventually picked her up.

"You're a friend of hers?" he asks.

"Yup."

"She's interesting, to say the least," he notes with wry amusement. "About 5:00 P.M. we expressed to her how important it was to 'raise yer hand now before the weather gets really snotty.' The straps that kept her comfy had broken, and she'd lost her drogue and sea anchor and bonked her head, and there were 15-foot seas with maybe 20-foot swells and winds at 35 to 40 knots and it was forecast to get worse over the next 96 hours—so that probably played a role in her decision [to be rescued]. We [flew out and] got on scene with about 20 minutes of light left. We lowered the swimmer in the water. She got in the water, and he put a strop [rescue sling] around her."

"They give me instructions to put on my immersion [survival] suit and jump in the water so the swimmer could attach me to a winch," Roz recalls. "So I'm sidling over the side and have a life ring from the tanker under my armpit and a [waterproof] pelican case off my hip, and the immersion suit is a hundred sizes too big with the feet flapping off me. I wallow toward the swimmer, and the *Brocade* seems to want to follow me. The wind is blowing her almost over on top of me, and he hitches me up to this hook and makes me let go of the life ring, and after a long time the line goes taut. As they're hoisting me into the helicopter, I look down on my boat, and she gets smaller and smaller. I felt horrible leaving her behind. It might be the correct and sensible thing to do, but I just hated being rescued, even though these were great guys, really nice, sweet guys, who did their job well and professionally."

Roz did almost everything right in preparing for her journey, which is why she lived to try again in 2008, becoming the first woman to row solo from San Francisco to Hawaii, the first leg of her quest. As the old salts say, though, "What the sea wants, the sea will have."

The oceans that cover 71 percent of our blue planet's surface are a rougher, more challenging frontier than any encountered by terrestrial or space explorers. The seas pummel us with an unbreathable and corrosive liquid medium, altered visual and acoustic characteristics, changing temperatures, depths, and pressures, upwellings, tides, currents, wild animals, shifting chemistry, sudden storms, and towering waves. The ocean is both the crucible of three billion years of evolutionary life and the generator of great tempests that can devastate our coastlines. It is the driver of climate, weather, rain, and snow, a source of recreation, transportation, energy, protein, security, and endless poetic wonder. The ocean's blank indifference to human endeavor also makes it awesome, inspiring, and deadly in ways few of us fully comprehend.

Among those who come close are people like Lt. Steve Baxter, Lt. JG Kevin Winters, Aviation Mechanic Second Class Jason Bauer, and Aviation Survival Technician (rescue swimmer) Chief Chuck Wolfe, who flew the mission to rescue Roz with the support of their operations center staff, two C-130 aircrews, and the crew of the cutter *Dorado*. They are among some forty-two thousand active members and eight thousand reservists of the U.S. Coast Guard.

Unfortunately, not all their search and rescue efforts go so well. My friend David Guggenheim is a widely respected marine explorer, conservationist, and licensed pilot of deep-diving research submersibles.

In the summer of 2007, this short, wiry scientist with a closely trimmed salt-and-pepper beard led a dive expedition into the unexplored Pribilof Canyon in the Bering Sea off Alaska, discovering hitherto unknown deep-water coral and sponge gardens amid swarms of aggressive squid fifteen hundred feet below the surface. In 2008 he continued his long-term efforts to identify and protect pristine reefs, mangroves, and turtle-breeding beaches along the Gulf Coast of Cuba.

Thirty-three years earlier, on November 28, 1976, he'd been a freshman at the University of Pennsylvania. "It was a miserable, cold, foggy, rainy, raw-to-the-bone day, and my dad [William L. Guggenheim] had gone fishing for stripers in Delaware Bay," he recalls. "I decided to be with my girlfriend that day, and everyone he asked had a different reason, so he went by himself. We had a 23-foot SeaCraft with twin 150 Mercurys, which were big [outboard] motors back then, and that boat was his pride.

"When I got back to my dorm room later, the phone was ringing. It was my mom, who was really worried. It was dark and he wasn't home. He usually called when he was off the water. So I said I'd call the Coast Guard and called the Cape May [New Jersey] station and said, 'My father's overdue. He's been fishing in Delaware Bay, and his boat registration number'—I still remember it—'DL111G.' As I was reading it off, the guy was saying it with me, '111 Gulf,' like he already knew the number, and that's when I knew this was something pretty serious.

"He said, 'Yes, sir, the Cape May–Lewes Ferry captain radioed in that he saw a vessel going in circles with no one aboard and a fishing line in the water.' It was about three miles from shore, and they were going out to recover the boat. This was the end of November, and the water [temperature] was in the forties. I had to get home by trolley, bus, and subway. My mother and brother and some family friends were all there, as well as 'Uncle Phil' and his wife, Elaine. I wanted to drive down but they said they would.

"We drove down in the rain, and it was after midnight, and they were just bringing the boat in. Later, looking at the depth chart, I could tell that at one point he was in very shallow water—probably trolling on Prissy Wicks Shoal, where there are a lot of fish, but it's a difficult place because of the chop and currents. I think he was setting the second line and got catapulted over the back.

"After waiting around a while, the rest of them went home and left me to keep watch as the Coast Guard did their search and rescue. I didn't have a place to stay. I just sat on some vinyl bench at three in the morning, and these guys would stop to say hello and talk to me. It was something I needed. They brought me a blanket to let me sleep on that bench. They also got me water and told me they'd have helicopters up the next morning at first light and not to worry, but at first light it was so foggy you couldn't see anything. They brought me food and coffee. It wasn't till the afternoon the helicopters could go up, but they didn't see a thing.

"It was clear he couldn't have survived, so, maybe it was the next day, I got his car and went up the beach and walked along the edge looking out, and I could see these guys were still at it. My perception as an eighteen-year-old kid was these guys were doing a major military operation with all this radio chatter and helicopters and boats for two days, and I couldn't believe all these people were working so hard for us even though it was a lost cause."

He pauses to have a gulp of his mojito in the D.C. bar where we're meeting. He stares at his drink but is really looking back at a hole punched in his heart more than three decades ago.

"They stayed in touch for a year or so just to check in to say if they found anything. They understood how, with no body recovered, how hard it is to lay things to rest. They found a skull two years later off Cape May, but it was of a younger person [his dad was forty-nine]. My brother and I are now resigned to not having that closure.

"Later I became a marine biologist, a scuba diver, a lot of things my dad would have enjoyed. At the synagogue I gave a eulogy, and I said I didn't want people to hate the ocean. It was the place we could be father and son together. It was the place he loved."

As for the Coast Guard, "Thirty years later I still remember their professionalism and how human they were to me. It wasn't a phony humanism. It was real."

Every day the U.S. Coast Guard responds to 123 distress calls for help and rescues some fourteen people who could tell you stories just like Roz's and David's.

The Coast Guard claims to have saved over 1.1 million lives since its founding more than two hundred years ago. It's even hung a banner to that effect on its boxy faded blue headquarters building at Buzzards Point in a run-down waterfront section of Washington, DC. Of course, that 1.1 million figure includes some 350,000 illegal migrants it's taken off the water, mostly Cubans, Dominicans, Haitians, and Chinese, who are generally not too pleased to see the white-hulled cutters of the Coast Guard unless they are in the actual process of capsizing and drowning.

So let's say the real number is closer to three-quarters of a million people saved. That's still a lot of lives saved, a lot of mothers, fathers, sisters, and brothers who made it back to shore alive thanks to America's Rescue Warriors.

So why have there been more books, movies, Web sites, and articles about the U.S. Marines, Navy, even Navy SEALs, than about America's preeminent lifesavers and multimission maritime service? What makes uniformed services that kill people seem more interesting than those whose primary mission is to save lives?

For thousands of years, warfare has been the main rite of passage by which young men proved themselves as warriors and heroes and, if they survived, went on to become the leaders of their clans, tribes, and nations.

Today, given the social and economic interdependence of an increasingly crowded planet, and faced with growing impacts from environmental disasters including extreme weather events linked to climate change, terrorism, droughts, bombings, migrant surges, industrial poisonings, and pandemics, we may be seeing the emergence of an alternative role model for our youth.

In the future our warriors, heroes, and leaders may more often arise from the ranks of young women and men willing to go in harm's way to confront a wide but unknowable range of catastrophes in unusual and dangerous settings on a planet that's more than two-thirds saltwater. That, to me, sounds very much like the definition of a "Coastie," a member of the United States Coast Guard.

Tracing its origins back to the earliest days of the republic (1789 or 1790, depending on whether you prefer lighthouses or wooden boats), today's Coast Guard has evolved into a service that, despite limited resources and overworked vessels and aircraft, seems genetically unable to decline any job involving moving bodies of water, be they fresh, brackish, or salty.

In addition to saving lives, the Coast Guard:

- conducts port and waterfront security patrols
- directs port traffic
- responds to water pollution and oil spills
- seizes illegal drugs and migrants at sea
- regulates and inspects recreational, commercial, and fishing vessels, as well as U.S.-flagged vessels under construction
- inspects offshore energy production and delivery facilities
- enforces fishing regulations and marine mammal protection laws
- investigates maritime and bridge accidents
- licenses mariners
- maintains and repairs buoys, lighthouses, and other vital aids to navigation
- provides boating safety courses to the public, largely through its volunteer auxiliary
- trains and works with foreign coast guards

- fights in foreign wars
- carries out icebreaking operations at both poles and on the Great Lakes
- supports scientific research at sea
- does whatever other jobs it's called upon to do in order to guarantee the safety, security, and stewardship of America's blue frontier

The Coast Guard's unofficial slogan used to be "You have to go out, but you don't have to come back." Today it takes a more measured approach to its search and rescue efforts, tempering its historic tendency toward iron-willed recklessness with a mission-based risk-assessment calculus married to constant on-the-job training.

As a result, Coast Guard men and women can do things like drop a rescue swimmer from a helicopter into a raging ocean as the pilot, flying blind to the action, trusts his or her winch mechanic to avoid ensnaring them in the wildly gyrating rigging, mast, or superstructure of a sinking vessel. Qualified surfmen can tow sailors out of harm's way in thirty-foot seas and fifty-knot howling winds or dash into big shorebreak to rescue a drowning surfer or kayaker without bottoming out and smashing their surfboat onto the rocks and sand. In places like New Orleans after Hurricane Katrina, they were able to repeat this type of "evolution," or task, for days on end, entrusting their lives to different people on different days thanks to their standardized training and practiced ability to surge resources almost anywhere needed or else improvise solutions on the spot.

"The normal average Coastie's attitude is 'I don't know how I can get it done, but I know I can do it, it's just figuring it out,' " explains Chief Warrant Officer David Lewald, one of the heroes of Katrina.

Of course, there are also bound to be problems in a service that has been perennially shortchanged financially, prey to the whims of Washington politicians, and the recent poster-child for contractor malfeasance in a fleet expansion program that left the sea lions guarding the salmon pens. Historically the Coast Guard has been shuffled between various government departments, most recently in 2003 when it moved from the Department of Transportation to the massive new Department of Homeland Security, whose short history of dysfunctional behaviors would embarrass a Jerry Springer or a Dr. Phil.

In addition, by September 11, 2001, the Coast Guard had gone through a decade of funding cutbacks and "streamlining" and was about to see another 10 percent hit on its budget. Coast Guard Commandant Adm. James Loy warned that the service, famed for "doing more with less," was at risk of becoming a "dull knife."

Since the Al Qaeda attacks of 9/11, the Coast Guard has seen its budget grow from $5 billion to $9 billion, but much of that has been for security-related functions and counterterrorism. There has been little parallel growth in its marine safety and environmental protection missions, whose historic core competencies have now been put at risk.

"We shifted assets to security, and we've failed to keep pace on the safety and environmental side," Adm. Craig Bone, commander of Coast Guard District 11 in Alameda, California, told me a few hours after a container ship hit the San Francisco Bay Bridge in late 2007, spilling fifty-three thousand gallons of toxic bunker fuel and inspiring widespread criticism of the Coast Guard's response.

At the same time, the Coast Guard opened up a new rescue station in Barrow, Alaska, to respond to increased maritime traffic on the Arctic Ocean, where climate change is turning the once icebound Northwest Passage into a viable shipping route and creating a fifth U.S. blue-water coastline for the service to guard.

To meet all its mission demands effectively, the Coast Guard will probably have to double in size and funding over the next decade and then double again by 2030 until it is closer in size to the U.S. Marine Corps than to the NYPD. This, of course, will be a hard thing to make happen in hard times, especially for a service that doesn't have many champions in Congress or the executive branch.

Still, despite many serious challenges, it's almost counterintuitive that what I discovered in reporting on the U.S. Coast Guard is a part of government that *works*. In terms of value per taxpayer dollar, it's up there with public libraries, national parks, water reservoirs, fire departments, and Fourth of July fireworks.

I first sensed I could write a good in-depth book on the Coast Guard while reporting from the post-Katrina hurricane disaster zone in the fall of 2005. As I traveled the devastated Gulf region, I made several calls to their 8th District Headquarters—which covers the Mississippi River basin and had relocated from New Orleans to St. Louis—to see if I could get onto the Coast Guard air station south of the flooded city. In the past, when working on stories involving the Navy, I'd always had to go through the Pentagon chain of command and sometimes wait as long as six months to get approval for interviews or air station or shipboard visits.

When I finally got through to St. Louis, however, the Coast Guard lieutenant at the other end of the line wondered why I didn't just go down to the station and ask at the gate for whoever was doing public affairs that day. He gave me directions. The PAO (public affairs officer) at the battered air station, which looked like a combination combat airstrip and refugee camp, buzzed me in, pointed me to the hangers, and apologized that she was too busy to escort me. In short order I was doing interviews, walking the flight line, and getting offers to fly over some damaged oil rigs.

What impressed me most that day was finding a military service that allows its people not only to act on their own but also to speak for themselves. Adm. Thad Allen, Coast Guard commandant from 2006 to 2010, insists that "total transparency breeds self-correcting behavior." He argues that because the Coast Guard has to work with the public and various maritime stakeholders every day of the year, it can't be operationally effective unless it's open and aboveboard in ways that would scare the security briefs off the other armed services.

So I was given an unprecedented amount of access for this book that I may have abused—only in the sense that I probably rode more rigid-hull inflatables, cutters, surfboats, fixed-wing aircraft, and helicopters than was absolutely necessary to complete it. On the other hand, how could I describe the mix of altruism and adrenaline that inspires so many Coasties if I didn't get out there and ride along with them?

Like most Americans, particularly the 53 percent of us who live within fifty miles of a coastline, I've always had some awareness of the U.S. Coast Guard and the fact that it works to save sailors in distress.

During seven years living on a cliff in San Diego, I'd been witness to and peripherally helped out in several rescues, including one with local lifeguards and a Coast Guard helicopter standing by. I've gone through Coast Guard safety inspections on friends' boats that sometimes seemed too exacting and heard more than one commercial fisherman complain about its enforcement of fishing and safety rules. I've heard environmentalists complain about its slowness to establish and enforce pollution regulations. I'd even heard some Navy folks speak less than respectfully of their fellow sea service.

For all that, I don't know of a waterman or woman, mariner, or sailor who doesn't feel a bit safer catching sight of the white and orange of a passing Coast Guard cutter or aircraft.

The men and women of the Coast Guard are the police, the frontier marshals, and the fire department of America's wild oceans, and like the heroes of our last great wilderness, theirs is a story as large and varied as the vast, often lawless waters they patrol.

Rescue Warriors

CHAPTER 1

New Orleans Saints

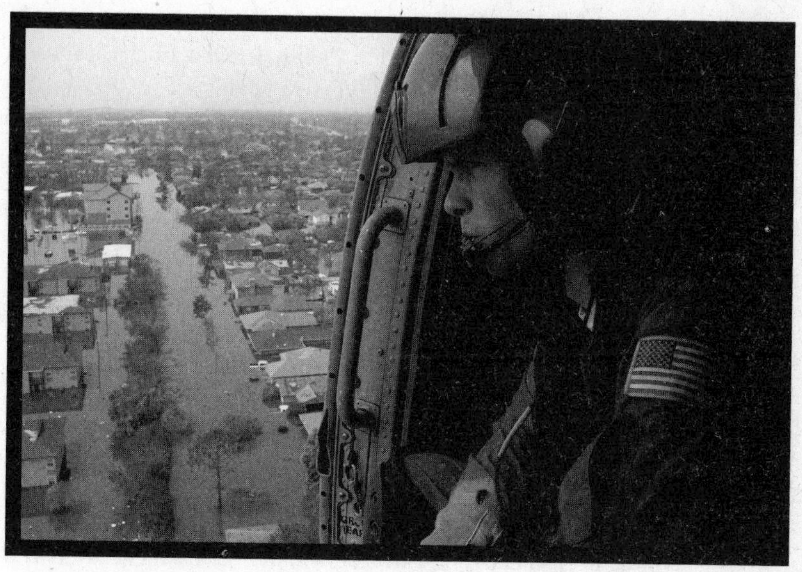

"They didn't wear their humanity on their patches, it was in their hearts."
—DOUGLAS BRINKLEY, *THE GREAT DELUGE*

"I'd blow up FEMA and ask the Coast Guard what it needs."
—ST. BERNARD PARISH SHERIFF JACK STEPHENS WHEN ASKED HOW TO IMPROVE THE FEDERAL EMERGENCY RESPONSE SYSTEM

Friday, August 26, 2005

The crew of the fishing boat *Mary Lynn* pitched and rolled in raging forty-foot seas, eighty-five miles west of Key West. With their controls gone and their vessel threatening to break up, they activated an EPIRB (emergency position-indicating radio beacon) buoy and hoped someone would hear its signal. They tried to launch a life raft, but the storm winds capsized it and dragged it away. All they could do now was hang on and pray for help.

At Coast Guard Air Station Clearwater, 210 miles away, their signal was received and an HH-60 Jayhawk helicopter launched in forty-knot winds around 10:00 P.M. Soon the big chopper was flying along the leading edge of the storm, blinded by heavy rains, clouds, and darkness, its crew unable to see the ocean rising and falling below them. It would take three hours of manhandling their aircraft through buffeting winds and ballistic rain before they finally arrived on scene. A big four-engine C-130 Hercules from Clearwater was already circling overhead.

Unfortunately, the rough trek had depleted the helicopter's fuel supply, leaving them only fifteen minutes on scene. Below they could see the *Mary Lynn* being tossed around in the rolling seas as the crew clung to the stern. Rather than try to rush things and risk someone being swept away, they decided to head to Key West to refuel. Battling 75 mph headwinds, the trip, which should have taken forty-five minutes, took two hours. They landed at 3:00 A.M., refueled, and were back over the *Mary Lynn* at daybreak. If anything, the storm had worsened in their absence. Pilot Craig Massello told Rescue Swimmer Kenyon Bolton that he was not to come off the rescue cable for any reason. This meant the boat crew would have to get in the water to meet him.

"The first hoist wasn't pretty," flight mechanic and hoist operator Robert Cain noted dryly. First they swung Bolton into the stern of the fishing boat, and then, as he came free, dangling like bait on a line, he was hit head-on by a monster wave. Still he managed to get in the water and swim to crewmember Anita Miller. He got a quick strop harness around her, but then the cable jerked them, dropping the strop's V-rings and jamming his hook open. He replaced the rings and made sure he had a tight grip on her, then got them lifted back aboard the helicopter and determined that his cable hook, though damaged, was still operable. He went back down for his second hoist. This time a lifeline from the foundering boat to the second crewmember in the water got entangled with the hoist cable. This was even less pretty. Were the boat to sink at this point, it could drag the survivor, the rescue swimmer, even the helicopter down with it. While Bolton and the fisherman remaining on the *Mary Lynn* worked to free the line, a shark two or three feet long swam through Bolton's legs. "I was surprised it was so close to the surface. . . . It made me think twice about what was out of sight," he later told *Coast Guard* magazine.

With the lines cleared, he was able to make the second hoist. The third hoist went without a hitch (or much of a functioning hook). The entire rescue took around thirty minutes. Rather than fight the winds to Key West, they headed toward Clearwater. With cyclonic tailwinds, they made around two hundred knots ground speed, "ridiculous for a helicopter," grinned copilot

Dave Sheppard who, like the rest of the crew, was now riding an adrenaline high.

The storm, which had already battered Florida, leaving six dead, would continue to pick up strength as it crossed the unusually warm waters of the Gulf of Mexico. The survivors of the *Mary Lynn*—Mark Gutek, Anita Miller, and Charles White—would be the first three of over thirty-three thousand people to be rescued by the U.S. Coast Guard in the coming days as Hurricane Katrina continued on toward the Mississippi Gulf Coast, New Orleans, and the history books.

More than two years earlier, on February 25, 2003, the Coast Guard had transferred from the Department of Transportation to the newly created Department of Homeland Security (DHS), as part of the Bush administration's post-9/11 "War on Terror." The administration had initially opposed the creation of what would quickly grow into a 22-agency, $40 billion, 180,000-employee color-coding bureaucracy. It was only when (then) Democratic Senator Joseph Lieberman of Connecticut introduced a bill for its creation that the White House, fearing it was being politically outflanked on national security, did an about-face and came up with an improvised plan for the new department.

When it was announced that the Coast Guard would be a part of DHS, its friends in Congress, including Senators Ted Stevens of Alaska and Olympia Snowe of Maine, got a provision attached to the Homeland Security Act, section 888, preventing the new department from interfering with the Coast Guard's maritime missions. Admiral Allen, who would take over Hurricane Katrina response before becoming head of the service, jokingly told *Washington Post* reporter Michael Grunwald that the Coast Guard's leadership had "888" tattooed on their arms.

Unfortunately, the Federal Emergency Management Agency (FEMA) had no such immunity. It was demoted within the new department and had billions of dollars of preparedness funding stripped away, along with a national disaster response plan. At the same time, a system of political cronyism had grown within the demoralized agency, with five of its top eight managers, including director Michael Brown (a former commissioner with the International Arabian Horse Association), having no previous disaster response experience.

The Coast Guard, by contrast, spends every day saving people in trouble in the water. As both a law enforcement and military organization tasked to do search and rescue, environmental response, and maritime commerce support, it didn't have to wait for an official disaster decree or federal letter of permit to do its job.

Nor, unlike President George W. Bush and Secretary of Homeland Security Michael Chertoff, did any Coast Guard officer claim the failure of New Orleans's levees could not have been predicted or a disaster of this scale foreseen. The Coast Guard had spent much of 2004 responding to a series of major hurricanes in Florida and along the Gulf and was keenly aware from its oversight of ports and shipping along the lower Mississippi of just how vulnerable the below-sea-level city of New Orleans was. If there were any doubt left, FEMA had staged a major interagency exercise to practice for just this type of disaster, dubbed "Hurricane Pam," a year before Katrina struck.

On the day of the *Mary Lynn* rescue, Friday, August 26, 2005, the National Hurricane Center announced Katrina had regained hurricane strength and shifted its track from a predicted landfall on the Florida panhandle to the Mississippi-Louisiana coastline.

That afternoon, Chief Warrant Officer David Lewald got a call at his home in Bay St. Louis, Mississippi, from his Coast Guard boss in New Orleans. Rebuilding of navigational buoys damaged by Hurricanes Cindy and Dennis had just been completed, and in 2004 there had been Hurricane Ivan. "I remember after Ivan thinking, 'Wow! If I lived through that I can do anything,' not realizing it was just a dress rehearsal," Lewald recalls.

Lewald was in charge of the cutter *Pamlico,* a 160-foot construction tender that looks like what you'd get if you crossbred a tugboat, a barge, and the *Mississippi Queen* riverboat. His boss wanted the *Pamlico* to escort their smaller boats upriver.

"One of our duties is to play mother duck to all the boats they can't trailer away. So for Katrina I had eight 41s [41-foot patrol boats], three 55s, and the *Clamp*."

The Coast Guard Cutter *Clamp* is a 75-foot construction tender designed to push a 68-foot barge. It was transiting from Alabama to Texas when a generator fire broke out and forced it to divert to New Orleans for repairs in late

August. As Katrina approached, the *Clamp* headed up the Mississippi with the *Pamlico*.

By end of day Friday, most personnel from Air Station New Orleans, Sector New Orleans, and Coast Guard District 8 had done their usual hurricane evacuations and were hunkered down from Texas to Missouri ready to surge back in as soon as the storm passed over.

New Orleans's shore command had just stood up its sector on August 14. This was a new approach to integrating Coast Guard activities previously divided between Marine Safety and Operations. It established a single sector commander who could move boats and aircraft, and oversee search and rescue, pollution response, maritime safety, and shipping control without having to book a conference room to do it.

Instead the new commander, Capt. Frank Paskewich, booked a convention center in Alexandria, Louisiana, a small city in the central part of the state with food, power, and hotel rooms for a couple of hundred of his staff, his Incident Command Post, and occasional displaced family members and pets. A year earlier when Hurricane Ivan had threatened New Orleans, he'd been unsatisfied with the location the Coasties had hunkered down in and determined to find a better one, which they now had.

The Louisiana National Guard, by contrast, stayed put at their Jackson Barracks compound in New Orleans, where they would have to deal with six feet of flooding before they could turn their attention elsewhere. In addition, a third of their force, 3,200 members, were deployed in Iraq—along with most of their high-water trucks, fuel tankers, and satellite communications gear.

Coast Guard District 8 is one of the service's nine regional commands, and one of the largest, covering the entire Mississippi watershed including all or part of twenty-six states, the Gulf of Mexico, and the river itself. As Katrina approached, the command moved upriver from New Orleans to St. Louis, where it would coordinate activities in the coming weeks and months without second-guessing its people closer to the front in Mobile (which became a major air hub), Alexandria, or New Orleans.

All along the Gulf of Mexico, Coast Guard stations and families from

Grand Isle, Louisiana, to Dauphin Island, Alabama, were now evacuating ahead of the storm.

Saturday, August 27, 2005

Tom Ostebo, the incoming CO at Air Station Cape Cod, was training on Falcon jets at the Coast Guard Aviation Training Center (ATC) in Mobile, Alabama, that Friday when the CO invited him to a hurricane briefing. Reaching New York the next day, Tom decided he should do something to help out and put in a call to his district commander in Boston. Between them they agreed to send a Jayhawk helicopter and a couple of crews from Cape Cod down to Florida.

"I was on vacation in New Jersey when I got a call asking if I wanted to fly," Lt. Jason Dorval recalls. He would end up making 332 rescues in the coming week.

By Saturday morning, Hurricane Katrina had reached Category 3 intensity. Mandatory evacuations were ordered in southern Louisiana's low-lying parishes. Mayor Ray Nagin of New Orleans announced a state of emergency and asked for voluntary evacuations. Governor Kathleen Blanco sent a letter to President Bush asking that he declare a major disaster and provide federal aid to the state.

"We left Saturday and spent the night on the river," David Lewald recalls of his flotilla's slow progress up the Mississippi out of harm's way.

Twenty-six-year-old Petty Officer Jessica Guidroz is from the New Orleans area. She'd joined the Coast Guard three years earlier because she loves boats and water and was tired of working construction like her dad. That Saturday she helped trailer three 25-foot boats from Station New Orleans north across the Lake Pontchartrain Causeway.

Sunday, August 28, 2005

On Sunday, fearing north shore flooding, Jessica and her station crew relocated their boats from the Maritime Museum in Madisonville, their usual evacuation point, to their CO's house closer to Baton Rouge.

Chief Warrant Officer Lewald's larger boats arrived in Baton Rouge, where they refueled at a commercial dock and set up to ride out the storm in a small cove behind a thick cover of trees.

Sunday afternoon, having kept a handful of aviators on scene for any search and rescue calls that might come in, the air station launched its five Dolphin helicopters and their crews to evacuation points in Lake Charles and Houston.

By Sunday night, August 28, Katrina had grown into a Category 5 monster with 175 mph sustained winds and gusts of over 200 mph. New Orleans ordered a mandatory evacuation and opened up the Superdome as a refuge of last resort; 80 percent of the city's population had already fled. The National Hurricane Center warned of a catastrophic event about to hit the Gulf Coast.

"Most of the area will be uninhabitable for weeks . . . At least one half of well-constructed homes will have roof and wall failure . . . The majority of industrial buildings will become nonfunctional . . . High-rise offices and apartment buildings will sway dangerously . . . Persons . . . pets . . . and livestock exposed to the winds will face certain death."

My colleague Mark Schleifstein of the *New Orleans Times-Picayune* had written about the risk of a Category 4 or 5 hurricane striking his city for so many years that his editor began calling his stories "disaster porn." On Sunday night, Max Mayfield, director of the National Hurricane Center, called Mark at work and asked nervously, "How high is your building and what's its structural integrity?"

"Are you saying what I think you're saying?" Mark asked.

He was.

Monday, August 29, 2005

The cyclonic hurricane dropped to a Category 4 just before slamming into the Gulf Coast and southern Louisiana early Monday morning, striking like the fist of God with 145 mph winds and storm surges up to thirty-five feet. It drifted slightly to the east of New Orleans, initially appearing to have spared the city.

"Monday morning when the storm hit, it was blowing good, but we were protected. Our cook was feeding a hundred people, and we had two toilets and two showers onboard. It was like camping," Lewald says, recalling the scene at his well-protected hurricane hole up in Baton Rouge.

At about the same time, farther south, a thirty-foot wall of water overtopped the sixteen-foot levees in the town of Chalmette in St. Bernard Parish, where thousands of people had failed to evacuate. In fifteen minutes the flood wiped out the town, killing dozens of people and rupturing an oil storage tank that inundated a thousand homes with twenty-five thousand barrels of oil. The storm surge then moved west, breaching the Industrial Canal, and drowning much of the Ninth Ward and East Orleans Parish just as the Seventeenth Street floodwall gave way, putting the Lakeview section of the city under eight to fifteen feet of water.

The scene was equally horrific at Coast Guard Station Gulfport in Mississippi. There they had been down to a skeleton crew of seven Sunday night. As the storm intensified, they got on the radio to warn mariners no one would be monitoring emergency frequency Channel 16. They then took their trucks and headed inland to an Air National Guard base, only hours before their station was torn apart by scythe-like winds and surging ocean waters; by early Monday, Katrina had reduced the main building to a metal frame. Their mascot, Mayday, a mixed-breed mutt who had been left tied up on the top floor, was thought lost to the storm but would be returned unharmed, months later.

Even as Katrina was savaging the Gulf Coast, crushing and drowning more than a thousand people who'd been unable or unwilling to evacuate, the Coast Guard began responding.

One crew and aircraft went down Sunday, and I came into Cape Cod Monday morning and boarded a Falcon with my crew, and we met up in Jacksonville [Florida] around 11:00 A.M.," Jason Dorval recalls.

They joined crews that had evacuated from Mobile with another HH-60 Jayhawk helicopter and six HH-65s, the smaller Dolphins. "We walked into the operations center and they looked at us like 'Where are you guys from?' They didn't know we were coming, but it turned out to be a good thing. It [the hurricane] was already ashore, and we were monitoring the weather the best we could, given all the stations along the coast were destroyed.

"We figured the two 60s were larger airframes, so we'd stick our heads out first. We flew across Florida and down the coast, and when we landed in Mobile around sunset we were in winds of fifty to seventy-five knots on the back side of the storm. They had no power, but they had fuel trucks, and the storm crew was there and ready for us. They said, 'Keep heading west and see what you find.' "

At 10:00 A.M. Monday, Lt. JG Shay Williams from Air Station New Orleans woke up in Houston, where two of their helicopters and crews had evacuated. With the storm moving over Louisiana, they took to the air, meeting their other three 65s in the sky over Houma, thirty-five miles southwest of New Orleans, bucking sixty-knot headwinds, looking like a scene from *Apocalypse Now*. They landed at Jack Hammond's fuel depot, topped off, and waited to relaunch on the back side of the storm. They were able to take off again around two in the afternoon.

"So we fly on, knock our bags out the door [at the air station, where the hangar roof has peeled back and rainwater is now flooding in], and start working the Mississippi River," he says.

Their first recorded rescue is at 2:51 P.M. in Port Sulphur, south of the city, where one of the helicopter crews battles high winds to hoist a woman, her daughter, and the daughter's four-month-old baby from an open skiff jammed under a tree. On the third hoist, a wind gust tangles the cable in a fallen tree. The mechanic lets out enough slack for the swimmer to free himself and return to the aircraft.

Shay's first rescue is of a man who's cut a hole through the roof of his house to keep himself and his dog from drowning. "That first day we saved twelve lives, plus twenty on this 600-foot tanker that was out on the river without power. It was hard to communicate with the Chinese on board, and I wondered what they thought they were doing on the river," Shay recalls.

Around 8:00 P.M. Monday, Jason Dorval flew out of Mobile in his Jayhawk. "The first thing that struck us as odd, the coast there is normally well lit up, but west of Mobile it was just a big black hole. I mean there was nothing! We'd see people waving flashlights. Then, about ten to fifteen miles west of the air station, we flew over a neighborhood with maybe two feet of water and twenty-five to thirty people waving flashlights at us. We lowered our rescue swimmer, and in the back of a minivan they had this quadriplegic they'd rescued from his house. So we hoisted him and two family members and brought them back to Mobile, and that was our first rescue.

"Later, over Gulfport-Biloxi, we could see the I-90 bridge torn apart and casino barges [by law, Mississippi casinos had to be "offshore"] pushed up onshore and total devastation, so we started going block by block. Hovering over one hotel, we saw a bunch of flashlights and a group of people rolling another person out to the pool area on a serving cart. These were people who'd tried to ride the storm out, and this fellow had had a heart attack, so we put our swimmer down. We called a 65 [that was flying in after them], and they radioed that just across I-90 there was a hospital. We find it, and it's all lit up on a generator, and we find a dry area of grass and land and expect hospital staff to come running out. Only no one comes out, so the swimmer runs up and pounds on the door, and after two to three minutes they roll out a hospital bed, and they tell us they can take him but are full beyond capacity and please don't bring anyone else. That's when it struck me this was pretty dire!

"Later we see some people walking along the highway, and we land and offer them water. I look up, and there's a Waffle House sign, so we put the searchlight over toward the beach and there's an empty foundation. Odd that that plastic sign is perfectly intact but the building is gone. We flew seven hours that night, went back to Mobile, and handed the aircraft off to another crew."

Lt. Lance Kerr, a big, tan former rescue swimmer turned pilot, was stationed in Miami the day Katrina struck. "The Miami ops [operations] officer said, 'Pick three people who have experience in New Orleans and we'll send them each with a team,' " he recalls. "So I picked myself, another swimmer, and Jeff [Lt. Jeff Vajda, an ex-Army pilot who'd transferred from New Orleans two weeks earlier]. Monday night a C-130 picks us up and we go direct to Mobile."

"That same night we went out. I thought we'd never get there, that we'd have so many survivors on the way." Jeff takes up the story. "Only there was nothing there. All along the [Mississippi] coast it was just devastation everywhere you looked, things just blown away. So we fly into New Orleans East, and we're light on fuel and there are flashlights everywhere. This guy had his grill lit up on his roof is what attracted us to him first, and gas lines are exploding, and there was this U-shaped office complex with too many people, dozens of people, on one side of the roof, so we took this gentleman and two ladies off the other side. There were lots of downed wires and trees, so we did a high hoist. You don't like to, but we did, like a hundred and fifty feet [the standard rescue hoist is from thirty to fifty feet and easier to control]. We did some sixty to seventy hoists down there, all at night wearing [night-vision] goggles."

Looked at through those goggles, the darkest night is transformed into an eerie lime green landscape. Rescue Swimmer Wil Milam, based in Alaska, recalls his first nighttime mission in New Orleans—being lowered into a flooded warehouse district. After his helicopter flew off to let him listen for cries for help, he saw something on the street, lowered his goggles to his eyes, and realized it was a coffin. There were more in the branches of downed trees, on front porches, even on the steps of a church. They had floated out of their crypts in a nearby cemetery.

After the wind and rain began to subside, Petty Officer Jessica Guidroz and her crew from Station New Orleans spent Monday evening driving around downed trees, power lines, and storm debris on the north shore of the lake, searching for a place to launch their 25-foot boats. Eventually they found a cleared boat ramp in the middle of a swamp in Robert, Louisiana. "By now it was 2:00 or 3:00 A.M. We drove back to our CO's house, and he said, 'We're going to be on the water at sunrise.' "

Tuesday, August 30, 2005

By the time Jason Dorval woke in storm-soaked Mobile Tuesday morning, New Orleans had flooded, filling up like the soup bowl it is. Closer by, a massive oil rig, torn free from its dry dock, had jammed under the Cochrane/Africatown USA suspension bridge, becoming one of the visual signatures of the storm's awesome power.

At the air station it was decided the 60s, with their greater range, should head toward the Big Easy.

"We took a maximum load of fuel, water, and MREs [meals ready to eat] and flew to the eastern end of New Orleans that night, out by Six Flags. All the houses were flooded and people were waving flashlights off the roofs. We came on this first family of four on top of their house—and it was hot, I mean it was 100 to 103 degrees in the middle of the night with humidity off the charts—and we lowered the swimmer, and the copilot says, 'Jason, look out in front of you, you won't believe this.'

"I'm concentrating on holding the aircraft where the mechanic wants me to, because I can't see back there [where the hoist is taking place]. When I look up it's like every third house has people standing on top, and they're all flashing lights at us from everywhere 'cause we're the first helicopter on scene, and there's just hundreds, thousands of these light beacons as far as you can see.

"So we start lifting people off roofs till there's no more room, twelve or fifteen people in back plus the crew. That first night there was no extraction point, so we were just putting people on highway overpasses and discovered the cloverleaf [interchange] where I-10 meets the lake. That was dry, and there were some ambulances there, so we began landing on the highway and off-loading people.

"There was also some desperation that night. People were to the point where we'd be hoisting someone and see someone else trying to light their house afire thinking maybe they'd be a higher priority. We also saw some houses just blow up like bombs where the gas lines broke and erupted.

"We'd move house to house and to apartment complexes with seventy people and more on the roof. The swimmers would enlist the larger individuals to help them, to keep things orderly. Where we couldn't take everyone at once, soon they saw that when the bare hook came down that meant we were leaving, and sometimes they'd rush the swimmer, and sometimes we'd have the swimmer hop in the [rescue] basket 'cause it was getting a little dangerous."

Later swimmers began working in pairs to maintain crowd control. Their standard gear for rooftop rescues, similar to cliff rescue gear, became a shorty wetsuit, helmet, knee pads, and work boots.

"People were also bringing belongings up with them and we were hoisting people with dogs and cats," Jason recalls. "We hoisted twelve dogs and four cats. Suddenly this cat, this brownish gray tabby cat, is sitting on the [control] console [between the pilots] with the switches and everything, and my copilot flips out and says, 'Control this cat or he's going out the door!' and the owners got ahold of it."

I took off from Mobile Tuesday morning and started picking people up and dropping them off at the [New Orleans] lakefront. There were Army Chinooks taking people out of the area, but we were the only ones flying who could hoist people," Miami pilot Lance Kerr recalls. "We lucked out in that we were working a daytime cycle, so we could see more. We did 133 rescues in four days, which is about what I did in eight and a half years as a swimmer."

I ask him what his most memorable rescue was.

"Just to the west of downtown we saw two gentlemen on a grassy knoll, and they told our swimmer there were fourteen children in this house. So we decide to see how many we can bring up, bringing the kids up two at a time in the basket, and we were pushing the limits. We were pulling 98 percent of power—you don't want to go over 90 percent—and we got everyone on board. Now we have eleven children and three teenage mothers in the back [of a small orange Dolphin], and I look and there's nothing but flesh back there, just all these eyes. We've got fourteen people plus me, the [other] pilot, the flight mechanic, and the swimmer.

"Every time at the cloverleaf these first days, you'd have no idea where you'd land, and I aimed for the grass and did this steep approach and came up to 100 percent power and I'm still descending [instead of hovering], which is not good! So I'm counting on this air cushion effect when you land. I aimed for the grass but came down on pavement, and the air cushion effect worked anyway, so we landed OK, and I put my hand back and they all gave me high fives!"

Jessica Guidroz and her station crew launched two of their 25-foot boats at dawn Tuesday with ten on board including her CO and a radioman.

"Approaching the city, what caught our attention was the loss of visual references. The Dock and Jaeger's, this bar and a seafood restaurant I'd gone to as a kid, were gone—they were just pilings in the water—and the marina's sailboat masts, instead of pointing straight up, were pointing in every which direction.

"So we come back to the station and tie up, and we had two of our guys drive our trucks and trailers back down. There were all these people randomly wandering around, and we initially put them on the ground [at gunpoint] 'cause we didn't know who they were or what was going on. They had been rescued by helicopter and dropped off at the base, but there was no one there, so they'd just taken over our duty rooms and broken into our lockers and taken our clothing and attempted to break into dry stores to find food. Someone also tried to break into the ammunition locker with a sledgehammer, but that's like a big safe bolted into the concrete, and there was no way they were going to crack it."

She helped corral the crowd of about sixty into the station courtyard. Among them were a pregnant woman, a diabetic, and a schizophrenic man off his meds. They placed a Coastie by the ripped-up security fence to keep other people out and began confiscating drugs and alcohol from the folks on base. "There was a lot of alcohol they'd taken from a bar down the street. There was lots of marijuana, hash brownies, we found prescription pills, knives, a few guns. We had a pretty good stash once we got done," she says wryly.

"So then we fed everyone, and more Coasties arrived with big F550 stake-bed [cattle] trucks, and we loaded these people onto them and dropped them at this FEMA station by the Causeway exit at Interstate 10."

Jessica then went to the Seventeenth Street canal bridge after someone came by to report an injury. They found a man with a gashed leg who, trapped in his Lakeview attic, swam down through his flooded house, kicked out his living room window underwater, and, after surfacing, swam to the bridge. They took him back to the station and later got him medevaced out.

"We had no sanitation or water on base, and the rooms were trashed. The building was pretty gross," she recalls. "Some of us had left cars by the seawall, and they'd all been pushed into a pile on the side of the building. I had a '98 Corolla in the pile and went and got my change out of its ashtray. For the first three or four nights, nine of us slept in this one room that wasn't too trashed, although that first night I don't think any of us really got any sleep."

Tuesday afternoon, Chief Warrant Officer David Lewald and his flotilla motored back into the drowned city. On the way downriver they saw thirty- and forty-foot trees snapped like twigs and ships and barges tossed on top of levees. Entering the Big Easy, his crew was impressed by the blown-out windows on the downtown high-rises and the people waving towels from the windows of hotels where they'd waited out the storm and were now trapped by the water. Smoky fires were also beginning to smudge the skyline. Lewald got through to Sector Command in Alexandria and was telling them about the levees being breached and the city flooded and was being told they didn't have any reports to that effect when his radio and cell phone went dead.

In response to a local marine radio request, his boats carried out their first evacuation of a hundred people from the Navy station on the west bank of the Mississippi over to the Naval Support Activity on the east side, where it was dry.

They next got a request from Sheriff Jack Stephens of St. Bernard Parish to help evacuate the traumatized Chalmette flood survivors. Lewald asked the Navy if he could take people to the Naval Support Facility in Algiers. He was told that they were in lockdown mode and didn't have the Marines to keep control of the situation and that there were criminals on the loose. "I told them we could handle security, but they said no, they didn't want anyone on their base."

The day after the storm, Air Station New Orleans was littered with debris. It had no power or water and only one tanker truck of aviation gas that was rapidly being depleted. The Navy had locked up its fuel depot before evacuating the adjacent airfield. Taking the initiative, Electrician's Mate Rodney Gordon got into the Navy fuel farm, found some tanker trucks, and, using a scavenged generator, forklift, and electrical wire, got the power working to siphon gas into the trucks.

With their fuel secured, the air station ops center now gave what would become its standard instruction to newly arriving aircraft, "Go out over the city and rescue people." The station's five helicopters would rescue more than fifteen hundred people that week, as many as they had saved over the previous twenty-two years.

Like the Marines in war, the Coast Guard is designed to go in first during disasters while larger forces are mobilized. Only in this case those larger forces—local, state, and federal—failed to mobilize due to incompetence, inattention, and jurisdictional disputes, particularly between the Bush White House and the State of Louisiana.

Meanwhile, Coast Guard resources—boats, aircraft, and people—continued to flow in from around the nation. By Tuesday, Air Station Cape Cod had sent six of its eight aircraft. The Canadian Coast Guard volunteered to provide backfill, taking over search and rescue missions out of Cape Cod for the next two weeks.

A Coast Guard C-130 was the first heavy transport plane to bring relief supplies into New Orleans. The pilot of another C-130, sent to do an environmental survey, decided her plane would be more useful acting as an air control platform linking helicopters with hospitals and improvised landing zones, so that's what she had it do.

"By now we had multiple calls going all the time," says New Orleans pilot Shay Williams. "A director at Tulane had forty people who needed evacuation, the medical center had patients to get out, and we'd just get aircraft anywhere we could—say, sixty people here, 'come here, take these patients' there. We took women and children off the roof of a Winn-Dixie downtown. You just do it till you can't do it anymore.

"We just kept working for two days straight. I flew so much that they grounded me on day three and dropped me off at the Superdome, where I represented the Coast Guard [among twenty-five thousand hurricane refugees]. That was a bad scene. No food, no water, no order.

"I don't want to get into the politics, but we found ten FEMA trucks with food and water and cut the locks and had our aircraft kick it out to people at UNO [the University of New Orleans campus, which had become a refugee center], the cloverleaf, the lakefront . . . Eventually, come day five, six, or seven, the Regular Army, the 1st Cavalry and 82nd Airborne, arrived."

I'm interviewing the square-jawed, brushy-blond lieutenant at the air station three weeks after Katrina and in the immediate wake of Hurricane Rita, which has reflooded the Ninth Ward and smashed through the western part of the state, including Lake Charles.

I ask the former Army Black Hawk pilot how the two services he's worked for differ. "The Coast Guard is more focused. I joined because it mixes flying and lifesaving, and that's a pretty thing," he answers.

He's still working nonstop amid what looks like a gypsy camp of RVs, trailers, office cots, communications gear, and pallets of canned water, soda, and brown plastic MREs. The roof of the hangar remains damaged, but running water and electricity have been restored. I ask about his apartment in New Orleans. He says he hasn't had a chance to get over there to check it out yet.

Outside the gates of the Belle Chase Naval Air Station, where the Coast Guard is based and a tan-colored tent colony is being erected, are scenes of vast devastation and some one million environmental refugees living under damaged bridges, in carports, moldy offices, rural barns, marine lab dormitories, tents, and refugee centers, and with families scattered across the nation. Daily I'm reminded of war zones I've reported from. The casualties are fewer (some sixteen hundred estimated dead) but the area of devastation far more extensive. Over 150 square miles of wetlands and barrier islands have simply vanished beneath the waves.

A big C-130 from Sacramento lands and taxis, as does a Jayhawk from Clearwater with a crew from the Weather Channel on board. Larry King's producer is calling for the captain, but he's on the phone with Fox News. The ops center wants a copter to check out a reported levee break in Abbeville to the west.

"Like many search and rescues we're going out without enough information," Shay gripes to me, nevertheless grabbing the chopper before another pilot gets to. I walk out on the flight line with him as he pulls safety tags and does a preflight check around an underpowered HH-65B Dolphin that looks like a big orange waterbug (or small plastic helicopter). A mechanic and copilot join him. So does a rescue swimmer, pedaling up on a big tricycle with his black gear bag in the rear basket, including wetsuit, fins, helmet, dive mask, etc. Early on the swimmers also started carrying fire axes to break through rooftops where people were trapped in their attics.

Standardization of training and language among the pilots who fly the helicopters, the mechanics who maintain them, run the hoists, and direct the pilots during a rescue, and the swimmers who deploy on a cable hook or by jumping into the water is now so advanced that crews are being mixed and matched as needed.

They begin revving up the helicopter's engines as the blue-helmeted copilot makes a quick call on his cell phone. "Hey, I'm getting launched out. Love you. 'Bye." A moment later they're airborne, being tracked by an Air Force AWACS plane circling over the Gulf of Mexico.

On the other side of the air station, twenty-one-year-old Rescue Swimmer Keola Marfil of Hawaii is playing catch with two hounds a young woman Coastie has just rescued. He joined the service at a high school job fair in Kona after they landed a Dolphin on the playing field, he tells me. He'd grown up bodyboarding and paddling an outrigger and already knew he wanted to be a rescue swimmer. His first assignment was at Humboldt Bay in Northern California, where the ocean's a lot colder than in Hawaii. "The first time I went in the water with only my board shorts I almost died." He grins. "Nice jump, buddy," he compliments one of the dogs.

Keola has light brown eyes, short brown hair, a creased brow, and bulging leg and calf muscles that Popeye the Sailor Man would envy. He flew out of Mobile during the first days of the surge.

"I was involved in about a hundred and forty rescues," he says. "A lot of rooftops on the first day, more balconies on the second. It was nonstop. We were just hoisting and fueling. It was surreal, like something you'd see in a movie."

I ask him if he had to get in the water at all.

"I only had to go in the water one time. There was this elderly man and his son, and we had to get him to the yard next to his house to get some clearance from the trees and power lines, so I got on the roof next door and jumped over to their balcony."

"You jumped from the next-door roof?"

"It was only about six feet, and I still had a line on to the hook, but his was a gated house, so his son and I walked him into the yard through this chest-high water. There was lots of stuff in the water, and it was warm, and I'm glad I only went in once. We lowered the basket, and there were still power lines all over the place. These pilots are pretty skilled. You realize these people you're helping have nothing left but they're still smiling at you, and that's the appreciation."

Keola, like many Coasties, has a talent for improvisation. "We carried axes to break through doors and roofs and windows, but I didn't have one, and I had to break through this locked sliding glass door three stories up in this apartment to get to three people on the next balcony over. I tried this piece of wood, but that didn't work, so then I found this aluminum crutch and used it to smash through and get them across the hallway so I could hoist them."

On Tuesday, August 30, Rescue Swimmer Joel Sayers landed on a steeply sloped roof to rescue an elderly woman from the floodwaters. She pointed to a small opening in the roof that she'd squeezed through. Her husband was still trapped inside the broiling attic. Unable to widen the hole with the helicopter's rescue ax (a hatchet, really), he tied a bright piece of cloth around a vent pipe and convinced the wife they had to leave. After touching down at an improvised landing zone where he was able to borrow a fireman's ax, they returned to the neighborhood, found the flagged house, and lowered Sayers back onto the roof, where he chopped away at the hole till it was large enough to bring the man out. One of his crewmates videotaped Sayers, and a fifteen-second clip of his roof-chopping heroics aired nationally on TV that night.

On another roof, where a dozen people had been waiting too long, some guy came up behind Sayers and smashed a bottle over his head. Luckily he was wearing his helmet. He immediately grabbed the biggest guy on the roof and said, "If anyone does that again we're out of here." The bigger man established order, and Sayers was able to get everyone safely off the roof. Sayers, Jason Dorval, and Shay Williams would be among thirty Coast Guard aviators to win Distinguished Flying Crosses for their Katrina rescue work.

Wednesday, August 31, 2005

"I don't want to take anything away from the aviators. They did a great job, and they're also very good at getting their story out," *Pamlico* CO David Lewald notes wryly. The fact that helicopters have video cameras attached to their hoists and are often back on land with dramatic rescue footage in time for airing on the evening news has been an occasional source of irritation for the Coast Guard's boat crews.

Beginning Wednesday morning, Lewald and his crews began moving people from the Chalmette slip in flooded St. Bernard Parish to the Algiers ferry landing in Jefferson Parish (despite objections from the Jefferson sheriff). They used their patrol boats, ferries, tugboats, and barges to transport flood survivors, stripping life jackets from a large ferry that had been tossed up on the levee and giving them to evacuees taking the three- to four-mile river trip on an open barge. Meanwhile, the air temperature never dropped below one hundred degrees.

Three of the *Clamp*'s crew, Jeffrey Worth, Chris Schwarz, and Blake Lena, were EMTs and, along with a volunteer nurse, set up a triage station that began treating victims of hypothermia (from extended water immersion), diabetes, broken bones, heart attacks, and gunshot wounds. They used smoke flares to bring in Coast Guard and National Guard medevac helicopters to a parking lot LZ (landing zone) they marked out with orange construction paint.

That evening, after they'd helped some two thousand people across the river and onto school buses to get them out of the area, there were still 120 evacuees left waiting on the Algiers side. Fearing for their safety, the *Clamp*'s crew hot-wired and commandeered two abandoned buses, one of which they discovered contained an unattended paraplegic and someone in a coma. Eventually they found everyone refuge and medical care for the two who needed it and returned to the buoy tender.

"They came back pretty shaken," Lewald recalls. "One of them said he saw what he thought was the beginning of a rape. The bad guys owned the night. We backed off the riverbank and set up a watch. We lit up the area with a searchlight, and if a vehicle approached, like a stolen police car, we'd talk on the loud-hailer—give a martial-law-type speech—basically telling them don't fuck with us."

In the morning one of the buses had been stolen and the other one trashed.

The Coasties began frisking the evacuees and setting up amnesty barrels for contraband. Drugs and alcohol got tossed in the river. Guns they initially handed over to the New Orleans police until they noticed one of the cops taking the guns from his patrol car trunk and handing them out to his buddies. After that, confiscated weapons were locked in the *Clamp* and eventually transported to Texas (like coals to Newcastle).

Jessica Guidroz and two of her stationmates spent Wednesday in an 18-foot jet boat cruising the flooded streets of the Lakeview section of the city, knocking on roofs and attic windows looking for survivors. At one point their depth finder read thirteen feet. "We'd keep looking over the front of our boat. We ran over some cars and stop signs and just hoped we wouldn't put a hole in the bottom."

Eventually they gathered ten people, among them a woman in a walker, a man in a cast, a nine-year-old child, an elderly man who didn't want to leave his third-floor apartment above the water, and a very old woman whose son had floated her out of their home in a small catamaran. They got them to Ochsner Hospital, which was full and would only take the old woman, who was in critical condition. The others they had to drop off at I-10.

By then their station boats had started evacuating twenty-five hundred people from higher ground at the University of New Orleans, taking them three miles to the base, loading them onto cattle trucks, and driving them to the Interstate 10 drop off. The Jefferson sheriff didn't want Orleans Parish people (predominantly black and poor) brought into his mostly white suburban parish, but the Coasties once again ignored him, doing what they felt was right and necessary.

In another part of town Jason Dorval, concerned about the slow pace of basket hoists, touched his HH-60 down on the roof of a two-story hospital between two air-conditioning units. He kept the Jayhawk's rotors turning so the full weight of the helicopter never came to rest on the roof, and that way he was able to evacuate twelve people at a time, ducking them under the churning blades.

"If there was ever a Coast Guard war zone, that would be downtown New Orleans those first nights," he says. "The first two days we were the only people you could find down there. The third day the DOD [Department of Defense] started flying and the airspace started getting congested. That Wednesday they got a forward air controller into the cloverleaf and cut down the light posts so we could set more helicopters on the grass. Then they told us to clear out a two-mile radius because people were shooting at helicopters, but we ignored that. It's a combat helicopter [the Jayhawk is a variation on the Army Black Hawk] designed to take small-arms fire. There were still a lot of people in there, so we just kept working, just kept hoisting."

Coast Guard Rescue Swimmer Sara Faulkner did fifty rescues that Wednesday, including twenty-five off a second-story apartment balcony. Mechanic

Doug Nash from North Carolina, who was flying with her, recalls, "The building's roof was ripped off, and we swung her into that balcony railing. It was tricky 'cause you're also dealing with debris and blowing rooftops. She was swinging on the cable and came up and physically handed me a three-year-old child by the arm."

In the first days of disaster, the Coast Guard divided the city into four sectors.

They had a lieutenant commander running more than fifty shallow-water skiffs, known as punts, out of Zephyr Field. Home to the New Orleans AAA baseball team, it was a predesignated FEMA disaster center, though when the Coast Guard arrived FEMA was nowhere to be seen. Disaster Area Response Teams (DARTs) brought the 16-foot flat-bottomed punts in from Texas, Missouri, Kentucky, West Virginia, Pennsylvania, and other "Inland Coast Guard" stations that protect America's rivers and waterways.

They began moving through the northern part of the city, including the Central Business District, with Louisiana Wildlife rangers guiding them. When one of the midwestern crews steered nervously away from what they thought was an approaching alligator, the rangers laughed. It was a three-foot plastic toy alligator, soon adopted as their mascot, Zephyr. However, sightings of live alligators, snakes, and at least one bull shark were reported from other parts of the flooded city.

Launched from bridges and highway ramps, Coast Guard punts helped rescue some six thousand people from the floodwaters. Also brought into the city were three ice boats from the Great Lakes, small flat-bottomed vessels driven by aircraft-type propellers, normally used for winter rescues on top of the ice but now put to work navigating flooded streets.

The air station, the second sector, covered the city and the river. Syndicated editorial cartoonist John Sherffius was so inspired seeing their work on TV he penned an image of an HH-65 lifting a man in a basket, replacing the rotor blades with a halo and labeling it "New Orleans' Saints."

Small Boat Station New Orleans on the lakefront became the third sector, designated Forward Operating Base New Orleans, while the *Pamlico* flotilla that was holding the fort at the Algiers ferry landing became the fourth.

Thursday, September 1, 2005

On Thursday, two big Marine CH-53 Sea Stallion helicopters from the assault ship *Bataan* landed on their parking lot LZ. The giant seventy-two-foot rotor blades threw up rocks and litter that smashed a yellow school bus's windows and cut David Lewald's scalp with a piece of flying glass. "This was the biggest helicopter I'd ever seen," he recalls. "The ramp drops down and this guy gets out, about six-eight with a head like a globe, and we walk away from the helicopter, and he says, 'I can take fifty people at a time, but don't keep us waiting,' and I say 'Pets, too?' and he says, 'Yeah, but they count as a person.'

"Diabetes is a real poor people's problem, and we had these obese elderly people in wheelchairs. It was real hard to get them on the buses, so we put them onto these helicopters along with other sick people and the bigger animals in kennels. We must have moved a thousand people that way. That was the only day we didn't have lines waiting for the buses in the heat."

That same day, Jessica Guidroz was put in charge of eight 23- and 25-foot boats with instructions to evacuate the people at the University of New Orleans. "We were moving people for the next five to seven days," she recalls.

Unfortunately, the I-10 exchange where most of them were being dropped off had become a pungent, trash-strewn refugee camp where crowds of angry, frustrated people were forced to sleep on the ground and forage for shade, food, water, and a place to relieve themselves. The helicopters landing on the overpass would take only the dying and the infants.

"We had no place to dock at UNO," she recounts. "You have this seawall and these very slippery [algae-covered] steps, so we'd push up the bow and load people one by one. We'd have crewmembers get off first and form people into lines and search them for weapons and walk them to the seawall. Then our eight boat drivers would push back in, and the crew would help people over the bows and into the boats. It was hot and miserable, but we'd adapt and overcome. We had all different races, classes, single moms, dads, everyone boarding those boats.

"There was this one lady who got on the boat with two or three kids and an infant in her arms without a diaper change in who knows how long, because that diaper stunk up the whole boat, and she was reluctant to hand the baby over to me. This other woman, who must have been on drugs or something, was trying to claw her way over the lady and was knocking the baby out of her arms, and I screamed at her to hold on a moment, and we finally got them out of there safely.

"Later I'm watching a CNN report from the Astrodome [evacuation center] in Houston, and there's that first lady and she's showered and her baby is in a clean diaper. Until then I wasn't sure if we weren't just shuffling people from one bad situation to another, and now I can see where these people are actually getting help, that we're helping them, and I probably did, I got a little emotional [and cried] at that point."

She and her shipmates worked sixteen-hour days under the din of helicopters dropping sandbags into the breach at the nearby Seventeenth Street floodwall. Their station rapidly expanded as the "original eight" enlisted personnel from Tuesday were joined by newer arrivals, including sixty armed Maritime Safety and Security Team members living in RVs, trailers, and tents erected by Coast Guard civil engineers.

Even as the Coast Guard was surging into the region, it was also taking care of its own. Early on CGIS, the Coast Guard Investigative Service, sent some twenty agents to search for more than 130 missing Coasties. Within four days they were all accounted for. Some had gone to stay with or search for relatives; others had reported to different units and were working the storm outside the chain of command. CGIS was able to track them using credit card data, interviews, and ingenuity. One agent got a cell phone out of a flooded house and went through its speed dial till he found the relative the missing man was staying with.

CGIS agents also helped secure Coast Guard facilities from looters, including an armory on the west bank of the Mississippi where millions of rounds of ammunition were stored. They helped provide security for rescue crews and later for Coast Guard Adm. Thad Allen, when he was named principal federal official (PFO) in charge of rescue and recovery. "Mostly we prevented him from being mobbed by fans and people wanting to hug him or put him in a liplock," CGIS Assistant Director Marty Martinez says, grinning at the memory.

They also worked with Hurricane Assistance Teams that spread out across the region in SUVs carrying hundreds of thousands of dollars in cash to help displaced Coast Guard families secure motel rooms, food, medicine, toiletries, and other essentials. The M-16-toting agents would sleep with the satchels full of cash between their knees at night.

Through it all, of course, the orange helicopters kept flying.

• • •

I was too low on fuel to make it back to the air station and had to stop at the New Orleans airport," pilot Lance Kerr recalls. "I landed by the fuel truck ahead of this line of contract helicopters. This one guy had a huge helicopter and was waiting in a folding chair with his legs up on its ramp, and I go up to him and say, 'How much fuel do you take?' It's like six hundred gallons, and I say, 'We're going to fuel up first,' He's like, 'No way, dude,' and I say, 'Yes we are, because we have something you don't and you have something we don't.' 'Like what?' he asks. 'We have a hoist and you have a chair.' His crew laughed, and we finished filling up our hundred gallons and took off."

"It wasn't all fun. There was also the dark side," Jeff Vajda reminds him.

"There was a gentleman we took off a roof, and the rescue swimmer asked if there was anyone else, and he said no, and as we're flying away he says, well, his wife and daughter and grandmother were still in the house. We kind of look at him and say, 'Why didn't you tell us this at the time?' He says, 'I wanted to make sure I was OK.' So we worked our way back and found the place. The hole he'd cut in the roof wasn't large enough to get them out, so the swimmer had to break through a window on the side of the house and cut his leg up pretty badly. After we evacuated them, we had to take him to the hospital to get stitches.

"Then we had these two men on a roof with three women, and they had two large black duffel bags and wanted us to take them, and when we said we're only taking people, not their belongings, they became aggressive. They tried to pay our swimmer. We hoisted the biggest guy but thought maybe he was going to try and take control of the aircraft, so we kept the basket outside. The other guy then became extremely aggressive, and I was thinking, 'How do you use the helicopter as a weapon? Can I use the downdraft to blow this guy off the roof into the water?' But when our swimmer held his own, the guy signaled for his friend in the basket to come back down, and we got our guy back and left them there."

"There was this multilevel parking garage with a hundred-plus people," Lance now recounts, "and some were sitting and others were lying in the corner. We later realized these were the dead people lying off to one side. We lowered our swimmer down to assess, and as he was coming down on the hook all of a sudden a mob was forming below him, and we aborted the hoist. The next morning an Air Force 60 with multiple parajumpers landed on the roof and got control of the situation and helped these people. Turns out they had given up and were just getting high, waiting there to die."

• • •

Swimmer Tim Kessell from Elizabeth City, North Carolina, recalls a similar moment. He found himself alone with a crowd of survivors on the roof of the New Orleans Days Inn. "One guy said, 'I have five bullets I'm going to put in you if you don't put me in the next basket.' I told him, 'I can't put you in a basket with a weapon, sir.' He went away, and we got two more swimmers put down with me. After that we always flew with another guy."

Another time Kessell had to wade back and forth a quarter mile through filthy chest-deep floodwaters stinking of natural gas to evacuate boatloads of old folks in wheelchairs from an elementary school to a Shell gas station where there was a dry patch of ground to bring in a helicopter. At one point he noticed a dead body floating inside a car. On his third trip he stepped into a pothole and sank above his head.

"Back at Air Station Mobile they set up these fifty-five-gallon drums of disinfectant with antibacterial solution, and we'd just dunk ourselves in them and then take a hose to shower off. It was nasty."

Friday, September 2, 2005

"On Friday, an Air Force parajumper came in, and he had this backpack sprouting antennas, and he was in touch with everyone." Chief Warrant Officer David Lewald recalls the scene back at the Algiers ferry landing. "So soon, he had helicopters coming in on the levee three at a time and bouncing onto our LZ, and this was great because by then people were getting tireder and hungrier and it was close to hell. We lost two dozen people [who died], most of them on that day, mostly diabetics and drug addicts. We didn't have medicine, we didn't have insulin or methadone, and all we could do is cool them down and get them on a helicopter.

"Around 3:00 A.M. this warehouse explodes across the river, and I'm thinking, 'This is the warehouse where we have our people' [the refugees from Chalmette]. I lost my cool and wanted to get everyone on the water. My senior chief talked me down and said, 'It's not our warehouse, just let it burn.'

"Until then I'd felt like 'This is America, we'll figure it out.' Now it was like 'Where is everyone? Are we the only ones here?' "

About that time the *Spencer*, a 270-foot Medium Endurance Cutter from Boston, came upriver from where it had been patrolling in the Straits of Florida. Lewald was piped aboard and taken to the Combat Information Center for a briefing. "It's air-conditioned, like forty degrees, and I'm stinking and shivering, and the commander is smiling and says, 'So what can I do for you?'

So I got some engineering help for the 41s and let them moor up and let their crews get four-hour naps in this nice air-conditioning. This was also the first time in days I could communicate with the chain of command in Alexandria."

By then the chief warrant officer, along with his boat team, had helped evacuate 6,600 people across the river. Friday evening, after helping the *Spencer*'s officers establish an evacuation route to the Convention Center, where ten thousand more storm refugees were stranded, Lewald was relieved as the city's on-scene commander. "My boss says to me, 'What do you want to do next?' and I say, 'I want to regain my anonymity.' "

Shortly thereafter the *Pamlico* and the *Clamp* headed south to the badly damaged Coast Guard station in Venice to help replace buoys and other aids to navigation that had been blown away by the storm and to reopen the Mississippi River to commercial traffic. On the way the *Clamp* caught fire again.

Saturday, September 3, and the aftermath

"Saturday they finally started getting things together," Lt. Jason Dorval recalls of the broader government effort. "They evacuated the Convention Center and the Superdome and divided the parking lot into six landing zones with forward air controllers. We'd fly people to New Orleans International Airport and see all these commercial and military jets like C-141s landing, and we'd taxi up to the terminal, and they'd pull out luggage carts and people would climb onto them, and they'd drive them into the terminal, screen them, and fly them out to Houston and Dallas. By then it was like an air show with some 250 or 300 military helicopters from every service flying over New Orleans."

David Lewald's house in Bay St. Louis, Mississippi, was badly damaged but not destroyed. Thirty percent of the Coast Guard men and women in District 8 lost their homes to Katrina, even as they continued helping others. Along the Mississippi-Alabama coastline, where whole neighborhoods and communities were reduced to piles of kindling, empty lots, and brick foundations, Gulfport became the major "Recovery Base." A convoy of Coast Guard reservists with five tractor-trailer trucks and three buses traveled twenty hours from Ohio to relieve local Coasties so they could begin rebuilding their station, their homes, and their lives and help their neighbors mourn.

"After the first couple of weeks we were mostly finding bodies," Jessica Guidroz recounts. "We'd go into areas that hadn't been checked and tie up our boats and walk around, search houses, but mostly just find victims, not anyone alive. It was pretty sad stuff."

I ask her about her own situation. "I was about to move from this town house, so I had all my stuff in boxes downstairs, and we got three or four feet of water. So I moved into my new place with three crusty Coast Guard uniforms and my kitten that had survived, and it was the easiest move I ever done."

By the time I arrive to do some environmental reporting, New Orleans has become a Woodstock for first responders, emptied of its residents but occupied by some thirty thousand troops, reporters, relief workers, and contractors from every part of the country and the world: New York firemen, Louisville sheriffs, Utah National Guardsmen, San Diego customs agents, Japanese TV crews, angry local cops.

The Big Easy has literally lost its color. It's sepia-toned, all mud brown, russet, and gray, and the smell I often encounter is not that of dead bodies but of a dead city: like dried cow pies and mildew with a strong chemical aftertaste. I take pictures of the brown waterline that indicates how high the floodwaters rose and runs across tens of thousands of homes, schools, banks, supermarkets, video stores, churches, and other ruined buildings, including the main sewage plant, that will have to be torn down. I share empty debris-strewn streets and freeways with abandoned cars and boats and with big Army trucks and Humvees full of red-bereted 82nd Airborne troops, their M-4 rifles at the ready. I cross paths with animal rescue crews, police patrols, utility crews from New York and Pennsylvania, and body recovery search teams (including Coasties) with K-9 dogs using orange spray paint to mark the doors of still-unexamined buildings, writing the date and adding a zero for no bodies or numbers where bodies have been found.

I travel the demographically and geographically altered landscape of the bayou, Mississippi and Alabama, the Dust Bowl of the 1930s now replaced by the Flood Bowl of 2005.

I ride with Deputy Sheriff Ken Harvey along the west bank in Plaquemines Parish, where towns of several thousand like Empire and Buras have washed away forever. In what's left of Port Sulphur, the sheriff's deputies are living in converted shipping containers. Where the road's cut by water, we drive up on the eroded levee and keep going. The world's turned upside down, with big shrimp boats on the land and houses in the water and a truck propped up in a tree and a semi pinned under a house. Still another flooded house has a speedboat jutting through its picture window. We stop and stare in awe at a 250-foot barge tossed atop the levee like a bath toy on a tub rim.

Approaching the Empire Bridge, I note that the white church facing north toward us is still intact and suggest that's a hopeful sign. "It used to face the road," he points out.

Later, in Biloxi, I stop by an 8,000-ton, 600-foot-long casino barge that the storm drove half a mile across Beach Drive. Somewhere underneath its barnacle-encrusted black hull is a historic mansion. Another casino barge has gouged a hole halfway up the stately six-story yellow brick yacht club before coming to rest next to it.

In Waveland, Mississippi, I drive over twisted railroad tracks, where the eye of the storm passed, into neighborhoods of jagged wooden debris. A middle-aged couple is trying to clear the drive to the lot where their half-million-dollar home once stood. A surfboard leans against one of the live oaks that seem to have fared better than the houses in between.

"Are you an adjuster?" the woman asks.

"No, a reporter."

"Good, because we don't like adjusters. Nationwide was not on our side."

"At least you've got your surfboard," I tell her husband, John.

"Oh, that's not my surfboard." He grins, pointing around. "And that's not my boat, and that's not my Corvette [buried to its hood in the rubble], and that's not our roof. We think it might belong to the house at the end of the street."

On the narrow west end of Dauphin Island, Alabama, I walk with Dauphin Island Sea Lab director George Crozier through an apocalyptic scene of some two hundred broken and vanished stilt houses, downed power lines, flooded roads, buried cars, shallow quicksand, and a massive oil rig, Ocean Warwick, that has grounded in the surf after floating loose for sixty miles. It's one of more than 180 rigs damaged, destroyed, or set adrift by the storm.

We're being sandblasted by the leading edge of Hurricane Rita as George, one of the nation's leading authorities on coastal processes, tells me about climate change and how warming seas will lead to higher flood tides and more Category 4 and 5 hurricanes like Katrina and Rita. "What happened to Florida in '04 and Louisiana in '05 is no longer the exception," he explains. "It's the new rule."

Between human-induced climate change, increasingly crowded coastlines, and loss of wetlands that act as storm barriers, are we ready for the new coastal reality we've helped create? I wonder. While prevention is key—

changing our approaches to wetlands protection, coastal development, and energy choices—our ability to respond and adapt is also going to be vital.

In its February 2006 report *A Failure of Initiative*, the U.S. House Select Bipartisan Committee to Investigate the Preparation for and Response to Hurricane Katrina stated: "We are left scratching our heads at the range of inefficiency and ineffectiveness that characterized government behavior right before and after this storm. But passivity did the most damage. The failure of initiative cost lives, prolonged suffering, and left all Americans justifiably concerned our government is no better prepared to protect its people than it was before 9/11."

By contrast, a Government Accountability Office (GAO) report published in July 2006 stated, "Of the estimated 60,000 people needing to be rescued from rooftops and flooded homes, over 33,500 were saved by the Coast Guard . . . Underpinning these efforts were the agency's operational principles that promote leadership, accountability, and enable personnel to take responsibility and action."

At the height of its response, the Coast Guard had thirty cutters, sixty-two aircraft, and 111 small boats operating in New Orleans and the Gulf along with over five thousand people. They saved more people in a week than they had in the previous six years. They also got the job done without a single casualty or major accident.

In the days, weeks, months, and now years following the greatest natural disaster in U.S. history, the Coast Guard has helped reopen the Mississippi River to shipping, upgraded sea buoys and other aids to navigation, restored offshore oil production, and cleaned up or mitigated some 8.1 million gallons of spilled oil, more than two-thirds of an *Exxon Valdez*.

"When I joined I was just going to do my four years, but I realized I absolutely love this job and got to participate in something that was a positive moment in Coast Guard history," says Petty Officer Jessica Guidroz. "And if this ever happens again I want to be the one to help again, not to be in front of the TV watching it."

So how do you train people like Jessica Guidroz, Jason Dorval, David Lewald, Shay Williams, and Keola Marfil to take the initiative and act autonomously while standardizing their ability to work as a team? Surprisingly, the process often starts with a group of tired, bus-weary teenagers.

CHAPTER 2

The Boot and the Factory

Sometimes I take them down to the beach with the company colors and make them taste the saltwater, and that's the best.

—Petty Officer Dave Knapp, Recruit Training Center, Cape May, New Jersey

Scientiae Cedit Mare *(The Sea Yields to Knowledge)*

—Motto of the U.S. Coast Guard Academy, New London, Connecticut

The Boot

Two buses from Philadelphia wind their way through the small towns and hazy salt marshes and along the tidal bays of South Jersey. Fall colors darken with the autumn sunset as V-formations of Canada geese fly honking overhead. The buses pull through the streets of Cape May, a tourist-friendly beach town closing in on itself for the winter. They turn left off Pittsburgh Avenue toward the fisherman's memorial and the red and white water tower with blue letters reading COAST GUARD. They slow down to maneuver around the cement security barricades at the gate before being waved onto the 450-acre training center campus and boat station that juts between the harbor and the sea. With its one- to three-story pebbled concrete structures and wide quads, it resembles a community college with a not very well-endowed building fund. It is in fact the common ground shared by every enlisted man and woman of the United States Coast Guard. The young men and women on board the buses hardly notice, their nerves are jangling so badly at this point.

Soon the buses pull up in front of Sexton Hall, and company COs in Smokey the Bear hats come aboard and loudly instruct them they have fifteen seconds to vacate the bus and form up on a series of yellow triangles that have been painted on the street between their transport and the yellow curb. They will shortly be marched inside, where they will be fed box meals and issued T-shirts, sweatpants, and running shoes and be placed in squad bays (living areas), where they will spend several days before being assigned to training companies, all the time being loudly directed, with "a sense of urgency," about what to do. They will have their hair cut—buzz cuts for men, no more than two inches on the neck by cutting or pinning for women—and they will be given a wide range of medical and dental shots and extractions (wisdom teeth out).

Watching the weekly Tuesday night processing is Master Chief Stephen Dykema, a seventeen-year Coast Guard veteran, tall, and thin as a blade. As battalion commander, he'll have very little direct contact with the recruits during their eight weeks of training. "If a recruit gets to my level it's a serious issue," he explains.

In the late '90s, Dykema served as a company commander (CC) after attending Cape May's in-house CC school. Among the skill sets they teach is how to shout without going hoarse. They practice at the far end of the property by the firing range, away from where the recruits might see them.

"Yelling wasn't me," Dykema recalls. "I wanted out but found that this was a small part of the job. So I learned to find my command voice. We have a CC here, Petty Officer Butler, she's about five foot two, but she found her . . ."

"Ability to intimidate?" I suggest.

"Her command presence," he responds with a thin, barracuda-like grin.

Among the recruits Dykema commanded was Nathan Bruckenthal, the first and so far only Coastie to die in combat in Iraq. "Last year we had a welterweight boxing champ join up. He accidentally killed his sparring partner and decided to come here. Some people used to join after seeing the Coast Guard on *Baywatch*. Post 9/11 we saw a lot of patriotic motivation. There's still a ripple effect of that. I expect we'll now see a lot of recruits wanting to be swimmers."

The Guardian, a film starring Kevin Costner and Ashton Kutcher as Coast Guard aviation survival technicians, or rescue swimmers, had recently come out. The night of its red carpet premiere in Washington, DC, I spotted a teenage girl skipping down the sidewalk in front of the Uptown Theater talking excitedly into her cell phone. "Ginny! I touched Ashton Kushner, I touched him!"

The morning after their arrival, the fifty-six new recruits are marched onto the second floor of Sexton Hall, named for Charles Sexton, a Coastie medic who died after trying to administer first aid aboard the fishing vessel *Sea King* when it capsized and sank near the mouth of the Columbia River in 1991. The Coast Guard's "Core Values"—"Honor, Respect, Devotion to Duty"—are painted in black letters on the room's white walls. The recruits are still in gray tees and blue sweatpants. They won't get their blue ODU (Operational Dress Uniform) work clothes for another day. They won't get to eat at the galley till tonight, after they've learned how to march and eat Coast Guard fashion.

Chief Dougherty, who's in charge of Sexton Hall, makes sure the recruits are given bag lunches and fruit drinks. He holds up a drink.

"Take these beverages and put them down and then sit down," he orders.

"Sir, yes, sir!" they shout, lining up at tables where questionnaires are being handed out.

"Take these forms, write your name, last name, and middle initial, put your age, weight, your company is K17S. Again, eyes on me! When we come around you will stand behind your bench. You will then have the bench pushed in with your dominant hand out and fingers spread. I'll give you your wrist size and you will line up for your weight and height. When you get to this aisle—this break in the tables—you will take your shoes off and step on the scale. You will put the shoes down next to the scale before being weighed. You will then put your back to the bulkhead and you will stand tall and proud for your height measurement. Sit down." There's a loud shuffling of benches. "Put your bag lunch in front of you [*swish, swish*]. Start eating until I come to your table."

As he gets to each table, the recruits rise and march to the petty officers waiting at the scale. "Put your pen in your left sock," one of them orders a young recruit. "We do not want you to hurt yourself falling with a pen in your hand."

While it can seem like unnecessary harassment to the new recruits, they're actually entering a highly structured program designed to get them fit, focused, and team oriented in a relatively short period of time.

Week one's indoctrination is followed by a complex pattern of recruit qualification standards to be learned (like time management for your average eighteen-year-old), required knowledge (drills, CPR, nautical terms), incentive training (including physical fitness), remedial instruction, classroom instruction, and exams. This will keep recruits busy from five in the morning till ten at night, every day for the next two months. They'll join one of seven or eight companies housed in Monroe, Healy, and James halls, also named after Coast Guard heroes. In recent years, new towers or wings have been added to house female recruits so that mixed companies remain in close proximity.

I end up spending most of my time with Lima Company, which, in its fourth week, is halfway through the training cycle. Their company commander is Chief Petty Officer Louis Bevilacqua, a bullet-headed thirty-seven-year-old, about five-nine, trim, with dark glasses, the big Smokey the Bear hat, and the rough look of an ex-felon, though he's actually spent the last fifteen years in the service, most recently inspecting lighthouses off the coast of Maine.

He's assisted by Petty Officers Second Class Craig Faw and Dave Knapp, both in their late twenties. Dave is a former Army reservist married to another Coastie.

The company has seventy-five recruits and is over 20 percent female. Like every class, it has to meet certain physical standards. Guys have to run 1.5 miles in 12 minutes 51 seconds or better, females in 15:26. Males have to be able to do twenty-nine push-ups and thirty-eight sit-ups, females fifteen and thirty-two. Everyone has to swim five hundred yards in under five minutes and tread water for five minutes in the center's big fifty-meter pool (where they also have to don Mustang survival suits in two minutes and float in them for ten). Each week about 25 percent fail their requirements.

"This generation is in terrible shape. We get people off the bus who can't hold themselves up in push-up position," Faw complains. We're watching Lima's recruits run around the outdoor track past a flock of disinterested Canada geese in the cool drizzle of a leaden afternoon.

Inside the gym, a recruit comes up to Petty Officer Knapp wanting to go to the clinic for an ingrown toenail soak he's missed. Another requests to run to the commissary for a razor. He's told no candy or soda, "and don't try to drink it outside real fast."

Another has gashed her head on a changing room locker (a small gash) and is holding a paper towel to the cut. An EMT team arrives with a gurney. One of them suggests she not cough into the wet paper towel and then reapply it to her head.

Faw is tracking his recruits' scores. Mustafa did thirty-two push-ups, Naavercut one, Williamson nine, Woods thirty-five, Kissinger twenty . . .

Next, they're marched off to class, where the other Petty Officer Knapp (Dave's twenty-one-year-old wife, Samantha) will coach them for their midterms on topics such as service missions, chain of command, and ranks. The classes are geared to an eighth-grade comprehension level.

Dave has returned to the third floor of James Hall, where Lima lives. He's searching for "scoosh" powder (an abrasive cleaner). He knocks on the door of one of the female towers. "Male on deck," he announces before entering the empty squad bay with its six double bunks. He finds the powder in a cleaning closet and goes into their head (bathroom). Taking orange pump soaps off the metal shelves, he unscrews the tops and starts splashing the goopy liquid across the mirrors and sinks. He throws paper towels into the sinks and turns on the taps to soak them. He then tosses the soaking paper towels around, shakes the scoosh powder in the showers and toilets, and toilet papers the stalls like it's Halloween.

"When they live aboard a boat and live like pigs they'll get sick. This will help educate them." He grins. "And hey, I'm not gonna lie. It's fun to do."

We move on to one of the male heads that is less well kept, with water stains on the sinks, toilets less than spotless, and underwear hanging on towel hooks. "Typically males are a lot dirtier than females," he admits, splashing the liquid soap around and trying to bomb the shower room with a plastic container of powder that fails to explode the way he'd like. He attempts to finger-paint CLEAN ME in orange liquid soap on the mirrors. He looks out the window and sees CC Bevilacqua bringing the recruits back. We rush to trash the other two squad bay bathrooms before they return.

"They were supposed to be gone half an hour. Unfortunately, that doesn't give us time to destroy their squad bays," Dave explains regretfully.

We return to the quarterdeck, the racetrack-like central hall with its glass-enclosed stairwell, bulletin boards, and CC offices. The recruits are run up the stairs and back to their bays.

"Do not transit my quarterdeck with a pen in your hand," Chief Bevilacqua warns one of them.

"Smith! This is not college. Do not walk around with one strap of your rucksack on. You have two straps. Use them both," Faw warns another.

"Weygand," Dave Knapp barks.

"Weygand, Weygand, Weygand," the recruits in the bays repeat till we hear her shouting, "Female transiting," as she fast-steps through the male squad bay and braces in front of him. She's in charge of one of the squads cleaning the area.

"Weygand, explain why the tops of these bulletin boards are dusty." He runs a finger above one and shows her the evidentiary smidgen of dust. "Is this acceptable?

"No, PO Knapp."

"Are we going to correct this?

"Yes, PO Knapp. Aye, aye."

"Well, let's do it." He then shouts to let them all know they have twenty minutes to undo his "White Tornado" trashing of their heads. It's also one of the remedial instruction drills every company gets to experience in the third or fourth week.

A recruit braces and asks permission to go to the clinic for an appointment.

"Why?" Bevilacqua asks.

"They removed . . ." He begins to point to his cheek.

"We all understand English. You don't need to point," he's told.

"They removed a tumor from my cheek and wish to do a follow-up exam, Chief Petty Officer Bevilacqua."

"Fine. Sign out and go directly to the clinic."

I wander back to one of the bathrooms to find a dozen recruits scrubbing and cleaning away as a team.

Back on the quarterdeck Faw tells me Recruit Salinas is having "sign-in and sign-out problems." Bevilaqua has her braced against the wall.

"I did this remedial last week," she says.

"I don't care. Shut your mouth!" he screams into her face. Speaking out of turn is strongly discouraged among the recruits.

"Jeckel," Knapp calls out. "Jeckel, Jeckel, Jeckel," the call reverberates through the bays.

Jeckel has to fill out a page of forms because he wrote over the line. He has to fill one line (taped to the chicken-wire-embedded glass of the stairwell), then run around the racetrack and fill out the next line till he completes the sheet. Recruit Lowe has to do fifty laps around the quarterdeck because he was late to formation.

Dave Knapp is now in his office playing tapes of Army Airborne cadences. "I just try to learn them and then use Coast Guard words when we march," he explains.

On the quarterdeck four recruits are reading out loud from the Coast

Guard Manual. In one of the adjacent squad bays they're passing web bags full of laundry.

"We just like to have a kind of controlled chaos." Dave smiles.

"Why'd you fail your push-ups?" Faw asks another recruit.

"My arm cramped up."

"Is that what you're going to tell the parents of some kid who died, who you were supposed to save from drowning but he died and you'll tell them, 'Sorry, I couldn't rescue him because my leg cramped up?' "

A squad leader named Herder approaches Faw. "Petty Officer, we found a gun casing in the squad bay." He hands over a casing from a 9 mm round.

"Someone probably took it back from the range as a souvenir and then left it in their clothing when it went to the laundry," Faw postulates after the recruit leaves.

In week six, Dave tells me, they'll take the recruits to the Cape May Boat Station and let them tour the 210-foot cutter and the 87-footers. "Week eight we'll give them pillow talk, talk to them in our civvies and answer any questions they may have about life in the fleet."

Another group of recruits is now writing zeros with slashes through them in boxes formed by the chicken wire embedded in the stairwell glass.

I wander down to the Seamanship Center close by the boat docks, where they have helm control simulators. Poles on the ceiling lower down so the recruits can practice knot tying. Outside there is a raised platform like a wooden dock with dolphins (metal stanchions) to practice heaving lines and tying up ships.

I head off to dinner in town. I love beach towns on gray rainy evenings like this when they've shut down for the season and begin to take on a slower pace determined by the tides and the weather. *The Guardian* is playing at the old Beach Theater down by the waterfront dunes.

"We all went to see it on our liberty day," Samantha Crane, a twenty-year-old recruit graduating basic this week, tells me. "It was cool, seeing the movie and then looking down and seeing myself in a Coast Guard uniform. I had tears in my eyes, and I wasn't the only one."

When I return to James Hall, I find another company conducting night drills out front. They're snapping to with their "pieces"—old M-1

Garand rifles that have had their rods pulled and barrels filled with lead so that they now function as 9.5-pound ceremonial props. "Port arms, shoulder arms . . . one mike, two mike, three mike, four."

Inside, Dave Knapp and Craig Faw have taken charge for the evening. A recruit is doing push-ups on the floor. Another is braced against the wall with his piece held out arm's length in front of him. On the far side of the quarterdeck, several recruits are staring at pictures of a ship taped to the glass. "Keep your eyes on the boat, shipmate. Shipmate, keep your eyes on the boat . . ."

"Mustafa, give me article 6."

"Yes, PO Knapp." Mustafa recites a pledge of loyalty to God and country.

"Do you believe that?" Knapp asks.

"Yes, PO Knapp."

"Because Coasties go to war every day. We never know when that container ship we're boarding will blow up or some fisherman will pull a gun on you and you have to disarm him. That's a pretty scary moment, looking at that gun as it's pointed at you. You think you'll be ready when something like that happens to you?" (Later Dave confesses that it wasn't him but his wife this actually happened to.)

In the squad bay to my left, recruits are sitting around polishing their boots. Others are working on their locker spaces under their mattresses.

"Can I ask you a question?"

The recruit's eyes dart toward the hall.

"It's OK with the POs," I assure him.

"Yes, sir?"

"How much space do you have in there?"

He starts explaining the different compartments. "It's about ten square feet," his shipmate interrupts.

"We literally have to fit our entire seabag in here," the first guy grins.

Squad leader Herder requests to speak privately with Petty Officer Knapp.

"This is as private as it gets around here. What is it?"

Herder tells him a shipmate's wife is pregnant with their second child and wonders who he should contact about family reimbursements. Knapp tells him but also warns that the recruit shouldn't expect he'll get to call her.

"He's in boot camp now and has to keep focused on that," Dave explains to me. "If he doesn't pass, he won't be in a position to provide for his family."

Recruit Kissinger is called on the quarterdeck to recite his piece nomenclature. He has memorized his gun's parts but keeps falling asleep during the day.

"How old are you?" Knapp asks him.

"One niner."

Dave pulls a copy of the *Navy Times* from his office. "Here's this Army PFC Christopher T. Blaney. He is just nineteen years old, and now he's dead in Iraq. He's never calling home. He's never talking to his mom or dad again. He'll never get married or have kids. Maybe he never had a drink. How does that make you feel? Are you going to stay awake?"

Kissinger's eyes are tearing up.

"Why are you about to cry?" Dave asks curiously.

"I don't like to hear about people dying, Petty Officer Knapp."

"Me neither, but he did it, right? And he did it for his country, and you have to ask yourself, am I ready to die for my country, to die for some fisherman or some kid who you don't know but is depending on your sacrifice? Are you willing to die so that others can live?"

Meanwhile Craig Faw is explaining to Recruit Vallejo why she's standing with a felt pen drawing slash marks through zeros on a glass window.

"In the U.S. Coast Guard you slash your zeros. So if we want to find people lost in ten thousand square miles of ocean we don't have to worry, 'Did she say *o* when she meant zero?' "

Dave goes into the port-side squad bay and stands up on a double bunk. All the recruits brace. "All present and accounted for," he's informed. Then they recite the Pledge of Allegiance louder than I've ever heard it said before.

Two days later, I'm talking with Louis Bevilacqua while his recruits are taking their midterms. "Last night we had a kid who snuck a cell phone in and they reported him, so that shows they're starting to understand integrity," he says. "We confronted him, and first he said he'd found it in the stairwell. We said we weren't born yesterday, tell the truth. So he did and he'll get a reversion [be set back] for one week. Otherwise, if he'd lied, that's more serious, and he would have gotten probably three weeks.

"Another kid complained of a stomachache. We sent him to the clinic, and now he's having his appendix out today, so he'll start with a new company when he recovers."

He expects about 80 percent of the company will pass the open book exam. For those who don't, there's a makeup on Sunday. If 93 percent pass, they get to put a pennant on their company stick (banner pole).

Before lighthouse tending, Bevilacqua sailed aboard the *Polar Sea*, an icebreaker. He traveled from Antarctica to the Arctic Circle and to Japan and

Singapore. He's sailed to Jakarta, Haiti, and New Caledonia with the Coast Guard, and also on a buoy tender on Long Island Sound. He did a tour on the *Rush*, a High Endurance Cutter doing fisheries patrols in the Bering Sea. He was on a boarding team that helped rescue a crew and then found out they were illegal migrants and busted them. "With fishermen and the Coast Guard it's a love/hate thing," he admits. He has a wife and three young kids but still comes across as a total hard-ass.

I'm in the classroom as the recruits turn their exam books in to PO Samantha Knapp. The first two rows then report to the back of the class for cleanup detail. The others head off to gym for their Cybex weight machine class.

Later, when I run into Louis Bevilacqua and Dave Knapp, they're looking pleased. They tell me all their recruits passed the exam, with six or seven scoring 100. The lowest score was an 86.

I talk with a couple of Lima recruits about why they enlisted and how they feel about boot camp.

Andrea Salinas is twenty-three and from Detroit. "I wanted to save lives is why I joined. I was doing odd jobs and construction work and woke up one day and decided I had to change my life. My dad's best friend was in the Coast Guard, so I knew they did valuable things. Basic training is difficult for me because a lot of times I know the information but I lose it with all the stress, so that's frustrating."

Amber Nethercutt is eighteen, a wide-eyed blonde from North Carolina who says she joined for the adventure. "It's the hardest service to qualify for, and I like the fact we don't kill people, we save people. Don't tell the POs, but I expected basic training to be a lot harder than it is."

"I think boot camp is harder for older recruits," claims Michael Ryan, who's twenty-six. "I realize the purpose for all this stuff, even as they yell at me, like left shoulder to the bulkhead will mean something trying to get through the narrow passageways on a ship, passing a shipmate. Still, basic's been going on a lot longer than I thought. I mean, the weeks do seem to fly by, but the days are excruciatingly long."

"But you're still having fun?"

"Smiling is not really allowed." He smiles at me.

"I was working for Southwest Airlines and going to school and had what's called an epiphany. I was just working to go to school and I didn't know why I was," says William Parker, a twenty-one-year-old African American who's also breaking the smiling rule. "I want to be a firefighter and use the Coast Guard for my training. I'm a military brat and know how the other branches can . . . stretch the truth with what they promise. I had friends who joined the Marines and thought they were going to get to play basketball at the service academies and were sent to Iraq. The Coast Guard is more honest. As far as basic, I didn't expect to be in class so much."

Mark Herder, the twenty-seven-year-old squad leader, has a more apocalyptic sense of mission. "I was the elite as a machinist for ten years making surgical tools for heart operations, and I began reading about peak oil. I was looking at what that means if, say, the Iranians cut off the Straits of Hormuz and our oil supply dries up. I want to be one of the ones who are able to respond, and the Coast Guard proved during Katrina that in the worst climate they'd be second to none."

Listen up, Lima Company. Your squad bays look like crap, so what I want you to do is bring all your seabags and rucksacks and everything you have loaded up onto the quarterdeck because we're going to change squad bays," Dave Knapp shouts to his charges back in James Hall. "If you lived like this on a ship it would get nasty. Gear adrift sinks ships. Pack everything you own. Bring your rucksacks and ditty bags. Pack your linens in your seabags. Leave your pillows where they are. You have ten minutes."

Recruits begin scrambling, flipping up their beds and emptying out their rack drawers. He goes back to his office and plays loud music, then pulls out a bullhorn and begins hitting the button that produces siren wails. "Oh-seven minutes," he announces. He walks into the starboard bay just as one of the recruits bumps his head on the top rack drawer he's lifted up.

"MISSON FIRST, SAFETY ALWAYS," Dave instructs on his bullhorn. "It's like we got a hurricane evacuation order and we're evacuating to Fort Dix." After a few minutes, the first recruits arrive on the quarterdeck with their big rucksacks on their chests, their seabags, smaller ditty bags, and rifles slung on their shoulders.

"Find room on the floor to put that stuff down," he tells them. As the space is jamming up with recruits and their belongings, a tall, neatly coiffed Navy chaplain, Lt. Cdr. Yolanda Gillen, arrives. Dave appears mildly dismayed.

"Place your crap on the deck and face the chaplain," he orders. She begins by reading a news story from today. A Coast Guard buoy tender saw a 16-foot boat going under and diverted to pull a sixty-five-year-old man out of the water.

"They rescued him. That's our mission. Wherever you are sent, be sure you bloom wherever you are planted. Do your best here so you'll be ready to help your shipmates out on the fleet." She asks if there are any specific prayers needed. A female recruit asks for a prayer for her cousin in Iraq. Others ask for deceased and loved ones. Someone asks if they can pray for sports. She gives them a few baseball and football scores and suggests that Detroit could certainly use some prayers. She says those who don't want to pray don't have to. "Those who want to pray, let's bend our heads." The girl whose cousin is in Iraq leans her head against the stock of her rifle and closes her eyes. I resist the desire to take a picture, as the flash would startle her.

"Let's pray for our ill and lost loved ones and let this company know they've come a long way and you [God] will see them through."

As soon as she leaves, Dave has them on the run again, switching their sleeping bays.

"They took money from the Coast Guard and gave it to the NSF [National Science Foundation], which hired a Russian ship for icebreaking in Antarctica, and the ship got stuck, and the [Coast Guard Cutter] *Healy* had to head out to sea to rescue the Russians and saved them." He tells the story not exactly as it happened but close enough to make his point. "So let's GET MOTIVATED," he shouts through the bullhorn. "I'll give you a minute thirty-five to finish. Let's be like we're getting under way to save that Russian ship!" He hits the bullhorn's wailing police siren again.

"*Healy*—must SAVE RUSSIAN VESSEL. Preparing to get under way. This is the captain speaking."

Crowds of recruits are hustling back and forth through the halls, top-heavy with bags and bedding and rifles.

"MISSION FIRST—SAFETY ALWAYS—LINES AWAY—FULL SPEED AHEAD!' Dave Knapp calls out, his blue eyes shining with delight.

On my last day, I attend a recruit graduation that has been moved indoors to the gym because rain had been predicted. Naturally, the parade ground is now awash in bright sunshine. Some five or six hundred family members are crowded onto the gym's bleachers as the graduating recruits march out in their dress blues. There's a band, a color guard, and a precision honor guard that performs with rifles and bayonets. My favorite part is where they form a circle around their instructor and point their bayonets at him shoulder high, a nice fratricidal flourish.

The Training Center's captain thanks the families of the recruits for "trusting us with their care and sharing them with our nation." The band plays a tune

I remember as "A duck must be somebody's mother." "That would be 'Stars and Stripes Forever,' " the bandleader archly instructs me.

As the recruits are called up to the front of the gym, their assignments are read aloud: Woods Hole, Massachusetts; Yorktown, Virginia; Cutter *Alex Haley* in Kodiak, Alaska; Barbers Point, Hawaii; Cutter *Boutwell* in Alameda, California; Miami Beach; Key West; Juneau; San Diego; Ohio; Venice, Louisiana; Cutter *Mellon* in Seattle; Cape May; Portland; New Orleans; San Francisco; Texas; New York; Omaha, Nebraska . . .

An Air Force dad hands his son his graduation certificate. A Coast Guard commander identified as a mentor gives a young man his. An Army Ranger gives his cousin her certificate. A diminutive Army mother in dark green uniform gives one to her son, a policeman to his nephew; a Marine hands one to his Coast Guard brother. There's the final muster. "What you learned may one day save your lives or the lives of others." After the retiring of the colors, families and friends swarm the gym floor to embrace their sons and daughters, now active-duty Coast Guard men and women.

The Factory

Now take boot camp and add four years of rigorous academics, at-sea training and sailing on a tall ship, various assignments in the fleet, leadership development, and senior projects that could pass for master's or PhD theses, and you have the Coast Guard Academy, the smallest and least known of the armed services academies, and also the most gender neutral.

The whiteboard on the big bridge simulator reads CONN: Steph DECK: Claire HELM: Jenni PLOT: Katie NAV EVAL: Virginia RADAR: Laura RECORDER: Ysabel BEARING: Tasha. An all-male crew in the academy's nautical science lab might not seem unusual, but we're still early enough in this century that I'm impressed to find an all-female crew operating the virtual bridge of a 378-foot High Endurance Cutter, a crew that wasn't intentionally formed around gender but just shook out that way because with women now making up 28 percent of the cadet corps, and friends selecting friends to work with, it will on occasion happen like that.

First a little background. The Revenue Cutter Service founded its School of Instruction in 1876 on board a 93-foot two-masted schooner named *Dobbin*. There were nine students. By 1890, they'd moved to a new ship, the *Chase*, and a land-based campus in Curtis Bay, Maryland. In 1910, they moved again, to Fort Trumbull, a New London, Connecticut, Army post dating back to the

Revolutionary War. The modern Coast Guard was formed in 1915, and in 1932 the citizens of New London donated the present 110-acre site of the academy, just above town on the Thames River.

New London itself is a somewhat down-at-the-heels working port with commercial docks and car ferries. Across the river is the General Dynamics Electric Boat Yard that builds nuclear submarines. Twenty-two operational subs are stationed upriver at the Groton Navy base.

The academy sits on a rise on the river above where the barque *Eagle* is usually berthed. Since the Coast Guard gave up Governors Island in New York Harbor in the 1990s, the 295-foot *Eagle,* the largest tall ship flying the Stars and Stripes, is now its most visible symbol. Every cadet will spend six weeks at sea on this floating classroom, sometimes crossing the Atlantic or sailing the deep Caribbean.

The academy, also known as the ensign factory, has around a thousand cadets, graduating some two hundred a year (after attrition). It's the only service academy that doesn't require a congressional nomination, which meant something back when politicians' letters of support were based more on favoritism than on merit. Even though it offers a free education (in exchange for five years' service), is a well-regarded engineering school with a STEM program in science, technology, engineering, and math, and has some thirty sports to choose from, the number of high school students applying has been in decline for years. As a result, in 2006 *U.S. News and World Report* lowered its rating from "highly selective" to "selective." It saw some application growth right after 9/11, but, as with the other military academies, that declined as the war in Iraq dragged on.

With its big white-columned redbrick buildings, parade field, flag-backed football field, boathouse, sailing center, and ceremonial guns that fire every Friday (setting off car alarms in nearby parking lots), the academy has the feel of the pleasant New England campus that it is, rather than the historic grandeur of a West Point or Annapolis. Still, most of the cadets seem satisfied with the choice they've made.

"I was chosen at West Point and here and decided I'd rather train to save a life than take a life," Lt. Elizabeth Ferry tells me. She's a 2002 graduate now working as an academy planning officer after a few years on a buoy tender.

"I grew up next to the ocean in Ocean Park, Maine, and so I was always aware of the Coast Guard and just felt I'd rather save lives than take them," agrees fourth-year (freshman) cadet Noah Hudson at the end of his civil engineering class.

"My feelings are similar to Mr. Hudson's," his classmate Ryan Flannigan concurs. "My family has been in the military for generations. My father was a Navy aviator, and I wanted to fly, and yet I'd rather not be bombing people. I'd rather be pulling them out of the water."

Of course, the Coast Guard's humanitarian mission is only one of the reasons cadets join, according to Lieutenant Ferry.

"Other academy graduates say, 'We love our academy but hate our service.' It's the opposite here because during the summers cadets get to do stuff with the operational Coast Guard and then they're just waiting to get out into the fleet and onto these awesome missions. To tell a twenty-two-year-old you could run your own ship in two years . . . It could be five to seven years before a graduate from [the Naval Academy at] Annapolis gets that kind of opportunity."

Coast Guard cadets go through a kind of reverse year order. Freshmen are called fourth class. They begin in July with Swab Summer, which is a seven-week version of boot camp except they also get to go sailing, including a week on the *Eagle*. After that they spend their freshman year learning to be "exemplary followers," in much the same way Lima Company recruits do. This includes squaring away their meals, meaning they have to look straight ahead while eating. The next summer they get to spend ten weeks working as an enlisted rank on a Coast Guard vessel, learning the finer points of scraping, painting, and sanding.

In their third-year sophomore class, they become mentors to the fourth class. That summer they get more time and experience with the fleet, including five weeks sailing aboard the *Eagle*.

Second-year juniors train (give orders to) the freshman class and run Swab Summer as "cadre." Trainers from Cape May teach them how to do this. They also get to spend time with Coast Guard units and take a 44-foot sailboat around Long Island Sound for two weeks with three or four classmates and a safety officer.

The first-class seniors run the Corps of Cadets. They also find out if they'll get their "dream sheet" assignments as newly minted ensigns. This is determined by their combined GPA and military rankings and by what's available.

Most seniors spend their last summer at sea as junior officers or divide their time between sea duty and an internship. Some act as division officers aboard the *Eagle*.

Since the school became the first service academy to admit women, it has established dating rules. Fourth class can only date other freshmen. Third can date third and second class. Second can date first, second, and third. First can also date recent grads who are now Coast Guard ensigns. You can also date outside the Academy, including anyone who'll have you at Connecticut College just up Route 32, one reason that in looking at flag officer bios you'll find that a number of admirals' wives are Connecticut College alumnae, or "New London Lovelies."

While the dating rules were established to prevent those with more power abusing those with less, it hasn't always worked out that way.

In December 2005, charges were brought against twenty-two-year-old First Class Cadet Webster Smith claiming he raped and assaulted his former girlfriend and three other women cadets. His court-martial in June 2006 was the first court-martial of a cadet since the academy was founded. During the trial he and his accusers admitted to having sex on campus and binge drinking, while he denied coercing or extorting the women. A military jury acquitted him of rape but found him guilty of indecent assault, extortion, sodomy, and two lesser charges. He received a six-month sentence and served five months with time off for good behavior.

In September 2006, the Coast Guard established a task force to examine race and gender issues at the academy (Cadet Smith was African American). It was headed by retired Rear Adm. Errol Brown, the first African American to make flag rank. In November 2006, nineteen-year-old Third Class Cadet John Miller was arrested by Groton police and charged with third-degree sexual assault and unlawful restraint. He was at an off-campus drinking party with other cadets where, the police claimed, he assaulted a female civilian. She claimed he attempted to force her to have oral sex. He ended up with a broken nose and a trial date. The academy dismissed him and another cadet who was at the party. In April 2007 Miller was placed on special probation that would see his record cleared if he stayed out of trouble for two years.

Ten days after Miller's arrest, academy superintendent Rear Adm. James C. Van Sice was reassigned as director of personnel management at headquarters. An investigation of Van Sice was initiated as a result of information that surfaced during the task force's review. It concluded he had made some "inappropriate" comments to staff. In January 2007, Van Sice announced his early retirement from the Coast Guard.

In March 2007, the task force released its report with the jargon-laden title *Comprehensive Climate and Culture Optimization Review Effort (C3ORE)*, stating that while sports and academics are important, the academy had to refocus on leadership and character development to distinguish itself from civilian colleges.

The Coast Guard also launched a civil rights investigation into the Smith case after Smith filed a complaint claiming whites who committed offenses similar to his had only received administrative punishments. Between 1993 and 2005, the Academy had ten reported incidents of sexual misconduct. Eight resulted in dismissal or resignation. Two lacked sufficient evidence to pursue charges. The investigators ruled there was no race bias. In April 2008, the Coast Guard Court of Criminal Appeals ruled Smith's sentence was correct in law and fact.

Capt. Tom Jones was president of the jury in the Smith trial. "It came out later he didn't have any friends in his years at the academy," Jones tells me. "In a group that tight, that should have been a red flag. There are some cadets who in their last two years, when they get to be in a position of authority, cross the line and abuse that trust. In his case he was way over the line."

That isn't to say racism doesn't exist among some on campus. In July 2007, a noose was left in the seabag of an African American cadet aboard the *Eagle*. The next month, a second noose was found on the office floor of a white female officer conducting race relations training in response to that first incident. Just as swastikas symbolize Nazi terror, nooses symbolize the murder by lynching of thousands of black people that was a common occurrence in the United States in the late nineteenth and early twentieth centuries. In October 2007, Coast Guard Commandant Thad Allen went to the academy to tell the cadets that "when you enter the Coast Guard you are held to a higher standard" and that spreading "symbols of racism . . . is conduct unbecoming an officer," which could lead to dismissal or court-martial. He vowed to find those responsible, assigning a dozen CGIS investigators to the case. After an extensive months-long probe, they were unable to determine who was behind the two incidents.

The first black cadets were admitted to the Coast Guard Academy in the 1960s. The first women were admitted in 1976. In 1979, the all-male graduating class announced their class motto as "LCWB—loyalty, courage, wisdom, and brawn," but everyone knew it really stood for "Last class with balls."

Capt. Anne Flammang, chair of the Humanities Department, was in the second female class, which graduated in 1981. "The first class had fourteen women. Mine had twelve," she says.

"Was there overt hostility?"

She rolls her eyes. "Absolutely."

One of the incidents at the time involved two drunken first-class cadets kicking down the door of two female cadets and groping them in their beds. The only action taken was that one of the women got demerits during a room inspection for having a damaged door.

"There are still issues of young men and women and adolescent attitudes that might include some hostility, but the adults don't struggle the way they did then," Captain Flammang explains. "Today I think Coast Guard errors are errors of cognition, misunderstanding, or ignorance ["male cluelessness," as my late love used to put it] and not of a malicious nature."

"This is a completely different corps of cadets than when I went here in the 1990s. They're far more diverse in terms of gender. There was still a 'boys will be boys' attitude in my day very hostile toward women," says Lt. Scott Borgerson, director of the academy's Institute of Leadership. "I'm amazed how today the male cadets embrace their female counterparts and work together—although their writing skills have gone down badly."

Chase Hall houses all the academy cadets. In its foyer there's an inscription in the marble deck: WHO LIVES HERE REVERES HONOR, HONORS DUTY.

The rooms, which have two and sometimes three bunks, include blue comforters and white pillows, waxed tile floors, white cinder-block walls, storage space, desks, and Dell computers. *U.S. News* calls them dungeon-like, although I'd go with Spartan. All the wings are coed, while the bathrooms are separate male/female.

I knock on open room doors (they're all kept open till 7:00 P.M.) and chat with cadets who are trying to study but too polite to blow me off. I ask if they have any thoughts about the Smith case.

"I don't notice any harassment. That's not the culture here," Emily Kurt tells me. She's a government major and member of the sail club.

"I didn't even know about it till they announced it," Jennifer Hom adds. She's into operations research and computer analysis (ORCA) and also sails.

"I think they made a big deal out of it, like to set an example," Kyle Schaffner theorizes. Kyle is a big, goofy-looking blond kid who's into naval architecture and a member of the swim team. He escorts me to the cadet wardroom, where I've been invited to have lunch by the cadet leadership.

"I'm from Sandy Hook, New Jersey," Kyle tells me. "I like the missions of the Coast Guard and growing up would see them flying by. I went to check out the Naval Academy, and it didn't feel the same as when I came here. This is more of a community. Also, with three younger sisters, my parents are glad not to pay that extra $30,000 a year [for college tuition]."

A female cadet begins shouting out "the Clock," announcing the impending lunchtime fare. "Afternoon meal formation. The meal will consist of lentil soup, buttered egg noodles, beef stew . . ."

I'm introduced to Rob Foos, the regimental commander of cadets, and his posse (staff). He's six-six, clean-cut, with short blond hair. A management major, he plays lock for the rugby team, which he's quick to let me know is the divisional champ. "I'm also a basketball player." He grins. I wonder if he has any friends in the world.

The cadets all stand to attention as we walk through the crowd to a podium area where we're seated, introduced, and applauded.

"Everything's regimented," Foos explains, assuming that at my age I must be vision impaired. I watch a fourth classman with a shaved head as he squares his meal, looking straight ahead and kind of down, silently raising his fork in front of his mouth and then bringing it straight back with some noodles and salad attached. Rather than try the beef stew, he wisely shifts to a peanut butter and jelly sandwich, followed by a banana and milk.

After lunch I visit McAllister Hall's electronics labs, where third-class cadets are working with biometric face recognition software.

In the networking lab, they're working on cyber defense. Every year, each service academy sets up its own network with its own e-mail and codes, and the National Security Agency tries to damage it. The hackproof system wins the contest.

In the antennas lab, I'm told about the real-world application of a cadet's senior project. The fleet's 110-foot cutters have a kind of electromagnetic doughnut hole where their midrange communications drop out. They're sending the cadet and a faculty member to Hawaii to test out the midrange "towel bar antenna" he designed. I can see it's named for its shape.

Two years ago, a cadet designed a new engine room for a 75-foot river tug as his senior project. Another got a 41-foot utility boat running on biodiesel. Still another is doing her senior project based on work involving ultrawideband radar that can see through walls.

Leigh Dorsey, a self-described Air Force brat, with a flip hairdo and an attitude to match, spent the summer working with the Navy's dolphins and sea lions and plans to do her senior project on Coast Guard applications for the animals.

We walk into the design lab, where a group of fourth-year students are stress-testing their crane barge constructions, adding weights until they break, much to everyone's delight. It takes sixty-three pounds to break Cadet Trevor Clark's crane.

We climb up a metal stairway to the tow tank that runs the length of the building. Here the cadets' foam model hulls are towed through the water and tested for durability. I wonder if they tried this before letting defense contractor Northrop Grumman stretch their 110-foot cutters to 123s (that then had to be scrapped).

In the construction bay/power lab, they've just completed the frame for an autonomous dune buggy that will race other robot cars in Baja come the spring. Other courses include terrorism, nuclear detection, and strategic intelligence.

At 1600 (that's 4:00 P.M. civilian time), the cadets get two hours for sports. More than nine out of ten cadets earned a team letter in high school. Half were team captains. Nick Custer, a ruddy-cheeked third-class cadet, tours me around the facilities. He's a lifelong offshore sailor who's here because he wants to work at sea. We visit the huge indoor track in Roland Hall, then go downstairs and watch some racketball games. Thirty-six cadets are sharing the swimming pool's six lanes, doing timed laps under the traffic-control-like supervision of their coach. The main basketball court is being cleared for a college game.

We hike over to the old gym past the observatory, where they used to keep their live bear mascot, Objee ("objectionable presence"). Actually Objee was a series of young bears first brought on board in 1926. The bears were often allowed to wander around Chase Hall, the showers, and the wardroom. Capt. Scot ("with one *t*") Graham was a cadet and football player in the late 1970s. "My friend John Ochs was the bear keeper," he recalls. "The bear was huge. We had a special room in the barracks with mattresses on the floor and walls, and we'd dress up in extra pairs of jeans and sweatshirts and gloves, and four or five of us football players would wrestle the bear. She'd just toss us around like rag dolls."

Adm. Tom Atkin remembers the time the bear was taken to a birthday party in a cadet's room and ended up half under the bed eating the birthday cake with the cadet standing terrified on top of the bed shouting for the bear keeper.

In 1984, new laws about keeping wild animals as pets forced the academy to replace its last Objee, a 250-pound black bear, with a cadet in a bear costume. Before that, Objee had often been seen growling at Coast Guard–Merchant Marine Academy football games, which academy folks describe as "our Army-Navy game."

There's a game of flag football taking place on Memorial Field in the twilight of afternoon. I can imagine Objee lurking in the shadow of the stands, licking mariner's blood off her paws.

At the old basketball court, dozens of cadets are playing pickup games and riding stationary bikes under a bear emblem reading SCIENTIAE CEDIT MARE (The Sea Yields to Knowledge). The upstairs weight room is crowded. Downstairs a dozen wrestlers are matched up on the mats. Every sixty seconds the coach calls "Ready," and they take new positions, then "Wrestle," and they grapple, sweat, and strain with unbridled intensity.

We go over to the attic of the Alumni Building, where the boxing club is training. Nick Custer is unimpressed. He got to sail the Newport-to-Bermuda race last summer and is just waiting to do it again. I ask him if he charts his own courses. "Charting is easy," he claims. "Sailors aren't the brightest people in history, so it has to be practical enough so anyone can understand it."

Course should be around 284, and tower's at 325. So plot 325, and now go to Tango Tango," the instructor directs the bridge crew. I'm in the nautical science lab of Yeaton Hall, on the smaller of two bridge simulators where groups of cadets are training to drive real ships.

This sim-bridge for a 378-foot High Endurance Cutter is about 175 square feet and looks out on a computer-generated video scene of Charleston Harbor while also generating matching electronic charting and radar displays.

"Thirty seconds to mark. Tango Tango 325," one of the third-class crew calls out.

"Freeze it for a second," their instructor directs, and the virtual winds and waters of the bay stop moving. "Will course or speed change the effect of drift?" he asks.

"Yes," the eight young men and women agree.

"Would missing that mark make you cry?" one cadet asks another.

"Why?"

"It would make me cry if I missed."

"It's so dramatic when men cry," she teases him.

Most of the crew are now humped around the charting table, working with their course plotters and two-pronged dividers.

"So record your bearings. Try shooting for the light on the other side of Fort Sumter," they're told. The fort and the Arthur Ravenel Bridge are straight up the channel, whose computer-generated waters have come back to life on the bridge's screens.

"Mind your helm," one of the guys says.

"Mind your helm, buddy," his shipmate replies.

Behind the "bridge" is the controller's room, where a second instructor sits in front of a row of five flat-screen panels. Above him is the computer imaging of the harbor, and in front of him are closed-circuit images of the map table, radar screen, and other indicators the cadets are also viewing.

I go over to the "main bridge," where the all-female crew is at work. This room is about 250 feet square, and with its 180-degree wraparound screen the water motion fools my inner ear into believing the bridge is actually swaying with the motion of the waves.

"Why are you standing here?" Lt. Andy Passic, their instructor, asks one of the crew who's leaning over the map table.

"I'm helping her get the bearings."

"She plots, you record." He turns to her shipmate. "How can you shoot a bearing if you don't have a fix?"

"We're in a narrow channel—"

He turns to the officer of the deck, another lanky, confident girl with her hair in a bun.

"You are in charge of everything. You have the bridge."

I follow him through a door to another controller station with a bank of screens, monitors, mikes, and digital recorders on a low console. In front of it, Eric Conley, a contractor for General Dynamics, the company that built the simulators, is seated.

"This group is doing better than the last," Lieutenant Passic tells him. "They don't seem lost out here. They're on point, set, and drift. Every three minutes, they're getting a fix and adjusting for current."

He teaches nautical science labs Monday, Tuesday, Thursday, and Friday. After graduating from the academy in 2001, he went aboard the *Mellon,* a 378-foot cutter out of Seattle, then got command of his own 87-footer in San Francisco.

Conley tells me they have more than twenty projections they can use on the simulators, including San Francisco Bay, Block Island, Seattle, Kodiak, the approaches to Boston, the open ocean, a fictional port, and Key West, which, like Charleston, is a popular one.

Passic is back on the bridge reminding the crew that it takes a while to turn a 378, "and your bearing taker is giving bearings before the fix is called."

"On a real cutter they'll need to learn to plot, shoot some bearings, do some visual piloting," he explains on his return.

"There's a buoy straight ahead. You need to bear left," the deck officer instructs the helm as we watch them on a fifteen-inch black-and-white monitor that reminds me of early live television plays.

"They didn't use enough rudder and ended up outside the channel. I think they just figured that out," Andy Passic notes.

They also realize they missed the buoy by twenty-eight yards.

"When they hit a buoy, there's a computerized ding. We used to bang a garbage can outside the door," Andy says. "They get into it and really think they're there. They get so stressed I've seen cadets cry when they've hit a buoy."

He presses a button and a tugboat horn sounds, a prompt that gets them to return an acknowledgment to the cartoonish-looking video tug now coming up on their port side.

"Cadets will do around sixty hours in the bridge lab during their four years, which is the equivalent of perhaps two hundred hours on a real bridge in terms of what the instructors throw at them. We intensify the experience." Andy grins.

"Ten seconds to mark," one of the crew announces.

The controllers freeze Charleston Harbor with its single-span bridge, and I follow Andy back into the simulator. "A couple of points," he says. "One, you said, 'Come around 365 [degrees]'?"

"Just keeping them aware." Claire, the officer of the deck, blushes and smiles.

"Also, you came within twenty-eight yards of the green buoy. You cut it a lot closer than we'd like. Also, start turns with a fuller rudder. You can always back off. Also, taking a fix on a turn is not very accurate. I think you guys figured that out. So let's do it again." They continue.

OCS

"Line, get ready. Is line ready?" The buzzer sounds. *Bam, bam . . . Bam, bam . . . Bam, bam.* The officer candidates blast their silhouette targets; two rounds in three seconds from three yards.

"Is there alibi?" the firearms instructor asks on his mike after the firing stops. The red-shirted coaches and safety crew raise one arm each to indicate there were no malfunctions of the weapons, ammo, or target. The three officer candidates holster their weapons and step back to continue shooting the practical combat course from seven yards and then from kneeling and standing positions at seventeen yards. I've never seen such safety control on a gun range.

"If there is a jam or other problem, we expect them to fix it themselves, drop the clip, clear the jammed round, replace it, and fire again," explains Gunner Mike Lechler, the range master. They're firing 9 mm Berettas. The academy hasn't yet received the service's newer .40 caliber handguns.

We're in one of the two old basement firing ranges in Chase Hall that are undergoing rehab to improve ventilation and reduce lead exposure. Lead pollution is why I'm a big fan of the Army's green bullets, which the Coast Guard will soon adopt. They're made of tungsten instead of lead. They still kill people but leave ducks unharmed.

Officer Candidate School residents live in the C and D annexes of Chase Hall. There are two seventeen-week OCS courses that graduate 160 ensigns a year. When the service needs to expand rapidly, as it did after 9/11, the OCS school can gear up to three classes a year.

Sixty percent of the candidates are enlisted Coasties up from the ranks. The rest are college graduates. Their average age is twenty-six. Today's class is 76 percent male, 24 percent female. Most of the class, however, is off on their two-week "long cruise," with the fleet.

Cdr. Patti Seeman, the assistant school chief, petite with short brown hair and glasses, is officious at first but quick to warm. She tells me about the college precommissioning program, for schools with student bodies at least 25 percent minority, that helps tutor and support potential officer candidates. The program is one of the Coast Guard's attempts to increase its racial diversity. Diversity is not only a moral but an operational requirement since this is the only armed service in daily contact with the nation's increasingly diverse public.

The school also runs three- to five-week direct commission officer (DCO) courses that bring in abut 110 officers from other services each year, mainly physician assistants and helicopter pilots, along with selected civilians such as lawyers and intelligence agents. They also transition about a hundred reserve officers to the regular corps.

"We graduate over four hundred people a year. More go through our doors than the academy's," Commander Seeman notes.

Still, while OCS grads make up about half the officer corps, the modern Coast Guard has long been dominated by admirals wearing academy rings, including all its commandants to date. The social and political networks formed within each year class at the academy generate strong currents in favor of career advancement that seventeen weeks in OCS cannot match. In addition, until 2004, all academy graduates went straight to sea duty, and serving on a cutter is one of the few assured ways of moving up in the service.

With only 75 percent of cadets now going to ship duty, however, more valued at-sea billets are becoming available to OCS grads, and while I've been told that, "there'll probably be a woman commandant before there's an OCS commandant," Vice Commandant Vivien Crea, the Coast Guard's second-ranked officer, is both female and an OCS grad. The new superintendent of the academy, Adm. Scott Burhoe, is also the first OCS grad to run the school. So things do seem to be changing—and change is, after all, what the Coast Guard is about, and has been for more than two hundred years.

CHAPTER 3

Hamilton's Legacy

"A few armed vessels, judiciously stationed at the entrances of our ports, might at a small expense be made useful sentinels of the laws."

—Alexander Hamilton, *The Federalist Papers*, November 27, 1787

"I did not think it possible for them to get to us, but somehow they did . . . I think it is a miracle that I am alive to tell this tale."

—Capt. Israel Hawkins, after he and his crew were rescued off New Jersey, January 20, 1903

"One wave I thought Willie washed overboard, and then a minute later he's up again, but I swore he was gone. I've never been that scared in my whole life," the jug-eared Larry Clements confesses to me. I'm three beers and three Stolis into the wind, which is when you really have to concentrate on your note taking, like that night in that whorehouse bar in Belize with those British army spies.

Anyway, I figure my last night in New London I'd better check out the local Coastie bars, the old Dutch Tavern with its tap beer and boiled eggs in brine where Eugene O'Neill used to hang out, and the Roadhouse with its pretty "tenders" behind the boat-shaped bar. Showing me around the foggy streets and alleys is Lt. Scott Borgerson, the six-foot-four professor. Having told me his most harrowing rescue adventure earlier in the evening, he's gone on to take the standard demur that it probably isn't worth putting in my book because "there are other Coasties who've been through worse."

Now we've run into one of his old crew from that creaky 82-footer in Grand Isle, Louisiana, on the tentlike back deck of the Roadhouse. Scott, who's otherwise brilliant, has come out here to cadge cigarettes from whoever has them. My sister's going to be dead of lung cancer in five days, the same thing that killed our mom, but I don't say anything because I'm a reporter and, drunk or sober, I'm working right now.

It's not a setup, his old shipmate showing up tonight. You just have to remember how small their organization is. If there are six degrees of separation in the world, there are rarely more than two in the Coast Guard.

So with Larry's arrival, Scott Borgerson decides to repeat the tale. "We got the call to stand by. It was really rough, but these divers were lost on this oil rig, and one of them was the station CO's cousin. So we're going out the channel and there's this sailboat—its sails are in tatters, and the people on board think they're going to die. We had this M-1 [rifle] with a line, and the guy who fired it—the wind just took it, and it got tied up in the rigging. So we then got another shot over, and that worked. We got them under tow, but we're in like thirty-foot seas, and they've got their anchor out and we can't pull the hook loose. We're on the radio saying, 'You have to cut the line'—and he's like, 'It's chain, I can't,' and I say, 'Then you'll have to get in the water and a helicopter will hoist you out.' Finally the hook broke loose, and we were able to tow them back in. We got on the radio, and the chief's like, 'OK, now go back out.' So we know we're not going to find those divers. We know they're already dead, but we're out there, and we're under way for seventy-two hours with these waves just washing over us, and no one can sleep or eat 'cause you can't make food in these conditions, and everyone's sick but me and this big Samoan chief and he says, 'It's just you and me.' "

That's when the big wave came that Larry thought washed Willie overboard, "and then a minute later he's up again, but I swore he was gone."

"So finally we're heading back in," Scott continues, "and there's another sailboat wallowing in the seas with no engine, no control, and you wonder what they're doing out here, and my crew's like, 'We don't see nothing, do we?' But I have to get on the radio and say, 'This is Coast Guard Cutter *Point Sal,* are you in distress?' They're like, 'We're dying here. Save us or we'll all drown.' The waves are so huge our props are coming out of the water, but we still manage to get a line on them and tow them in for like twelve hours more, and when we get to the dock it's still so rough we have to kind of accelerate and whipsaw them up to the seawall, where these sailors are able to grab their lines. Happened back in 2000."

"What about the divers?"

"They found one of the bodies. Don't think they ever recovered the other one."

Scott thinks it's like war, but it's not. It's like its own thing.

A few minutes later, we run into the crew of the 110-foot cutter *Bainbridge Island,* up from Sandy Hook to escort a nuclear submarine out from the shipyard. Their engineer tells us they have an officer candidate on board doing his long cruise.

Scott puts on his loudest command voice. "OC FEDERER, FRONT AND CENTER." Nothing. "FEDERER, STAND UP." Officer Candidate Jerry Federer, a muscular guy in civvies with a swooping wave of short dark hair and intense blue eyes, peeks nervously around the curtain, then saunters over to brace in front of Scott, smiling uncomfortably with a beer in one hand, not sure if this guy's for real. Scott lightens up, offers to buy him a round, and asks if he has a cigarette. "I was thinking of jumping over the side of the deck when I heard you call out like that," Jerry confesses. He's worked in law enforcement until now, he tells me, but he'd like to get into marine safety, environmental stuff, oil-spill response, become one of the "duck scrubbers."

So what makes these guys who they are, and how did they form such a colorful cast of characters, from Ida Lewis to "Hell Roaring" Mike Healy to "Jug Ears" Larry Clements, protecting our maritime domain? Turns out it takes about two hundred years to salt them properly.

The origins of the Coast Guard can be traced back to the establishment of the federal Lighthouse Service in 1789, though the organization prefers to date itself from the establishment of the Revenue Cutter Service a year later. Both were the creation of Alexander Hamilton, America's first secretary of the treasury and a founding Federalist. Long before his fatal duel with Aaron Burr, he and Thomas Jefferson differed over whether the new nation should be a loosely affiliated confederation of states supporting an agrarian culture of independent farmers (and slaves) or whether, as the Federalists argued, there should be a strong central government and bank to protect and nourish a growing market economy driven by urban merchants dependent on sea trade. Jefferson claimed Hamilton was supporting "a new aristocracy of monied corporations" but in the end lost his argument at the Constitutional Convention in Philadelphia. He and the other anti-federalists did force an important compromise, however, getting the convention to adapt the first ten amendments to the constitution, known as the Bill of Rights.

Still, for a strong central government to function, it would need revenue, and during the early years of the republic the states were unwilling to share theirs. As a result, import duties accounted for 90 percent of federal revenues. To ensure navigational safety for merchant traders, Hamilton oversaw the maintenance and construction of a string of lighthouses along the eastern seaboard.

To prevent the smuggling of untaxed goods, he got Congress to approve the construction of ten single-masted patrol vessels called revenue cutters to intercept contraband. With the disbandment of the Continental Navy in 1790 and until the U.S. Navy was created eight years later, the hundred or so revenue marines manning these ships were America's only seagoing military force. In a June 4, 1791, letter of instruction, Hamilton cautioned the new officers that "[your] countrymen are freemen, and, as such, are impatient of everything that bears the least mark of a domineering spirit. [You] will, therefore, refrain, with the most guarded circumspection, from whatever has the semblance of haughtiness, rudeness, or insult . . . [You] will endeavor to overcome difficulties, if any are experienced, by a cool and temperate perseverance in [your] duty—by address [skill] and moderation, rather than by vehemence or violence." Thus the Coast Guard's forbears began to adopt an attitude of quiet professionalism that would serve them well in the coming centuries.

Even before the Lighthouse and Revenue services were established, along the rugged shores of the great fishing, shipping, and whaling commonwealth in whose statehouse hung a golden cod, a voluntary organization, the Massachusetts Humane Society, was formed in 1785 to help mariners in distress. Its early members and supporters included Governor James Bowdoin, Harvard Medical School founders Drs. John Warren and Ben Waterhouse, and Revolutionary veterans Paul Revere, John Hancock, and Sam Adams. Thomas Jefferson exchanged letters with the Humane Society; George Washington called its efforts "highly estimable." These initial efforts consisted of establishing a string of "refuge" huts for stranded sailors.

Only much later, in 1848, would the federal government become involved in the shore-based rescue business, providing funds for volunteer lifesavers along the wild New Jersey coast.

From 1798 to 1800, the United States and France carried out a "Quasi-War" from the waters of New Jersey to the tropical West Indies inspired by Revolutionary France's unhappiness over increased U.S.-British trade. French seizures of U.S. ships convinced President John Adams to reestablish the U.S. Navy, with the Revenue Marine (as the service was known early on) coming under the Navy's command during times of war, a pattern later followed by the Coast Guard. During the Quasi-War, which included dozens of real casualties, the U.S. Navy captured eighty-five French ships, twenty of these seized by the Revenue Marine, ten by the Revenue Cutter *Pickering* alone. The *Pickering* sailed under the command of Lt. (later Navy Commodore) Edward Preble. In a brilliant nine-hour engagement, he led his ship with its crew of seventy and fourteen four-pounder guns against the much larger French privateer *L'Egypte Conquise*, with a crew of 250 and eighteen six- and nine-pounders. In the end, the *Conquise* was forced to surrender. The *Pickering* was later lost at sea with its entire crew after being transferred to the Navy.

The U.S. Congress prohibited U.S. vessels from engaging in the slave trade beginning in 1794 and by 1807 had banned the importation of any new slaves into the United States. Unfortunately, Eli Whitney's invention of the cotton gin in 1793 made expansion of slavery in the cotton-growing South economically beneficial to that region's economic elite. The Revenue Service began seizing slave ships and freeing their captives, but the owners and crews were rarely convicted in U.S. courts, and the illegal trade continued. In a cruel irony, until the 1840s, U.S. slaves served as cooks, stewards, and seamen on board a number of revenue cutters chasing down the slavers.

From 1807 to 1809, the Revenue Service also enforced the Embargo Act that froze almost all commerce with Europe. It was President Jefferson's attempt to influence Britain's restrictive trade policies and impressment (forced recruitment) of thousands of U.S. sailors at sea, short of war. The Embargo Act and the service's attempts to enforce it proved hugely unpopular, particularly in maritime New England, where a mob in Gloucester, Massachusetts, destroyed a cutter. America's Rescue Warriors would not see their reputation fall so low again until the Prohibition era of the twentieth century, when the U.S. Coast Guard was tasked with stopping the illegal importation of alcohol.

With the outbreak of the War of 1812, the Revenue Marine saw additional military action. The most dramatic encounter was that of the *Eagle* and the

British brigantine *Dispatch* off Long Island on the morning of October 11, 1814. The *Eagle* was badly outgunned in the initial encounter, its flag three times shot away and replaced by volunteers. Capt. Frederick Lee finally beached the ship to prevent it from sinking. He and his crew then dragged their four-pounder cannons up a 160-foot bluff under fire. From their new position, they continued fighting the *Dispatch*. When they ran out of cannonballs, they retrieved balls that had been fired at them and lodged in the ground, tearing up their ship's logbook for wadding. Finally, in late afternoon, they were forced to surrender.

After the war, the Revenue Marine would go on to battle pirates from New Orleans to the Leeward Islands of the Caribbean. In late August 1819, in the Gulf of Mexico, the cutters *Alabama* and *Louisiana* captured the pirate ship *Bravo* and its master, Jean LaFarge, a lieutenant of Jean Lafitte. In 1820 the cutters attacked and burned the notorious pirate enclave on Breton Island, off southeast Louisiana; 185 years later, 80 percent of Breton Island would be washed away by Hurricane Katrina.

The Revenue Cutter Service (its official name as of 1863) would see additional action in the Seminole Wars of Florida (1817–58), the Mexican-American War (1846–48), the Civil War (1861–65), and the Spanish-American War of 1898 before being incorporated into the modern Coast Guard just in time for the maritime horrors of World War I.

America's other sentinels of the coast were its lighthouses and, where there were no islands or promontories of land available on which to build a warning beacon, lightships. America's first lightship, actually a small boat, was anchored in the lower Chesapeake in 1820. By the end of that summer, it was so battered it had to be relocated. Three years later, the first "outside" lightship was anchored off Sandy Hook, New Jersey. Between 1820 and 1983, 119 lightships would stand duty off America's shores before being replaced by automated platforms and buoys.

Life aboard lightships often involved seasickness, boredom, dreary meals of "scouse" (salt beef, potatoes, and onions), endless card games, and occasional terror. Some were sunk in storms, including Buffalo's Light Vessel 82 and its six-man crew on Lake Erie in November 1913. A few days later, a board washed ashore with a message from the captain to his wife. "Good-bye, Nellie, ship is breaking up fast—Williams."

A number were also lost to collisions, like the Nantucket lightship that was run down in the fog by *Titanic*'s sister ship *Olympic* in 1934 with seven of its eleven crew killed.

In 1832, the revenue cutters expanded their mission to search and rescue when the treasury secretary ordered them to begin winter cruises to provide aid to sailors in distress.

However, nineteenth-century sailors faced danger not only from shoals and storms but also from a new maritime propulsion system, the steam engine. Once American inventor Robert Fulton built the first commercial steamship, the *Clermont,* running it up the Hudson from New York City to Albany in 1807, the age of steam bubbled forward with breathtaking speed, expanding from Mississippi paddlewheelers to oceangoing steamships carrying the first great wave of Irish, German, Italian, and other postcolonial immigrants in the 1840s, many of them riding below deck in low-cost "steerage," by the stern rudder that steered the ship.

Unfortunately, when too much steam pressure built up in their boilers, these ships tended to explode, often with horrendous loss of life. From 1811 to 1851, over 20 percent of U.S. river accidents were caused by boiler explosions. In 1832, 14 percent of all steamships exploded, resulting in more than a thousand deaths. In 1838, with an appalled public demanding action, Congress enacted a steamship safety act that would lead to the eventual creation of the Steamship Inspection Service.

Today, when the Coast Guard establishes safety standards for recreational or commercial vessels, licenses mariners, inspects oil tankers or cruise ships, formulates rules for hazardous waste and petroleum transport, or carries out its many other efforts to improve maritime safety and prevent disaster at sea, these efforts can be traced back to that first navigational law of 1838.

Later, in 1884, the government would establish the Bureau of Navigation to oversee construction, operation, and documentation of all U.S. merchant vessels and those who crew them. It would combine the two as the Bureau of Navigation and Steamship Inspection in 1932 and then, following the Lighthouse Service in 1939, would be incorporated into the Coast Guard in 1942.

By 1839, the British navy was targeting the pirate slave trade from its African ports of embarkation to its New World destinations with a vigor unmatched by its American counterparts. That summer, the British navy delivered four American-flagged slave ships to New York Harbor in an attempt to embarrass U.S. courts into enforcing their own anti-slave-trading laws.

On August 27, the Revenue Cutter *Washington* seized a slave ship named *Amistad* off Long Island, but only after its African captives had rebelled and taken control of the vessel. They would be brought into New London, Connecticut, and put through a series of trials leading to an 1841 Supreme Court ruling upholding their freedom to return to their homeland (a story retold in the 1997 Steven Spielberg movie *Amistad*).

In 1843, the Revenue Marine gained an inspirational new leader in the person of Capt. Alexander Fraser. During his five years in command he oversaw the construction of the first steam cutters, standardized operations, abolished shipboard slavery and flogging, raised salaries, established a merit system for promotion, and advocated unifying the cutter service with the Lighthouse and Life-Saving services, envisioning a multimission maritime Coast Guard that would not come into existence for another ninety years.

In 1848, with the end of the Mexican War and the U.S. annexation of California, Fraser was ordered to sail a revenue brig around Cape Horn to San Francisco, arriving eleven months later, after many adventures along the way, just in time for the gold rush, at which point most of his crew deserted him to join in the digging. In San Francisco he became a key enforcer of civic order, trying to secure revenues, enforce shipping laws, and suppress mutinies amid some five hundred gold rush vessels filled with thousands of rowdy, violent '49ers anxious to make their fortunes no matter what. Later he'd sail down to San Diego and on to Hawaii, a true adventurer. Unfortunately, with his absence from Washington the Revenue Marine fell back under the influence of the patronage-ridden Customs Service.

The year 1848 also saw the first effort to bring federal dollars to the all-volunteer lifesaving system that, at the time, consisted mainly of Humane Society rescue boats and boathouses in Massachusetts. Dr. William Newell, a congressman and physician from New Jersey who'd been witness to one of the frequent and terrible shipwrecks then taking place along the shore, added an amendment to the lighthouse appropriations bill to provide $10,000 for lifesaving stations and apparatus between Sandy Hook and Egg Harbor, New Jersey.

Apparatus used in lifesaving included metal surfboats and 30-foot whaleboats, lanterns, rockets and mortars, heaving sticks, shooting and hawser lines, block and tackle, sand anchors, breach buoys, and life cars, as well as boat carts and big two-wheeled beach carts to carry all that gear in.

Where shipwrecks were close enough to shore, a small line would be thrown or fired by rocket or gun to sailors on board, who would then pull a manila hawser line and tail block onto the ship and tie it as high up in the rigging as they could. Secured at the beach end by a sand anchor, the lifesavers would then rig a two-line pulley to bring the survivors ashore. They would often come in a breeches buoy, a life ring with canvas pants sewn into it, or sometimes in a life car, a small galvanized metal boat with a sealable hatch on top that could carry two to four people lying flat inside. When it was first used, in 1850 at the wreck of the *Ayrshire* off the coast of New Jersey, the life car saved 201 of the 202 people aboard.

The most famous of the line-throwing devices was the Lyle gun, a short-barreled cannon designed by an Army ordnance officer named David Lyle. It could fire an eighteen-pound shot with line attached up to three hundred yards with a full charge of gunpowder.

Of course, when a shipwreck was too far offshore, the lifesavers, in their cork vests, had to take to their surfboats to effect a rescue.

Another regular source of rescue was lighthouse keepers, whose primary mission was maintaining aids to navigation but who also, because they lived on coastal bluffs or rocky offshore isles, were well positioned to help save the victims of tumultuous seas. The most famous lighthouse keeper/rescuer was Ida Lewis, known in her day as "the bravest woman in America" and recipient of the kind of accolades later awarded Amelia Earhart and (to a lesser degree) astronaut Sally Ride.

She was fifteen years old in 1857 when she joined her father, Hosea, who had recently been appointed keeper of the Lime Rock Lighthouse just off Newport, Rhode Island. Within months, she had made her first rescue of four men whose boat capsized. Shortly thereafter, Hosea suffered a stroke that effectively made her the lighthouse keeper. She would be given the official appointment some years later, after her father's death. Along with tending the light, she also helped take care of her family, including three siblings that she rowed to and from school every day. During her many years at Lime Rock, she was officially credited with saving eighteen lives but may have saved as many as twenty-five, including a friend who fell off a boat and almost drowned when Ida was sixty-three. Among her rescues was that of four young men from well-to-do families who capsized their sailboat while roughhousing. In 1867, three sheepherders went into the harbor to save their boss's prizewinning sheep. She saved all three plus the sheep. During a fierce storm in 1869, she saved two soldiers whose sailboat had overturned. Articles about her then appeared in *Harper's Weekly*, *Leslie's* magazine, the *New York Tribune*, and other periodicals. President Ulysses S. Grant and Vice President Schuyler Colfax (whose sister was a light keeper in Michigan) came to visit her at Newport, as did thousands of others over time. Girls began to pin their hair in "the Ida Lewis fashion," while "Ida Lewis" hats and scarves flew off store shelves (with no profit returned to her). Several pieces of music and poetry were penned in her honor. Still she remained an essentially private person, a valued trait for a keeper. In 1907, she wrote, "Sometimes the spray dashes against these windows so thick I can't see out, and for days at a time the waves are so high that no boat would dare come near the rock, not even if we were starving. But I am happy. There's peace on this rock that you don't get on shore."

When she died of a stroke on October 24, 1911, all the boats in Newport Harbor tolled their bells in her honor.

Today the Coast Guard is rightfully proud of having a higher proportion of active-duty women than any of the other armed services and of having no position in which a woman can't serve. Still, the Lighthouse Service was exceptional in that it had over four hundred women serving as keepers and assistant keepers throughout the nineteenth century, a time during which few women worked outside the home other than as clericals, maids, field hands, school teachers, or factory workers, and none could vote. Yet Ida Lewis said she was not comfortable being made a hero and exemplar by the nineteenth-century feminist movement that grew up alongside an increasingly militant abolitionist movement. She was too reclusive for that.

The abolitionists argued there was a basic contradiction between America's claim that all men are created equal and the holding of human beings as chattel slaves. That contradiction also played out in the economy between the labor-dependent, manufacturing-oriented industrial North and slave-dependent, cotton-exporting South, leading to increasing violence, political division, or "sectionalism," and finally to war.

In 1858, seven months after being launched, the Revenue Cutter *Harriet Lane* seized a suspected slave ship, the *Wanderer*, outside New York Harbor. The fact the schooner had been outfitted with tanks designed to hold fifteen thousand gallons of fresh water was one indication of its intended use. Even so, federal officials released the ship for lack of evidence. A few months later, it picked up five hundred captives on the Congo River in Africa during a yellow fever epidemic and was briefly chased by a U.S. Navy ship at the river mouth before escaping. Eighty of its prisoners died before the *Wanderer*'s "cargo" was delivered to Jekyll Island, Georgia, in November of 1858. This was one of the last smuggling runs of "black gold" before John Brown's raid on Harpers Ferry, Abraham Lincoln's election, and the outbreak of the Civil War.

In April 1861, the *Harriet Lane* steamed into Charleston Harbor along with other warships to help relieve the siege of Fort Sumter, which followed on South Carolina's secession from the Union. On April 12, they were witness to Confederate batteries opening fire on the fort, in a bold act of treason and rebellion against the United States of America.

While the bombardment continued, the *Harriet Lane* observed a sail steamer like itself approaching the harbor. It signaled the unknown vessel to hoist a flag. When the ship failed to respond, the *Harriet Lane* fired a shot across its bow, the first maritime shot fired in the Civil War. The target ship then raised the Stars and Stripes to identify itself as American and was allowed to pass. That ship, the *Nashville,* would quickly reveal its true allegiance, taking action as a blockade-runner under Confederate colors. The *Harriet Lane* would go on to join the August attack on Confederate forts at Hatteras Inlet, North Carolina, lending fire support to ground troops in the war's first Union victory. In 1862, the Navy sent the *Harriet Lane* to blockade the coast of Texas until Confederates captured it a year later and converted it to a blockade-runner.

Of the twenty-eight revenue cutters at the start of the war, six were seized by or defected to the Confederacy, while the others came under Navy control. Some of these, including six built in 1863, continued patrolling the nation's shipping lanes looking for Confederate privateers, assisting sailors in distress, and protecting federal income derived from tariffs and customs.

The American Civil War stimulated an industrial and technological expansion that included large-scale steel production, the growth of railroads, and the introduction of steam power, gun turrets, and metal armor on American ships of war, including the Revenue Cutter *E. A. Stevens.*

The "Hoboken Ironclad," built in New Jersey, was a prototype warship, a 110-foot semisubmersible twin-screw gunboat with a large forward-facing gun and two boat howitzers on pivots. Unfortunately, it arrived in the waters off Hampton Roads, Virginia, too late to participate in the deafening but inconclusive battle between two other ironclads, the USS *Monitor* and CSS *Virginia,* on March 9, 1862. It did get to fire on the *Virginia* a month later, before spending much of the rest of the war guarding New York Harbor.

The Lighthouse Service also provided help to the Revenue Marine and Union cause, assisting in the capture and control of more than a hundred Southern lighthouses and destruction of Southern lightships, some of which were then used as harbor obstructions by blockading Union forces.

The end of the Civil War saw rapid economic growth for the United States as railroads opened up not only the West but the seashore to vast numbers of day-trippers and families from all classes. Areas such as Coney Island, Cape Cod, Atlantic City, and the Jersey Shore became holiday destinations for growing numbers of beachgoers and recreational boat owners, thousands of whom would later come to depend on the U.S. Coast Guard when they got into trouble.

The United States also grew geographically. In 1867, it purchased Alaska from Russia for just over $7 million. While some condemned the deal as Secretary of State William Seward's Folly and President Andrew Johnson's Polar Bear Garden, most were supportive of American expansionism.

The story of the Revenue Cutter Service and the Coast Guard in Alaska is an epic tale in its own right. Until World War II, they were the major representatives of federal authority in the territory. As such they did law enforcement, search and rescue, oceanographic research, fisheries and wildlife protection, dispute resolution, and a host of other essential jobs, many of which the Coast Guard continues to carry on today.

For close to forty years, two revenue cutters named *Rush* patrolled the Bering Sea chasing outlaw hunters who threatened to wipe out the fur seal population of the Pribilof Islands. The poachers, trying to maintain their black market in skins, coined what would become a popular phrase, warning each other to "get there early to avoid the *Rush*."

More famous than the *Rush* was the cutter *Bear* under the command of Capt. "Hell Roaring" Mike Healy, long a heroic figure and symbol of rough justice in territorial Alaska. The *New York Sun* wrote, "Captain Mike Healy is a good deal more distinguished person in the waters of the far Northwest than any President of the United States or any potentate of Europe has yet become . . . and if you should ask in the Arctic Sea, 'Who is the greatest man in America?' the instant answer would be, 'Why, Mike Healy.' "

Healy was a master sailor, and he and his crew created navigational charts, tracked ice, and rescued hundreds of mariners in distress including, in 1888, 160 whalers after their ships were smashed against massive sea rocks during a violent gale at Point Barrow, Alaska, three hundred miles north of the Arctic Circle. Several years later, noting how commercial hunting of seals, whales, and caribou was threatening Native Alaskans' food sources, Healy sailed the *Bear* to Siberia. There he negotiated the purchase of seventeen reindeer from a local Chukchi village chief, then had his crew row them out to the *Bear*, where they were hoisted aboard by sling. Back in Alaska, he then helped introduce reindeer herding to the native people.

The Coast Guard identifies Healy, the son of an Irish immigrant father and slave mother, as one of its heroes of African American descent, though clearly, at the time, he and his more illustrious brothers, the president of Georgetown University and the bishop of Portland, Maine, were "passing," for white.

"If they [the Revenue Service] had known he was African American, there's no way they'd have let him be in command of white officers," says Dennis Noble, a retired Coast Guard senior chief, professor, and author working on a Healy biography.

Healy got his "Hell Roaring" reputation in saloons up and down the West Coast and was twice court-martialed for abusing his crew. Reviled by both outlaw sealers and temperance crusaders, he would lose command of the *Bear* before having an Alaskan cutter command returned to him only to lose it again. Arguing in his own defense, he insisted that "I take all the responsibility, all the risks, all the hardships that my office would call upon me to take. I do not steer by any man's compass but my own." Restored to honor and retired as number three in the Revenue Cutter Service in 1903, he died of a heart attack less than a year later.

Healy's introduced reindeer, a mobile source of food, would prove fortuitous when, in 1897, 273 whalers in eight ships were trapped by early ice near Point Barrow. With the threat of mass starvation growing, President William McKinley ordered the Revenue Cutter Service to take action. The *Bear* sailed north to within fifteen hundred miles of the stranded men. From there a relief party consisting of Lt. David Jarvis, Lt. Ellsworth "Bully" Bertholf, Dr. Samuel Call, a Russian guide named Koltchoff, seven dogs, and two sleds began the Overland Relief Expedition. Three and a half months later, in March 1898, having hired more dogs and Native Alaskan drivers and purchased and herded 448 meaty reindeer along the way, having fought through blinding snowstorms, fallen down dangerous crevasses, and endured temperatures of forty-eight degrees below zero, they reached the whalers, fed and treated them, and protected some native villagers they'd been harassing.

After the ice broke in June, the three surviving whale ships sailed free. In July, the *Bear* arrived, and the last ninety-seven whalers sailed with it for Seattle. Seventeen years later, relief-party member Ellsworth Bertholf would become the first commandant of the U.S. Coast Guard.

In 1871, the Revenue Cutter Service was put under the newly created Revenue Marine Bureau, headed by treasury official Sumner Increase Kimball. Kimball was a highly competent lawyer and public servant with a receding hairline, a steady gaze, and a mustache that would shame a walrus. Along with professionalizing the officer corps and upgrading the fleet, he also began to take control of the Life-Saving Service, sending Capt. John Faunce (former CO of the *Harriet Lane*) on an inspection tour of the lifesaving network. Among other things, Faunce found "apparatus rusty for want of care and some of it ruined."

Neglected during the Civil War, the volunteer system was now rife with politics and patronage, its stations decayed and far too few, too isolated, and too undermanned to work in a coordinated manner. Kimball began to campaign for a paid, professional service as increased U.S. migration and shipborne trade also led to an increase in the number of lives lost and cargoes sunk.

With congressional support, he instituted the stationing of paid six-man boat crews at the stations, set standards and regulations for "surfmen," introduced new equipment like the Lyle gun, and rapidly expanded the number of stations from the rocky coast of his home state of Maine to the sandy Outer Banks of North Carolina. Still it was too little.

On a stormy night in November 1877, the Navy ship *Huron* ran aground off Nag's Head, North Carolina. Although they were only two hundred yards from shore, the crew stayed aboard hoping for help that never came. Due to a lack of funding, local lifesaving stations were closed until December. By the next morning, ninety-eight men had lost their lives to the freezing cold waves that roared across their battered decks. Two months later and twenty-three miles to the north, the steamship *Metropolis* ran aground with the loss of eighty-five lives. Congress, under pressure from an outraged public, the insurance industry, and shipping companies, soon authorized construction of new lifesaving stations and the establishment of the U.S. Life-Saving Service as an agency within the Treasury Department.

Sumner Kimball became its first and only superintendent. Soon he was overseeing 189 lifesaving stations: 139 on the eastern seaboard, 38 on the Great

Lakes and Ohio River, 5 along the Gulf, and 7 on the Pacific coast. As eastern stations were set closer together, the service initiated a system of overlapping beach patrols during which surfmen from adjacent stations exchanged "checks," small metal badges, to prove their patrol had been completed.

In his commitment to honesty, professional standards, and effective execution of mission, Kimball would both foreshadow and live to become a part of the Progressive Era that marked the opening years of the new century. At the same time, he reflected many of the prejudices of his time, once telling Mike Healy he had no business being a revenue cutter officer because he was a Catholic (it's no wonder Healy forgot to mention he was also black).

Nonetheless, records show the Life-Saving Service did employ a number of "colored surfmen" along the Maryland, Virginia, and North Carolina coasts. In 1880, African American Richard Etheridge, a former slave, a Civil War combat veteran, and "as good a surfman as there is on this coast, black or white," according to one of Kimball's inspectors, was appointed keeper of the Pea Island, North Carolina, lifesaving station on the Outer Banks. Pea Island was the only all-black station in the service and carried out numerous heroic rescues. Etheridge's constant military-like drills assured that the Pea Island men were among the best trained in the service.

One of their most renowned rescues took place on a storm-wracked night in October of 1896 when the schooner *E. S. Newman,* having survived a savage hurricane and drifted almost a hundred miles without sail, managed to ground two miles north of the station. When Etheridge and his crew arrived on the scene with their beach cart, they found the water too high and the sand too wet to mount their Lyle gun. With nine survivors, including the captain, his wife, and their three-year-old child, clinging to the wreckage, Etheridge directed two of his strongest men to tie heavy line around themselves and move into the crashing surf while the rest of his crew secured the beach end of the rope. The two made it to the ship, where, amid mountainous breakers, they managed to tie on to one of the crew. The three of them were then hauled back through the raging surf to the beach. Switching off the two lead swimmers on each turn, this operation was repeated nine more times until all, including the child, were saved.

For their efforts the Pea Island crew received the Gold Lifesaving Medal, the highest award for lifesavers. Unfortunately, the medal wasn't awarded until 1996, a century after their action. The belated recognition came as a result of the efforts of a Coast Guard reservist, two graduate students, and a fourteen-year-old North Carolina girl, Kate Burkart, who wrote letters of inquiry about the rescue to her state's elected officials.

The toughness that was demanded of station keepers and surfmen like Richard Etheridge was reflected in the 1899 Blue Book Regulations of the Life-Saving Service, which read in part, "The statement of the keeper that he did not try to use the boat because the sea or surf was too heavy will not be accepted unless attempts to launch it were actually made and failed."

This inspired Cape Hatteras station keeper Patrick Etheridge (no relation to Richard) to tell one nervous young surfman as they prepared to launch on yet another seemingly impossible rescue: "The Blue Book says we've got to go out, and it doesn't say a damn thing about having to come back."

The coming of the twentieth century was marked by a series of marine and maritime disasters. The year of the century, 1900, brought one of the costliest when the wealthy Victorian port town of Galveston, Texas, built on a sandy barrier island, was devastated by a storm-driven sea surge that killed more than six thousand people, about a third of the town's population.

Four years later in New York, the excursion steamboat *General Slocum* caught fire, burned, and sank in the East River. Of the 1,350 or so passengers on board at the time, 1,021 died as a result of the fire. A presidential commission found that lack of fire drills and boat drills, a complete failure of onboard fire hoses, defective life preservers, and inefficient inspections by the Steamboat Inspection Service all contributed to the tragedy. The service was cited for failing to meet even minimal requirements for testing hose pressure, engine, boiler, and hull worthiness and for being too close to the industry it was supposed to regulate.

That kind of corruption and incompetence was the bane of the new Progressive movement that saw preventable disasters such as the *General Slocum* fire, urban slums, industrial monopolies, and unsanitary food, air, and water as part and parcel of a political economy in need of scientific and professional reform. Efficiency was a byword of this often contradictory movement that opposed child labor but frequently failed to support trade unions, embraced women's rights but excluded Jews, Catholics, and blacks, and saw both social work and alcohol prohibition as equally effective ways to improve society. Leading Progressives ranged from muckraking writers and journalists like Ida Tarbell, Lincoln Steffens, and Upton Sinclair to political leaders including William Jennings Bryan, Wisconsin's Robert La Follette, and New York's Theodore Roosevelt.

The Life-Saving Service's Sumner Kimball certainly fit the Progressive mold, as did George Putnam, appointed by President William Howard Taft to head the newly created Lighthouse Service in 1910, and Capt. Ellsworth Bertholf, appointed captain-commandant of the Revenue Cutter Service in 1911.

George Putnam was an engineer from Iowa who as a U.S. Coast and Geodetic Survey scientist helped establish the Alaska-Canada border line, examined the world's largest meteor with Robert Peary in Greenland, and directed the first coastal survey of the Philippine Islands. During his twenty-five-year tenure as the Department of Commerce's commissioner of lighthouses, he worked tirelessly to make the service a model of efficiency. During his time, the number of aids to navigation (ATONs) doubled, and he created a retirement plan for lighthouse personnel, oversaw the electrification and initial automation of lighthouses and other ATONs, and introduced a range of new safety technologies, including radio beacons, lighted buoys, and foghorns.

"The lighthouse and lightship appeal to the interests and better instincts of man," he argued, "because they are symbolic of never-ceasing watchfulness, of steadfast endurance in every exposure, of widespread helpfulness."

After participating in the Overland Relief Expedition in Alaska, the square-jawed, bald, and ruggedly handsome Ellsworth Bertholf traveled in Siberia and commanded the *Bear* on Bering Sea patrol before being appointed head of the Revenue Cutter Service. Raised in New York City, a graduate of the Revenue Cutter School of Instruction, he was also the the service's first officer to attend the Naval War College in Newport, Rhode Island. This was at a time when the work of one of its faculty, Capt. Alfred Thayer Mahan, was electrifying the Navy and the nation. In his book *The Influence of Sea Power Upon History* (1890), Mahan rejected the naval traditions of commerce raiding and brown-water coastal defense as less than worthy of a great power. America's navy, he argued, should be a blue-water force able to engage foreign fleets in direct battle. Bertholf couldn't have failed to notice how this might leave the role of coastal patrol and defense in the hands of the Revenue Cutter Service.

Ironically, his service almost fell victim to the Progressive movement. At the beginning of 1912, President Taft's Commission on Economy and Efficiency recommended the service be abolished and its missions and vessels be distributed to other agencies for a savings of at least a million dollars a year. Whether this would have come to pass and the Coast Guard never come into being cannot be known. What is known is that the Revenue Cutter Service was rescued by yet another famous tragedy.

On April 14, 1912, nine days after President Taft sent his commission's report to Congress, urging its recommendations be enacted, the White Star liner *Titanic*, owned by American industrialist J. P. Morgan, hit an iceberg in the North Atlantic and sank with the loss of some 1,500 lives among its 2,224 passengers. As survivors reached New York on April 18, more than forty thousand people jammed the city's docks to witness their arrival. They were swarmed by press and newsreel photographers, their faces splashed across newspapers and later appearing in "flickers"—movies—across the nation.

Follow-up investigations and hearings into the tragedy, led by Progressive Senator Robert La Follette, among others, resulted in a number of changes in maritime practice, including mandated lifeboat space for every passenger on a ship, regular evacuation drills, better lookout systems, twenty-four-hour radio watches, and the establishment of the International Ice Patrol.

In the immediate wake of the tragedy, the Navy sent two cruisers to patrol the Grand Banks of the North Atlantic to look out for icebergs and warn off shipping but also made it clear it didn't have the vessels to spare for this type of work. The Revenue Cutter Service, with its vast experience in the ice floes of Alaska, quickly stepped forward to take on this new role, beginning in 1913. Today the Coast Guard continues the Ice Patrol using C-130 aircraft, although in the near future it may rely solely on remote sensing satellites to watch the drifting bergs.

President Taft's secretary of the treasury, Franklin MacVeagh, fighting to defend his turf, which included the Revenue Cutter Service, recommended Captain Bertholf and Sumner Kimball work together on a proposal to combine it with the Life-Saving Service into a new more efficient service. The seventy-eight-year-old Kimball and forty-six-year-old Bertholf proved a good team, drafting a workable proposal for a hybrid new agency, the type of multifaceted maritime operator Alexander Hamilton would have approved of.

After Woodrow Wilson was elected president in 1912, the merger proposal was sent to Congress, where it found great favor. The Senate adopted it on March 12, 1914. With encouragement from President Wilson, the House voted for it 212 to 79 on January 20, 1915. On January 28, President Wilson signed the Act to Create the Coast Guard into law. It would "constitute a part of the military forces of the United States . . . under the Treasury Department in time of peace and operate as a part of the Navy, subject to the orders of the Secretary of the Navy, in time of war or when the President shall so direct."

For the civilian-oriented Life-Saving Service, this would prove more of a stretch than for the already militarized Revenue Cutter Service. It would take some years for the two cultures of lifesaving and law enforcement to truly merge, if in fact they ever have. Meanwhile President Wilson named Ellsworth Bertholf as captain-commandant of the Coast Guard, a position he would serve in until his retirement in 1919.

Seven weeks after Wilson established the new agency, just before dawn on March 17, 1915, the three-masted schooner *Silvia C. Hall*, carrying a load of cypress logs from Florida to New York, wrecked on Cape Shoals, North Carolina.

As waves began breaking over the ship, a crew from Station Cape Lookout, under the command of keeper Fred Gillikin, ran the half mile to their new 36-foot motor surfboat. The foundering ship was too far offshore for a line shot, so they launched into stormy twenty-foot seas in below freezing temperatures and better than forty-knot winds.

After several hours, they were able to maneuver close in to the wreck. Then a couple of waves broke over the surfboat, flooding its engine and injuring one of Gillikin's men. After pulling into deeper water and trying to outwait the storm, they were forced to head back into shore.

Returning before dawn on the eighteenth, they used the motorboat to tow a 26-foot surfboat closer in to the battered schooner. A team of surfmen then rowed through the outer break. Amid piles of floating wreckage, they were able to get two of the survivors on board the ship to rig a line to the jib boom and then slide down to the surfboat. Only after they'd pulled away were they told there were three more men still aboard. Less than happy with this news, the surfmen took another run through the breakers and debris, back to what was left of the schooner, where they retrieved the last of the *Silvia C. Hall*'s crew.

As the motor lifeboat towed the rescue boat, surfmen, and survivors toward shore, a crowd of fishermen and townspeople who were gathered on the beach let out a mighty cheer. The U.S. Coast Guard had carried out its first major operation. Its greatness and its story were only just beginning.

CHAPTER 4

Calling All Boats

"With oceans to the east and west and friendly neighbors to the north and south, the United States has been untrammeled by enemy boots on our ground. Those carefree days are now over."

—Former Coast Guard Cdr. Steve Flynn, *America the Vulnerable*

"Most of our talk and everything now is homeland security. It's kind of become an industry, really."

—Senior Chief Ross Fowle, Coast Guard Cutter *Line*

History has a tendency to come up and bite you when you're least expecting it. Coast Guard Station Battery Park at the foot of Manhattan is a three-story brick and faded blue Kleenex box of a building that inspires shivers of disdain from the area's historic restoration crowd, though Robert Moses would have liked it. It houses the Regional Examination Center (the Coast Guard acts as a salty DMV, licensing merchant sailors), the bridge inspection program, and Sector New York's public affairs office, among others.

Public Affairs Chief Petty Officer Brandon Brewer went up on its roof on a bright September morning in 2001 right after he heard that an airplane had struck the World Trade Center a few blocks away.

"There wasn't a lot of smoke at that point. There was some papers and debris floating down from the top of the building, and then we heard this really loud noise, so we turn around and this airplane flies right by us so close we could see people in the windows. It flies up through this canyon of buildings, and I'm thinking it's coming in to take a closer look, and I'm thinking this guy is cutting it awful close, and it doesn't click for me what is going to happen, and then we see it hit. It seemed to take place in slow motion from when the nose of the plane hit the tower to when it exploded and you realize people and their things are now exploding out of the tower."

Just off Governors Island, Petty Officer Carlos Perez was at the helm of a 41-foot utility boat sent from Staten Island to check out the initial report of an airplane hitting the World Trade Center when that second hijacked plane, United Flight 175, flew directly over him. He looked up at its aluminum underbelly and watched it fly into the South Tower and the giant orange fireball that followed. He thought it was like something from a Steven Spielberg movie. He then took his boat closer in to Battery Park and watched through his binoculars as people on the upper floors of the towers began jumping to their deaths.

At Cape Cod Air Station in Massachusetts, CO Capt. Richard Yatto watched the second plane strike the South Tower on TV and knew America was under attack. He also remembered a hotel fire in San Juan, Puerto Rico, where people had been trapped on the roof and couldn't get off. At full speed it would take his HH-60 helicopters about an hour to reach New York. He told his operations officer to call the district command in Boston for permission to launch two birds. By now F-15 fighter jets were screaming off the tarmac of the adjacent Otis Air National Guard base, their afterburners blazing like dragon tails. When he couldn't get clear directions from Boston, Yatto cursed and ordered the helicopters launched on his own authority. They headed south at over 150 knots.

As the lead helicopter reached Long Island Sound, its crew tuned in to emergency radio channels and heard that the South Tower had just collapsed. They were continuing toward the North Tower when New York air traffic controllers ordered them to land immediately.

"We're the rescue helicopter!" one of the pilots argued. They were told Air Force F-15s were clearing the skies over Manhattan and would shoot down anyone they encountered. After some more arguing, the Coast Guard helicopters landed at Gabreski Airport on Long Island. Their pilots went to the control facility to get on the radio and keep arguing. There they saw the North Tower burning on TV. A few minutes later it collapsed. The crews and their CO, Richard Yatto, believe they could have saved a number of lives if they'd been allowed to proceed on to the roof of the North Tower that morning.

The Coast Guard Captain of the Port of New York, Adm. Richard E. Bennis, was at his doctor's office that morning for a follow-up exam after brain surgery. In his absence his deputy ordered the harbor closed to all vessel traffic at 9:10 A.M., seven minutes after the second plane struck. Coast Guard boats loaded with armed responders were launched from Staten Island, from Rockaway, Queens, and from Sandy Hook, New Jersey. They were well positioned to secure the city's borders. New York is a maritime town, and 80 percent of the city is separated from the U.S. mainland by bodies of water.

In Washington, DC, Coast Guard vessels closed down the Potomac following Al Qaeda's attack on the Pentagon, where the Navy Command Center, overseen by Coast Guard Adm. Jeffrey Hathaway, was destroyed, killing forty-two people, twenty-seven under his direct command. In Boston Harbor, they refused to let an LNG tanker dock for fear it might be used as a weapon of mass destruction. In LA, Houston, Seattle, and San Francisco, Port Security Units made up of Coast Guard reservists with M-60 machine guns took to the waters on highly maneuverable 25-foot Boston Whalers. In Virginia, half a dozen 38-foot 65-knot antidrug raider boats were taken out of their winterized plastic wrap and placed on trailers and were on New York's waterways by the next morning, as was a larger cutter, the *Bainbridge Island*, flying an oversized American flag as its battle ensign.

On maps showing the location of Coast Guard cutters on September 10 and September 12, you see what looks like a belt being cinched tight around the continental United States as the service quickly shifted from a peacetime to a wartime footing.

After contacting his boss, the secretary of transportation, and asking for permission to mobilize five thousand reservists, Coast Guard Commandant James Loy received an unusual call from the chief of naval operations asking what the Navy could do to assist the Coast Guard. It was decided that placing Coast Guard cutters in New York Harbor would reassure the public in a way that putting Navy ships of war there would not.

During those first minutes and hours of 9/11, the Coast Guard's surge response depended largely on the bottom-up capabilities and top-down trust of its people in the field and on the water.

Quartermaster Bruce Dickinson, in addition to working at Battery Park Station, was also a volunteer fireman. As soon as the first plane struck, he ran the six blocks to the towers and worked with firefighting crews until the building fell. Barely escaping with his life, he headed back to the water and got on board the Coast Guard Cutter *Hawser*, a 65-foot tug that was the first command vessel on scene. From there he helped evacuate civilians, transport emergency workers, and direct water traffic. He then transferred to his old patrol boat, the *Adak*, to do armed security work.

September 11 was Lt. Rob Mutto's first day as an accident investigator on Staten Island. After the second plane hit the towers, he directed people and vehicles to the Staten Island Ferry at the St. George Terminal. "We inspected the ferryboat and took it across with a fire brigade aboard. As the first tower collapsed, this cloud enveloped the upper bay, and the ferry entered the cloud and the captain had to use his radar to land. We got off at Old Whitehall Terminal, and everything looked like ash, like a volcano had gone off."

By now thousands of people were swarming the Battery to escape the collapsing towers and their choking dust clouds.

"I was looking out the front window and watching this cloud coming down and saw this couple with two small children go between these cars, and they huddled over the children as the dust caught up to them. We got them inside, and they turned out to be German tourists," recalls Herb Haeger, an older Coast Guard Auxiliary volunteer who was working at the station that morning. "One of our admirals [retired Adm. Richard Larrabee, who escaped from the sixty-second floor of the North Tower and went to the Marriott Hotel just as the tower fell on top of it] was let into the building covered in white. It was like it had been snowing. You couldn't even recognize him."

In fact, the CO of the station didn't recognize his old boss and demanded to see Larrabee's ID before letting him enter the building. A Coke machine was then pushed in front of the main door to block any further entry.

"After the towers fell, thousands of people were running toward our building," Brandon Brewer recalls. "It was like we were in a bowl of soup with all the ash and debris. A couple of people were trying to get into the parking lot, trying to come over the barbed wire. We gave first aid to one guy who cut his hand doing that. Someone else tried to break the glass on our front door, and they were yelling at the security guard to let them in. On the river side, people crowded the seawall, and one guy tried to climb around our fencepost and fell in the water and was rescued by an NYPD boat. It was a mad rush of terrified people, and they just kept adding up 'cause the [outbound] ferries had been taken out of service."

It was around this time that the Coast Guard's Vessel Traffic Service (VTS) New York put out a call on the marine radio for all available boats in the harbor to go to Battery Park and begin evacuating people.

A few minutes later, Public Affairs Officer Jim McGranachan, who was inside the building, turned his chair toward the harbor-facing windows. "I felt like that German general in that D-day movie *The Longest Day*, because suddenly through the fog, through the smoke, appear all these boats: ferries and tugboats and Circle Line [sightseeing] boats, all coming toward us."

Dozens of boats, including a Coast Guard buoy tender, began nosing up to the seawall in what would become one of the largest waterborne evacuations in history, larger than the British evacuation at Dunkirk, with more than half a million people taken off Manhattan Island (while tens of thousands of others fled across the Brooklyn Bridge).

As the tugs, fast ferries, police launches, fireboats, and other working and recreational watercraft pulled up to the foot of Manhattan, their crews would hang handmade signs on their railings saying where they were headed—to Sandy Hook or Hoboken, Brooklyn or Staten Island. Teams of Coast Guard inspectors, cops, and firemen ashore started organizing the crowds into boarding lines and helping them over the seawall. Just offshore aboard the pilot boat *New York* and harbor tug *Hawser,* other Coast Guard personnel were directing the growing boat traffic through the smoke.

With visibility around five feet due to the ash cloud, and stories of new attacks both real (a hijacked plane down in Pennsylvania) and rumored (a car bombing at the State Department), the crowds remained anxious to get off the island. Still, tugboat captain Gordon Young told *WorkBoat* magazine of one passenger who, when informed they were headed to Sandy Hook, New Jersey, complained that he needed to get to Staten Island. "I couldn't believe it. I told him, 'Get the fuck on here now, anyplace is better then here!' Then he jumped right on."

Brian Walsh, a mate aboard the Staten Island Ferry *Samuel I. Newhouse,* told the magazine that once on the water the survivors were generally subdued. "They were mostly sitting in circles, holding hands and praying or crying . . . We kept telling them over and over again that it's going to be okay, you're safe." By this point more than twenty-seven hundred Americans, mostly civilians, had died in the attacks.

"The evacuations went on all morning, and eventually by around three in the afternoon downtown was emptying. We ventured out to look around, and it was a ghost town," Brandon Brewer recalls. "In a few hours it had gone from more packed then I'd ever [seen] to more empty than I'd ever seen. A fire department boat dropped off supplies on our pier for the rescue workers, and we loaded some vans with food and water and went up to Ground Zero, and just seeing the destruction was pretty overwhelming. There were still these other big buildings on fire and collapsing and firefighters working to fight those fires. You'd pick up something—a notebook or photograph—and realize it was something personal, something you'd have on your desk or in your cubicle, and now it was just this pile of debris. I saw the landing gear from one of the planes on the street, and that was weird—all around it looked like snow had fallen, and everything seemed just somehow off."

"As a photographer the hardest part for me was seeing pictures of children and family pictures you'd pick up in the rubble, and they were everywhere, with the edges blown away," recalls Coast Guard photojournalist Tom Sperduto, who spent two months documenting Ground Zero. "I saw a fireman pick up a picture and look at it, and I snapped that. It wasn't my best picture, but it's the one I always come back to."

Station Battery Park (along with North Cove Marina) soon became an emergency staging area with its conference room covered in sleeping cops, FBI agents, and exhausted Coasties unwilling to go home. Admiral Bennis, ignoring his terminal illness, began working twenty-hour days and telling friends that maybe this was what he'd been spared for. Bennis would eventually pass away on August 3, 2003, at the age of fifty-three.

The Coast Guard's Atlantic Strike Team from Fort Dix, New Jersey, which specializes in environmental response, was quickly mobilized on the day of the attacks, followed by elements of the Gulf Strike Team. They were the first unit to establish a mobile Incident Command Post (on the back of a tractor-trailer truck) and begin monitoring air quality and worker safety at

Ground Zero on the night of the eleventh as ground fires still raged. Unfortunately, within days, responsibility for hazardous-materials-related issues at "the Pile" was handed over from the Coast Guard Captain of the Port to the Environmental Protection Agency (EPA).

The result was EPA Administrator Christine Todd Whitman going on TV assuring the public that the air quality in lower Manhattan was fine (a declaration encouraged by the White House), even as the Coast Guard Strike Team was monitoring a witches' brew of airborne toxins and dangerous elements at Ground Zero including asbestos, PCBs, compressed gases, chlorinated compounds, hydrogen cyanide, mercury, lead, blood, and human remains that they occasionally stumbled over.

Although the Coast Guard required its own people to wear respirators, goggles, and hearing protection while searching abandoned buildings or working at Ground Zero and Fresh Kills Landfill, where debris was being moved, and also required them to go through decontamination afterward, it did not have the authority to order others to do the same.

"Whenever I was with the Strike Team we had to wear masks. You thought of it as an annoyance at the time, but they knew what they were doing," says photographer Tom Sperduto, who still suffers from reduced lung capacity resulting from his time at the Pile.

Chief Warrant Officer Leo Deon described his frustration to professor and reservist Pete Capelotti, author of the Coast Guard's internal book on 9/11, *Rogue Wave*. Deon set up hazmat washing stations at Ground Zero, but "we could not mandate that these rescue workers, whose shifts had just concluded, go through and decontaminate. We were not allowed to even use the word 'decontaminate,' which is the proper term for a site of this nature . . . Through some entrepreneurship, we were able to entice people to the wash stations, with cold drinks, with rehab areas where they could actually sit down, and through this aggressive approach a visit to the wash station eventually caught on."

Years later, thousands of people, including firemen, police officers, and rescue and recovery workers, are still suffering and dying from respiratory illnesses associated with exposure to hazardous materials generated by the 9/11 attacks that the government failed to address at the time.

A few weeks after the attacks, the strike team would be called down to Washington, DC, to respond to the release of "weaponized" anthrax in the Capitol Building, an act of domestic terror the FBI would, seven years later, attribute to an Army scientist who committed suicide while under investigation.

The strike team would return once more in February 2004 when ricin, a lethal toxin, was discovered in the Dirksen Senate Office Building.

In the days, weeks, and months after 9/11, Coast Guard cutters and small boats would work around the clock doing security patrols, boarding ships as the harbor was reopened, guarding the Indian Point nuclear power plant, the Statue of Liberty, and other potential targets, and transporting emergency workers and supplies. Some of the small-boat operators would put the equivalent of twenty-two years of service on their craft. Nearly 50 percent of the service's 7,500 reservists would be mobilized (by the beginning of the Iraq war that figure would rise to 70 percent). Port security would grow from 2 percent to 58 percent of Coast Guard activity before gradually scaling back to around 25 percent.

The Coast Guard, which had seen years of cutbacks in funding and personnel during the 1990s and was facing an additional 10 percent cut in its 2002 budget, was hard-pressed to adjust to the new reality of post-9/11 America, of guarding and protecting ninety-five thousand miles of coastline and over three hundred major ports. As it began to respond, it also began to transform into a more militant, surveillance- and intelligence-oriented organization. "We regained what we'd lost in more specialized capabilities" is how Vice Commandant Vivien Crea explains it.

"It was a busy year. All we were doing morning, noon, and night was 9/11 and homeland security work," Brandon Brewer recalls.

The Other City by the Bay

I began to see the Coast Guard's transformation six months after the attacks when I set off from Yerba Buena Island on San Francisco Bay on a 41-foot utility boat almost as old as its blue-eyed, thirty-year-old coxswain, Chuck Ashmore. I was writing a port security story for *Popular Science*, while Chuck was waiting to have a Vietnam-era M-60 7.62 mm machine gun delivered to the boat as he and his crew carried out daily security patrols past the new waterside ballpark, the bridges, and the airports.

On the eastern side of the bay, among the brick buildings and quays of Coast Guard Island, a wooden-beamed theater hall had been partitioned into work cubicles for the new Sea Marshal escort program. Here more than twenty people, including marshals in blue jumpsuits, reported to Cdr. Jeff

Saine. Until he'd been mobilized six months earlier, the stout, balding reservist had worked as a Safeway supermarket manager in Chico, California. Now he oversaw armed boarding teams that escorted about one-third of the large vessels, including oil tankers and cruise ships, transiting the bay. "We'll put people on the [ship's] bridge from twelve miles out at sea to the ports of Stockton and Sacramento," he explained.

Before 9/11, incoming ships had to give the Coast Guard twenty-four hours' notice of their arrival. This had been extended to ninety-six hours, with more information required on their cargoes and crews. That information was being sent to the newly established National Vessel Movement Center in West Virginia; from there it was e-mailed back to local users like Saine who could evaluate which ships to target for boardings.

Meanwhile, Special Forces troops had found a mariner's license in a cave in Afghanistan. As a result, Coast Guard Investigative Service personnel were reviewing some 270,000 merchant mariner documents by hand to see if they could identify anyone with links to terrorism and compare those names to the crew lists provided to West Virginia. They identified seven names and also managed to track down hundreds of salty criminals the Coast Guard had previously licensed, ranging from deadbeat dads to a couple of homicide suspects. To meet the demands for this paper chase, dubbed Operation Drydock, CGIS had to call up sixty reservists.

Other reservists from Port Security Units (PSUs) continued to patrol key U.S. harbors in their machine-gun-mounted Boston Whalers while the Coast Guard trained thirteen SWAT-like Maritime Safety and Security Teams (MSSTs) as required by the newly enacted Maritime Transportation Security Act of 2002. Beginning in 2003 in Seattle, MSSTs (pronounced "Mists") would patrol America's ports and harbors in matched pairs of 25-foot Defender class law enforcement boats, hundreds of which were now placed on order. Older technologies were also being adapted to meet the Coast Guard's new security demands.

Yerba Buena is a pine-, lupine-, and eucalyptus-covered island that divides the two sections of the Bay Bridge. At the top of the island, in a prefab metal structure beneath a field of microwave and radar antennas, is San Francisco's Vessel Traffic System. Established in the 1970s following the collision of two oil tankers below the bridge that released close to a million gallons of oil, VTS is the functional equivalent of an air traffic control tower with computer and video terminals manned twenty-four hours a day tracking some 350 to 400 ship transits on the bay and under the Golden Gate Bridge, considered a prime terrorist target after 9/11.

VTS operators were, by the turn of the twenty-first century, using digital chart overlays of radar video imagery to track vessels that were color-coded (onscreen) by their type and size. If any ship attracted a controller's interest, he or she could then pull up a database describing what vessels had come into the bay since 1990.

"Prior to that we had to write all the information on index cards," VTS operations officer Lt. Dawn Black explained, as she showed me one of their other capabilities—panning and zooming powerful video cameras located around the bay looking into, among other places, the inner harbor of the Port of Oakland, America's fourth busiest container port.

"Container ships are not always punctual, so this way we can keep an eye on what they're doing," she noted dryly. She became more enthusiastic as she described plans for Automated Information Systems, or AIS. Under rules adopted by the International Maritime Organization, a UN agency responsible for maritime law, by 2010 the vast majority of oceangoing commercial vessels (over three hundred tons) would be equipped with transponders that broadcast real-time information about their identities and activities. The United States was pushing hard for quicker implementation of AIS as part of its new homeland (homewaters?) strategy.

After visiting VTS, I hit the docks of San Francisco with the U.S. Customs Service, which had been given security oversight for millions of shipping containers arriving in the United States each year. On an aging pier, Customs inspector Steve Baxter took me aboard a truck-mounted machine with a cherry-picker arm that shot gamma rays through selected containers, giving its operator a medical-film-like image of the contents, displaying shapes and densities. A container that was supposed to be filled with empty wooden pallets showed a dense field above them. They broke into it and found that sheets of plywood had been piled, unreported, on top of the pallets. The Customs inspectors next took battery drills and began boring holes in the plywood, looking for hidden compartments that might contain other dense materials like drugs or explosives.

"Without this machine, that's our main technology," Baxter said, pointing to a pair of heavy-duty bolt cutters and a pry bar lying on the ground. Today, despite overseas inspectors and improved intelligence, container security, like port security as a whole, remains problematic.

My own suspicion is that as long as America remains at the vortex of a continuously expanding consumer-based trade, in which unneeded amenities like bottled water are shipped in from France, Italy, and Fiji, our port operations will remain, by dint of scale, vulnerable to disruption from pollution, weather, sabotage, or terror.

In 2007, I returned to the Coast Guard station on Yerba Buena to find that AIS had been implemented several years ahead of schedule and that vessel traffic management was now a key element in U.S. port security efforts. The island also had a new Sector Command Center down by the boat basin linked to the Vessel Traffic System up on the hill.

Com Center duty officer Lt. JG Neptwim Rosario points to a large wall-mounted monitor with a live AIS feed of ships that appear as circles, squares, and triangles on a map of the bay. "The AIS gives us the name of the vessel, ID number and call sign, what type of vessel it is, its tonnage, crew size, flag country, location, course, and speed," he explains. "The ferries also broadcast their capacity or their actual number of passengers. Any ship [over three hundred tons] without AIS gets our attention. If you don't have it functioning, you will be ordered to repair or replace it by the next port."

We wind our way up the hill, past some of the island's feral cats that have been neutered and microchipped and a foraging raccoon that wouldn't put up with that kind of nonsense.

Since I was last in VTS, they've opened up the windows to let the sun shine in and installed newer flat-screen monitors. There's also a fifty-inch plasma screen over the supervisor's desk that displays a "transview" of AIS feeds from major ports around the nation, broadcast in real time from the Coast Guard's R&D Center in Groton, Connecticut. Every port authority can now receive these AIS signals from its region. With a wireless laptop or handheld device a fishing boat captain or recreational sailor can also get a better sense of the commercial traffic in the vicinity and hopefully avoid being run over by a seagoing behemoth. At the same time, these civilian boaters are being encouraged to participate in the Coast Guard's America's Waterway Watch program, reporting any suspicious activities they see along the shore or on the water.

I look at one of the VTS controller's twenty-one-inch screens and see the *Del Norte*, a high-speed Larkspur Ferry color-coded in blue, and the *Miki Hana*, a tug pulling an oil barge. Scott Humphries, the VTS training director, uses a mouse click to shift the monitor's map to a different part of the bay complex. He can stack charts onscreen or bring up video images from a growing number of camera locations. He shows me live video of the *Delta Pride,* a bulk carrier carrying steel upriver to Pittsburg, California, close to where a couple of stray whales will soon pass.

He switches to a picture of the *Sirius Voyager,* a 900-foot oil tanker offloading at the Richmond Long Wharf. Another controller, Henry, tells Scott there's a tug waiting to go in there. I ask about a green dot in the Port of Oakland. They click on it and tell me it's the *Genoa Bridge,* a 920-foot container ship with Panamanian registry. Along with a ship's AIS information, they can call up the Maritime Inspection and Law Enforcement database, if they get a funny feeling about a vessel such as the *Angelica Schulte,* a 797-foot Liberian-registered tanker that's now headed toward the bay.

They retain their video files for thirty days and, thanks to the R&D Center's servers, have playback capability allowing them to retrieve earlier information on ship movements from their own or other major ports around the country.

Along with improved surveillance, today's Bay Area Coast Guard has its own Maritime Safety and Security Team that, along with Vessel Boarding and Security Teams (VBSTs), does ship boardings and harbor patrols so reservist "sea marshals" no longer have to. The MSST has more than seventy operators, half a dozen 25-foot Defender boats with M-240 machine guns, and over a dozen trucks for towing them. Lt. Cdr. Greg Thomas, their thirty-five-year-old CO, agrees to let me go out on patrol. He's a compact, youthful-looking officer with gelled brown hair. After donning body armor, we head down to the MSST dock on Coast Guard Island just south of Oakland to meet the rest of his crew: Coxswain Brian Hughes, Burt Wells, who's responsible for the M-240, and Josh Bly, who's carrying an M-16. Not only am I the only one unarmed, I realize, I'm the only one not wearing Oakley sunglasses.

They do a standard risk assessment before we head up the estuary past a great blue heron and into the harbor channel past a big container ship. A sailboat cruises by with a bikinied young woman at the wheel. She waves. Burt waves back, " 'cause she waved at me first." We cruise past the *Chinese Eagle,* a cargo ship loading scrap metal. America, of course, has a huge trade deficit with China. While they ship toys, clothing, and electronic goods to Wal-Mart and other U.S. retailers, we export scrap metal, waste paper, and air (empty containers) back to China.

"Coming up," Brian warns. The boat's nose drops as the twin Honda 225 outboards kick in, throwing up a roostertail of spray. We speed past the *Hanjin Miami,* another container ship, as Greg starts telling me about his MSST unit. "I got divers, dogs, assaulters, ROVs [robot subs], and swimmer systems to put hurt on them ["bad guys"] with sonic blasts. I've got entangling systems with nets to tie up [propeller] screws. We can also use vertical insertion [fast rope assault teams dropping from helicopters]."

At this point the boat's radar fails. We keep going. Then the depth finder and radios short out; the whole heads-up suite in the metal wheelhouse fries. They try to reboot the system. No luck. We take a fast turn over our own wake, then slow down, limping back to the dock.

Greg, disappointed, transitions into confessional mode, telling me about "a big raccoon problem" they're having on the island. "They screw with my dogs. They steal their food and water." I ask him how good his two working dogs are. "They're great. If a dog's not good at bomb sniffing or acts crazy, he ends up doing mine decommissioning in Africa or somewhere. It's rough, but better than some kid losing his legs." I later read an article about the work of these "second chance" dogs.

At Air Station San Francisco I talk to post-9/11 helicopter pilots qualified in Airborne Use of Force and others recently trained to fly in mummy-like CBRN—chemical, biological, radiological, and nuclear—environment suits.

Up at Hamilton Air Field in Marin County, the Pacific Strike Team shows off their tractor-trailer trucks, oil skimmer boats, and a new 48-foot trailer by Featherlite, "the same guys who build NASCAR trailers." Walking up its rear ramp, I'm shown racks of new Tyvek moon suits with hoods, air tanks and compressors, air quality monitors, radiation detectors, and a built-in lab, kitchen, and communications shack that can be sealed off from the outside world.

"It's hazmat response on steroids," Cdr. Anthony Lloyd explains. It's also ready to respond to oil spills, chemical plant explosions, or weapons of mass destruction, including dirty bombs and loose nukes. Plus, they have a dozen team members qualified as commercial truck drivers in case a state trooper pulls them over on the way to the apocalypse.

I get to enjoy the upside of this "new" post-9/11 reality when I'm invited onto the 87-foot cutter *Hawksbill* as it sets up a security zone for one of the thousand or so "special events" that take place on the bay each year. This one is off Crissy Field at the Presidio. A stunt pilot will be flying over the bay for Oracle, the computer database company, which is having its convention in town. We motor past Oracle CEO Larry Ellison's 192-foot white yacht, *Ronin*. The *Hawksbill*'s CO, Senior Chief Stephen Tierney, radios over, asking the yacht to relocate, which it does. "Our job is to keep people out of the [safety] box," the plainspoken forty-two-year-old chief explains.

There are four San Francisco police boats and one Marin sheriff's boat to help out. They all "energize" their blue lights to signal the establishment of the box. This way, if the stunt plane crashes there will only be one casualty, the pilot. "During Fleet Week [when the Blue Angels fly over the bay] there are thousands of radar blips [boats] and a huge box," Tierney tells me.

The *Hawksbill* has two .50 caliber machine guns mounted on its bow and a deck well at the stern holding a 17-foot RIB (rigid inflatable boat) with a 200 hp jet drive diesel. This pocket rocket has a centerboard control console and three saddle-like seats that you straddle while grabbing onto a handgrip.

The oil tanker *Angelica Schulte* is now sailing in under the Golden Gate as a red biplane appears overhead and begins trailing white smoke. It etches elegant loops and heart-stopping stalls and wild spirals through the blue sky above. Machinery Tech Wes Coulter hands me a float coat and red helmet as the biplane ends a big loop flying upside down fifty feet off our deck. "Oh my God, he's out of control!" one of the *Hawksbill*'s crew exclaims appreciatively.

Three of us quickly climb into the RIB. Coulter takes the driver's position at centerboard while I straddle one of the rear seats. Someone opens the gate, and we slide backward off the ramp, as the cutter is under way. Hitting the water, the jet diesel roars to life and we take off, shooting past the *Hawksbill* and leaning over in a tight g-pulling thirty-five-knot turn so that, like a crazed dolphin, we leap over our own bow wake. We begin chasing around the box, jagging and thumping hither and yon in a highly professional manner. I catch glimpses of the red biplane flying above, boats steering clear of us, and two sheriffs laughing as we shoot past them. I'm grinning wildly. "This is your job?" I shout to the young Coastie next to me, Bosun's Mate Third Class Skip Aldrich. "It's not suck time," he agrees.

All too soon the sky is clear and we catch up to the *Hawksbill*, which is cruising along at fourteen knots. We aim for the stern ramp and clunk-slide up it at twenty-some knots. A young woman Coastie tosses a thick loop over the RIB's bow post, capturing and securing the $150,000 joy ride before it back-slides off the cutter. I'm just glad these young Coasties have been able to do their part protecting Larry Ellison from Al Qaeda.

On the Set of *"24"*

Seattle Sector commander Capt. Steve Metruck leads me into a secure conference room, part of the Puget Sound Joint Harbor Operations Center, a $5 million suite jointly paid for by the Coast Guard and the Navy. Twenty black leather chairs are pulled up around a long blond wood table with sleek speakerphones opposite a gray glass wall. A screen on the far end of the room allows for secure videoconferencing. Underwhelmed, I'm thinking that a conference room is a conference room when Steve hits a switch and the gray wall's "magic glass" turns transparent, revealing what looks like the set of the TV show *"24"* on the other side. Some twenty people, none of whom look like Kiefer Sutherland, are moving around three banked rows of workstations with flat black screens facing a large video wall. The wall is divided into a dozen live images including the afternoon Fox and CNN news shows. Others include a wide digital navigation map of Puget Sound, scrolling AIS listings, and real-time black-and-white video feeds showing different parts of the sound. We go out onto the watch floor.

"After all the fiber-optic cables were installed, we could barely get this floor battened back down," Steve says, pointing at the blue industrial carpeting below our feet.

Off to our left are half a dozen glassed-in cubicles, including the sector's search and rescue communications center. To the left, behind another wall of "magic glass" and cheaper matching gray glass, is the VTS center.

A Navy tech sitting in a Herman Miller chair at one of eighteen workstations brings up some video that was shot a few hours ago from a state police aircraft with a Navy camera mount aboard. The image pans from one of the Seattle commuter ferries under way to the new sector building we're now standing in. The image changes from standard video to ghostly infrared and zooms in. "No heat coming from my office," Steve jokes. With all the Ops Center's video and graphic displays, they use Dell gaming consoles for their CPUs.

Along with the Coast Guard, Navy, Border Patrol, and police, the Harbor Ops Center works with state, city, and county emergency planners. Just now they're getting ready for a major earthquake drill.

We go into the VTS center, where Coast Guard Chief James Smith and his crew show me more digital wall maps and explain that Puget Sound has the largest area of responsibility (AOR) of any Vessel Traffic System in the nation, one they run jointly with the Canadian coast guard in Victoria, British Columbia. He shows me live images from eight video cameras spread across forty miles of the sound.

"Our AOR could fit all of San Francisco, LA/Long Beach, Miami, New York/New Jersey, and several others," he brags.

The Big Oyster

Back on the East Coast, I'm not surprised to find that Sector New York's VTS also rocks, though in a less flashy "look what Hollywood inspired me to do" sort of way.

New York remains among the most vulnerable targets for terrorist attack and so has been forced to innovate. Its VTS center has twenty-eight flat-screen monitors arrayed around the room plus two big screens above the watch desk, using live video feeds, radio, radar, and digitalized AIS to track the city's thirteen hundred daily ship transits. That's the kind of traffic you might see spread across all of Puget Sound and San Francisco Bay combined, only squeezed into ten square miles of complex urban waterways.

This global armada of trade is monitored by three civilian operators, a watch supervisor, and a uniformed watch officer. The operators switch positions every hour tracking Channel 11 (the getting under way and harbor entry calls), Channel 14 (the Lower and Upper Bay calls), and Channel 12 (the anchorages, the East River, and Arthur Kill, on the skinny side of Staten Island) calls.

VTS training coordinator Matt Holiday points out ferries (green squares), cruise ships (blue triangles), and other on-screen traffic symbols. "I started out with a single radar screen and punch cards back in 1995," he grins. He uses a keyboard to manipulate one of twenty-four cameras housed around the city, zooming up the East River past Roosevelt Island.

He tells me National Park Service and other cameras will soon be linking to the Vessel Traffic System. He then switches from a shot of Hell Gate, in the East River, to one from the Brooklyn Navy Yard. He shows me a container ship, then pushes in from several miles out to where "it looks close enough to see someone picking his nose on the bridge."

We go over to a map of the New York area. "San Francisco VTS bases their rules on tonnage. Here it's more about length and draft. We don't have the warning signals when they come within five hundred feet of each other. Here it could be fifty feet. In Kill Van Kull, in Arthur Kill, it's maybe five hundred to eight hundred feet wide with 145-foot-wide ships passing each other at the same time."

With New York's hairpin turn, we go into America's second busiest port, Newark: river traffic, narrow channels, major dredging projects, and low bridges; I'm impressed at these controllers' ability to track as much as they do, even with the kind of high-tech cameras and playback systems you can't buy at Radio Shack.

As with many computer labs, I'm less than awed when I get to visit the Coast Guard R&D Center's AIS program on the Avery Point campus of the University of Connecticut. It's housed in a large beige room full of computer towers and screens, with lots of exposed cables, a few big monitors, and a few bored-seeming people drinking coffee. Their nonergodynamic pink, red, and blue swivel chairs provide what little color the room has to offer.

"This time of day we're looking at about fifteen hundred ships," AIS program manager Dave Pietraszewski tells me (it's 10:30 A.M. EST). "We have about five thousand ships in the U.S. EEZ [two-hundred-mile Exclusive Economic Zone] on any given day and are working toward a nationwide AIS system to monitor all their signals. Right now we're getting VTS inputs from Seattle, San Francisco, New York, LA/Long Beach, New Orleans, Houston, and elsewhere [including the National Oceanic and Atmospheric Administration and the offshore oil industry]. The final system will include several satellites, but the Russians, who are supposed to launch one of them, are concerned about being part of a U.S. surveillance system."

I ask about their ability to capture past AIS activity. "That's got lots of uses," he explains. "Like San Francisco just had a speeding problem where one ship passed another under the Golden Gate Bridge. With our server we can go back and review it. You can bet they're going to get slapped hard. Or there's the LNG debate on Long Island Sound [a proposal to place a liquefied natural gas terminal in the sound]. We can go back and look at the [vessel] traffic there to see the impact a restricted area might have and use that as a planning tool."

He tells me they're now past the R&D stage so that the AIS servers will be moved to West Virginia, while control of the system will go to the Coast Guard's Navigation Center in Alexandria, Virginia.

The room's central display screen is of a map of the United States. With clicks on a wireless mouse, he takes us through several levels of resolution from the nation to the Northeast, New York, New York Harbor, and then down to a dot and a square sitting offshore. We click on the little pink square and its AIS information pops up.

"It's the *Atlantic Surveyor*, a 597-foot-long cargo ship moored off New Jersey. It's not displaying the proper code for its radio transmission. In San

Francisco they'd beat him up, not let him come into port without correcting that," Dave notes. He clicks on the dot next to it. "That's the *Princess One*. With a name like that you'd think it's a cruise ship, but it's another cargo ship. You never know."

We certainly didn't know what was coming on 9/11 and probably won't know what's coming next, despite our best surveillance efforts. Eighty-five years before the September 11 attacks, New York's Black Tom Island disappeared in a horrific earthshaking blast that showered the Statue of Liberty with hot shrapnel, caused the evacuation of immigrants from Ellis Island, and could be felt a hundred miles away in Philadelphia. That July 1916 cataclysm was the result of German saboteurs setting off some two thousand tons of munitions stored on the island for shipment to Britain during World War I. In the wake of that now forgotten act of covert war, Congress gave the newly created U.S. Coast Guard authority to establish Captains of the Port to try to prevent similar incidents from taking place.

Today it's well-armed Maritime Safety and Security Teams that are guarding our ports. I join Lt. Matt Ross, XO of New York's MSST, at Boat Station New York, just down the road from the historic Fort Wadsworth on Staten Island. I'll be riding with Matt, Bosun's Mate First Class Jeff Fallon, a big shaven headed ex-Marine, and Machinery Technician Second Class Rich Bassin, a short, swarthy New Yorker. We'll be the observer boat riding along with a safety boat for two other 25-footers that will be firing their M-240 machine guns to keep up their training proficiency. The shooting range will be set up in open seas fifteen miles outside the Verrazano-Narrows Bridge. Down by the dock, the safety briefing includes a report of fifteen-knot winds and two- to three-foot chop offshore. Due to the weather, it will take us about an hour to get on scene.

Our four-boat convoy heads out under the bridge, coming up quickly to thirty-five knots. Even braced against the padded wheelhouse seats it feels like we're experiencing a fender bender every three to five seconds. Jeff Fallon slows down to call in our location. "Sector, Position is 40 degrees north, 073 degrees west along with other three vessels."

They radio back that the 210-foot Medium Endurance Cutter *Dependable* is nearby practicing vertical insertions (commando-style rope landings from a helicopter onto their deck). We speed up again, banging along in our mini collisions with the sea, before slowing and positioning ourselves near the shooter boats.

The first boat goes off about two hundred yards and starts firing at a floating tube target they've tossed over the side, *brat-tat-tat-tat-tat-tat*. Plumes of water spout between the bow gunner and the bumper-like target as he walks the bullets toward it. He empties the first box of 7.62 mm ammo and preps a second hundred-round can. Each boat's gunners will qualify on a day shoot and a night shoot. The bow gun can fire in a 120-degree arc. When switched to the aft mount it can fire in a 180-degree arc. Right now a second shooter with an M-16 is poised on the rear of the boat.

I step out on our aft deck with Matt, as it's feeling a little tight inside the rolling metal cabin. The air clears my head, but tomorrow my thighs and buttocks will be black and blue. The second boat starts blasting away, a female MSST gunner harnessed to the M-240.

The first boat calls the safety boat to report a contact on their starboard side. "Looks like they're coming into our line of fire."

The safety boat gets on the radio and contacts the distant white ship.

"This is the [Coast Guard] Cutter *Dependable*," comes the reply.

"Could you go to channel A-3, please."

"A-3, roger." They switch to a secure channel.

"We are off your port bow. A 240 exercise is being conducted," the safety boat reports.

"Roger. What's your range?"

"We're about three to four miles off."

"Roger. We're four-point-five to five miles, and we're gonna continue north by northwest, so we should be well out of your way."

"Thank you and roger that."

The ride back into shore is less thumpy. I look forward to tomorrow, when I'll be riding flat water with what I think of as the "traditional" Coast Guard.

Back in Manhattan, I take the IRT from 125th Street to Chambers, then a shuttle bus in the rain past Trinity Church, where Coasties carefully cleaned the grave of Alexander Hamilton after 9/11. I ride the ferry to Staten Island's St. George Terminal and catch a 6:00 A.M. cross-island ride with Jim McGranachan, past tank farms and rail yards full of black chemical cars and over a high span to the Bayonne, New Jersey, Ocean Terminal.

Inside, across a gunmetal gray channel from the big gantry cranes of the Port of Newark, is the New York Aids to Navigation Station with its black-hulled tugs, buoy tenders, and icebreakers. Here I'm introduced to the six-man crew of the Coast Guard Cutter *Line*, a 65-foot small harbor tug.

A classic multimission boat, built in 1962 in North Carolina, it's part of the Coast Guard's little-known "black hull fleet," which maintains the nation's navigational aids, buoys, and lighthouses.

Senior Chief Ross Fowle is in charge, MK (mechanic) 2 Charlie Wells, a big ginger-haired thirty-three-year-old Irish guy with a thoughtful fleshy face, is his XO. Kevin Thomas, Brian Leghorn, Dan Wishnoff, and Sean Cody make up the rest of the crew. Before heading out they do a premission GYR ("gar"), the standard green-yellow-red risk assessment.

On a scale of 1 to 10, they collectively rate Supervision a 2, Planning a 3, Crew Selection a 3, Crew Fitness 2, Environment (lousy weather) a 5, and Event and Evolution Complexity a 4, for a total of 19. They don't want to go over 25, though if someone were drowning they'd modify the formula and find a way to save him.

We make our way up the channel within sight of the Statue of Liberty and enter the harbor headed toward Manhattan. Along with their Ports, Waterways, and Coastal Security (PWCS) patrolling, they've been asked to fix one of their twenty-five assigned ATONs, this one a four-pole marker in Flushing Bay by LaGuardia Airport. One of its red day boards has apparently been knocked off. In the winter months, they'll head up the Hudson River behind a big icebreaker and clear channels into the smaller river port towns.

This is the third time "Senior" Ross Fowle and Charlie Wells have worked together. Their first time was in Tactical Law Enforcement, riding aboard U.S. Navy ships.

"I was on the *Thomas S. Gates*, and we seized the motor vessel *Love* and found three thousand kilos of coke on board," Fowle recalls, "but then their engineer snuck down to the engine room and opened all these valves, and this 270-foot coastal freighter starts sinking. We were able to keep it afloat long enough to take off some drugs for evidence, along with all the people, and then the *Gates* sank it using its five-inch guns. Since it was the MV *Love,* the ship's PA began playing the theme song from *The Love Boat* as they were firing the guns."

I ask Charlie, the son of a New York fireman, how he ended up in the Coast Guard. "I was a summer lifeguard at Jones Beach, and we had a loss, a death, and I remember this orange helicopter coming over the water with guys jumping out of it, and I said, 'Who are they?' and my dad said, 'That's the Coast Guard,' so I joined."

We cruise past Governors Island just off lower Manhattan. "This would have been a perfect operating base on 9/11," Charlie grouses. Like many in the Coast Guard, he regrets the service's decision to give up the old harbor fortress in 1996. "I was here on 9/11, and it would have been a lot easier. Instead we launched our boats from Sandy Hook [New Jersey]," he recounts. "I went in a 21-foot RHI (rigid-hull inflatable) and our 41 and 47 [-foot] boats set up a security zone and were transporting firemen and other emergency workers. We had to use radar to get through the smoke. I lost my uncle and a number of friends, four guys I went to school with, that day. I got a day off to go to the funerals, but our other guys kept working thirty days straight."

We head up the East River, passing under the BMW—the Brooklyn, Manhattan, and Williamsburg bridges. Through the chill mist we pass a towboat and a crane barge. On the barge is a 70-foot commercial fishing boat lying on its side. Its broken rails and crushed doors suggest it sank and was hauled up off the bottom.

"Sixteen miles to LaGuardia. Maybe we'll get to work the aid while we still have this break in the weather," Senior suggests hopefully. Five minutes later it's pouring again and visibility has dropped below a quarter mile.

I admire the tug's old beveled compass and metal steering wheel, which contrast with its newer digital charting, radar, and communications gear. The Medium Response Cutters that are replacing older 41-foot utility boats don't even have wheels; instead they have throttle controls built into their armrests and can be docked using a computer mouse.

Charlie takes the helm and talks about his seven-year-old daughter who's doing fractions and an emergency fire call he went on last night (he's also a volunteer fireman) where they responded to a house full of carbon monoxide and rescued a woman who was foaming at the mouth.

We pass the Domino Sugar refinery and a big Con Edison power plant opposite a petroleum fuel tank farm on the Brooklyn side, both rated as critical infrastructure to be watched by the Coast Guard. We cruise on past the United Nations. They show me the apartment building that Yankee pitcher Cory Lidle's plane ran into in October 2006. The burn marks where it impacted are still being worked on.

At Ward's Island we turn into Flushing Bay, moving past the big prison barge by Rikers Island. The rain continues in a steady downpour.

They call the airport so its security response force doesn't go after us while we're fixing the marker. "Most of our talk and everything now is homeland security," Senior notes while dropping anchor. "It's kind of become an industry really."

They lend me a Mustang suit and a bill cap. Charlie, Kevin, and Brian dress out, with Kevin and Brian strapping on climbing harnesses and ropes. Then they prep the 17-foot skiff secured in a cradle on the back of the boat, lifting it over the side on the *Line*'s small crane. I climb over the side and join them in the flat-bottomed craft, stepping over a big red triangular board.

Kevin helps Charlie get the Johnson outboard started, and we shoot off around a muddy bend and along runways where jets are taking off in the cold pelting rain. Charlie is driving, wearing a black skullcap and goggles, while Kevin is checking the navigation map. With the thump and biting chill and white furrowed wake rolling behind us, I'm suddenly reminded of a similar moment riding a Zodiac with Chilean marines in Antarctica.

"I love the smell of fish," Kevin remarks as the winds shift and a pungent piscine odor hits us. We nose up against a rocky isle with a four-post metal tower supporting large red navigation signs. Kevin and Brian leap onto the slippery rocks as Charlie holds the boat in close. They take the big red triangle board from the bottom of the boat. Kevin attaches a line to the tower's slick ladder and climbs up to a raised platform. Brian follows, handing him the sign. They then angle and attach it with a battery screwdriver. The twelve-degree outward angle of the sign "keeps the birds from crapping on it," Charlie explains. We head back to the *Line*, jumping the wake from a passing tug and garbage scow.

Back aboard, we sit around the galley table drying out as Senior gets us under way. Charlie talks about when he was boarding freighters in the Persian Gulf with his Tactical Law Enforcement team and "the Iranians were always pushing us." Brian puts on a sweatshirt that reads USCG LINE—SLOW BUT STEADY. They reheat some Chinese food and down carrots and chips.

Heading back down along the east side of Manhattan, Charlie tells me about his early career involvement in a famous migrant smuggling case, the *Golden Venture* back in June of 1994.

"I was watch stander at Rockaway [Station] and the U.S. Park Police called saying there was a fishing boat with seventy-five people on board, and that didn't make sense. I grabbed our truck and drove over to the beach—it was less than five minutes away—and saw this 200-foot freighter [the *Golden Ven-*

ture] and people jumping into the water. There were some Park Police and NYPD, and initially we were handcuffing people like it was a law enforcement thing, but when more people started dropping off the ship, I called on the radio and we drove back to the station and got life rings and lines and started pulling people out of the water. We did medevacs for four or five who were in cardiac arrest. A fireman came up and said, 'Can we get a helicopter to get people out?' and handed me a phone, and someone says, 'Who is this?' I say 'Coast Guardsman Charles Wells,' and he says, 'This is Fire Captain Charles Wells,' and it's my dad!" He grins at the memory. "He asks how it is, and I say it's pretty wild, 'cause it was chaotic at that time. I called in the Coast Guard helicopters, and I think six people died, but we got the rest who were critical out of there and to the hospitals."

We go up the Hudson River to a sports complex where the *Sanibel*, a 110-foot cutter from Group Woods Hole, is moored up. They call Dan Wishnoff to the wheelhouse because he's fresh from Cape May boot camp and has never seen a 110. We then head back down to the Battery, checking the currents and looking for a dock where they can drop me off. They bring the cutter in close to Pier 16 and hand me a life jacket. I put it on, hop onto the pier, return the jacket, and shake hands good-bye. They back out into the channel. I climb a fence and duck into the shopping mall at Pier 17 to get out of the rain.

Moments before, an NYPD patrol boat had cruised past us. "Since 9/11 they're doing more SAR and the Coast Guard more homeland security, and I got a huge problem with that!" Charlie, the dyed-in-the-wool New Yorker, complained. "Our job is search and rescue!"

For a rapidly growing force within the Coast Guard, however, the job and the mission are not primarily about saving lives anymore but about arming up for violent confrontations in the maritime domain.

CHAPTER 5

Gunners

"That movie Navy SEALS, *there's the scene where one of them says, 'If I wanted to play it safe I'd have joined the Coast Guard.' That irritated me."*

—Cdr. Mark Ogle, Pacific Tactical Law Enforcement Detachment, USCG

"Homeland Security officials and the Coast Guard say they're enforcing the law and accept no responsibility for the casualties."

—*Wall Street Journal* story on Cuban migrants killed during high-seas chases

On the day Al Qaeda attacked the United States, the Coast Guard had about three hundred full-time armed responders, mostly Tactical Law Enforcement Teams (TACLETs) going after drug runners and an antidrug Helicopter Interdiction Squadron called HITRON. Aware of a change in focus, they quickly renamed their mission CNT—Counter Narco-Terrorism.

Today's Coast Guard has over three thousand armed responders, including Tactical Law Enforcement Teams, Maritime Safety and Security Teams, Boarding and Security Teams, Port Security Units, and a two-hundred-strong and growing Maritime Security Response Team (MSRT), a kind of SEALs Lite, designed to board potentially hostile ships in U.S. waters and beyond.

"It's like we were always the bridesmaid and now we're the bride," says the otherwise extremely macho John Daly, CO of Tactical Law Enforcement Team South in Miami.

Coast Guard gunners now train at their own Special Missions Training Center on the Marine Corps base at Camp Lejeune, North Carolina. Here a small team might shoot off a hundred thousand rounds in a week, practice special boat tactics with armed pairs of 25-foot Defenders, or enter and clear a "kill house" or simulated "ship in a box," made of stacked shipping containers. They also train on how to quickly dump their body armor and other heavy gear if they end up in the water. Tactical flying has also become a specialty at the Aviation Training Center in Mobile, Alabama, where tactical aircrews have begun practicing for joint air/surface counterterror operations. In Chesapeake, Virginia, the Maritime Security Response Team has its own elaborate weapons training facility where its Direct Action Teams hone their ability to "neutralize enemy personnel." MSRT even has its own small air wing in Elizabeth City, North Carolina. Establishment of additional MSRTs is being considered for the West Coast, the Gulf Coast, the Great Lakes, and the Mississippi River.

Coast Guardsmen can also now apply to become Navy SEALs and retain their active-duty status in the Coast Guard (this is the only service career option not open to women). The template for today's increasingly militarized post-9/11 Coast Guard can be found in the service's decades-long participation in the "War on Drugs."

Drug Gunners

"We were hundreds of miles off Latin America when we came upon this unmarked go-fast boat. It was dumping bales of coke as it tried to escape. We fired warning shots across its bow, but it still wouldn't stop," says Lt. John Kousch, recalling the time he was in charge of a LEDET, a Coast Guard Law Enforcement Detachment, in the eastern Pacific. "After about forty-five minutes, and after it almost came into contact with our ship [the Navy frigate USS *Boone*] three rounds of disabling fire were fired into its rear engine compartment. Then it came to DIW—dead in the water—status, and one of the go-fast's crew jumped overboard. We picked up the guy in the water and boarded the vessel, and my guys went down below and found the drug rep had committed suicide, had blown the back of his head off. Over the next two to three hours, calculating set and drift, we were able to use the [*Boone*'s] helicopter to search and recover the bales of cocaine that were now spread over miles of ocean. There was approximately three tons of it."

The eastern Pacific is where most of the Coast Guard's big cocaine busts now take place, including a twenty-one-ton seizure from the Panamanian freighter *Gatun* in March 2007, the largest-ever coke bust at sea. Recent smuggler tactics have included liquefying cocaine and hiding it in their fuel tanks and using semisubmersible submarines to transport it.

Another time Kousch and his team were trying to secure the flooding engine room of a 65-foot fishing vessel, the *Simon Bolivar,* when it slammed into their Navy frigate, smashing its own bow while leaving only superficial scrapes on the warship. A Navy rescue and assistance (R&A) team was able to keep the drug boat afloat long enough for the Coasties to do a space accountability search and find the secret compartments hiding five or six tons of cocaine that was intended to go down with the ship.

Eight-man LEDET teams (there have only been a few women) operate as part of Tactical Law Enforcement teams in San Diego (PACTACLET) and Miami (TACLET South). A Chesapeake, Virginia–based TACLET North and an MSST unit were reorganized as the counterterrorist Maritime Security Response Team in 2004.

Coast Guard Law Enforcement Detachments ride aboard U.S., British, Dutch, and other allied warships and military oilers for thirty to sixty days at a time, mostly in the Caribbean and eastern Pacific. There they pursue and board suspected drug vessels, sometimes sneaking up on them in small boats in the open ocean at night. They also spend part of their time working as trainers with the Iraqi navy and other armed forces in the Persian Gulf.

Among their two hundred or so members, they account for half the cocaine seized by the U.S. Coast Guard, which is more than all the cocaine seized by the DEA, FBI, Customs Service, and all local and state police combined. In 2007, the Coast Guard seized a record-breaking 355,000 pounds of cocaine (over 160 metric tons) with an estimated street value of $4.7 billion.

Of course, the Coast Guard was also highly effective at chasing down rumrunners during Prohibition. That didn't stop Americans from drinking a sea of alcohol brought in by cagey smugglers like Capt. Bill McCoy, whose product was so admired by the public it came to be known as "the real McCoy."

Less attractive are some of today's smugglers, people like Francisco Javier Arellano-Felix, the head of a ruthless Mexican drug cartel known for its intramural executions, the accidental murder of a Catholic cardinal, the torture-murder of several drug agents, and a half-mile-long drug tunnel it excavated between Tijuana and San Diego. In August 2006, Arellano-Felix, then thirty-seven, fell into a fish trap laid by the Coast Guard and DEA. He took his family and friends (including two alleged cartel assassins) on an offshore fishing holiday aboard the U.S.-registered 43-foot yacht *Dock Holiday* (a play on the name of a famous American gunman). They left the port of Cabo San Lucas not realizing they were being observed. Nearby an undercover DEA "sports fishing boat" operated by a couple of Coast Guard agents was watching, waiting, and passing secure message traffic north.

The *Monsoon* is an angular, lethal-looking 179-foot coastal patrol boat, one of eight the Navy lent the Coast Guard after 9/11 (it still has use of four). The *Monsoon* spent weeks offshore with a LEDET team waiting for Arellano-Felix to decide to go after that big trophy fish beyond Mexico's twelve-mile territorial sea. They waited so long they had to drop most of the team ashore, as they were scheduled for duty in Iraq.

"It was an on and off operation," the *Monsoon*'s CO, Lt. Cdr. Troy Hosmer, admits. "We were south of Cabo and starting to patrol back north when we [finally] got word [that the *Dock Holiday* was headed out to sea]. The opportunity was just right. I think part of how it went down is we have a gray hull that looks like the Navy [as opposed to Coast Guard white]. They probably thought we were the Mexican navy when we stopped them and got on board.

"We used seven people for the actual boarding. While we [the *Monsoon*] blocked them from making a run toward (Mexico's) territorial sea, our small boat came up on them. I'm not even sure they saw it. I mean, it had to look impressive as we pulled up with all our guns manned and loaded. We knew some of those guys with them were their bodyguards and knew what we were going to do if any of them pulled a weapon. They didn't. So we detained eleven people, eight adults and three children. It was unfortunate the kids were exposed to this, but pretty soon we had them on Sony PlayStations and were feeding them candy."

I asked about the fishing. "I think they had one hooked when we boarded," he said. Later one of the boarders tells me they'd actually just lost a blue marlin when they were arrested and so were already in a bad mood. Either way, it was a victory for America and for that fish.

• • •

Even before former commandant Paul Yost volunteered the Coast Guard for the Reagan administration's War on Drugs in the 1980s, its cutters were chasing down maritime smugglers. Before the rise of the cocaine cartels, it was marijuana smugglers in the Caribbean.

"We were chasing old shrimp boats piled high with marijuana. The best tactic was just to be downwind of them," former Coast Guard commandant Jim Loy recalls of his time chasing pungent loads of ganja in the 1970s.

Where the big cutters used to display marijuana leaves representing their seizures, they now display snowflakes representing tons of coke they've busted.

"Last summer everyone was getting a case," Cmdr. Mark Ogle, head of the Pacific Tactical Law Enforcement Team, tells me. "Nothing big, but a ton here, a ton there. Then we got the submarine case [a fishing trawler hauling a steel-hulled semisubmersible containing 3.5 tons of coke]. Just our seizures [PACTACLET's] have been $2.7 billion in two years. That's some real money." He grins.

We go in the back room of one of his unit's single-story yellow cinder-block buildings located inside the Marine Corps Recruit Depot in San Diego.

Past Iraqi and Colombian flags and photos of burning drug ships and heavily armed boarding parties are half a dozen buff young guys in their twenties listening to thrash metal music under a wall-sized Dutch flag. They'd just spent much of the last year on a Dutch warship busting drug runners in the Caribbean. Their only complaint: too many sandwiches on Dutch ships. Those who ride with the British grouse about all the curry and potatoes.

In the Caribbean, where the distances are relatively short and a drug runner can deliver a load, sink a boat, and fly home within twenty-four hours, there are "more runs but fewer tons" of coke being smuggled. In the eastern Pacific, go-fasts, fishing boats, and coastal freighters out of Colombia and Ecuador may travel thousands of miles out past the Galápagos Islands to try to bypass U.S. antidrug patrols. They'll then work their way north up a ladder of fueling vessels, or "floating gas stations," to Mexico, where the drugs are off-loaded and taken by land (and sometimes by tunnel) across the U.S. border. Because of the added logistical costs involved, the drug cartels tend to run larger loads in the Pacific.

"We'd captured two go-fasts in two days and to build the [legal] case wanted their fueler," recalls Chief Mark Quinlan of Miami's TACLET South. "Generally these [fuel ships] are fishing vessels with radar on board, so we had to do a UNB, an unannounced nighttime boarding. So we climb down the ladder [off the Navy frigate *De Wert*], my team and a Navy coxswain and swimmer/engineer, into this small boat in the middle of the ocean six hundred miles west of Ecuador.

"There were two- to four-foot seas, and here we are heading sixteen miles over the horizon at night. We're driving for two and a half hours and we're soaked and we're miserable. We're sitting on the RIB's [rigid inflatable boat's] sponsons [pontoons] hanging on to the ropes. We couldn't use our [night-vision] goggles as we got near because they were covered in salt. We came up on the port aft section [of the target vessel], and this Navy coxswain was good. He pulled up and stuck it against the boat, and we all leaped over the rail. The gunwales were so low in the water, there was so much gas on board, that the deck was almost awash.

"So all eight of us jump onto the boat at the same time. There was this head [latrine] at the end of the boat, a curtained shack, and this guy stuck his head out, so two of my guys took him down. I went to the engine room with another guy [to see if the boat had been scuttled or set afire, as their crews are instructed to do if boarded], but it was empty. Four of my guys were going up the port side to the bridge and past the crew cabin when one of the crew woke up and reached out of the porthole and grabbed at one of our rifles and knocked the magazine out of the weapon, so two of our guys dealt with him, and the other two secured the bridge and called me on the radio. It took us one minute and twenty-eight seconds to gain control of that ship.

"There were nine people aboard. It was a 67-foot-long wooden trawler with two tanks of gas; one held seventeen hundred gallons and the other twenty-eight hundred. We had to search for a while before we found the fuel port in the crew quarters. There were triple bunks, and under one of the bottom beds was this port [gasoline pipe] and two electric leads. The fuel pump was disassembled around the boat, but all the parts were painted red—the hoses, flange, wires—so that an idiot could put it together, which is what we did." He grins. "It even had a gas-pump-style handle. We took fuel samples to compare with the go-fast boats we'd seized. Then we uncuffed our one suspect at the head and let him finish up his business."

Lt. JG Todd Taylor tells of another unannounced nighttime boarding, in December 2005, in which one life was saved but two lost.

"We had a team of eight and two Navy officers. We were approaching an 80-foot fishing boat eight hundred miles south of the Galápagos at 3:30 A.M. There were two dogs aboard, a sheepdog type and a Doberman, and they came to the side of the boat as we approached and were barking and snapping at us. We probably emptied fifty ounces of pepper spray at them. Finally they took a break, and we climbed aboard.

"It was a high freeboard, because I'm about six-three, and I had to raise both my arms to pull myself up and over with my full kit [about sixty pounds of gear]. As we came on board, the crew started coming out on deck and lying down with their arms raised. One of them told us there were eight people on board, and my team took control of the bridge without any resistance.

"I went into the engine room, and there were these four wooden plugs that had been pulled to scuttle the ship and also this pump on deck that was pumping water into the ship so that I was waist deep when I got there. I found debris, garbage, and stuff floating around the room, and we got the pump reversed, so the water was now pumping out.

"The Navy was two miles off, and they sent a small boat team to start dewatering the boat and try to keep it afloat. I went back on deck and counted seven people and got the interpreter to ask the guy who said there were eight about the missing man, and this is ten minutes into it, and he says, 'Well, the master dove over the side when you boarded.'

"It was about dawn, just getting light, and the Navy coxswain begins to search in the direction we'd come from and finds him six miles behind the boat treading water and brings him back to us. So he's a lucky guy even if he is in jail today.

"We were still searching, and the Doberman wouldn't allow one of my guys access to this space and was attempting to bite him, and so he shot the dog in the shoulder, and it ran to the back of the boat, laid down, and died.

"We got on that boat at 3:30 A.M. and kept it afloat till we could offload the eight detainees and twenty-one thousand pounds of cocaine we found on board which took about one and a half hours moving these 244 double-sized bales onto small boats. They even put a Navy diver in the water to try to patch it [the drug vessel] from below, but thirty-six minutes after we left the boat it filled with water and sank."

I ask what happened to the second dog.

"The Navy captain said no way we could bring it on his ship. We'd locked it in the master's cabin, and it went down with the boat."

I ask why they didn't at least shoot the dog rather than let it drown. He says they have to account for any shots discharged. I suggest putting a dog down humanely ought to be considered a justifiable use of force.

• • •

While not allowed to shoot dogs, specially trained Coast Guard snipers are allowed to use .50 caliber rifle fire from helicopters to shoot out the engine blocks of fast-moving boats during high-speed ocean pursuits. This is done by the Helicopter Interdiction Tactical Squadron (HITRON) based out of Jacksonville, Florida. They pioneered the service's Airborne Use of Force doctrine in 1998, deploying eight aircraft on Coast Guard cutters in the Caribbean and the eastern Pacific. Until recently these were Sting Rays, sleek Italian helicopters built by Agusta Aerospace and leased by the Coast Guard along with civilian contractor/mechanics who went out on the cutters but didn't fly. Each aircrew included two pilots and a gunner who'd fire warning shots from an M-240 machine gun in front of an escaping drug boat and then, if peppering the water in front of it with hot lead failed to stop it, would shoot its outboards with a laser-mounted .50 caliber sniper rifle.

Lt. Greg Mouritsen went from flying Black Hawks for the Army to Sting Rays for HITRON. "Actually the mission's not that different. This is the only non-SAR-capable mission in the Coast Guard," he explains. "Generally when we run into these boats we fire on them. They generally stop. They know we're not shooting to kill, but if I knew you were going to shoot out my outboard and there's going to be shrapnel and it's fifteen feet from where I'm standing at the console, I'd stop."

Bosun's Mate Mark Collison tells of finding a Caribbean go-fast dead in the water at two in the morning. His LEDET team snuck up on and surprised the three men on board who had earlier escaped from a HITRON helicopter. One of them had a bloody tourniquet around his thigh where metal fragments from one of their shot-up outboards had penetrated above his knee and exited just below his buttocks.

"I had my EMT look at the injured guy. We then put them on our boat, and one of our guys got on their boat, but coming back it sank in six-foot seas. It was a pretty good chop, and our communications had gone down, so we decided to pick our way toward where we thought our ship [the USS *Ticonderoga*] was, and three hours later we finally made contact."

In other cases, drug runners being pursued by HITRON have died flipping their boats at 40 and 50 mph trying to evade capture.

In 2007, HITRON's Sting Rays were replaced by upgraded Dolphins. With the use of this standardized Coast Guard helicopter, more aircrew men and women are now being trained to function as snipers.

• • •

The Coast Guard has also committed five Dolphins to National Capitol Region (NCR) security flights over Washington, DC. Based out of Air Station Atlantic City and flying out of Reagan National Airport under the command of NORAD, the North American Aerospace Defense Command, they're equipped with hailers and side-mounted electronic message boards, essentially flying billboards to warn off small aircraft that stray into or intentionally enter restricted airspace over the Capitol. Filling the gap between what high-speed Air Force F-16 fighter jets can identify and what Secret Service agents with Stinger missiles can stop from the roof of the White House, NCR aircraft are supposed to identify a threat early on and, if it proves real, back off and let the Air Force do the actual shootdown.

The Cuban Connection

Since joining the Department of Homeland Security in 2003, the Coast Guard has expanded its own use of live fire to include boat crews firing shotgun slugs into the outboard motors of migrant-smuggling go-fasts. To date, only boats filled with Cubans have been fired upon. Haitians and Dominicans know that if caught by land or by sea they will be deported home and so tend to surrender when confronted by U.S. authorities. Since 1994, however, the United States has had a "wet foot/dry foot" policy that allows Cuban migrants leaving the island by boat to claim refugee status only if they make it onto U.S. soil. If caught at sea they will be returned to Cuba. Previously all Cuban migrants were given special refugee status as part of the United States' Cold War confrontation with Cuba.

Wet foot/dry foot was the result of a 1994 Clinton administration deal with Fidel Castro to end the huge surge of maritime migrants the Cuban government was permitting to leave the island. It ended when the United States increased the number of legal entry visas to twenty thousand a year but made it harder for Cubans without visas to gain access by sea. Since then wet foot/dry foot has had the same impact on immigration policy as "don't ask, don't tell" has had for gay members of the military.

In 2006, in a peculiar example of how this ongoing policy can be interpreted, fifteen Cubans landed on the old Seven Mile highway bridge in the Florida Keys that runs next to its modern replacement. Since some of the old bridge's spans are missing and the Cubans were unable to walk to shore, the

Coast Guard ruled they were not technically on U.S. soil. They loaded them on a cutter and sailed them back to the Cuban port of Bahia de Cabañas, where the majority of Cuban migrants caught at sea are repatriated.

A short time later, a flotilla from the "Conch Republic" (a hard-drinking faux nation based in Key West) sailed out to the highway bridge and claimed it as their territory, since no other nation seemed to.

Dry-footing is a much quicker way to U.S. residency than joining the Cuban lottery for a U.S. visa or applying from a third country. I know of one Cuban scientist who, in order to escape the economic hardships of life in Cuba, got a travel permit to Mexico, where he snuck across the U.S. border. From San Diego he rode a bus to Miami. Once there he put on an old pair of cut-off jeans and went to the beach, lying in the sun for twelve hours till he was severely sunburned. He then slipped into the water, swam offshore, and swam back, splashing around loudly, announcing that his raft had sunk and demanding political asylum, which he got. He didn't know he could have simply asked for it at the Mexican border.

A far more serious result of the wet foot/dry foot policy has been the growth of between twenty and thirty criminal gangs of smugglers (often new arrivals themselves) who charge $10,000 per person to get people into the United States. They'll pull up on a Cuban beach, jam thirty or more people onto a 10-meter cigarette boat, and then head for Florida at breakneck speed, not bothering to stop if confronted by the law.

While a majority of Cuban refugees still come in what the Coast Guard calls "rustic vessels" or "chugs" (as in chug-chug) that can range from a raft of innertubes to a '59 Buick with pontoons (intercepted in 2004), the go-fasts represent a newer, more dangerous mode of transport.

Sitting in the Coast Guard Investigative Service office at an old communications station in south Miami, I watch a black and white FLIR (forward-looking infrared) video shot from a Coast Guard Falcon jet. It shows a large speedboat bumping across open water.

"We were looking for him for two days [based on intelligence tips] and found him five minutes from shore with a Black Hawk in pursuit," Special Agent in Charge Jon Sall tells me as the scene unfolds.

The boat slows down only slightly before running up on a sandy beach amid high-end estate condos and manicured palm trees. It's Miami's Fisher Island, one of the local retreats for wealthy celebrities. You see twenty-five whitish figures spilling out of the boat, running across the deck of a condominium owned by wrestling entrepreneur Vince McMahon. At the same time, a Black Hawk helicopter appears in the foreground of the video, hovering menacingly next to the beached boat. A man from the boat pulls another whitish figure, that appears to be a woman, off the vessel. She stumbles, and they take off into the dark between the condos. Two gunmen jump from the Customs and Border Patrol helicopter and begin to examine the beached and abandoned $130,000 boat. The video ends. The Cubans get to stay.

I look at a map on the office wall that shows the waters around Puerto Rico, including a flyspeck island forty miles to its west. Mona Island is a barren, waterless U.S. wildlife refuge, but since it's easy for Cubans to get permits to visit the Dominican Republic, which is close to Mona, a growing number have begun arriving on the island from there.

They risk the treacherous Mona Passage in order to land and claim their right to "political asylum" from the local ranger, who is otherwise kept busy counting iguanas. Dozens of Cubans are thought to have drowned attempting this journey. The Coast Guard spends a lot of time trying to block landings here or else delivering food and water to desperate, dehydrated Cubans who made it ashore.

Recently, however, the Coasties have been able to reduce traffic in the Mona Passage by 50 percent with new biometric technology. They use handheld satellite-linked scanners to transmit photos and fingerprints of people they've picked up on the water to a U.S. criminal and immigration database. Getting instant "hits" back, they are able to sort out the smugglers for prosecution. This has discouraged other smugglers from using this route. This Biometrics at Sea Program has now been extended to the Florida Straits.

Agent Sall shows me a couple of recent photos taken by a U.S. Wildlife ranger on the Marquesas Keys Refuge, only thirty miles west of Key West, where twenty-eight people were dropped off. They're mugging happily, smiling and waving to the camera, knowing they're now on U.S soil, a fact that gives no similar joy to millions of Mexican, Haitian, Dominican, Chinese, and other migrants who once in the United States are still forced to work as "illegals" in America's low-wage underground economy.

Agent Sall, dark-haired with lively blue eyes, gray slacks, and a black shirt that could only work in Miami, claims that a week earlier off Key West a Cuban woman draped her infant child over the cowling of a go-fast boat's outboard engine so it wouldn't be shot out. A few migrants have tried to set themselves afire, knowing that if they're taken to a mainland hospital they get to stay.

There have also been a number of documented incidents of Cubans violently resisting arrest at sea, trying to fight off Coast Guard boarders with spear-like fish gigs, clubs, and hatchets.

"We have maybe fifteen to twenty attacks on Coast Guard members a year [on the water], but now we make federal assault cases, and recently one perp got ten years in prison, so that's something," Sall says, appearing satisfied. "For the smugglers it's not about the migrants, it's organized crime. You get thirty people in a 30-foot boat, that's a three-hundred-grand [$300,000] load, and unlike drugs, you get caught and maybe have your wrist slapped, though that's beginning to change . . . Right now there are more boats stolen in Georgia and Florida than the rest of the country combined. Within eighteen months of starting one investigation, we recovered forty boats worth over five million dollars.

"The typical organization is involved in stealing boats, smuggling migrants, and maybe committing Medicare fraud. They'll make up phony stickers for the outboard engines or use real numbers from another engine. I tracked one number and called it up, and it's a guy in Washington state, and he says, 'Yeah, that's my engine number and it's on the engine of my boat sitting here in my yard.' That was from a case out of Jacksonville. Or with boats they'll change the HIN number—that's the Hull Identification Number, like a VIN number on a vehicle—and then they'll register it with the state so when you look it up it comes back as legal. So they steal a boat, use it for a smuggling run—not a lot of start-up costs there—then sell it to a friend, report it stolen, collect the insurance, and 'round it goes."

Frustrated with the smugglers, the Coast Guard Investigative Service initiated Operation Triple Play.

"The majority of landings have been on the Keys, so we tried to deny them the Keys as an operating area," he explains. "We brought in fifteen to twenty agents from around the country and had a profile—I know that's not a good word, but it wasn't ethnic. It was, say, a 30-foot go-fast boat with three outboards and no fishing gear aboard [being towed by a twenty-four-year-old Cuban in a Hummer]. We'd get with state and local police, and they'd enforce statutes on registration and brake lights and see if the driver had a valid license. We had boats stopped with sixty-five-gallon gas cans, and we pulled one back to the Coast Guard station in Miami, and none of the three guys with the boat was the owner, so we asked them to call him. He shows up in this SUV, and we tell him you can't have all this gas on the boat, so he loads three hundred gallons of gas in the back of his Chevy Tahoe and puts his boat on the hitch and drives off. We called the Dade County sheriff to say there was this bomb driving down the highway, but they didn't care."

During its four months of operation, Triple Play led to a lot of traffic citations and brake light tickets, a couple of fishing violations, and the recovery of dozens of stolen boats and engines.

Still, most of the active confrontations—and several migrant deaths—have taken place not on land but at sea, partly as a result of the Coast Guard's increased use of force.

In the summer of 2007, the *Wall Street Journal* reported on the case of Amay Machado Gonzalez, a twenty-four-year-old newlywed who was one of more than two dozen migrants on a go-fast boat that was trying to outrun two Coast Guard vessels and a helicopter. When a Coast Guard gunner shot two copper slugs into one of the outboards, the boat made an abrupt left turn before stalling out. It was during that turn Amay hit her head against the side of the boat in what would prove to be a fatal injury, the third fatal head injury of a Cuban migrant resulting from a high-speed ocean chase within a year.

Right before the Coast Guard opened fire, over the sound of sirens wailing and engines roaring, Amay had turned to her new husband, Agustin, and said, "Pray for me, my love, because I'm praying for you." A moment later, she lay dying in the bottom of the boat.

The Coast Guard blames deaths such as Amay's on the human smugglers trying to avoid arrest, and, as with high-speed police chases on land, so does the law. Three U.S.-based Cubans involved in smuggling Amay and the other migrants were sentenced to twelve years in prison, two of them for contributing to her death.

However, *Wall Street Journal* reporter Robert Block suggests there's no evidence that harsh methods like shooting out the engines of go-fast boats result in any greater success. More than half the Cubans who attempt to sneak into the United States still make it.

So why is the U.S. Coast Guard so actively involved in maritime drug and migrant interdiction in the first place? It's because, as a multimission maritime agency, the Coast Guard has both U.S. Title 10 (military) and Title 14 (law enforcement) authority. The other armed services are prevented from carrying out any domestic law enforcement under the Posse Comitatus Act of 1878. As a result, the Coast Guard gets to enforce criminal statutes that the Department of Defense cannot.

One effect is that when an at-sea drug boarding is about to take place, the Coast Guard ensign is raised over the Navy warship carrying its team, and that ship officially becomes a Coast Guard vessel. This is something the U.S. Navy generally doesn't like to talk about. During migrant pulses like the Mariel boatlift of 1980 or the Haitian and Cuban boatlifts of 1994 and 1995, Navy ships have also functioned as Coast Guard holding pens.

Today the Coast Guard's mixed law enforcement and military authority is viewed by the Department of Homeland Security as a way to ramp up its domestic firepower in the War on Terror. Unlike other military helicopters flying over our cities and ports, the Coast Guard's HH-60s and HH-65s wouldn't require a federal declaration of martial law to open fire. This is one reason they're now equipping all Coast Guard helicopters with Airborne Use of Force capability.

Aerial Gunners

The rotors whir, and AC steam begins to run like a waterfall in the space between the cockpit and the main cabin. Struts up, we roll down the runway as the blades roar, and suddenly we're shooting up like a fast freight elevator two hundred feet above the air station. We head out over the water with a breeze blowing through the open door, over the bay and marinas full of sailboats, running past Harbor Island and the channel and the big North Island Navy air base and out past the Coast Guard lighthouse at the tip of San Diego's Point Loma. It's a beautiful blue ocean afternoon for flying.

Ten minutes into the flight, Sector Control announces an EPIRB—an emergency position-indicating radio beacon—signal has been picked up. On a small monitor linked to a rear-tilted camera, I see the other HH-60 peel away to respond. Looking out the side window, I can see it flying toward shore above a gray-hulled Navy frigate.

"25 and 37 have broken formation. 25 returning to San Diego to investigate," the Coast Guard pilot announces on the radio.

"Sector understands. Out."

"Ninety-nine percent of the time it's a false alarm, but we always treat them as the real thing until we know better," Capt. Chip Strangfeld explains from the front of our craft.

A few minutes later, we hear a call between 25 and base.

"Believe we located the source. We're over North Island [Naval Air Station], and the signal is coming from the hangars."

"From the hangars, is that correct? Over."

"Correct. That double dome area."

"Thank you. Please stand by."

Shortly, 25 is released to rejoin us.

The light is fading as we circle over the Navy firing range on San Clemente Island, having chased a state Fish and Game boat out of Horseshoe Cove. I can see blue waves breaking along the rugged marine terraces to one side, an improvised shooting range on the other. Randy, lying in the open door, takes aim with his M-14 EBR. The high-tech 7.62 mm rifle, all composite, steel, and laser sight, is tethered to the side of the door with the same type of woven lanyard you might have found on a nineteenth-century revenue cutter. We hover about twenty-five feet off the ground fifty yards out from four paper targets of male torsos on wooden supports, each spray-painted 1 through 4.

"Ten shots from fifty yards, then ten shots from one hundred," Travis Marsh, the thickset blond gunnery mate, instructs over the ICF internal radio line that plugs into our helmets.

"Commence firing." The pilot makes the call. Randy takes aim. Even with the helmet's ear protectors, there's still a loud series of pops and static whines on the headset, along with air pressure pulses, orange muzzle flashes, and a whiff of cordite that's quickly washed away through the open door. "Cease firing." The Jayhawk pulls back and a little up till we're hovering thirty-five feet off the ground. Randy clears his weapon. A video camera on the helicopter's nose zooms in to show close-ups of the plywood-backed targets so Travis can count the hits. We tilt up and pull back to one hundred yards for another ten shots. Randy puts his weapon away in its case.

Next it's Tyson Finn's turn. He has to unravel his radio line from his safety line before taking a kneeling position in the open door and blasting away at fifty yards. After "Cease firing," the chopper backs up, and he fires another clip at a hundred yards. Randy scored fifteen, Tyson ten. Seventeen out of twenty is required to pass this shooting qualification. The radio tells us the shooters on the other helicopter scored thirteen and seventeen. One out of four has qualified on the daytime shoot.

As twilight turns the desert scrub of the island to gold and ocher, Randy turns on the weapon's laser sight and walks its red dot across the ground, up to the target, and "between the legs." Between the helicopter's vibrations and his point-and-shoot style of firing from the hip, the laser dot is bouncing around like a firefly on methamphetamine. Each shot's impact sets off a spout of dust on the slope behind the targets.

"This is my second time on this course, and I don't think I've even qualified," Travis, now the aerial gunner, assures the others as he blasts away from a cross-legged lotus position in the door.

After the cease-fire order, a blue light is turned on in the cabin and all the spilled brass cleaned up. We then land, and I accompany Travis and Randy through the cactus, sand, and shrub, following his flashlight beacon to the targets. Most of the shots are bunched low. Travis sprays glue on the targets and covers them with new paper torsos from a cardboard stash box nearby. Randy follows with a staple gun, then relabels them 1-4 in black spray paint. We hike back to the HH-60 and remove cactus stickers that have bunched on the sides and bottoms of our shoes. "One guy didn't and got a cactus spine stuck in his ass when he squatted down in the cabin," Travis warns.

By the time we lift off again it's pitch-black. On the next run, the pilots and shooters are wearing night-vision goggles attached to their blue helmets. All I can see is the muzzle flashes as Randy fires into the darkness . . . *Pop, pop, pop, pop, pop.*

"You hit nine out of ten," Travis announces. He must see my look of disbelief and reaches over to let me look through his night-vision-rigged helmet.

I put it on and see the rugged landscape of the island transformed into a globe-shaped lime-colored world that reminds me of the psychedelic rock posters of my youth. There's a bright white targeting dot that, unlike the ruby red laser dot, is only visible to the night-vision goggles' wearer. Also, this dot's much larger, pea sized rather than pin sized.

Tyson is still kind of herky-jerky, letting the uneven weight of the weapon and the copter's vibrations jump the dot around when he gets the white pea into the body mass of the target. He proves better at a hundred yards.

Someone asks what I think about their stealthy night-vision targeting system. I say I think I'd still rather be the guy on the ground hidden in the rocks shooting back at a big, noisy orange helicopter hovering just off the ground.

We land a final time and load the wooden target frames and shooting supplies onto the helo. The low-slung interior of the HH-60 now looks like a pickup on a trash run.

"We need more training," Travis admits at the end of our four-hour flight. The station's last range training was in February, and it's now September. The Coast Guard is in the process of arming its entire helicopter fleet with belt-fed M-240 machine guns and ride-along shooters.

"It makes no sense in post-9/11 to not have this capability," reasons Capt. Chip Strangfeld, our pilot and San Diego's sector commander. "Others think that's what we have the Department of Defense for, but the National Guard and DOD are not there right away, while we are on the scene and operating above America's waters every day."

"We'll put ballistic armor on the floor and armored plates under the pilots' seats and on the sides," Travis explains. "We'll have M-240 mounts and also a FRIES bar, which is a big bar and pole for fast rope descents [for tactical teams]. The idea is to have it as a modular package so we could reconfigure the cabin in an hour with armor and the M-240."

Travis was one of the first nine flight mechanics to be trained as aerial gunners at the Coast Guard Aviation Training Center in Mobile, Alabama. "We started training in January '06," he tells me. "Actually on Martin Luther King weekend."

Walking the DOG

Coast Guard stations, sectors, and districts, I've quickly come to notice, are very reflective of the areas they operate in. So it doesn't surprise me that in a Navy town like San Diego, the Airborne Use of Force doctrine is being eagerly embraced. Coast Guard aviators in Kodiak, Alaska, on the other hand, a place famed for its larger-than-life search and rescue cases, are concerned about the extra workload after being chosen as the second station to be trained and armed for Airborne Use of Force. "I'm now doing more AUF training than SAR training," Kodiak flight mechanic John Inman tells me.

In July 2007, most of the service's paramilitary units, including the Tactical Law Enforcement Teams, Marine Safety and Security Teams, and Maritime Security Response Team were put together to form the Deployable Operations Group, or DOG. The DOG also includes the Environmental Strike Teams, Port Security Units, Naval Coastal Warfare Squadrons, the International Training Division that works with other nations' coast guards, and several dozen scuba divers. The DOG staff is working to add additional assets like the Patrol Forces deployed in the Persian Gulf, the HITRON helicopter squadron, and the Redeployment Assistance Inspection Detachment (RAID) that helps the military load sea cargo for shipment to and from places such as Afghanistan via the Port of Karachi, Pakistan (Hint: Remove the U.S. flag and ARMY STRONG decals from your shipping containers).

Coast Guard Commandant Thad Allen, who has been thinking about "adaptive force packages" and "deployable commands" since 2001, envisions the Coast Guard functioning as "a three-pronged force with shore-based operations, maritime operations, and deployable operations."

Tom Atkin is the very tall, Hollywood-handsome one-star admiral put in charge of the DOG. "We will respond to all threats and all hazards all the time," he says, quoting a Coast Guard slogan. "It could be a hurricane or a security threat. What we're doing is laying out lots of scenarios, writing plans [with a staff of 147], reaching out to DHS and other partners so as events unfold, they roll with us."

Of course, some partners are famous for their inability to roll with others. The FBI, after working with the Coasties on various counterterrorism and port security task forces, established their own Maritime SWAT Teams, then located them in all the same ports as the Coast Guard's MSSTs.

More recently the DOG has, without irony, provided dog handlers and other assets to the Transportation Security Administration for airport sweeps and in turn got support from TSA and CBP (Customs and Border Protection) during a heightened security watch over Seattle's commuter ferries, which carry ten to twelve million passengers a year.

The multiagency operation, labeled Sound Shield, was launched after two young Middle Eastern–looking men were seen "acting suspiciously" on area ferries. Even though a ferry crewman took their pictures, which were then distributed to law enforcement and shown on local TV, the authorities were unable to locate them for questioning. Almost a year later, they contacted the U.S. Embassy in Lisbon. Portuguese software consultants who'd been attending a business conference in Seattle, they now feared they might be picked up as terrorists if they returned to the United States. They explained to the FBI that they had never been on big ferries that carried vehicles before, and that was why they were on the car deck taking pictures, to show their friends back home. "It was perfectly normal [behavior] once we knew what was going on," an FBI agent concluded.

While the Coast Guard works to expand its interagency collaborative efforts, it's historically been able to confront most challenges on its own. Mark Ogle, the PACTACLET chief who's moved on to the DOG staff, recalls deploying to St. Croix in the U.S. Virgin Islands after Hurricane Hugo devastated that island in 1989.

"We were just supposed to show the flag. We got three-quarters of a mile off the coast [on a 110-foot cutter] and two guys, two reporters, swam out to us from the beach with a waterproof capsule containing the names of seventy people barricaded in the center of town. They were under siege. So four of us went into the beach in an RIB [raft] with M-16s. We were given keys to cars and drove into town, where we found the local police and National Guard were looting. When the storm was approaching they'd opened up the jail and let out all the criminals, and now people had broken into the liquor shops and gun stores, and it was a real scene. We reached the people who were trapped."

I ask if they were white, as I recall reports of racial conflict on the island. "There was definitely a racial element," he admits. "We formed a caravan of cars to get out, and other vehicles would block the road, and we had to get out and knock on their windows with our M-16s to get them to clear out. We got to the pier and called for reinforcements and then went back for more folks who were on the southern tip of the island. These folks were real relieved to see us when we showed up. We got the evacuation under way, and then gunshots erupted. It turns out this shop owner had discharged his shotgun [at a looter] and there was one dead. Then other shots were fired, and the evacuation, which had been going in a lackadaisical manner, really picked up speed as people jumped into [Coast Guard small] boats and abandoned their cars and just got on board."

It used to be that with the exception of wars, riots, and interventions—a Coast Guard cutter led U.S. forces into Haiti in 1994—the service was a largely unarmed one.

Incidents involving Coast Guard shootings during the Prohibition era, including the killing of at least twelve rumrunners between 1924 and 1928, proved hugely unpopular. The Coast Guard killed four more men in 1929, including three aboard the British motor launch *Black Duck,* headed into Narragansett Bay with a load of liquor. That incident resulted in protest meetings and newspaper editorials across New England demanding the resignation of the service's commandant, Adm. Frederick Billard. There were also mob attacks on off-duty Coast Guardsmen in New London and angry confrontations with Coast Guard recruiters.

The hanging of rumrunner Horace Alderman at the Coast Guard base in Fort Lauderdale, Florida, that same year generated local protests and national outrage, even though he had shot and killed two Coast Guardsmen and a Secret Service agent during a boarding. A Coastie in Key West was threatened with lynching after he was falsely accused of shooting another smuggler. By the end of their thirteen-year-long "Rum War," the service had dramatically expanded in size but lost much of its hard-earned credibility with the public.

The introduction of sidearms during the early years of the "drug wars" of the 1970s and '80s also generated lots of controversy.

"The boating public was up in arms about our armed boarding parties. It was a hard sell," recalls retired Adm. Roger Rufe, now with the Department of Homeland Security. "It's like the fire department versus the police department, except in the Coast Guard we're both, and the public prefers the fire department aspect, the search and rescue."

Surfman Ricky Spencer remembers odd attempts at compromise when he was serving in Port Angeles, Washington, thirty years ago. "I wore my gun belt with a .45 and was told not to have a clip in it and to cover it over with my long float coat. That didn't make any sense to me at all."

The Coast Guard also got into trouble for getting too deeply into paramilitary activities overseas. Adm. Paul Yost, Coast Guard commandant from 1986 to 1990, volunteered the service for the War on Drugs, the Cold War, the looming Gulf War, and any other war in sight. The Vietnam combat veteran's swing toward all things military, starting with a ban on beards (including then–Lt. Cmdr. Thad Allen's) had service members grousing about the new "Yost Guard." He even began placing antiship Harpoon missiles on Coast Guard High Endurance Cutters. The first demonstration launch blasted observers on the cutter's bridge with heat, smoke, and debris.

One of his most troubling legacies was the International Maritime Law Enforcement Team (IMLET) created for the War on Drugs. It was supposed to be a part of the Coast Guard's overseas training program but by 1990 had married up with Army Special Forces, DEA, and Ecuadorian, Colombian, and other military units that were targeting and attacking cocaine processing labs deep in Latin America's countryside.

"It was not a smart idea having Coast Guard guys running around in the jungles of Panama and Colombia. It was not a great moment in the Coast Guard's career," says Mark Quinlan of TACLET South.

When *Soldier of Fortune* magazine ran a September 1990 story on IMLET, "Coast Guard Fires Up Narcos," and *60 Minutes* started investigating, the new commandant, Adam. J. William Kime, shut the program down. Kime, a maritime safety expert, also removed the Harpoon missiles from the High Endurance Cutters.

Today, for the average coastal resident, the most commonly seen Coast Guard vessel is likely to be a 25-foot Defender class RBS, or Response Boat Small (there are some seven hundred), often mounted with one or two machine guns.

Still the public remains ambiguous in its attitude about how militarized it wants its Coast Guard to be.

One of the biggest controversies to date erupted in 2006 around the Great Lakes. That August, the Coast Guard posted a notice in the *Federal Register* of plans to establish thirty-four permanent live-fire training zones on the Great Lakes. The service had already begun temporary training on the lakes with M-240 machine guns following an agreement between the United States and Canada stating that this did not violate an 1817 treaty to keep the lakes demilitarized.

The *Federal Register* notice established a thirty-day period for public comment, but, of course, most of the public doesn't read the *Federal Register*. When word began to get out, recreational boating groups, ferry operators, fishermen, environmentalists, and others started to complain. Boaters and fishermen feared people accidentally entering the live-fire zones and getting shot. Environmentalists expressed concern about the impact of the lead bullets (up to six hundred rounds per minute) on wildlife and water quality.

The Coast Guard's 9th District Headquarters in Cleveland, which oversees the Great Lakes, extended the public comment period while arguing that the machine-gun training was essential and that the zones would be at least five miles offshore and used only two or three times a year for two to six hours at a time.

At the public hearings and town meetings that followed, hundreds of people, while stating support for increased security on the lakes, condemned the planned firing ranges. Eighty lakeside mayors from eight states and Canada criticized the plan, as did members of Congress. Even the residents of Grand Haven, Michigan, one of a handful of "Coast Guard Cities" and host to the largest annual celebration of the service, were not on board for this one. In December 2006, the Coast Guard announced its live-fire exercises would be suspended indefinitely and its proposal withdrawn.

"It's simple," Coast Guard Commandant Thad Allen tells me when I ask about the decision. "If the public won't tolerate it, we won't do it."

Yet the public doesn't know much about the service's commitment to Airborne Use of Force—or about Coast Guard gunners in general and their expanded role from our major ports to the most obscure maritime reaches of the global war on terror.

On April 29, 2005, in the Bay of Aden off the coast of Somalia, sixteen members of TACLET South were working off two Navy patrol boats, LEDET 404 aboard the USS *Firebolt* and LEDET 406 on the USS *Typhoon*.

They were under the command of Naval Task Force 150 out of Djibouti. Their group included the U.S. guided missile cruiser *Normandy* and German frigate FGS *Karlsruhe*. For several weeks they'd been stopping, searching, and questioning local mariners, ranging from Egyptian trawler crews to small Yemeni fishing boats with armed Somali guards on board, trying to develop intelligence on a reported Al Qaeda training camp ashore.

While working with Navy SEALs and CIA types, the Coast Guard gunners brought their own unique skill sets into the War on Terror that day, including well-honed instincts for search and rescue that are imprinted into the very DNA of the organization.

Late afternoon on the twenty-ninth, the *Karlsruhe* came upon a poorly maintained fiberglass boat, about forty feet long with high canvas siding, and more than a hundred Somali refugees squeezed aboard trying to make the dangerous eighty-mile transit to Yemen. Somehow by the time the German ship radioed the *Normandy* and the *Normandy* radioed the *Firebolt*, the message had been scrambled so that LEDET 404 was armed up with M-16 rifles and shotguns, believing they were about to do a tactical takedown of a hostile vessel.

"We got on scene and through our binoculars saw this grossly overloaded boat and realized this was actually an urgent SAR case," recalls Jeremy Obenchain, the lieutenant jg in charge of the team. "The boat was rocking even in calm water, and we knew we needed to get them off of it." Among his team were Bosun's Mate First Class Pete Rossi and Machinery Technician First Class Dale Stauffer, both experienced in rescue and recovery of overloaded migrant boats in the Caribbean.

An RIB was put in the water. A second smaller boat was dispatched with additional life preservers and rescue gear to approach from the other side. The Coasties knew that if you approached an overloaded boat from just one side all the migrants would run to that side and capsize it. Their rescue plan was taken up the chain of command to the *Karlsruhe* and the *Normandy*.

It turned out that if any refugees were taken onto the German ship they'd be in a position to demand political asylum in Germany. As a result, an order was issued for the refugee boat to be turned back to Somalia. Within a minute of trying to come about, however, the crowded, unstable boat capsized and the water was suddenly filled with panicked drowning people.

I watch clips from a color video taken by a Navy public affairs cameraman who happened to be on the *Firebolt* that day. It shows the sudden turnover and a ridiculous amount of people leaping and tumbling over the boat's canvas walls into the water, then dozens and dozens of heads floating like dark seeds upon the water and the two small inflatable boats from the *Firebolt* tossing them life rings.

"It was chaos. I had three guys in the RIB and five topside throwing life rings and vests, anything that would float," Jeremy Obenchain recalls. "By this time we had the other small boat in the water. You could see a lot of the women and children and some men were not able to swim, and it was pandemonium. Our PC [patrol craft] had a dive platform at the back and a pilot's ladder lowered on the port side, and the stronger men who could swim there climbed up the ladder, and the small boats picked up other people. The Navy rubber boat was designed to hold an eight-man SEAL team, and it had sixteen people on board."

The next video segment shows life rings being tossed from the *Firebolt* to people who have made it closer to the patrol craft. Parts of the water are dyed bright green, and a few men are clinging desperately to a pole being held by a Coast Guardsman along the side of the patrol craft. Some women are floundering. There's a brief shot of a baby floating facedown, and then you see someone jump from the *Firebolt*.

"I was back on the fantail helping pull guys up [the ladder], and we had a Navy corpsman and EMT there who started treating people," Jeremy recalls. "Four or five women made it to the ship, and I saw the men were trying to go first up the ladder and pushing them off, and I could see they [the women] were fighting for their lives and to keep their heads above water, and I could see the panic coming into their eyes, so [against orders] I took off my boots and jumped in and took them around to the dive platform.

"There was also a baby floating in the water, and a Navy chief jumped in, but the baby was already deceased. I grabbed these women and did a standard lifeguard swim around to the dive platform, just maybe ten or fifteen feet, and these other guys helped them up. It was a real team effort."

The video shows the Navy chief jump in and the baby's head lolling back as he lifts the infant up in the water. Women lie on the deck amid green water; a man throws up seawater; exhausted refugees crowd on deck. A sailor starts passing out plastic bottles of water, and off-camera someone says, "I got fifty-nine, but more came on since I counted."

The mixed Coast Guard/Navy crew managed to save eighty-six people that day and recover three bodies. A woman and small child they rescued didn't make it and died on the fantail. Some twenty other people were probably sucked down with the boat and their bodies never recovered.

Chief Mark Quinlan arrived on scene with additional emergency medical technicians from his LEDET team ten minutes after the boat capsized and began treating the survivors. The video shows him bandaging an older man's injured leg and washing his feet.

"We listened to their blood pressure, took their vitals. They were happy just to have care. There were about sixty to seventy injuries caused by other humans: cuts, scrapes, scratches, gouges, from people panicking to escape. There was a German doctor who came aboard. The German boat had thrown dye marker in the water, and I remember all these people we treated, their skin was covered in this fluorescent green and yellow."

Search efforts continued through the night without success. Meanwhile, the Coasties and Navy sailors provided their own food, water, blankets, and dry clothing, including socks, T-shirts, and underwear, to the survivors huddled on deck.

"The next morning, we were loading the survivors and the body bags up onto this Somali cargo dhow," Mark Quinlan recalls. "They were going to take them back, and as we reached up this child's body slid inside the bag—it was so small. That's stuck with me."

"To have started that incident as a noncompliant [armed] boarding and ended it saving eighty-six people was tremendous," says Jeremy Obenchain, now working as a Coast Guard staffer for the House Committee on Homeland Security. "We literally had to pull a couple of our guys out of the [inflatable] boats [that night]. They didn't want to quit searching. Before they even bothered to put on dry clothing, they would go down and try to find stuff for these Somalis, these people, these refugees who were just trying to improve their lives. Any Coastie would have done the same, 'cause it's how we're bred."

No matter how heavily armed, Coast Guard gunners, like their service shipmates, tend to remain lifesavers at heart. This is how we know and think of the men and women of the Coast Guard, when we think of them at all.

We know far less about their history and ongoing operations as combat warriors from the storm-tossed North Atlantic of World War I to the Persian Gulf of today.

CHAPTER 6

Warriors

"Why they didn't kill everyone in our boat I will never know,"
—COAST GUARD COXSWAIN DESCRIBING GERMAN GUNFIRE HITTING HIS LANDING CRAFT ON D-DAY

"They killed three people, but that RHI [rigid-hull inflatable] kept turning that boat away so it couldn't accomplish its real mission."
—CAPT. GLENN GRAHL, COMMODORE, PATROL FORCES SOUTHWEST ASIA

Nate Bruckenthal and Joe Ruggiero were part of an Australian-led Coalition effort to secure Iraq's two big offshore oil terminals close to the coast of Iran. When the two Coasties showed up on a Navy patrol craft the morning of April 24, 2004, there were hundreds of local fishing dhows working the waters around the terminals. The sailors began directing the fishermen away from the oil complexes in order to establish a two-mile exclusion zone.

"After about five to seven hours, most of the dhows had cleared out. After lunch we did a boarding on a converted cruise liner acting as a RORO [roll on/roll off cargo ship] and found the bridge all shot up," Joe recalls over breakfast on the beach in Fort Lauderdale, where he's now stationed. "The captain told us Ali Babas [thieves, pirates] had opened fire on them after they refused to open the [water-level] pilot's door to let them board.

"At dinner chow [on the USS *Firebolt,* later to be used in Somalia], we set up a rotation and decided we'd have two-man watches, and me and Nate took the first watch. Twenty minutes later, we had a boat in the area. Our ship tried to pull alongside it, but it was too windy and we couldn't get close, so seven of us got into a small boat, me, Nate, and five Navy guys, and we were craned over the side.

"We went out and found two boats. They had no documentation, just a Koran and fish all over the decks and fishing gear and nets, and the men were in cutoffs and tank tops or bare-chested, just regular fishermen trying to earn a livelihood.

"Then we get a call to come all the way around the terminal, and there's another boat, a very shiny boat a half mile into the exclusion zone. It's just about sunset, and it's approaching us out of the sun, maybe thirty feet [long] with a fifteen-foot beam and no marks on anything. It's freshly painted in gray with double outboard engines, which is unusual, and just these three crab pots that look almost decorative, and there's this one guy on board, and as we get closer we signal him over the engine noise to slow down [downward hand movements] and to cut his engine [finger across throat]. He took our slow-down signal as one to go away, and he starts heading away, and I notice he's putting off dark smoky exhaust, which could come from a heavy load or wrong-type engines, and then he turns and heads back toward the terminal.

"Me and Nate stand up, signaling for him to stop the boat, and he's cupping his ear like he doesn't understand, then starts to turn away. Then he cuts hard right like he's going to hit us. I was on the opposite side from Nate, who was facing it. We're leg to leg, there's so little room, and I turn to the coxswain and say, 'Cut out of here,' and we get about ten to fifteen feet from the boat.

"Then this huge explosion goes off, and it all went slo-mo with the heat and noise and then total silence as our eardrums were blown out and I saw debris flying. I was hanging onto the RIB with my left arm and must have raised my right arm to protect my head and got this impact from something that just split the skin open, and the arm swelled up like a football was stuck up my shirtsleeve. I was pushed into the water by the blast but with my legs and feet still in the boat, and then the outblast, the return suction, just flipped the boat over in the air in the opposite direction.

"I bounced off the sponson [pontoon] as it was flipped and remember spinning and spinning and spinning underwater and not knowing which way was up. I popped the lanyard on my life jacket, but it was shredded. I heard the air from the CO_2 canister going out, and there were bubbles everywhere, so I couldn't follow them to the surface. I got in a fetal ball, and gravity took me to the right, and I followed in that direction and finally surfaced. Our ship was about two hundred yards away. People said it was forty-five to sixty seconds before they saw anyone surface, so I guess that's how long I was down.

"The ship didn't know if we or the other boat [the suicide bomber's] had hit a mine, so they couldn't get close to us. All I could see was blood out of my left eye and this edge of skin from my face, and the only person I could see was Nate, who was maybe thirty to thirty-five feet away. I swam to him, and there was a big open wound on the back of his head, and he was mumbling 'no' very slowly, and when he realized I was there he said, 'Joe, what happened?' His eyes kept rolling in his head. I got his life jacket inflated and braced him against my chest and swam him to the RIB and started working my way around it. Coxswain Daly was holding on to it and screaming about his arm, and his whole face was covered in blood. I lifted his arm and like 90 percent of his triceps was gone, all the meat was just gone and part of his hand, and he was there in the middle of this pool of blood. I slung Nate across the overturned RIB with his arms and upper body on it, looked around, and could see Christopher Watts with this other break-in coxswain closer to the ship. There was this Australian helicopter that came over and was hovering over them, and I saw the rescue swimmer in the door, and Christopher was flailing his arms waving like he was in trouble.

"I looked in the opposite direction and fifty to sixty yards away saw [Bosun's Mate] Michael Pernaselli floating facedown in the water, and I grabbed Nate and pushed him up on the RIB and told Daly to keep talking to him and swam to Mike. This [fast] current got me to him real quick, and I roll him over and see there's this huge slice across his face. The skin is peeled away, and I could see the bone and tissue and brain matter, and the only intact part is the jaw structure. He was almost decapitated, and I just started screaming, I was so mad at the people who had done this, and I was shouting and then realized the other people [back on the ship and in the water] didn't know he was dead.

"So I stop shouting and just put him on my chest and start towing his dead body, and now I'm fighting the current and the copter is coming my way and the prop wash is hitting me and I'm getting killed by this sea spray from the helo, like I'm just breathing saltwater. Eventually I got back to the RIB and straddled the keel and put Mike's body over it.

"I guess the Australian small boat must have picked up Nate and Daly when I swam for Michael. I saw John Fox, one of our [Coast Guard] team [on the *Firebolt*], strip down to his boxers and jump in the water, and he swam to me and asked if I was OK."

It would take another half hour to get Joe Ruggiero back to the ship with Michael Pernaselli's body. Joe, John Fox, and another rescuer had to swim against the current in the darkness with the sound of sirens and another explosion going off in the distance.

Nate Bruckenthal was evacuated by helicopter from the 170-foot *Firebolt* to a larger Australian warship thirty miles away in deep water. When Joe and the other less seriously injured survivors arrived there by RIB, there were a dozen people working on Nate in the helicopter bay.

"I squeezed through and squeezed his hand, and they had a regular doctor there who said he'd be all right. Another helicopter came and took him and Daly and a third guy with a compound fracture of his leg to Kuwait. They took two of us to Camp Wolverine, an Air Force/Army base [also in Kuwait]. My ears were bleeding, and they X-rayed my arm and were amazed nothing was broken. They found metal structures in my head and also embedded glass.

"The next day I found out Nate had passed away at 4:00 A.M. I spoke to one of the docs, who said it was a closed-head trauma, where his skull bruised on the inside and the pressure on his brain killed him. They'd considered drilling into his head, but that was a fifty-fifty thing. A third death was that of Chris Watts, who'd been flailing in the water, and the cause there was death by drowning."

Twenty-four-year-old Nathan Bruckenthal, whose wife was pregnant with their first child at the time of his death, and whose previous posting had been Neah Bay, Washington, where he'd grown close to the Makah Indian tribe, was the first Coast Guard service member killed in combat since Vietnam. It was his second tour of duty in Iraq.

He and Joe Ruggiero were given Bronze Stars with combat V's for valor, as were Pernaselli and Watts, the two Navy sailors who died. Joe, curly-haired and medium-sized but buff, became a weapons trainer for two years before returning to duty in the waters off Iraq in February of 2006. Today, along with his battle scars and tats of a trident eagle, barbed-wire-entangled anchor, and mariner's cross, he's thinking of getting a tattoo of the events of April 24, 2004. Because the Coast Guard now restricts visible tattoos, he's thinking of having it etched across his back.

Coast Guard service members like Nate and Joe are not unique but rather have played their part in every war fought by the United States since 1790.

The Jaws of Death

Two years after the modern Coast Guard was established in 1915, it was transferred from the Department of the Treasury to the Department of the Navy for the duration of World War I. During the "Great War," Coast Guard cutters carried out escort and patrol duties in the Atlantic and Mediterranean while also handling port security on the home front. Six weeks before the end of the war, in September 1918, a German U-boat torpedoed and sank the Coast Guard Cutter *Tampa* with the loss of 115 crewmen. It took a year after the war ended for the Navy to finally return control of the Coast Guard to the Treasury Department.

The Coast Guard played a larger strategic role in World War II, escorting supply convoys in the North Atlantic and the Pacific, protecting the U.S. coastline, and piloting landing craft for every major amphibious landing of the war, including North Africa, Sicily, D-Day, Guadalcanal, and Iwo Jima. Over 240,000 people served in the Coast Guard during the war. Close to two thousand of them were killed. One of the bloodiest days in the service's history was June 6, 1944, D-Day at Normandy. Probably the most famous image of the D-Day landing, a photo of soldiers slogging through the water toward Omaha Beach framed by the open bow ramp and sides of their landing craft, was taken by Coast Guardsman Robert F. Sargent, a member of the landing craft crew. Its title is "The Jaws of Death."

In the early years of the war, when German submarine "wolf packs" tried to strangle the vital U.S.-British supply lifeline by sinking hundreds of merchant vessels, 180,000 Coasties were involved in convoy duty, including the Battle of the North Atlantic. Coast Guardsmen were armed with deck guns, depth charges, and newly developed sonar signaling to track their enemy below the surface. They disdainfully referred to the Nazi subs as "hearses" and were credited with sinking or helping to sink thirteen of them. They also sank two Japanese submarines in the Pacific.

One of the earliest subs sunk was U-352 off the coast of North Carolina in May of 1942. The crew of the Coast Guard Cutter *Icarus* that sank the U-boat then rescued thirty-three of its surviving crewmen, the first German POWs taken in the war.

The Coast Guard seized the only two German surface ships to be captured by U.S. forces in World War II, the *Buskoe* and the *Externsteine,* both taken off of Greenland. The Coast Guard also suffered a major loss not far from there when the 327-foot cutter *Alexander Hamilton* was torpedoed and sank in the frigid waters off of Iceland. Twenty-six of her crew were lost.

The Coast Guard's only Medal of Honor winner to date, twenty-two-year-old Signalman First Class Douglas Munro, was the officer in charge of a group of Higgins boats (small landing craft) at Guadalcanal. On September 27, 1942, he organized the evacuation of five hundred Marines trapped by the Japanese at Point Cruz. He led five of his boats toward shore, then used his plywood Higgins boat with its two old-fashioned Lewis .30 caliber machine guns as a shield for the beachhead as the Marines and their wounded were evacuated under intense fire. On the way out, he noticed a grounded landing craft full of Marines. He directed a second craft to tow it off the beach while his boat again provided cover and he again manned one of its machine guns. After twenty minutes, the grounded craft was free. By then the Japanese had moved one of their machine guns onto the beach and opened fire, hitting Munro once in the head despite a shouted warning from a wounded comrade. He died a short time later.

It was not unusual to see Coast Guardsmen functioning as both combatants and lifesavers during the war. The Coast Guard saved over a thousand merchant mariners, British sailors, and others whose ships were sunk while it was on convoy duty. Its "Matchbox Fleet" of sixty 83-foot patrol boats saved another fifteen hundred men on D-Day and later on the English Channel.

Still, the one Coastie who captured the public's heart and imagination wasn't a combatant or a rescuer but a four-legged mascot named Sinbad whose illustrated biography, *Sinbad of the Coast Guard,* was published in 1945. Sinbad, a mixed-breed mutt, served aboard the Coast Guard Cutter *Campbell* from 1937 to 1948. His book, written by Coast Guard publicist George Foley and illustrated by Coast Guard artist George Gray, used the popular dog as a way to portray real-life stories from the war, including the *Campbell*'s epic battle with a German wolf pack on February 22, 1943 (during which Sinbad allegedly scampered, barked, and snarled at all the appropriate times).

It started with heavy seas and gale force winds as Convoy ON-166 was being stalked by German submarines. When the *Campbell* received orders to pick up survivors from a torpedoed and sinking freighter, it came into the sights of a Nazi sub lying in ambush. Luckily the sub's torpedo exploded just before reaching the 327-foot Coast Guard cutter. With the rescued seamen aboard, the *Campbell* went after its would-be killer. It dropped a number of depth charges and saw the sub rise near the surface before diving again. An oil slick was then seen on the surface, but the *Campbell* had no time to pursue its quarry, as it had now fallen twenty-five miles behind the convoy.

Halfway back it joined a Canadian corvette that was firing on another sub. As soon as the *Campbell* joined in, the sub dove, and the Coasties dropped more depth charges, or "ashcans." This time large oil patches appeared on the surface, but that wasn't enough evidence to claim a kill. By then the Allies were aware of the German trick of dumping oil to make their pursuers think they were crippled or dead.

Within minutes of securing quarters, another sub was spotted surfaced at some distance. The *Campbell* opened fire with its deck guns. With its conning tower shot up from the cutter's accurate long-range fire, the sub dove. The *Campbell* quickly closed the distance and began dropping more ashcans. Just before sunset, they spotted and attacked a fourth sub, suggesting their convoy was being trailed by a very large wolf pack. Just before 8:00 P.M., a fifth sub was spotted outlined against natural phosphorescence in the water. Again the *Campbell* attacked with depth charges, and again an oil slick appeared. "All those Jerries bleed is oil," one gunner complained.

The cutter caught up with the main body of the convoy just before midnight, taking up its outrider position. Within minutes a lookout called out that a sub was surfacing off their starboard bow. Amazingly, this one appeared in the churning sea some ten yards from their ship. The *Campbell*'s gunners opened fire from point-blank range. "This one won't get away," one of the men shouted above the cacophony, as the U-boat captain tried to cut across the *Campbell*'s bow too close for its forward guns to come into play. "Ram the thing. Break its back," Cdr. James Hirshfield ordered his helmsman. The *Campbell* shuddered as it hit the U-boat, crushing its black hull. The German sub sank in less than two minutes, being chased by Coast Guard gunfire all the way down.

The *Campbell* did not come out unscathed, however. It had holed itself at the waterline, and the seas were now rushing in, flooding the engine rooms. Captain Hirshfield, who'd been wounded by ricochet fire, maintained command, directing the emergency repair efforts. Dead in the water and vulnerable to attack, they soon heard the approach of another vessel. It turned out to be the Polish destroyer *Burza,* sent to render aid. The crew worked on through the night to fix their cutter. To lighten the load, equipment was thrown overboard and half the crew, along with the rescued merchant seamen, transferred to the *Burza*. The captain, Sinbad, and the rest of the crew remained on board. A British tug was dispatched and, over several days, was able to tow the *Campbell* into a Canadian port.

When Commander Hirshfield, who was awarded the Navy Cross, was later interviewed in New York, he spent much of his time talking and joking about their mascot, Sinbad, and his canine courage. The New York press, loving a good angle, ran headlines including "Hero Dog Brings Back Cutter" and "Mascot Mutt Helps Lick Sea Wolf Pack."

At the end of the conflict the Coast Guard claimed itself a war prize, the 295-foot German training sail ship *Horst Wessel,* renaming it the *Eagle*. Today it's America's largest tall ship and the Coast Guard Academy's training vessel. Built in the Blohm & Voss shipyard in Hamburg in 1936, it was keel number 508. The next keel laid, 509, was for the infamous Nazi battleship *Bismarck,* later sunk by British warships—with the Coast Guard Cutter *Modoc* stumbling into the middle of the epic battle and getting a too-close-for-comfort view.

World War II established the United States as a world power and acted as a driver of human and technological innovation. On the home front the need for expanded war production at a time when many workers were going off to fight meant the doors to factories and shipyards were opened for the first time to working women, symbolized by "Rosie the Riveter," along with African American, Hispanic, and other minority workers who had previously been denied employment. Unfortunately, with the end of the war many of these doors of opportunity would be slammed shut again.

The Coast Guard was the first service to integrate its operational activities, thanks to the efforts of Reserve Lt. Carlton Skinner of the *Sea Cloud,* a weather patrol cutter that became the first seagoing command to include both black and white officers and men.

In 1943, the Coast Guard graduated its first black officer, Reserve Ensign Joseph C. Jenkins, a year ahead of the Navy. The Marine Corps didn't accept its first black officer candidate till the end of the war. Still, African Americans made up only 2 percent of the Coast Guard compared to 5 percent of the Navy and almost 10 percent of the Army. In addition, at the end of the war over 60 percent of black Coast Guardsmen were still serving as stewards (as were all Filipino members). The Coast Guard Academy would not start admitting African American cadets until ordered to do so by President John F. Kennedy in 1961.

Back in 1942, the Coast Guard also established a women's reserve force called SPARs (an acronym for Semper Paratus—Always Ready), which would only begin accepting black women in 1944. While mostly doing clerical and administrative duties in order to free up men for sea duty, some SPARs worked as airplane fuelers and loran operators. The women's reserve was disbanded at the end of the war. It would take another generation before women were welcomed into the regular ranks of the service, beginning in the early 1970s.

In terms of technological innovations, World War II saw the development of radar, sonar, and all-weather long-range aids to navigation (loran) that used timed low-frequency radio transmissions from several stations to determine the position of ships and aircraft. The manning of loran stations, highly classified during the war, became a key Coast Guard responsibility. Loran is still used on a limited basis even as new aids to navigation such as GPS, digital charting, and improved direction-finding antennae (the Coast Guard's Rescue 21 program) have come online.

Along with helping to develop loran, the Coast Guard was also the first service to recognize and develop the potential of the helicopter, both for search and rescue missions and as an antisubmarine weapon for convoy duty. Today Coast Guard helicopters have become as integral to the service as its small boats and cutters (more so, according to some aviators).

The Coast Guard was not transferred to the Navy during the Korean War, or "police action." Instead it expanded its regular duties relating to port security, maritime inspections, search and rescue, ocean stations (for weather reporting and to help downed aircraft), and loran stations.

Vietnam would prove different, involving the Coast Guard in eight years of river and coastal combat, arms interdiction, search and rescue under fire, training missions, and other wartime activities.

Adm. Edwin Roland, Coast Guard commandant from 1962 to 1966, pushed hard to get the service into Vietnam in order to maintain its "military credibility" after its reduced role in Korea.

Navy and Special Forces operators quickly came to appreciate the Coast Guard patrol boats they worked with in the "brown water war" fought in Vietnam's shallow, rain-soaked Mekong Delta. The Coast Guard was also active along the coastline, where, as part of Operation Market Time, they worked to stop the smuggling of arms from North Vietnam to National Liberation Front (Viet Cong) forces in the south. More than eight thousand Coast Guardsmen would serve in Vietnam aboard 82-foot patrol boats, High Endurance Cutters, and rescue helicopters. Seven lost their lives, and fifty-nine were wounded.

The worst single incident, which killed two and wounded eleven (including a South Vietnamese officer and a freelance journalist), involved a case of friendly fire. At 3:15 A.M. on August 11, 1966, the *Point Welcome,* an 82-foot patrol boat, was stationed three-quarters of a mile south of the 17th parallel, the demilitarized zone (DMZ) that divided North and South Vietnam. It was on a Market Time patrol, lingering at the mouth of the Cua Viet River with its lights off, when it came under attack from an Air Force jet directed by a C-130 command aircraft. Over the next hour, attempts to reach the planes with signal lamps and by radio failed as the *Point Welcome* took desperate evasive action under strafing attack from 20 mm cannon fire. After the CO was killed and his XO and helmsman badly wounded, Chief Bosun's Mate Richard Patterson assumed command. He put out a deck fire, got the wounded below, maneuvered to avoid the repeated attacks, and, when he realized that two Phantom jets had been called in to bomb them, ran the cutter close ashore and got the crew, including the wounded, over the side. Once in the water they came under fire from South Vietnamese forces ashore until another Coast Guard patrol boat, the *Point Caution,* finally came to their rescue and the Air Force stopped trying to kill them. Patterson was awarded a Bronze Star for his courage. Former commandant Jim Loy thinks that, along with a communications breakdown between air and marine operators, the *Point Welcome*'s attempt to warn off the first attacking aircraft with a blinking signal light might have been mistaken for muzzle flashes from a gun barrel and encouraged the jet to continue its attack.

Another tragic loss during the war was that of Lt. Jack Rittichier, a Coast Guard pilot shot down and killed in 1968 attempting a rescue behind enemy lines. He'd already carried out several rescues under fire earlier that year. His crash site was located and his remains and those of his three crewmates recovered in Laos in 2003, twenty-five years after their deaths. Lieutenant Rittichier was buried with full military honors on Coast Guard Hill in Arlington National Cemetery on October 6, 2003. He was the recipient of the Air Medal (four times, the first for a 1967 rescue on Lake Huron), three Distinguished Flying Crosses, a Silver Star, a Purple Heart, and a Presidential Unit Citation.

Four future commandants of the Coast Guard would also serve in Southeast Asia during the war. John Briggs Hayes commanded a Coast Guard boat squadron in South Vietnam from 1966 to 1968. Paul Yost won a Silver Star for leading his men through an ambush during a nine-vessel Swift Boat operation on the Bo De River on April 12, 1969. One of his captains and a number of Vietnamese marines were killed. Yost took two boats back to the ambush site to rescue the crew of a third boat that had run aground on a mud bank and was under fire from enemies ashore.

Jim Loy would spend fifteen months in country doing combat patrols on an 82-footer. He would win a Bronze Star and later train Vietnamese to take over Coast Guard vessels the United States left behind.

Thad Allen took command of a loran station in Thailand toward the end of the war, working to keep it up and functioning as Communist troops took control of South Vietnam in the spring of 1975. Because President Richard M. Nixon had declared the U.S. role in Vietnam over in 1972, he didn't get a service ribbon for his Southeast Asia tour—but I figure if not getting a uniform ribbon to wear is one of your life's regrets, you've led a pretty good life.

Still, many who joined the Coast Guard during the 1960s did so to stay out of this divisive and unpopular war. When I mention that many service members I've interviewed speak of joining the Coast Guard because it's a service that saves lives rather than takes them, an admiral's wife expresses sympathy, pointing out that her husband joined during Vietnam to get out of the draft.

The Coast Guard has gone on to play an active role in various post-Vietnam conflicts, including Grenada, Panama, Haiti, Kosovo, and the Persian Gulf wars.

In 1994, the 378-foot High Endurance Cutter *Chase,* which had seen duty in Vietnam and the invasion of Grenada, led U.S. forces into Port-au-Prince, Haiti, in an intervention that restored the democratically elected president Jean-Bertrand Aristide to power during the Clinton administration. Ten years later, the United States provided tacit support to the rebels who overthrew Aristide during George W. Bush's administration. The Coast Guard then surged into local waters, creating a blocking force to prevent a new wave of Haitian refugees.

More Coast Guard reservists were mobilized at the start of 2003's Operation Iraqi Freedom than had been mobilized after 9/11, mostly to guard military ports and cargo. In addition, over sixteen hundred Coast Guard members, several large cutters, six patrol boats, Port Security Units, Law Enforcement Detachments, and other assets have been deployed and redeployed to the Persian Gulf.

Even though the Coast Guard was forced to mothball eight 123-foot cutters in Florida in 2007 as a result of a botched "Deepwater" contract and deploy some buoy tenders in their place, its six best-maintained 110-foot cutters remain in the Gulf, along with about three hundred service members. This inspired one sector commander I interviewed to wonder, "Did we win homeland security so that we can now send our best resources over there?"

The NAG

Two more red flares go arching over the water. "Motor vessel, this is the coalition warship. Turn immediately or you may be subject to defensive action including warning shots. Come starboard thirty degrees immediately," warns the CO of the Coast Guard cutter *Monomoy* to the freighter now crossing our T two hundred yards out. This is the second time today the 400-foot North Korean–built *O Un Chong Nyon Ho* has headed toward the two-mile security zone around one of Iraq's two big offshore oil terminals, and tolerance is growing short.

Gunnery Mate "Thunder" Dann Merrick exposes the 25 mm Bushmaster chain gun on the bow loaded with high-explosive incendiary rounds. The double .50s off the bridge are uncowled and cocked. The freighter begins to turn to starboard.

"He's gonna get boarded," someone behind me predicts. Not an untypical day in the North Arabian Gulf, or NAG, as Coalition forces call it. The Iranians, just a few miles away, call it the Persian Gulf.

I arrived on scene a couple of hours ago, but it took some doing. After twenty-five hours traveling from California to Washington to Qatar and on to Bahrain, I'd caught a few hours' sleep at a Coast Guard villa in the capitol of Manama before heading to the "Mil-Air" base adjacent to the airport at 2:30 A.M. From there I caught a Desert Hawk (UH-60A) flight two and a half hours north, landing on the helicopter deck of the missile cruiser USS *Vicksburg*. After a short break in the hangar bay, Coast Guard photographer Nate Henise and I climbed down an orange rope ladder off the fantail and joined seven others on a Navy rigid-hull inflatable under the command of Ensign Nate Mitica. Seemed like a lot of Nates following in Bruckenthal's path, I thought.

Before heading over to the *Monomoy*, we make a fast bumpy run toward a fishing dhow that's gotten too near the *Vicksburg*. "I want to manage this but not get too close," Nate Mitica explains, reflecting lessons learned in blood. The dhow prudently changes course.

Climbing aboard the *Monomoy*, I'm greeted by its XO, Lt. JG Meghan Hague. At twenty-four, the blond, ocean-blue-eyed 2005 academy grad is lit up with enthusiasm, offering me a firm handshake and quick tour of her boat. It's like many stateside 110s except for three extra-heavy machine guns, an automatic grenade launcher, and ten thousand extra rounds of ammo. This is the only one of six Coast Guard cutters out here at present with a mixed crew (of men and women), though in a few months there will be three out of six, luck of the draw. As executive officer, Meghan has her own stateroom. The other six women (out of the *Monomoy*'s crew of twenty-two) share the forward berthing by the bow, the infamous antigravity chamber famed for its bronco-like bucking in rough seas. They've posted a cartoon by their head of a rockin' granny with a caption reading "Life's too short to dance with ugly men."

Of the six cutters in the theater, there are usually two in the NAG, each covering a slice of the no-go sectors around the al-Basrah (ABOT) and Khawr al-Amaya (KAAOT) terminals that pump over $100,000 of oil a minute, over 1.5 million barrels a day, accounting for 80 percent of Iraq's gross domestic product. The security sector around KAAOT overlaps with waters claimed by Iran, and the Iranian Revolutionary Guard Corps Navy (IRGCN) has been active in the area. In March 2007, they seized fifteen British sailors and marines who were inspecting a ship without their normal helicopter backup. Three months later, the *Monomoy* had its weapons loaded and aimed at Iranian speedboats headed toward them in the dark. "I thought we were really gonna shoot somebody," Gunny Dann Merrick admits. The Iranians turned away at the last moment.

A month after my visit, three IRGCN speedboats get into another near-fatal confrontation with U.S. Navy warships farther south in the Gulf. That confrontation, it turns out, may have been the result of a hoax radio transmission from a third party.

While I'll see one poorly maintained Iraqi patrol boat during my visit, it quickly becomes apparent that long after the last ground troops have left Iraq, U.S. forces will still be guarding these oil terminals.

•

When I return to Bahrain I'll talk to Commodore Glenn Grahl, who runs the Coast Guard expeditionary force in the Gulf, and the DOG's Adm. Tom Atkin, who's touring the area with an acquisitive eye on these "deployed" forces. I'll also visit with law enforcement training teams, including LEDET 408 from Miami, aboard the British Royal Fleet Auxiliary ship *Sir Bedivere,* which has Iraqi navy patrol boats secured to its deck.

One of the team suggests the Iraqis might be ready to take over oil terminal security in five or six years. "Ten years," another jumps in quickly. They tell me how a week earlier an Iraqi broke one of the ship's washing machines when he tried to use it to clean his helmet and machine gun.

I also tour a "ship in a box," a training site in the port (there's a second in Umm Qasr, Iraq) made of stacked shipping containers laid out like a commercial vessel (latched doors, an engine room, ladders, radio room, ladders, bridge) where the trainers just finished working with a team from the Royal Saudi Naval Force on how to take control of a hostile ship.

They tell me that after years of rotating in and out of the Persian Gulf they much prefer doing drug busts in the eastern Pacific.

So why can't the U.S. Navy do the job the Coasties are over here doing? I'm told the Coast Guard represents a less threatening profile, that they have more ship boarding experience, that they're better small boat handlers, that the 110s are perfect vessels for fast, responsive picket duty, that most of the world's navies are the size of the Coast Guard and so they make better trainers and ambassadors (one of the 110s just visited Oman for the sultan's birthday). I know Commandant Thad Allen believes the Coast Guard should be the sole provider of patrol boats for all the military sea services, and while I'm certain the Navy will never let that happen, the Coast Guard presence here at least works as a proof of concept.

Oil platform or, "opat," sector defense usually involves one "big deck" (a U.S., British, Australian, or other warship with its own helicopters) and two smaller, more maneuverable platforms, usually a 110-foot Coast Guard cutter and 179-foot Navy patrol craft.

The larger ships carry more punch but are slower and potentially vulnerable to small boat attacks like the 2000 attack on the USS *Cole* in Yemen that killed seventeen sailors.

Bosun's Mate 2 Emily Ernst, decked out in a black snowboarding helmet, tactical body armor, and a drop-down holster, backs the *Monomoy*'s 17-foot small boat away from the cutter, makes a tight turn, and leaves a roostertail of spray as she and her crew bounce off across open water to pick up some radar graphic software from the *Wrangell*, the other 110 guarding KAAOT, six miles away. Before lowering the boat, they do the usual risk-assessment briefing on the bridge, where they're told two cowboys have been seen hanging out by Maple Tree. "Cowboys" are Iranian Revolutionary Guard boats, and Maple Tree is a sunken crane that marks the disputed line between Iraqi and Iranian waters. Along with speedboats armed with small missiles and machine guns, the IRGCN has a couple of oversized armored dhows whose extended prows make them look like Viking ships. The Coasties used to call them "super-dhows" until psy-ops officers in Bahrain decided that made the Iranians sound too powerful and ordered they be called "red dhows."

I join Machinery Technician Second Class Chris Dias, a big, shaven-headed engineer who's grilling steaks on the *Monomoy*'s fantail. Meghan joins us and explains the protocol for dealing with security zone intruders. First they use the L-RAD, the long-range audio device (loud-hailer) that looks like a big black drum bolted onto the bridge deck. The L-RAD blasts taped warnings in Arabic and Farsi. On the *Wrangell* they also use it to blast music by AC/DC, the Hives, and Audioslave so their small boat crews can hear their tunes while practicing on the water. At night a cutter might spotlight an intruder. If that doesn't work, they fire off their red pencil flares like they just did at the Korean freighter. After that they use shell-cracker (flash/bang) shotgun rounds before resorting to warning shots and disabling fire.

That evening there's a birthday party in the galley for Electronics Technician Second Class Beth Keough on her twenty-sixth. Care packages of candy, nuts, and movie DVDs get passed around. Half the crew camps out on the padded benches to watch the movie *Anchorman* and episodes of *Rescue Me*.

I'm in my rack at 8:30 when a nervous voice announces, "Man overboard," on the pipes (PA system), followed by a delayed alarm. This break from protocol convinces several crewmembers that it's for real. I undog (unlatch) a couple of watertight doors and climb two sets of ladders to where I can watch from the open bridge as the crew scrambles topside, tossing three life rings with blinking strobe lights over the side that drift in the cutter's wake. Others are manning the small boat crane. A spotlight plays over the dark waters, and two crewmen with long poles work the port side until they hook and recover Oscar, a dummy made up of stuffed pants and a shirt in a life vest. It's their fastest recovery to date, just over five and a half minutes on a moonless night.

At 5:00 A.M., unable to sleep, I go up on the bridge with its softly glowing radar display where Lt. JG Mike Maas has the watch. Mike spent four years in the Army, then quit the first week of September 2001, thinking America would never go to war again. He entered the California Maritime Academy and later enlisted in the Coast Guard.

"Why didn't you go back into the Army after 9/11?" I wonder.

"I'm from a diving family, and my brother was killed in a diving accident in 2001. After that I lost my desire to kill people. I still wanted to be part of a military service, but this is one with an ethos of lifesaving. Funny thing is I've seen more real gunfire in the eastern Pacific [aboard the High Endurance Cutter *Boutwell*] than in four years in the Army."

"Doing drug operations?"

"It's like being pirates. You run up with guns, take them prisoner, and burn their boats down, but all within the law." He grins. He then tells me how on one patrol they and the Costa Rican Coast Guard rescued 160 Peruvian and Chinese migrants whose "snakehead" smugglers had deserted them and set them adrift to die on an 83-foot fishing boat. Being the majority, the Chinese had begun preying on the Peruvians. To avoid further ethnic conflict, they'd had to remove the half-starved survivors one Chinese and one Peruvian at a time.

The next morning, Nate and I pack our gear and catch a ride on the 17-footer to the cutter *Wrangell*, which is getting set to do a couple of operations. Four massive oil tankers now occupy the berthings at ABOT. I can smell crude oil wafting through the air from the petroleum terminal like roofing tar on a hot day. To date I've seen almost no sea life, only a handful of gulls.

"You see tons of sea snakes out here in the spring, also jellyfish," our driver, Bosun's Mate Third Class Dusty Banazzilo, offers brightly.

After a twenty-minute ride we approach the KAAOT terminal, where we'll be picking up a Bahraini interpreter. This badly damaged petro-island reminds me of the movie *Waterworld* with a little *Mad Max* thrown in. It's a mile of concrete pilings, catwalks, military antennas, stacked shipping container/barracks with air conditioners (average summer temperature 120 degrees), and an Indian supertanker named *Ankleshwar* tied up at its only working berth. Heavily bombed and shelled during the Iran-Iraq war of the 1980s, it was seized by Navy SEALs and Polish Special Forces at the beginning of Operation Iraqi Freedom, then had an accidental explosion and oil spill in 2006.

As we approach, we pass an Iraqi army post and machine-gun nest made up of two containers covered in tan camouflage netting. We pull up by a three-story barge next to a seagoing tug where an Aussie officer in desert camo is waiting with our interpreter. KAAOT is the Australians' command and control center for the platforms and has its own missile battery and unmanned spy plane. Rami, the hefty Bahraini interpreter, climbs aboard, and we head on to the cutter *Wrangell.*

Climbing aboard, we're greeted by its CO, Lt. Matt Moyers, a buff, intense, dimple-jawed weight lifter and '02 academy grad with a slight stiffness to his gait since he broke his leg fast-roping out of a helicopter. His XO is Lt. JG Gordon Hood, twenty-four, five-nine and stocky with a fuzz of light hair cut close to the scalp. His last assignment was on a buoy tender out of Kodiak, Alaska. Their lanky, more laid-back ops chief, Bosun's Mate First Class John "Harpoon" Harker, sounds and even looks a bit like the actor Ray Romano, though he's actually a born and bred New England sailor from Maine.

It doesn't take long to figure out that this is a gung-ho operations-oriented boat. After a quick briefing in the galley, Matt takes me up on the flying bridge and lets me drive. The 110 has the clunky throttle and quick pickup of a 47-foot surfboat. Leaning it over in a fast turn, I can understand why the designers of this narrow-beamed greyhound traded comfort for speed. Straight ahead we spot the *Chinook,* a 179-foot Navy patrol craft with two Coasties from TACLET South riding on board to help train and assist its crew.

"They probably wonder what we're doing," Matt says as I move his cutter around in random patterns. I decide I've had enough VIP treatment and give the controls back to the bridge.

It's time for the Operation Short Walk briefing for their daily game of chicken during which Coalition forces assert Iraqi sovereignty along a stretch of water close to the oil terminals that Iran and Iraq have been arguing over since the 1970s.

"Breakfast Time" will be the password to commence the operation, "Miller Time" to end it, after which it will be lunchtime, meaning time to eat lunch. Rather than the usual armed helicopter support, a six-foot unmanned aerial vehicle, the *Scan Eagle,* will be flying over us today. It's controlled from a trailer on KAOT. "This is a little abnormal," Matt warns his crew. "It'll just be us, us, and us out there."

They uncover the double .50s on the bridge wings as we leave the dhow box (where fishermen congregate) and begin running along the seven-and-a-half-mile line of dispute where the British marines were seized.

"Breakfast Time," Matt announces on the pipe. John shows me where we are on the radar with its graphic displays labeled DHOW BOX, THUNDER VALLEY,

NEXTEL, and FENWAY. Iran and the outflow of the Tigris/Euphrates (the Shatt Al Arab River) is off our port side twelve miles. Twenty miles to our rear is the Iraqi deepwater port of Umm Qasr, where a Coast Guard team from San Diego has been training Iraqi sailors and marines. Marsh Arabs live in between and on either side of the border. I scan the hazy waters to our left looking for Iranian speedboats. At 12:30 they call "Miller Time."

"They didn't come out to play today. Fifty percent of the time they show," Matt explains apologetically. "It was probably because of the heavy fog this morning. Fog or anything above three-foot seas they don't like."

"They're fair-weather militants?"

"None of the locals like any kind of rough water. So what we sometimes do with boats entering the security zone is run up to them and then stop and push them out of the way with our wake."

The *Wrangell* hasn't yet fired its guns in anger, though it's come close four times. "We've had big merchant tankers beelining for the terminals, and you worry about that kind of gross tonnage. You have to be ready to stop them pretty far out," he explains.

To keep sharp, they do lots of live-fire practice at high speed while executing tactical turns. "We've done twenty gun shoots in the last six months, and with that much gunfire things will happen," Matt says, referring to Bosun's Mate Second Class Frank Benetka, one of their shipmates, who was wounded in the thigh three months earlier by a fragment from a .50 round that misfired in the barrel. Frank's now in Bahrain recovering.

We pass a wooden dhow flying the Iranian flag. In late summer, the *Wrangell*'s cook and another EMT boarded an Iranian dhow to resuscitate a fisherman who'd collapsed from heatstroke on an otherwise typical 120-degree day.

We next brief for an HIPAT, or human interaction patrol, in which they board dhows and talk with local mariners to gather intelligence on terrorists, pirates, smugglers, the IRGCN, or any other potential threat to the platforms. One recent concern is car smuggling. They think older cars are being taken into Iraq to be used as improvised explosive devices. The XO, Gordon Hood, will be the boarding officer in charge. The crew assembles on the aft deck with black helmets, armored tactical vests, pistols, and M-4 rifles.

We climb down a short ladder to the small boat, the six-man boarding team, the two boat drivers (one is John Harker), the interpreter, and myself.

The Iraqi dhows have an elegant shape, but many are metal rust buckets up close. The first one we approach is wooden and about 80 feet long with a rag-tag crew hand line-fishing off the back. A white-bearded elder in a red-and-white-checkered headdress smiles down at us.

Gordon gets the master's permission to come aboard through the interpreter. Their freeboard is about chest high from where we come alongside and stand on our boat's pontoon. We muscle up from our elbows. Once on board, Gordon smiles and asks for permission to do a safety search before sitting down on the raised rear platform with the boat's master, Ahmed, a slim, black-bearded man in his thirties wearing a faded T-shirt and baggy pants.

Gordon asks questions off a list. Have they seen any international terrorist organizations operating in the area? How many days have they been here? How's the fishing?

The nine men on board, including two teenagers and the old man, have a small pile of snapper and undersized groupers in a red plastic laundry basket by the rail. One of Ahmed's crew lands another small grouper and tosses it into the basket. Later they'll put out their trawl net.

Ahmed says he's been fishing for seventeen years.

"Have you had any encounters with the IRGCN? How about Ali Babas [thieves and pirates]?"

"There was an Iranian attacked by Ali Babas yesterday. They only go for the Iranians," he tells us, "because they have cash for buying fish."

Since the Kuwaitis won't buy fish from Iraqis (whom they hate), the Iranians buy the Iraqis' fish at sea and then resell it in Kuwait. Another reason the Iranians are attacked is that most of the Ali Babas are Iraqi.

MK 3 Eugene Peters asks if I want to take a look below deck. We drop through a hatch into the dank, low-slung engine room where they live. There's a sick man lying on a thin mat, carpet scraps that the others sleep on, buzzing flies, bags of clothing hanging on nails, and flat breads tied to the far wall. It could be a dhow from any of the last ten centuries except for the old diesel engine at the center of the room.

The forward fishing hold has foam coolers full of small fish and some ice. There's one larger grouper they caught that's about thirty pounds.

There are six thousand to ten thousand fishermen working these waters. Unable to get fuel at home, they buy it at sea from the Iranians. Before we leave, the Coasties hand out life jackets.

"They call it psy-ops gear," Gordon explains. "The Navy gives out candy bars and stuff. We want to get boating equipment to these people, life vests, flares, and the like."

The next boat requires a climb up a truck tire being used as a bumper. This crew is hand fishing for shrimp. They've been out for six days. Their master, Ali, compact, bearded, and in a short-sleeved cotton shirt and Western slacks, says he's been fishing for twenty years.

Gordon asks if he's had any interaction with the IRGCN. He says last week the Iranians boarded his boat, "right here in Iraqi water."

"And they took our fish and shrimp," a voluble middle-aged man with rough skin and a salt-and-pepper beard adds.

Gordon asks if they've heard of any international terrorist threats to the terminal, which they haven't. He asks about car smuggling.

The loud guy goes off on how the Iraqi government does nothing and the Coalition forces support the government but if they weren't here you wouldn't have all this smuggling and killing going on. "The Coalition doesn't do anything about the fuel problem. You only talk, nothing's being done."

"We can't get fuel back home," Ali explains quietly.

"How do the cars move through?" Gordon asks.

"On big vessels."

"You understand we're here to protect the terminal and train Iraqis, right?"

"We know that if you leave, the Iraqi [navy] can't protect anything," Ali tells him. "If we see pirates and call the navy, they won't come, and besides, the Ali Babas have better weapons than they do."

Through the interpreter I ask Ali if the fishing was better twenty years ago, expecting to hear about overfishing or the impact of oil spills.

The fishing was better during the Saddam time, they all respond.

"You could fish anywhere."

"It was all open water."

"During Saddam, we went to Kuwaiti waters to fish."

As Shiites from southern Iraq, you'd think they'd hate Saddam's legacy, but they're also fishermen, and more than anything fishermen universally hate being told where they can and can't fish. They're now trapped in a narrow band between the terminals and Kuwaiti and Iranian waters.

We cruise up to another rusted dhow, whose green cotton nets are being repaired by its crew. One of them says, "Sure, come on aboard." Then the master walks over. "We can't talk. We're fixing nets. We have work to do." The crewman looks disappointed as we motor on.

The next boat, the *Madeena*, is a challenge to get aboard. We have to climb up onto a big truck tire, then stand on top of it, grab a chain, and stretch a leg around a post and netting to get on. Its master is named Muthana. He's short with a trim black beard, soft brown eyes, and an easy smile. They left a fishing port yesterday, he tells us. They heard someone was attacked, but only from the radio.

How long has he been fishing? "Since we were born we fish," he says. "Last week the Iranian coast guard [not the Iranian Revolutionary Guard] was here in this line [of fishing boats]. The Coalition didn't stop them. They came in two boats," he complains.

"We saw those boats," Gordon says, surprised they came this far south of the line. "You see any international terrorists or threats to the oil installations?" he asks.

No, Muthana says, before offering his opinion that the Iraqis can't protect the terminal or the fishermen on their own. He thinks the Coalition warships need to stay.

The Coasties give one of his crew some ointment for a blister and two life vests. Gordon asks if Muthana has seen any smuggling.

"There's camel smuggling from Iraqis to Iranians to Kuwaitis," the fisherman reports.

"Camel smuggling," Gordon writes down in his small notebook. I wonder if camels get seasick.

"There's also car smuggling, but the Iraqi border people are paid off, so what can you do?" Muthana adds. "All the problems, the smuggling, the stealing, all came after Saddam."

The next boat has a clean new layer of brown paint and very high sides. They say no, we can't board. I'm not sure we could have anyway without a boarding ladder. We move on.

"That's two noes today," Gordon notes, surprised. "I guess down here [south of the terminal] they're more independent." As if to confirm this, a third fisherman tells us we can't board his vessel either.

John tells me that Navy guys would take these refusals as a challenge, but the Coast Guard is used to dealing with fishermen and mariners. "We get better intel than the Navy 'cause we're friendly and joke with them and we interact better. This Navy guy says to me, 'What can you tell us about boardings?' 'Well, I did six hundred at my last station [in New Hampshire],' I say."

Our last boarding of the day is the *Sayad Shuda*. Its master is a man named Zuhar with a short black beard, stained white undershirt, and shorts. This dhow lacks the usual raised platform behind the pilothouse. In its absence Gordon sits cross-legged on the flaking yellow painted deck. Zuhar tells him they have been out two days and will stay out eight to ten. One of his motley crew brings out a couple of hand-sized jumbo shrimp. Rami, the interpreter, is interested. He says they're selling them for two dollars a kilo. They plan to catch about five hundred kilos.

"Your face is familiar," Zuhar tells Rami. "You've boarded us before."

Zuhar is a member of a fishing co-op. His dad is its manager.

What benefit do they get from the co-op? Gordon wonders. None, except it lets the authorities know they're real fishermen. Oil smugglers are giving fishermen a bad name.

There are bags of onions and potatoes hanging from the back of the boat and a water pipe by the wheelhouse.

Gordon asks about the IRGCN. Zuhar says the problem is that if Iraqi fishermen go into Iranian waters they jail them. Kuwaitis don't fine or jail Iraqi fishermen, they shoot and kill them. "They hate Iraqis because of the Saddam invasion. So why doesn't the Coalition do something to stop the Kuwaitis?" he wonders.

Has he seen any terrorist activity? Gordon asks, pretending he didn't hear that last question.

No, but Zuhar knows that hamor [grouper] hide under the rocks by the terminals, and there are big ones there, and if the Coalition let the fishermen in for just one day they'd leave them alone and stop trying to sneak into the zone after that.

"We can't," Rami tells him. "You know what happened in 2004"—the killing of Nate Bruckenthal and the Navy sailors. He talks some more to them in Arabic. They laugh.

"They feel happy you're close," he tells Gordon. "You protect them from the pirates." They bring out a slab of white squid about the size of a paperback book that looks like it's been sitting on the deck with the flies for a while.

Gordon gets a look of restrained horror on his face like they're about to chop it up and offer him a hunk. Luckily they don't, only telling him how good it is for your virility.

They give him the coordinates where the Iranians came by the fishing boats the other day. The *Sayad Shuda*'s wheelhouse has a threadbare sleeping carpet, a large wooden steering wheel, two small GPS units, and a child's stuffed dog and bear. We climb back down onto our RIB and return to the *Wrangell*.

After a break we transition from dhows to a supertanker, approaching the *BW Noto*, which is at anchorage waiting to fill up at the terminal.

Every oil tanker approaching the terminals first has to go through a security boarding.

The *Noto*'s hull is painted green and red. The red will drop beneath the waterline as it takes on oil. Fully loaded it's 286,000 tons. Empty it stands seven stories high with its white superstructure rising another six stories above its deck. At 1,100 feet it's more than three football fields in length. We sail around its massive bow. Bosun's Mate Jason "Oz" Ozolins will be leading the first boarding team. I'll be following in a second boat. I watch as the tanker lowers its accommodation ladder close to water level. The first boat races toward it like a sardine approaching a whale. The boarders jump onto the ladder platform on a rising wave and begin ascending like mountaineers. We head over and look up at the twenty-five crewmen and officers gathered far above us by the fantail railing. One crewman has been allowed to stay on the bridge and another in the engine room while the security and sweep teams do their work.

We time our approach to the ladder platform, leap aboard, and begin the steep climb up its eighty metal steps. The rails are gritty with sea salt and tar. We reach the main deck and look back down. A roll on/roll off freighter is passing near the *Wrangell* as the sun drops low on the horizon, turning the sea's surface a burnished copper and tin. We follow a yellow walkway painted on the green deck to the looming white apartment-sized superstructure. Below it the crew, in their orange and white coveralls, are waiting patiently by the stern rail.

Bosun's Mate Third Class Adam "Duck" Mallard, looking like a brick wall with the hard, flat face of a Spartan, stands guard with his M-4 held barrel down across his armored chest.

The tanker crew is called forward one by one, frisked with their arms stretched out, and questioned as their passports are examined. "Mr. Lee . . . Mr. Negazi . . . James Sullivan?"

"Yes."

"What's your birthday?"

"November 9."

I talk to the bald British captain, John Bardsley. He's wearing a white uniform shirt, white shorts, and running shoes. He works three months on and three off, he tells me. His Filipino crew work nine months straight. He says the Panamanian-registered *BW Noto* is owned by a Singapore shipping company. Its next stop after loading up will be Korea.

"Why are you here?"

"Why do we come here?" he replies archly. "You know. Because it's where the oil is." They'll be loading two million barrels beginning tomorrow. That's $200 million of product at the time, or eight *Exxon Valdez* oil spills, or a hellacious amount of CO_2 pumped into the atmosphere, depending on how you look at it.

The captain is the last to be frisked and questioned. Everyone is then escorted through interior hallways to the galley area. I opt to sweep the engine room with Machinery Technician Second Class Wally Waldron and Seaman Sheridan "Rook" Roebuck, who at twenty, with big biceps, bangs, and freckles, is the youngest member of the *Wrangell* crew.

It's about eighty-five degrees on deck and over a hundred by the time we climb down into what shouldn't really be called an engine room but a six-deck-deep propulsion atrium larger than some hotels I've stayed at. It's eerily empty, also noisy as hell with its 32,000 hp engines turning. We descend several more ladders and enter the glassed-in control room with its banks of switches and consoles. Here a crewman has been left to monitor the main power plant. Wally and Rook search around, checking through drawers and file cabinets, even the fridge.

We descend a few more flights to the main engine area and behind it into a cavernous room with open metal lattice flooring above the main propeller shaft as thick as a mature Douglas fir. The only ship I've ever been on of comparable size is the U.S. aircraft carrier *Stennis,* which has also sailed through these waters. The *Stennis* has a crew of over five thousand. This supertanker is crewed by twenty-seven. Redundancy in personnel is not a safety feature of the world's oil tanker fleet.

"You should have been here doing this with us in the summer, when I saw a temperature reading of 127," Wally says to me, almost shouting, as he pokes around some thigh-thick coils of rope and barrels of paint.

We spend the next hour in various rooms that ought to be occupied by giants. When they find two lockers with dead bolts on them that the crew were supposed to have removed, Rook first tries to smash them with a pry bar, then grabs and peels back the doors' metal corners with his hands and peeks inside with a flashlight (he's in competition with Matt, the CO, over who can bench-press the most on the *Wrangell*'s improvised fantail gym).

Eventually we climb back to the tanker's deck, wiping sweat from our eyes. It's now dark outside and cooled down into the seventies. There's a half-moon reflecting off the Arabian Sea, the *Wrangell* is playing a red spotlight across the water, and in the distance the terminal is lit up with colored lights like it's a holiday—Ramadan at the Manama shopping mall.

At dinner in the *Wrangell*'s galley, I ask the CO how much he bench-presses, which sparks gales of laughter from the crew. Matt's a competitive guy. He says, "315 pounds," not sure if he's been set up.

Later, on the darkened bridge, I notice the screensaver image for their Web log-in is a photo of "Our fallen hero," Nate Bruckenthal, in the same desert camo they all wear out here. The XO, twenty-four-year-old Gordon Hood, reflects on what a unique opportunity this mission is for "new guys" like twenty-year-old Rook Roebuck to get experience.

"The service trusts our people very young. It trusts mankind and the training that they give us. We're looking at the pain and war that surrounds oil, but still when people say it's a war for oil I don't think it's that simple, because most of these supertankers are not going from here to the States. They're going all over the world."

He's right. It's not that simple, although much of this Iraqi oil will in fact find its way to the United States. The production and distribution of fossil fuel has at the beginning of the twenty-first century become the largest industrial combine in human history. The armed protection of that global system of energy commerce is the largely unquestioned reflex of a U.S. foreign policy that all too often undermines the very principles of democracy these young men and women have come here pledged to defend.

The next morning, a British Lynx helicopter buzzes us, making several attack profile runs, the door gunner so close you'd think he could knock the digital cameras out of the *Wrangell* crew's hands with his machine-gun barrel.

Later they call general quarters and fire off the .25 mm bow gun with its thump and blast, big spouts of water appearing ahead of us amid whiffs of cordite that wash away as we surge forward. Twice they have to cease firing and change course as real targets, dhows and freighters, pop up on our horizon.

Over the next two days, we head south, first to KNB, the Kuwait Naval Base, and Camp Patriot, where U.S. troops play sand volleyball behind concrete blast walls. From there it's on through fields of oil platforms burning off natural gas and the crowded shipping lanes of "Tanker Alley" to the small island kingdom of Bahrain, where rich Saudis cross the causeway every weekend to drink and whore.

On the last leg of the trip, Lieutenant Moyers and Lieutenant JG Hood muster their crew on the Foc'sle. Matt reminds them that they have to keep their anthrax shots up to date—the military's very keen on that—and also details the ammunition offload at the pier and emphasizes they have to have paperwork for anything taken off the boat when it goes into dry dock.

He then gives out Iraq Campaign Medals to the crew for their just completed deployment. "This is a big deal," he tells them. "Less than one percent of people in the Coast Guard will ever see this."

After the crew's dismissed, John Harker reminds Matt that he still needs to reenlist. Matt administers the oath to him, there by the bow with a freshening breeze. At 7:50 A.M., John "Harpoon" Harker raises his right hand and swears his allegiance to the Constitution of the United States, to uphold and defend it.

"Sorry we couldn't do this in a more interesting place," Matt says as they shake hands, "but at least you did it at sea where it matters."

John, a qualified heavy weather Bosun, tells me his next assignment will be as executive officer of the 87-foot cutter *Flyingfish*, out of Boston. The Gulf's been interesting, he says, but he's really looking forward to getting back to New England, to his wife, kids, and family, and to doing what he and the Coast Guard do best—and are best known for: rescuing people and saving lives in big, angry, dangerous seas.

CHAPTER 7

Surfmen

"Twelve- to sixteen-foot waves are good conditions to train in. Above that you're more surviving than training."

—Bosun's Mate Bill Armstrong, instructor, Coast Guard Motor Lifeboat School

"You can only do what you can."

—Chief Warrant Officer Ricky Spencer recalling a rescue in which two people were saved and one died

The coast off the Columbia River on the Oregon/Washington border is known as the "Graveyard of the Pacific," the site of some two thousand shipwrecks over the last two centuries. With a watershed draining a quarter million square miles, the Columbia holds the second-largest volume of river water in North America, in some years even surpassing that of the Mississippi. It can discharge 262,000 cubic feet per second into the ocean, creating a four- to seven-knot current and depositing thousands of tons of sediment, generating large standing waves along with "sleepers" that can grow from flat calm to triple overhead in the few minutes it takes for the winds to shift or a long ocean swell to meet a sandy shallow.

"Mere description can give but little idea of the terrors of the bar of the Columbia: all who have seen it have spoken of the wilderness of the ocean, and the incessant roar of the waters, representing it as one of the most fearful sights that can possibly meet the eye of a sailor," warned Navy Cdr. Charles Wilkes, who, as a lieutenant, led the famed U.S. Exploring Expedition of 1838–42. His small fleet made it through the waters of the western Pacific and Fiji, Antarctica, and the Southern Ocean only to lose their sloop of war *Peacock* to the Columbia bar. The deadly break where that ship foundered is now known as Peacock Spit and its nearest buoys as Death Row. These are the big wave generators where the Coast Guard regularly trains its heavy weather boat drivers.

Predictably, the Graveyard of the Pacific is quiet as a grave with lumpy six-foot swells the week I visit the Coast Guard's famous Cape Disappointment National Motor-Lifeboat School in the small fishing town of Ilwaco, Washington.

"Should have been here last week. It was breaking sixteen to eighteen feet," the CO, Chief Warrant Officer Ricky "Spence" Spencer, tells me, sounding like every surfer I've ever known. Indie, his black lab, gets up from under the desk and gives me a couple of compensatory licks on the hand.

In the front hall of the station is the Master Board with rows of surfman's "checks," small brass badges that a hundred years ago were exchanged by surfmen from adjoining lifesaving stations to prove they'd completed their beach patrols. In 2002, individually numbered checks were brought back to recognize newly certified surfmen. There are around eighty-five of these elite boat drivers now in the Coast Guard, including three women. It can take four to seven years to get certified and prove in the eyes of your fellow surfmen that you can—as a matter of course—manage a rescue in thirty-foot seas with fifty-knot winds, or take your boat into eight-foot shorebreak and make a rescue without getting smashed onto the rock and sand. Those kinds of conditions require that the best boat drivers get stationed at the Coast Guard's twenty-one surf stations, sixteen of which (including the school) are located on the West Coast between Morro Bay, California, and La Push, Washington, on the Quillayute River. There are also fifty heavy weather stations, on the Great Lakes and elsewhere, that can see equally wild conditions, just not on such a regular basis.

The lifeboat school conducts six heavy weather classes for about seventy-two students a year. It's also wrongly famous for its rollovers and the idea, subtly reinforced by a generation of Discovery Channel documentaries, that flipping a boat is something its instructors encourage.

"I rolled a boat as a student in 1991. That may be the last time a boat rolled here," says Scott Lowry, the school's tall, shaven-headed executive officer. "The [newer] 47s are so buoyant I'm not sure they could even do a 360. I was in a 44[-foot-long motor-lifeboat]. We were in eight- to ten-foot surf, and I started the inbound run, and all of a sudden the seas stood up to sixteen foot and a wave broke and we did a 360 roll and 180-degree turn and I was blown out of the seat and just remember I held my breath and I was going to breathe and realized I was underwater and it was light, dark, light again and we were back up with the swell and I could taste and smell diesel fuel. One guy said he'd counted to fourteen seconds. The surfman [instructor] grabbed the helm, and I was able to reach up and push the throttles for power, and we got out of there. The mast had broken off and gave one of the crew a goose egg on his leg, and we were all, the eight of us on board, all a little banged up and bruised."

Spence, the CO, may hold the world record for rollovers. He got what he describes as "bubble massages" in 1977, '83, and '86. "I was never driving when I rolled," he quickly adds. "The Surf community looks down on people who've rolled boats."

Still, the school has its occasional "knockdowns," where the self-righting boats go over more than ninety degrees.

"Last year we had a knockdown. No injuries or anything," Spence recalls. "This year we had someone take a break too hard and the boat went airborne and we had a young gal break her wrist."

I sit in on a classroom discussion on how to do a safe tow and how to pass a metal drum with a dewatering pump to a flooded fishing boat.

In the engineering locker, next to the barn (boat garage) where they have an aluminum-hulled 47-foot surfboat up on blocks waiting for an engine replacement, I'm given a red and black Mustang drysuit to climb into through its zippered waist. Bosun's Mate Bill Armstrong will drive the boat I'm on, one of four doing today's training rotation. Bill's a hefty guy with a shaved head, now covered in a black balaclava as the air temperature has dropped to around twenty degrees.

The boathouse is at the end of a steeply wooded peninsula of fern, Sitka pine, and Douglas firs shared by the school and the Cape Disappointment Surf Station with its less than tourist-friendly motto, "Pacific Graveyard Guardians."

Bill drives the boat from atop its open bridge as our small flotilla pulls away from the dock, out through the channel, and past an ocean buoy. Some of the students have yanked their balaclava hoods down over their faces, making them look more like death-squaders than lifesavers.

"Coming up," Bill announces as we surge forward into the biting wind, passing a big inbound car ship.

We set up for towing exercises in a seven-foot swell. The 47 we've partnered with is rolling with the seas. We circle around to approach it from up swell with student coxswain Michael Daray of the Michigan City, Indiana, station at the controls.

"Remember the Fifty-Fifty Rule. Keep fifty percent of your attention on the line, fifty percent on the [approaching] swell," Bill instructs.

As we close in on the other boat, a few students and crew on our fantail gather up the line. One of them tosses it to a fellow student on the bow of the other boat.

"Now watch that line opening up," Bill tells Michael, watching his student's hands on the double throttles.

Off in the distance I see the black-hulled Coast Guard buoy tender *Fir* heading out from Astoria, Oregon.

"OK. Stop. Let's go forward twenty-six."

From the fantail the line tosser calls, "Thirty feet on deck."

"Close it up. Square it up. You'll still have to back down a little more."

"Forty feet out."

"Pivot on port. More power on the pivot. You don't want to be left in the trough."

"Crab pots on starboard bow about twenty-five yards," one of the students warns Bill.

"I'll keep an eye on them," he responds. "Make the boat do what you want—square it to the swell and tow point to tow point," he instructs as they tie off the towrope to the cross-shaped Samson post on our stern.

The other 47 closes suddenly, approaching within feet. A student wonders if they aren't too close.

"I'm watching [fellow instructor] Scott [Slade]," Bill tells him. "I've been working five years with Scott. If he's looking nervous, he'll indicate that, and I'll back our boat off."

Heading in to shore a few hours later, Bill points out a big red buoy with its cage missing and bell exposed.

"Last month we had 115-mile gusts and forty-foot waves that took the top off that buoy."

Nearby the two-thousand-ton *Fir* is listing over, working hard to pull up a similar surf buoy onto its buoy deck for inspection and cleaning.

"It's different out here," Bill explains. "Sometimes it can get all jumbled up. Twelve- to sixteen-foot waves are good conditions to train in. Above that you're more surviving than training." He's from North Carolina and joined the Coast Guard after graduating from college. I ask why he didn't enter Officer Candidate School.

" 'Cause I got a job I don't hate, and that's worth a lot," he says. Like rescue swimmers, surfmen are all from the enlisted ranks. They also run most of the surf stations, which is why the officer corps has sometimes neglected them. As we pull back into the Ilwaco channel, a bald eagle watches us from atop one of the wooden poles where the old canning docks used to be.

The surf station, down cove from the school, does over three hundred rescues a year plus, since 9/11, escorting ten freighters a day heading upriver to Portland with cars and fuel or to pick up grain. The station has two 47-foot rescue boats, an old 52-footer, and three fast, highly maneuverable 25-foot Defenders with twin Honda outboards.

"The Coast Guard plays the role of both maritime police and fireman. The 25 is like our police cruiser, the 47 like our fire truck," explains the station's chief, Lt. Jamie Frederick, a rare officer in charge.

When I get back to Spence's office at the Motor Lifeboat School, he's on the phone with his wife. She wants him to pick up a hundred-pound bag of feed on his way home.

"They bought a third horse," he tells me, hanging up. "She says, 'It's the one you said looked so nice.' I don't know." He shrugs, grinning in contented defeat, the crow's-feet around his eyes crinkling. Since his last assignment was the Coos Bay Surf Station in Oregon, and since they have two teenage girls in high school there, the rest of the family decided to stay put when he transferred. Now he's what they call a geographic bachelor, driving five hours south on weekends to be with them. When he finishes up at Cape D, he'll have thirty-four years in the service and retire.

Looking out the window, I see the 52-footer cruising in, one of four still in service here in the Northwest. Built almost fifty years ago, it has the charm of an old single-action Remington revolver, solid, heavy, and dependable. It's not just for show, however. It can tow up to 750 gross tons where a 47 can only tow 150. A year ago, this low-slung workhorse towed a 220-foot fish processing ship out of harm's way after it lost power near shore in twelve-foot seas.

"Today it was out laying a memorial wreath," Spence informs me. The day before, there'd been a memorial service marking the January 11, 1991, sinking of the trawler *Sea King* off Peacock Spit during which two fishermen died and EMT Charles Sexton sacrificed his life so that others might live, including the *Sea King*'s two surviving crewmen.

Today marks an even greater loss. On January 12, 1961, a crab boat, the *Mermaid,* was caught in monster surf near Peacock Spit. Two Coast Guard vessels from Cape D, a 40-foot utility boat and a 36-foot motor-lifeboat, went to assist. They called for additional assistance, and the *Triumph,* a 52-footer, arrived from the Oregon side and took over the tow. The 40-footer then capsized, but its crew was rescued by the 36-footer. Unable to get back across the bar, they headed out to sea and found refuge on the storm-tossed Coast Guard Columbia River lightship before their boat also went under. Shortly after that, the *Triumph* capsized. The fishermen aboard *Mermaid* were able to rescue one of its crew. Two more 36-foot lifeboats arrived from the Oregon side and put the *Mermaid* under tow. Then another giant wave hit, snapping the towline and sinking the *Mermaid*. Five of the six Coast Guardsmen aboard the *Triumph* died: John Culp, John Hoban, Joe Petrin, Ralph Mace, and Gordon Sussex. So did the two fishermen aboard the *Mermaid*. Miraculously one of *Triumph*'s Coasties made it to shore alive, where he was found by a search team below the Cape D lighthouse a few hundred yards from where we're now seated.

Indie, the Labrador retriever, walks around the desk to visit Spence.

"Now he's going to put his head in my lap and look up at me to let me know he wants to be fed," which is what the dog does. "He's been out on some rescues. I got him a red light for his collar 'cause he wants to jump in and join in the rescues."

I ask Spence about his best rescue.

"I get emotional about it because of the father-son thing," he tells me up front. "I was in Tillamook [Bay Surf Station in Oregon] in August of '87. I remember the swells were like canyons, but [Machinery Technician Third Class] Steve Meshki and I had to take the faster boat, the 30-footer, because we knew that there was a capsized craft out there and that there were people in the water [and time was of the essence]. So we made it across the bar, and we had to zigzag up the coast [10 miles among mountainous breakers] to Nehalem Bay. What was real weird is we got on scene and we're in the middle of the breaks and can't see where they are and this voice I heard says, 'Turn left ten degrees and go,' and I was in the middle of the breaks and just did that, and there they were. The father was lying on top of this capsized 18-foot boat. We picked him up, and he'd already lost his dad, but he begged us to get his son and we saw him [the boy] just kind of lying there in the water with his eyes open and staring and his arms out.

"We threw the heaving line and it landed between his arms, and we hoped he'd reach for it, but he didn't. Then we got close enough and we threw the ball [attached to the front of the heaving line], and it crossed his arms and it kind of hooked him, the line tangled in his arms, and I managed to hold the 30-footer steady as I'd get hit by the breaks till he was close up. Everything was in slow motion, it seemed like, and Steve is kind of dragging him in gently, and then Steve yells, 'He's sinking!' and I shouldn't have, but I left the helm, and we both went over to the starboard side and just kind of reached down into the churning water and felt something and grabbed him by the hair and pulled him up and into the boat. Steve started CPR, and the kid started coughing.

"There was a helicopter on scene, but we couldn't get him up into the basket in those conditions, so we took the boat back to Tillamook and had an ambulance waiting and when they were taken off in the ambulance I went to the locker room and—it was such an adrenaline thing, I think—I started just crying.

"Later the father was released from the hospital and thanked us, and he broke down crying, thanking us for saving his son. I felt bad that maybe if we'd been there five minutes sooner we could have also saved his dad, who went under, but you can only do what you can.

"It was pretty strange. The other time I sort of heard that voice was a few years later. We had these divers go missing southwest of Tillamook by the Netarts River in Netarts Bay, and we kept updating Tillamook but couldn't find them, and it was getting dark, and we were told to return to station. We were heading back in another 30-footer and something told me, something said to turn back around, to look one more time because they were there. I went back, and the station calls for our location, and we say we're heading back to Netarts. When we get there I tell the crew to turn off the engine and shut the boat down, and I start yelling and then hear people yelling back, 'Yeah, we're over here!' There were the four of them bobbing at night off this rock, hundreds of feet offshore and not knowing where they were, out of air except for their buoyancy vests. So we pull them out, and we call back to station and say, 'We're heading back with four divers aboard,' and I guess that's the difference between being applauded and getting reprimanded is that we found them. It feels like I always get these things happening to me, though, that voice that told me to take that course or to turn back for those divers. Or maybe it's just we have this messed-up gene that makes us who we are."

Everyone Volunteered

If it's a recessive gene, it could have been inherited from a host of earlier surfmen such as Joshua James, Rasmus Midgett, or Bernie Webber.

Joshua James was called "the best-known lifesaver in the world," during an era in which the Life-Saving Service rescued over 150,000 people.

James was only ten in 1837 when he saw the schooner *Hepzibah* capsize, taking his mother and baby sister to their deaths. At fifteen he snuck aboard a Massachusetts Humane Society surfboat and helped rescue the crew of another stricken vessel, the *Mohawk*. He would spend much of his life as a mariner and volunteer lifesaver until, in 1876, the Humane Society appointed him full-time keeper of their lifeboats and mortar (line-throwing) station in Hull, Massachusetts. Among the countless daring rescues he carried out, one of his most famous occurred on the stormy days and nights of November 25 and 26, 1888, during which he braved blizzards, sleet, rain, and mountainous waves to lead his crew in the rescue of twenty-nine men from six different ships.

It started on the afternoon of the twenty-fifth with the three-masted schooner *Cox and Green* trapped in the surf. James's crew dragged a mortar and surfboat half a mile to the site. James fired the line to the ship and soon had rigged a breeches buoy that brought all nine crewmen safely ashore. Just as they were finishing that rescue, the schooner *Gertrude Abbott* slammed into the rocks a little farther up the beach in wild surf beyond range of the line-throwing mortar. James asked for volunteers to man the boat. Everyone volunteered, although the risk of a watery death was quite real. Several times their boat filled with seawater and was tossed back onto the beach before they were able to fight their way through the shorebreak. Finally they reached the bow of the ship, where eight sailors, timing themselves to the rising and falling of the waves, managed to jump into the rescue boat. Heavily overloaded, the boat hit a rock and nearly capsized two hundred yards offshore. Approaching the beach, a giant wave took the boat "over the falls," smashing it to pieces on the cobble shore. Amazingly, everyone escaped injury. It was now nine at night. Shocked, exhausted, and hypothermic, James and his men continued their beach patrol.

At 3:00 A.M., another schooner, the *Bertha F. Walker*, grounded in the surf. Horses and volunteers dragged a new surfboat to the site of the wreck from a station four miles away. James, at the sweep oar, led his crew in the rescue of the seven sailors aboard. The captain and another crewman had earlier been swept away. As they were bringing the survivors ashore, a man on horseback brought them the less than thrilling news that two more ships were in distress five miles down the beach. By the time they'd dragged their boat to this next scene, two other rescue crews had managed to foul their shot lines in the rigging of the schooner *H. C. Higginson*. James's crew silently launched their boat, only to be driven back ashore forty-five minutes later holed in two places. After patching their ruptured boat they launched again, almost flipping over backward off the near-vertical faces of the waves.

The crew of the *Higginson* had been lashed to the rigging for fourteen hours and could barely move by the time Joshua James and his crew reached them. They had to pry their hands free of the wooden masts and spars before returning them to the small rescue boat and bringing them back through the crashing surf safely to shore. The other wrecked ship was stranded high enough aground not to need their help. Still, on the long march back to Hull, James and his crew had to launch their boat yet again to pull two salvagers off the grounded brigantine *Alice* that had slipped its moorings in Gloucester the day before. James and his men would be awarded Gold Lifesaving Medals for their work and also allowed to sleep in the next day.

Sumner Kimball waived the retirement age requirement in order to let Joshua James become keeper of the Point Allerton Life-Saving Station in Hull at the age of sixty-two. In 1898, at seventy-two, he led Humane Society and Life-Saving crews in the rescue of twenty men from four ships during the famous "Portland Gale" that took five hundred lives. In 1901, just before turning seventy-five, the white-bearded waterman won admiring praise from the *Boston Globe* for passing the service's rigorous physical exam with better scores than the twenty- and thirty-year-olds under his command.

The following year, panicked merchant sailors and big seas led to the loss of a crew from the Monomoy Point Life-Saving Station on Cape Cod. Determined not to see anything like that happen at Hull, Joshua James assembled his crew for a boat drill off Stony Beach across from the Allerton station.

After an hour's workout in rolling, windy seas, he directed them back to the beach. Stepping onto the wet sand, he looked once again out to sea. "The tide is ebbing," he noted, then fell dead upon the shore, a fitting ending to a legendary life.

At dawn on August 18, 1899, Surfman Rasmus Midgett carried out one of the more extraordinary rescues in the annals of Coast Guard lifesaving. During a wild hurricane with howling 100 mph winds, the barkentine *Priscilla* grounded and broke in two three miles south of the Gull Shoal Life-Saving

Station on North Carolina's Outer Banks. Surfman Midgett was on a sand-blown beach patrol that he'd begun in the dark when he spotted flotsam in the water and then heard cries of distress from somewhere beyond the thundering surf. Looking out across the breakers, he saw a group of men clinging to the wreckage of the *Priscilla.* He decided there was no time to make the three-mile trek back to the station. He'd have to save them himself.

Timing the lulls between the big whitewater breakers, he waded into the ocean close enough to the wreckage to where he could shout orders to the men. He had them jump into the water and then dragged them back through the thundering surf to the beach. This worked for the first seven men, but three of them were too weak to get off what was left of their ship. Struggling to its side, he hoisted himself aboard, lay exhausted on the buckling deck for a time, then threw the first sailor over his shoulder, dropped back into the sea, and carried him to shore through the pounding surf, ducking under crashing torrents of water. He repeated this effort two more times until all ten men were safe upon the beach. For his morning's work he received the Gold Lifesaving Medal.

Rasmus was part of a long-established family of Outer Banks mariners, pirates, and fishermen, more than 150 of whom would go on to become lifesavers and Coast Guardsmen.

On August 16, 1918, other members of his family would win Gold Lifesaving Medals. That day, Chicamacomico Lifeboat Station Keeper John Allen Midgett heard a powerful explosion and spotted the British tanker *Mirlo* sinking after being hit by a German U-boat torpedo. He and his crew spent almost seven hours battling heavy surf and burning oil to pluck dozens of survivors from the sea. Five of the six-man rescue crew with him that day were named Midgett.

"Back then, there wasn't much to do down here," one of the family later explained. "You could either set around and fish, or you could go out and save lives. The Midgetts chose to save lives." Today, in keeping with the changing tides of history, a couple of Midgett brothers have become Outer Banks real estate brokers.

Yet another hero of the Coast Guard, and model for its "act first, call me later" management style, was Bosun's Mate First Class Bernie Webber.

At 5:30 A.M. on February 18, 1952, during a wild nor'easter with billowing snow and up to sixty-foot seas, the crew of the 503-foot-long T-2 tanker *Pendleton,* heading south off the tip of Cape Cod, heard the explosive crackling noise of rivets coming undone like a giant zipper. Their ship, loaded with

122,000 barrels of kerosene and heating oil, lurched suddenly before breaking in two. The bow section, with the captain and seven others aboard, floated off into the night. The stern section, with thirty-two men on board, also stayed afloat, its lights, machinery, and rudder control still functioning. No one had had time to radio an SOS. Now the bow had the radio, and the stern the power to operate it. Strangely, the *Pendleton* wasn't the only World War II–built T-2 tanker to break apart off Cape Cod that night.

In the morning, the Coast Guard surf station at Chatham, Massachusetts, got word that a ship, the *Fort Mercer*, had broken in two and launched a 36-foot motor lifeboat to join two larger cutters and Coast Guard aircraft searching for it. Then word came that half a ship was drifting off of Orleans, more than twenty miles from the reported breakup of the *Fort Mercer*. An experimental radar system at Chatham confirmed two targets that would later be identified as the bow and stern sections of the *Pendleton*. Twenty-four-year-old Bernie Webber was ordered to sea that night with a volunteer crew of three.

As they took off from the harbor into the dark, storm-tossed night, his crew began singing "Rock of Ages." Then they hit the thundering sandbar, and a wave tossed their 36-foot lifeboat into the air before it crashed down into the trough. The next wave broke over them, smashing their windshield and compass and soaking them in freezing seawater. They were then knocked down, and the motor stalled, but the engineer was able to get it started again. By now they were beyond the bar, climbing mountainous waves and surfing down their back sides, reversing power to keep from fishtailing out of control.

No one was sure where they were. Then something large loomed out of the night ahead of them. Their searchlight illuminated the black, gaping interior maw of the *Pendleton*'s exposed stern section, groaning weirdly as it rocked through the waves, heaving up and then settling down in a "frothing mass of foam," as Webber later described it.

They spent the next forty-five minutes maneuvering along the port side of the stern section, seeing no signs of life. As they rounded the stern, lights appeared on the deck and a crewman far above began waving frantically. Soon the rail was lined with people. Webber thought they looked a lot safer than he felt. Then a Jacob's ladder dropped down the side of the ship, shocking Webber into a "Good Lord!" as he realized they wanted to get onto his small rescue boat. The first sailor down the ladder got dunked in the sea and then, still hanging on to the ladder, shot up fifty feet as the half-ship rolled with the heavy seas. Webber timed his boat's position with the waves. Coming in close, he saw that same sailor drop hard onto his deck, then backed the 36-footer away to avoid having it smashed against the ship with the next wave. He kept repeating this maneuver, even as the sailors on the rope and wood ladder swung free and were smacked back against the side of the ship with each rolling wave.

Soon the lifeboat was filled up, its freeboard sinking toward the waterline, but Webber decided he'd have to take all the survivors aboard to avoid panic and death. Five missed the boat, falling into the sea, where Webber's crew hauled them out like tuna. The last man down the ladder was the ship's 350-pound cook, George "Tiny" Myers. He jumped too soon, missed the boat and, after going under, surfaced by the stern, clinging to one of the eleven-foot propeller blades. Easing toward him, Webber's boat was picked up by a giant wave. The young boatswain tried to back the engine off, but to little effect, as the rescue boat smashed Myers hard against the *Pendleton*. When the next wave drove the motor lifeboat away, Myers was dead. A few moments later, the entire stern section of the *Pendleton* rose up and rolled over.

Now Webber and his heavily overloaded lifeboat, with thirty-six men crammed in every space, including the engine compartment, had to find a way back to shore. He got on the radio, and "every cutter within earshot had orders for me, wanting me to deliver my cargo out to them no matter where they were," he later explained to maritime author Dennis Noble. He heard "arguments going on between units as to what we should do, and in typical government service fashion, who was responsible for what and who outranked whom." He reached over and turned off the radio, thus ensuring his immortality among the enlisted ranks and all those who trust on-scene initiative now and forever.

He told his crew and the *Pendleton* sailors he was heading toward land and planned to ground the boat on the nearest protected beach he could find. They all agreed to his plan.

Despite a following sea that kept breaking over them so that they were often chest deep in icy seawater, he actually managed to bring his "cargo" safely back into Chatham Harbor, an amazing feat of seamanship.

A cutter and a second boat reached the bow of the *Pendleton* later that night. One sailor jumped off but was not recovered. No other signs of life were seen. Later a body would be removed from the bow. The next day, four survivors were rescued from the bow of the *Fort Mercer* and twenty-one more from its stern, with thirteen others electing to stay aboard while it was towed into port. In total seventy-one people were saved and six lives lost between the two tankers, including Tiny Myers, whose death would haunt Bernie Webber for the rest of his life. Bernie and his three crewmen were all awarded Gold Lifesaving Medals.

Station Golden Gate

"You should have been here this morning!" Chief Kevin Morgan tells me as I arrive at Surf Station Golden Gate just below the famous bridge. "We had fourteen- to sixteen-foot waves outside the Gate. We broke the windshield on the flying bridge on one of the 47s. We had both of them in the surf zone off Ocean Beach to see if we could hook a towline in theory, but . . ." He grins. They weren't training so much as surviving and having a great time of it.

I'd spent the morning touring the Coast Guard's Pacific Strike Team at some old airplane hangars in suburban Novato. I got to see lots of trailers and oil containment booms, plus big eighteen-wheelers (the Coast Guard has a squadron of licensed commercial truckers) loaded with safety gear and ready to respond to any spill or disaster. They even gave me my own copy of the U.S. Coast Guard Incident Management Handbook. Still, I'm beginning to feel like the gods of big surf have turned against me.

Station Golden Gate is located in a red-roofed, two-story yellow wooden building at Fort Baker on the Marin headlands, a short jog around Horseshoe Cove from their boathouse with its three 47s and two 25-footers. It's the busiest search and rescue unit on the West Coast, with some six hundred cases a year and a crew of fifty-four, including eight surfmen. In the hallway I'm greeted by a golden retriever named Wallace and a four-month-old black Lab pup named Sierra, the station mascot.

There's a map on the hallway wall of San Francisco Bay, the Golden Gate Bridge, and the Pacific with color-coded stickpins for different responses. Crossing the Gate it's thick with black pins—suicide jumpers. Along Crissy Field just inside the bay is an even larger clump of pink pins—wind- and kite-surfers who get in trouble and have to be rescued before the tide drags them out to sea. Fewer and more scattered are other colored pins, including green for disabled vessels and blue for "taking on water/capsized," some of which are stuck in the turbulent "Potato Patch" that stretches several miles offshore.

"Don't talk about the bridge jumpers, that's the guidelines," Chief Morgan informs me, as has the district public affairs officer.

"Because there are so many?"

"It happens something like thirty to forty times a year. We pull up [about] half, and that sucks. You have to recover and do CPR on them, but survivors are few and far between [which is why they call the litter they use for recoveries the "dead sled"]. It [the Golden Gate Bridge] is 220 feet high, like jumping off a twenty-two-story building, and the same as hitting cement. We've had two people live I know of. One kid was seventeen or eighteen. One of our station guys saw it [the jump] driving home over the bridge. Usually someone sees it and calls the bridge sergeant on an emergency phone and then he calls us, but our guy got on his cell and called us, and we were already under way a half mile from there, and the kid landed next to an ER doc who was surfing off Fort Point and who dragged him on his board. He started CPR, and we were there in a minute and pulled the kid and the ER doc aboard, and again, just this amazing alignment, there was a Highway Patrol helicopter passing over, and the helo came down and landed on the parade field, and that young guy was probably in the ER five minutes after he jumped. The second one who survived had a broken arm. He was messed up, but that was basically it."

The surf station is really where you'll find the heart of the Coast Guard," thirty-one-year-old Marine-turned-Coastie Jim Summers tells me, recounting some of the more adventuresome rescues that have gone on here.

In lieu of high drama I get to join Jim, Aaron Harris, Scott Mackey, Daniel Stanley, and a reluctant Sierra for a patrol around the bay in one of the 47s.

We head out around the Golden Gate Bridge. Its cement pier bunkers are home to dozens of lounging cormorants.

"We had a drunk sailboater run into the bridge the other day," Aaron notes. A year later it will be an 901-foot container ship hitting the Bay Bridge.

There are dozens of windsurfers and kite-surfers slicing through the bay by the Presidio. "When the wind dies they get pulled out through the Gate," Jim explains. "One day we had fourteen on the boat at one time with all their gear. We looked like some kind of kite sale."

A small wooden trawler passes by on its way to fish. We watch some sailboats heel over in the winds as a massive Evergreen container ship heads out to sea. We pass an old Liberty ship and submarine permanently docked by the maritime museum. The waterfront is an aquatic ballet, alive with boats and gulls and diving pelicans going after herring. We check out Pier 39 and the sea lions hauled up on the old marina floats barking contentedly as the tourists watch them from dockside and wave to us. Sierra has her front paws up on the console, looking interested.

"Hey, Sierra. You want your own seal? You want your own pet?" Jim asks.

"You love her," Daniel teases.

"No, I don't."

"Well, you don't hate her."

"Yes, I do."

"Coming up," Aaron warns as he turns out of the inlet, gunning the boat to over twenty knots, taking us out past Alcatraz.

"Hang on, dog. Here we go."

When we get back to the station we find that the operations center by the front door has become very focused. Sector has received a vessel assist request. The crew is working their radar screens and navigation charts.

"Call Sector, see if we're required to launch."

"Sector says they have them."

"Dude, Sector has its head up its ass as usual."

"There's a sailboat off Montara," the watch officer explains. "All we have is it's a 35-footer. No information except it's nasty out there. Eleven-foot seas at Point Montara, 16.1 at the [sea] buoy."

Jim gets on a cell phone while Aaron begins working the landline.

"Guy is requesting [a commercial] vessel assist, not the Coast Guard, but they'll probably decline. We'll know in the next five minutes," he reports.

"The harbormaster at Half Moon Bay says there's a big groundswell, north winds ten to fifteen knots, but if they can sail it into the harbor they could go out and get him," the watch stander notes after another radio check.

Sector is back on the frequency. ". . . guy said it would be about twenty-one hundred dollars to come out and tow him." A few minutes pass. "He's accepted the $2,100 offer. Sector will monitor."

"Why wouldn't he just ask for your help for free?" I wonder.

"Maybe they're sketchy," Aaron speculates. "Maybe they have something on board and don't want us out there."

"I'm glad not to do it." Jim smiles as their workaday tension fades, quick as a passing squall. "It would be a long haul, three hours to get there and a ten-hour tow. We'd also have to rig a drogue [small trailing sea anchor] so he wouldn't sail down on us."

Aaron, who is working to become a surfman, sports a tattoo of a tall ship with the name of his twenty-month-old daughter, Bernice Jean, scripted below it. The Coast Guard has banned tattoos covering more than 25 percent of your exposed skin, as well as any between your wrists and fingertips, on your neck, or on your face. So Aaron plans to do a tat of an octopus on his back with one tentacle reaching over his shoulder and another around his belly.

Six months later, I've moved back to the Bay Area and begun hanging out at Station Golden Gate. Sierra, the station mascot, has grown tall and lanky and more water-friendly, as a Lab should be. I also get to meet Wallace's owner, Petty Officer First Class Jessica Shafer. Jessica is only the second of three women to qualify as a surfman (to date). She's also just recovered a mentally disturbed bridge jumper who survived the 220-foot drop, the first survivor in three years.

I get under way with Surfman Jason Gale, who's training up a new coxswain, practicing side tows with two 47s just off Horseshoe Cove below the fog-shrouded bridge.

He tells me about his favorite SAR case, which reminds me of Bernie Webber and his famous radio protocol.

"It was during the millennium fireworks on the bay [December 31, 1999]. There were three barges loaded with fireworks and tens of thousands of people lining the San Francisco waterfront and also just tons of sailboats all rafted up and Coast Guard boats fifty feet apart maintaining this thousand-yard safety perimeter around the barges. I'm in this RIB with three guys, and the fireworks go off, and halfway through the show all you can see is smoke and ash and burning stuff raining down, and I see there's a small boat getting too close to the security zone. I realize everyone, including our guys, is looking up at the fireworks, and I look again and see that boat disappear into the smoke. So I call the patrol commander, and he says, 'Roger,' and calls the boat over in that area, and they say they didn't see anything. I figure no one in their right mind is going to go into that smoke unless they drifted in there, like if their engine failed, but the commander's not interested, he tells me to mind my own helm. So I call the 41-footer that's closest by, and he [the commander] comes back on the radio, only now he's annoyed. 'I told you to leave it alone.' Only my crew is like, 'We got to go get those people.' So my engineer reaches over and starts hitting the security button on the radio that turns the transmission to static unless you have a descrambler at the other end. Now the patrol commander is saying, 'I have you broken and unreadable,' and I answer, 'Roger, I'm responding,' like I got the go-ahead.

"So we head over to where we saw this boat go in, and there's even more smoke and burning debris. We just have this crappy little radar and can't see or hear anything, but on the radar we see three big blips, which are the barges, and a little blip. So I ask the crew if they're OK with it, and we pull our float coats over our heads and head into this thick acrid smoke. Soon we start hearing screaming, and we come alongside this small motorboat maybe fifteen feet long. We see this woman with her life vest smoking, and there's smoke coming off the boat seats and sides, and she's got two children under this beach towel she's thrown over them, and they're screaming and it's smoldering, and there's a guy leaning over, trying to crank the outboard, and his vest is smoking and he's cursing. So we throw a bowline and a towing line on them for a side tow, and I gunned it out of there.

"We couldn't see a thing, so I went where I thought it would be safe, and later realized we went right between two of the barges but missed their cables, and while we'd started on the Alcatraz side somehow we came out on the San Francisco waterfront.

"I realize the fireworks have stopped, and the only sound is these two screaming girls who are maybe five to ten years old. It turns out the patrol commander has stopped the show and explained to people what's happening. As we emerge from out of the smoke, the girls stop screaming and peek out from under their blanket, and here are these thousands of strangers staring back at us and this moment of silence and then this huge uproar as everyone starts cheering and clapping, the whole crowd. It was goose-bump city, I tell you. Then all these other Coast Guard boats converge on us and take them [the rescued family] away.

"Of course, I didn't get an award for that. I just got chewed out. The patrol commander started screaming, 'Your ass is mine!' and my crew's saying, 'Don't give him your name,' which is ridiculous because he could read our boat number. He tried to bring charges against me, but my captain said, 'Don't worry about it,' so I didn't."

The winter of '07–'08 sees California battered by a series of gnarly Pacific storms. On December 4, "Black Tuesday," well-known big-wave surfer Peter Davi drowns at Ghost Trees, a famous surf spot in Monterey, and two crab fishermen are lost when their boat breaks up in thirty-foot waves at Pillar Point by Half Moon Bay. By the time one of the station surfboats gets on scene, all they can find is chunks of wood and a floating survival suit.

In January 2008, Northern California is hit by a larger winter storm. I call the station from back east but am told Chief Morgan's out on one of the boats.

By the time I get home two days later, the nearby Richmond Bridge has reopened after a semi truck flipped, the downed trees are being removed, the floods have receded, and power has been restored to 2.5 million people. There'd been twenty-five- to thirty-foot seas outside the Gate, Chief Morgan tells me. "We were in Richardson Bay with anchor-out boats drifting around and grounding in seventy-knot winds. We got a woman off one boat. Another boat took out a dock. Two sank. Three or four went aground."

I don't say anything.

"Don't worry. There'll be more storms this winter," he promises.

A month later, another powerful storm front is heading toward the bay. I get to the station on Saturday, but the storm has stalled offshore. I return Sunday, but they've called off surf training because the seas are now over twenty-five feet at Ocean Beach and bigger to the south with wind gusts at sixty knots, well above their training limits. Kevin is back in Richardson Bay, where another sailboat is dragging anchor and a cabin cruiser has sunk at its mooring. I listen as the com center coordinates between his 47 and a 25-foot Marin sheriff's boat ("Rescue One") that has a shallower draft and can get in closer to where the sailboat has gone aground by Blackie's Pasture in Tiburon. They try hailing it just to make sure no one is aboard.

Then a call comes in that a surfer's in trouble off Pacifica (south of San Francisco). The SAR alarm goes off, and a crew including Aaron Harris, Surfman Jessica Shafer, and Surfman Greg Babst, a big slab of a guy with a shaved head, scrambles around the cove road to the boathouse, zipping up drysuits and strapping down helmets. They won't let me ride along with the waves at thirty feet. So, a little aggrieved and disappointed, I watch them take off from the seawall and then return to the station to follow the action on the com center radios. Kevin's 47 returns to the pier and immediately takes off again to pair up with the first boat that's gotten under way.

They head offshore rather than try to cut across by Ocean Beach and get crunched in its giant shorebreak. Going around the San Francisco peninsula that way means it will take them about an hour to get on scene. Meanwhile a helicopter from Air Station San Francisco has taken off and is heading south as coordinates are being read to everyone on the radio. A couple of Coasties have pulled out a navigational chart in the com center and are now using a metal compass to figure out where the surfer might be located.

The radio reports the fire department and police have a visual on the subject trapped in the surf.

Shafer and Babst get on the radio and, over the sound of breaking waves, complain the coordinates they were just given are north of the Golden Gate (Pacifica is south). "Be advised there are two swells out here both breaking," they warn Kevin's boat.

"We'll be there in a few minutes," he responds.

A radio update on the surfer says he's a little south of Rockaway Beach by the big rocks.

"Roger, we'll be on scene in four minutes," the helicopter responds.

Meanwhile the two 47s are climbing thirty-foot groundswells with twelve-foot cross-waves making for a giant washing-machine effect.

A few minutes later, the Dolphin pilot is back on the radio.

"He's paddle surfing. He's doing fine. We're gonna make another pass, but he's in there with a purpose for surfing."

"Can you confirm that?" the sector SAR controller wants to know.

"Surfer just gave us the universal A-OK sign. He's doing fine," the pilot responds.

"Coast Guard helicopter, abort."

"47 hanging out by buoy two till we get stand-down from Sector," Greg Babst radios.

"3-4, you may stand down from the case," Sector responds.

The two surfboats head back in.

A short time later, their crews are walking down the hallway soaking wet and buzzing with adrenaline.

"How was it?" I ask Greg grudgingly.

"Shitty! It's OK when someone's actually in trouble, but it bugs me when we get into it like that and it turns out to be nothing.

"In twenty-five- to thirty-foot steep seas like that, it's all about throttle management," he goes on to explain as we sit down in the galley. "You're constantly thrusting and backing off till you're squatting on the wave. You get into the wave and let it break underneath you. You don't let the engine bog down climbing up it, and you don't surf down it either. It's a controlled drop, but that's the easy part. It's when it's chasing you from behind that's harder. You look at the shoulder of the wave and ride over the saddles [shoulders] and try to never take a break[ing wave]."

"You took some breaks, though."

"We took some waves breaking over us."

"A couple broke on us," Jessica points out.

One of the crew, Jerry Eaton, is a rangy sixty-two-year-old member of the Coast Guard Auxiliary, one of the few volunteers qualified to crew on a 47-foot surfboat. "They've sort of adopted me like a mascot," he explains. "They've got Sierra, Wallace, and me."

The boat crews hold a briefing in the training room, where they're joined by the dogs.

"With these two swell patterns, this is already nastier than Black Tuesday," Kevin points out, going up to the whiteboard to write out a GYR risk assessment. He's changed into his standard khaki shorts, T-shirt and flip-flops. The others are still wearing their comfy black liner suits that go underneath their red Mustangs.

They agree on a 3 for Crew Selection as he writes down the numbers. A 7 for Planning, a 3 for Supervision. Crew Fitness they give a 5 because people are getting tired three days into it. Environment is a 10, Mission Complexity a 9, Equipment a 2. It adds up to 39, or high amber. Generally you don't want to go over a 25, or green, a low-risk evolution.

"It's definite SAR degradation. We'll need waivers to get under way," Kevin says. "Pipe all hands."

The rest of the station crew joins them. "The weather out there is exceeding the limits of the 47, so we'll not be the first resource sent out if something happens," he tells them. "They'll send the helos or the cutters. Still, I want everyone to chill, take it easy, and rest up in case we are called out again."

"Luckily none of the fishermen, none of the commercial guys are going out in this," Aaron notes.

"Surfers are the only real idiots who'll go out in this kind of shit," Greg claims.

"And us," Kevin points out.

"Yeah, and us."

CHAPTER 8

Aviators

"There's a fine line between a Distinguished Flying Cross and a court-martial."

—HH-60 Pilot Dan Molthen, recalling how his crew squeezed a record-breaking twenty-six survivors from a sinking ship into their helicopter

So Others May Live

—Motto of the Coast Guard Rescue Swimmers

Bob Watson is a compact guy with silver-blond hair and eyes the color of newly mined mercury. Now retired from the Coast Guard, he's a legend among fellow swimmers.

Over breakfast in Elizabeth City, North Carolina, I ask him about his most memorable rescue. Not surprisingly, he recalls one in which he almost died.

"We got the call about 8:00 P.M. A young boy was hanging by his arms in a waterfall a thousand feet up Horsetail Falls [in Whittier, Alaska]. I grabbed a body bag 'cause we were forty minutes away and I'm thinking, 'Who can hang on for forty-five minutes?'

"We start brainstorming on the way out—we had these old Navy harnesses that pull around your chest, and I grabbed a litter and hung that on the side of me with the cable attached to it. We get up around thirteen hundred feet and see him there. He's facedown in this wash by the falls. Turns out the kid is also epileptic and has no meds.

"Ethan Curry was the flight mechanic. He lowered me down and kind of swung me on the cable, swung me out in an arc till I was able to grab on to some alder branches that were growing out from the side of the mountain. With the basket hooked onto me, I began working my way over to the kid. He's [sprawled] facedown hanging next to Horsetail Falls in gravel and steep scree [broken rock], and the helicopter's hovering as I get closer. I'm grabbing onto branches 'cause it's straight up and down. Then there's this washed-out area between him and me. So I figure I'll kick out on the cable and swing over, and as I'm getting ready to jump, the basket disconnects and sails off into space with the cable. An alder branch must have unclipped the safety hook. So now I'm hanging on to this mountain on an eighty-degree angle. I'm telling the kid, 'It's OK, we're going to get you out of here,' like this is all part of how we do things.

"Soon the helicopter is dropping the litter from above, but they're in front of us and can't see the litter, so they're kind of fishing blind. [After a while] I see the basket is bouncing around on the kid's thighs and legs, so I say 'Get in the basket,' and he turned and spun around and grabbed it. He got his upper body into it as it pulled out into space, and I see where he then flips into the basket. Though they couldn't see us, the helo knew he'd gotten in the basket but didn't want to bring him up till I was also recovered, because a basket can take two people. I remember his eyes were just locked on mine. He didn't want to look down.

"They'd back off and then bring the helicopter forward so that the rotors were actually hitting alder branches. I'm still clinging to the mountain, mostly face to the rock. Then I felt the cable hit the back of my helmet as it swung in. I thought, 'This is probably my only chance.' So I let go, spun around in the air, and grabbed the cable. I slide down it and land on the kid. I landed on top of him, and he didn't even say anything. I sat on him and hooked back into the cable, and they started to bring us up only it [the litter] was snagging on the side of the mountain and rocking. There was this rock overhang like a nose, but the floatation [pads on the rescue litter] caught the rock and acted like a roller, and we're hanging on as the basket tilts ninety degrees.

"The helicopter backs off at that point. We're now hovering at sixteen hundred feet, and we get [winched] up to the door and are pulled in. This fifteen-year-old kid—his eyes were still so big, and [pilot] Harl [Romine] looks around and says, 'Why are you cradling your hand like that?' I look down and realize I've smashed a finger but hadn't noticed till then. So we land in this little town of Whittier right below the mountain, and the whole town is there, and his mom was crying like she didn't know whether to kill him or hug him.

"Later that night [back at the air station], I woke up screaming, and one of the crew in another rack says, 'What happened?'

" 'I fell,' I told him. 'Only it was in the dream. In real life I survived.' "

Rescue Swimmer John Green had a similar moment on a jack-up oil rig called Ocean Crusader back in the summer of 2000. An explosion and gas fire had trapped more than fifty crewmen twenty-five miles off the coast of Louisiana. His Dolphin 65 was the first responder on scene that night. After they landed, Green volunteered to stay on the burning rig so they could start to evacuate four men at a time (the 65 was notoriously underpowered at the time). After the first eight men were flown to another rig, a workboat arrived, and additional men were lowered 120 feet down to it on the rig's crane. Working in tandem, the workboat and helicopter were able to get most of the crew off the burning platform. A second 65 arrived and, pushing its capacity, was able to take the last three men. Green waited behind for his copter to finish refueling on a nearby platform. Soon it was making its final approach toward him.

Just then the Ocean Crusader exploded in an orange fireball that enveloped the entire platform. Knocked to his knees but partially protected by a steel shipping container converted to an office, Green grabbed a radio and called the 65, whose crew was convinced they'd just seen him incinerated. "If you guys are going to come get me, this would be a good time," he told them.

Green made his way back to the helicopter pad, which was now completely engulfed by thick black smoke. The 65's crew couldn't see him or the pad and told him he should maybe jump, but dropping over a hundred feet into a dark ocean didn't appeal to his survival instinct.

As the helicopter inched its way toward the rig, its rotor wash cleared some of the smoke away from the landing pad so that its mechanic was able to lean out the door and direct the pilot even closer. At that point Green decided he couldn't wait any longer. He took a running leap off the platform's edge and through the 65's open door next to the startled flight mechanic, slamming hard against the opposite bulkhead. "He's in! Up! Up! Up! Let's go!" the mech screamed. As they lifted away, they were rocked by a second massive explosion. The heat and blast from this one actually pushed them out of the death zone of the now raging inferno.

Martha LaGuardia-Kotite, a former Coast Guard officer whose book *So Others May Live* profiles fourteen swimmer rescues, titled her chapter on John Green's cinematic escape "The Perfect Rig."

That was before rescue swimmers got their own Hollywood action movie, *The Guardian*, released in 2006 and starring Kevin Costner and Ashton Kutcher. In the previous fifty years there had been only two feature films about the Coast Guard, both highly forgettable comedies, 1958's *Onionhead*, starring Andy Griffith ("The ship's cook who has the Coast Guard in a stew!"), and Walt Disney's 1970 *The Boatniks* ("Man the laffboats!").

Still, a number of books have been written about Coast Guard aviation rescues, including the rescue of more than five hundred passengers and crew from the cruise ship *Prinsendam* that caught fire and sank in the Gulf of Alaska in 1980. The mostly elderly passengers were successfully airlifted onto the deck of an oil tanker.

Two books were written about the attempted rescue of five fishermen forced to abandon their boat, the *La Conte*, in mountainous seventy-foot seas in the Gulf of Alaska in 1998. Three survived the great storm and two died, including the captain, who hung on to the bottom of a rescue basket as another fisherman was being hoisted into a Jayhawk helicopter in 100 mph winds. After being repeatedly banged, unseen, against the lip of the aircraft door by two crewmen trying to pull the basket in, the boat captain made momentary eye contact with one of them before falling a hundred feet back into the raging sea below. Three HH-60s and a C-130 participated in that harrowing search and rescue effort.

Along with its 144 helicopters, the Coast Guard depends on thirty-three muscular C-130 four-engine Hercules aircraft that can stay aloft for twelve hours at a time, as well as over a dozen agile but aging Falcon jets (gradually being replaced by two-engine Spanish CASA transport planes). It also owns two business jets, a Challenger and a Gulfstream for the admirals.

While best known for search and rescue, HH-65 Dolphin helicopters deployed on cutters and icebreakers also carry out counterdrug, fisheries, scientific, and migrant interdiction missions. HH-60 Jayhawks are used for search and rescue, marine safety, and homeland security, Falcons and CASAs (now known as Ocean Sentries) are good for search and rescue and surveillance, and

C-130s act as flying air-control platforms, do long-range fisheries and ice patrols, and provide logistical support for the full range of Coast Guard missions.

It's not surprising that Coast Guard Aviation, which makes up around 10 percent of the service with some 4,100 people, including 1,200 pilots and 380 rescue swimmers, plays such a significant role in the service, given that the Coast Guard was there at the birth of modern aviation.

Flying Boats, Pelicans, and Dolphins

The Wright brothers, Wilbur and Orville, launched the first heavier-than-air flying machine on a cold, empty Outer Banks beach near Kitty Hawk, North Carolina, on December 17, 1903. That first short, transforming flight of 120 feet by brother Orville lying prone on the lower wing was photographed by Surfman John T. Daniels from the nearby Kill Devil Hills Life-Saving Station.

The station's captain, Jesse Etheridge Ward, allowed his crew to help the brothers out when off duty. They brought mail and supplies and shared meals with the brothers and also acted as the first powered aircraft's first aircrew, helping to assemble the "Wright Flyer" and carrying it to its launch rail. After the first flight, the surfmen helped drag the Flyer back to the rail until, on its fourth and final flight, it flew over 852 feet, staying airborne for almost a full minute.

When a gust of wind then began to flip the aircraft, John Daniels jumped on a wing to try to hold it down. He was flipped and tumbled with the machine, falling fifteen feet to the sand, becoming the first modern aviation casualty if you count bumps and scrapes. He picked himself up, and he and the other surfmen helped the Wright brothers drag the damaged aircraft back into its hanger. That would be John T. Daniels's last flight until, in 1953, on the fiftieth anniversary of that historic day, he agreed to ride along as a passenger in a Coast Guard helicopter.

In 1916, the year after the modern Coast Guard was founded, two lieutenants, Elmer Stone and Charlie Sugden, began experimenting with a Curtiss flying boat thinking it might be useful for search and rescue. They won over their boss, Capt. Ben Chiswell of the cutter *Onondaga*, to the value of airplanes. He was eventually dubbed "the father of Coast Guard Aviation," even though he was a boat driver, not an Airedale (an early term for fliers still favored by sailors).

The Coast Guard ran a naval air station in France during World War I, although the service didn't establish its own until 1920. That was in Morehead City, North Carolina. Today there are twenty-four Coast Guard air stations throughout the United States, including major ones in Elizabeth City, North Carolina; Clearwater, Florida; Mobile, Alabama; and Kodiak, Alaska.

An early aircraft rescue involved a boy in a skiff who drifted thirty miles off Cape Canaveral, Florida, in January 1933. By the time the seaplane *Arcturus* located the small boat, the boy was fighting rough seas and trailing sharks with darkness approaching and the closest Coast Guard vessels over eighty miles away.

Lt. Cdr. Carl Von Paulsen, the pilot of the *Arcturus*, decided to make a water landing in twelve-foot seas, twice what the plane was certified for. The impact crumpled the left wing. Four of the crew stood on the right wing to keep the aircraft balanced while the radioman entered the shark-infested waters to retrieve the boy and begin repairs.

After a rough patch job and with the recovered survivor aboard, they took off again, though this time the rolling seas tore a pontoon away. Unable to keep the plane stable, they were forced to make a crash landing that damaged the flying boat's hull. Attempts to taxi the plane or deploy a sea anchor failed, though they were able to jury-rig an antenna and signal an SOS. After that the aircraft drifted for hours until it hit surf and beached itself on a sandy shoal at about one in the morning. The crew waded ashore with the boy. They all received Gold Lifesaving Medals.

Two years later, in 1935, Chief Warrant Officer Charles "Daddy" Thrun, the service's third pilot and first enlisted pilot, became the Coast Guard's first aviator to die in the line of duty after his Grumman F-2 Duck overturned on takeoff in the cold waters off Cape May, New Jersey.

Forty-seven years later, Lt. Colleen Cain, the service's third female pilot and first female helicopter pilot, would become the first woman aviator to die in the line of duty. She was copiloting a Sea Guardian helicopter on a rescue mission when it hit the side of a mountain on Molokai, Hawaii. Her two crewmates, Cdr. Buzz Johnson and Aviation Survivalman David Thompson, were also killed.

While fixed-wing aircraft would change the nature of transportation and warfare in the twentieth century and beyond, it was a different kind of aircraft that would come to be identified with Coast Guard search and rescue.

On December 7, 1941, as Japanese pilots launched their surprise attack on the Pacific Fleet at Pearl Harbor, Coast Guard pilot Lt. Frank "Swede" Erickson stood in the air control tower on Ford Island, watching the precision slaughter taking place around him.

"The control tower did not prove to be a target[;] however, it could have been destroyed with one bomb," he later wrote in a letter to the Sikorsky helicopter company. "These Japs were plenty accurate with their dive bombing and strafing. Every dive looked as if it were coming our way but evidently their plans did not include our tower. Within a radius of a mile and a half 2,000 men were killed and many thousands of others were wounded, most of whom were burned by the thick fuel oil covering the harbor. The long lines of oil covering wounded men coming ashore stand out in my memory."

Erickson was frustrated and angry seeing these sailors struggling and drowning in the water, knowing the Coast Guard had no easy way of saving them. He recalled an article he'd read in *Aero* magazine about Dr. Igor Sikorsky and the helicopter he'd invented and made a conceptual leap that day of infamy, seeing the helicopter as a future tool for maritime rescue. "It is perfectly feasible to equip these machines with a stretcher which can be lowered 25 or 30 feet in hovering flight to remove men from jungles, very high ground or the open sea where even the helicopter cannot land," he wrote the company in that letter, which he mailed a short time later.

Along with Erickson, a big bulldog of an extrovert, several other Coasties, including his friend Cdr. Bill Kossler, chief of aviation engineering, became advocates for rotary-wing aircraft. They saw the helicopter as having all the advantages and none of the drawbacks of large unwieldy Navy blimps. Still the service's seaplane pilots remained skeptical.

In 1943, Coast Guard Commandant Russell Waesche went to Bridgeport, Connecticut, to observe a Sikorsky helicopter in operation. He was so impressed he got the Navy to put the Coast Guard in charge of helicopter development for both services.

By then Kossler had arranged Erickson's transfer to Air Station Floyd Bennett Field, Brooklyn. As the military's first helicopter pilot, he began training other Coast Guard pilots and working on the use of helicopters for antisubmarine warfare, including techniques for landing on and taking off from ships' decks. By the end of 1943, all Allied helicopter pilots were training in Brooklyn. Among his many innovations, Erickson developed flight simulators and a rescue harness to winch a person into a helicopter. There's a 1944 picture of Dr. Igor Sikorsky dangling in a harness just below the door of a copter being piloted by Erickson. Swede Erickson also developed the first Coast Guard rescue basket and flew the first actual helicopter rescue mission on January 3, 1944.

The USS *Turner*, a destroyer anchored off Sandy Hook, New Jersey, exploded and sank that day in an unexplained accident that killed 100 crewmen and injured 163. The survivors were brought to a hospital, where blood plasma was soon running low. With roads and runways blocked by falling snow, a call went out to Erickson, who, along with Lt. Walter Bolton, volunteered to pick up plasma at Battery Park and fly it across the New York Bight. They made it from Brooklyn to the southern tip of Manhattan in buffeting winds and near zero visibility, at which point Bolton had to get out to keep the helicopter light enough to fly on with two cases of plasma strapped to its landing floats. Erickson lifted off, flying backward away from the trees until he was able to spin around over the water and fly on through the snow squalls to a successful landing in New Jersey, where the plasma was put to immediate use.

In April 1945, a Royal Canadian Air Force PBY crashed in Labrador, Newfoundland. All nine men aboard survived, although two were burned. Ski-equipped planes tried to rescue them. One crashed, and the other was able to get the two injured out but got bogged down on its next attempted takeoff from the isolated crash site.

With only eight days of food left, a new approach was needed. A helicopter was disassembled in Brooklyn and flown on board a C-54 cargo plane to Goose Bay, Labrador, where it was reassembled. U.S. Coast Guard Lt. August Kleisch then hopscotched the helicopter 184 miles to a frozen lake, where he refueled out of jerry cans of gas he'd brought along, flew on to the survivors' camp, picked up the first of the stranded crew, and then flew on to an isolated Canadian air force base thirty-eight miles beyond. It took him nine trips over three days to get everyone safely out of the wilderness.

Still, within the Coast Guard debate was growing more heated over which was the right aircraft for SAR, the helicopter or the seaplane. While Swede Erickson remained a staunch and unyielding defender of the rotary wing, he found a more than equally stubborn opponent in the outspokenly aggressive, cigar-chomping Capt. Donald B. MacDiarmid, a legend in his own time and, pretty obviously, in his own mind.

"Cap'n Mac" had perfected open-ocean seaplane landing and takeoff techniques in World War II (winning a Distinguished Flying Cross in the process). He was so frustrated with his inability to get a combat transfer he once launched a mock air raid on his own station in Port Angeles, Washington, to test his men's defense readiness. Unfortunately, his collaborators' use of flares, gunfire, and dynamite convinced a nearby Navy ship the Japanese really were attacking. They opened fire on his plane with heavy machine guns, forcing him to detour to Canada. At the same time, a war alert about the "invasion" of Port Angeles spread up and down the West Coast. In 1943, MacDiarmid finally got his combat assignment flying antisubmarine patrols out of Greenland.

After the war, he argued there was no need to replace PBY seaplanes or newer amphibians that could roll in and out of the water like the rugged Grumman Albatross, also known as "the Goat." Helicopters, he insisted, were nothing more than "mechanized Pogo sticks" that were only good for "county fairs and hauling Santa Claus."

Throughout the 1950s, however, the helicopter kept proving itself a great SAR asset. In 1955, Coast Guard helicopters rescued over three hundred people from flooding rivers in New England, and on Christmas Eve of that year a single HO4S Chickasaw helicopter saved 138 people from floodwaters in Yuba City, California, plucking them off rooftops and out of trees.

Coast Guard mechanics had already adopted the policy of flying the planes they fixed and also handling the hydraulic hoists on the newer helicopters. That night one of them, Petty Officer MK2 Victor Roulund, rode a hoist down onto the roof of a mobile home that had begun to float away. Using an ax, he chopped out a ventilator and lowered himself inside the dark trailer, where he found a paralyzed, terrified old lady floating on a mattress. Meanwhile his pilot, Lt. Henry Pfeiffer, had flown off to rescue some other people. On the helicopter's return, Roulund was able to signal with a flashlight from where he'd carried the disabled woman to a doorway. A rescue basket was lowered into the swirling floodwater, and she was placed inside it and lifted to safety.

In 1953, recognizing that the winds of change were now shifting vertical, Capt. Donald MacDiarmid reluctantly qualified as a "helicrapper" pilot. That same year, a Coast Guard rescue seaplane crashed on takeoff in open ocean waters off the coast of China, killing twelve of the people on board. By 1961, seaplanes were no longer flying for the Coast Guard, though the amphibious Goats would hang on until 1983.

The Coast Guard went on to fly a series of other planes including the Provider, Hercules, Samaritan, Guardian, Falcon, Condor, and Sentry fixed-wing aircraft and the Flying Banana, Seahorse, Seaguard, Chickasaw, Pelican, Jayhawk, Dolphin, and Augusta helicopters.

Coasties tend not to be overly romantic about their "assets," seeing their historical succession of boats and aircraft as so many useful tools needed to meet their maritime missions.

Still, pilots who flew the HH-3 Pelican, a variation on the Vietnam-era "Jolly Green Giant," tend to keep an open hangar in their hearts for it. They speak of this large, amphibious helicopter with admiration whether they've used it as a rescue boat in rough seas or a transport wagon for sedated grizzly bears.

Capt. Chip Strangfeld in San Diego keeps a framed picture of his old H-3 Pelican on his office wall. He recalls landing it in seven-foot seas during a rescue off Cape Cod in the early 1980s. "We had one survivor who made it probably because he was fat. His thin buddy died of hypothermia. We didn't have time to get the swimmer outfitted, so we did the water landing. I had the radioman take the window out in the rear so he could look back at the tail, 'cause if the tail went under we were gone, and a couple of times with the waves rising up behind us he'd call, 'Up! Up! Up!' and I'd lift off before we were finally able to land [long enough] and pull these guys in."

"It was a great helo—a little underpowered, and the avionics were not very advanced by today's standard, but it was a dump truck. You could load anything into it," recalls now retired Capt. Mike Moore, a former Alaska pilot and service chief of aviation forces.

"We had this Canadian goose [the dusky Canada goose] that was an endangered species nesting near Cordova, near the Copper River delta, and Fish and Game told us the brown bears [were] eating the goslings, and [they asked us] if they could bring them to our forward deployment site, could we move them away? So they'd bring these bears they'd darted two or three at a time and we'd forklift them into the back [of the H-3 Pelican], shackled and muzzled, and fly them to Yakataga. A vet flew with them with an extra hypodermic in case they came to, and there was a Fish and Game officer with a high-powered rifle between the bears and the cockpit. We moved about fifteen of them [sixteen, in fact], and by the time they made their way back to the Copper River the geese would have grown their feathers and be able to escape from them. Today you couldn't fit more than one grizzly in an H-60, I figure."

Ever the skeptical reporter, I confirm his story in the scientific literature. The helo-bear relocations took place in May 1987. Wildlife scientists, apparently having little in common with rocket scientists, later figured out it would be easier to relocate the newly hatched goslings than the grizzlies.

While the Pelican was a much beloved aircraft, little love was lost on the early production models of the HH-65 Dolphin, a Coast Guard version of the French company Aerospatiale's 1982 Dauphin. Under the "Buy American Act," passed by Congress back in 1933, over 50 percent of an aircraft purchased by the Department of Defense or Coast Guard has to come from American sources. Since the 65's advanced U.S. aviation electronics package wasn't enough to meet that requirement, the service decided to buy its composite airframe without the Turbomeca Arriel engines it came with and instead installed less powerful American-manufactured Lycoming engines. The result, while legally defensible, had all the engineering elegance of a Porsche Boxster with a Saturn Ion engine.

"The old 65s were a piece of shit. I never felt safe flying in one. They were just underpowered," says Russ Scheel, an otherwise taciturn Montana-bred rescue swimmer.

"It flew at the edge of the envelope all the time. It made for very 'finesse-ful' pilots, if that were a word," says the more diplomatic Capt. Dave Brimblecom, a longtime 65 pilot who now directs the Coast Guard Academy's Leadership Development Center. "The model A was at maximum weight almost every takeoff. You had to be careful with the A's and B's. You couldn't come in too fast or too steep [or they'd crash]. The B's had the same engine, just different avionics. The C model [first introduced in 2005 by Eurocopter and now the fleet standard] changed the engine and the nose."

There were other problems as well.

"We had core engine power turbine cracking [in 2003 and 2004]. The engines blew up," recalls Capt. Werner Winz, CO of Air Station San Francisco. "We fixed some of those core engine problems, but the engine control system was not so well fixed. 'Buy American' handicapped it [the aircraft]."

Also, along with gearbox problems, the 65's side doors tended to pop off in flight.

The obvious solution to the major problem was to retrofit the Dolphins with the more powerful engines they were designed for. By the early twenty-first century, with the global helicopter market expanding, Turbomeca USA was manufacturing its gas turbine engines in Grand Prairie, Texas. You couldn't buy more American than that. The engines were purchased and installed at the Coast Guard Aircraft Repair and Supply Center (ARSC) in Elizabeth City, North Carolina. These new "Charlie" models saw their earliest action in the wake of Hurricane Katrina and have since won over their flight crews with their improved power and reliability.

I ask Captain Brimblecom if he has any complaints about the new version, which continues to be upgraded.

"It used to look more like a dolphin with its extended nose," he grins. "The new C model [with a larger nose, housing cameras and avionics] looks more like a platypus."

The only problem with the Coast Guard's HH-60 Jayhawks is that they're aging. When I was in Alaska, three out of four were in the hangar for maintenance or repair. When new, Coast Guard Jayhawks required twenty hours of maintenance for every flight hour. Today it's more like forty. Still, with many 60s having already flown two-thirds of their useful lives, there's no replacement aircraft under serious consideration—though a few Jayhawk pilots keep pictures of the new Sikorsky H-92 Superhawk posted on their walls like pinups of some unattainable supermodel.

You're Going to Puke on Yourself

Among the Coasties' best-known heroes are the aviation survival technicians (ASTs), or rescue swimmers, who drop out of helicopters in order to pluck people from stormy seas and drowned cities. The program's origins can be traced back to February 12, 1983, when the coal ship *Marine Electric* sank in a storm off Virginia. By the time the first Coast Guard helicopter arrived on scene, the ship's crew of thirty-four had been in the frigid water so long they'd become hypothermic and were unable to grab on to the lowered rescue basket. By the time a Navy helicopter with a rescue swimmer was dispatched to the scene, only three of the crewmen were still alive. In 1984, Congress ordered the Coast Guard to establish its own rescue swimmer program to prevent this type of tragedy from recurring.

I drive to Building 33 at Air Station Elizabeth City, where five AST students are outside the nondescript sand-colored pool house doing chin-ups. They drop off the bars and begin doing push-ups on small medicine balls. "Twenty-five, twenty-six, twenty-seven, twenty-eight . . ." Tim Kessell, one of their trainers, counts out the pace. To qualify as rescue swimmers the students will have to do sixty push-ups in under two minutes, seventy sit-ups, and eight pull-ups and chin-ups and to run two miles in under fourteen minutes, swim five hundred yards in under ten, do four twenty-five-yard laps underwater with thirty-second breaks, and tow a buddy two hundred yards.

After their push-ups they do crunches with their knees up on a wooden rail, then resistance training and wind sprints before a forty-five-minute run. I look over at the Pasquotank River, notice a flock of Canada geese, and wonder if they're a required part of Coastie physical training.

Today's class will do one and a half hours of outdoor PT, one and a half hours of pool conditioning, and thirty to forty minutes of "water confidence."

"Confidence" techniques listed in their instructor's manual include Hypoxic

Laps, Underwater Laps, Underwater Knots, Brick Laps, Brick Tread, Brick Swim, and Buddy Brick, which involves two students pushing a brick across the bottom of the pool. Only one at a time can surface to take a single breath. The manual also directs the instructor that during the Buddy Breathe exercise (where a snorkel is passed between two students treading water facedown), "no more than two breaths in a row can be taken away from a single student" (by placing a hand over the snorkel when the student is desperately trying to get air).

The Coast Guard began setting its own training standards after the drowning death of a nineteen-year-old Navy recruit held underwater by his instructors at the Navy's rescue swimmer program back in 1988.

"In the real world you're going to puke on yourself, your heart rate will go through the roof, and you'll get really tired," instructor Jason Bunch tells me. "We fatigue them before they go in the pool, then toss them and turn them around, which is like a heavy sea state. They learn that the fatigue factor doesn't matter. Fear of failure is a motivator just like fear that you will die."

Jason is five-nine with a closely trimmed mustache, a shaved head, intense blue eyes behind dark shades, and a lean swimmer's body. Tim Kessell also has the shades and shaved head but tends more toward a harbor seal's physique.

The class started out with ten students six weeks ago. One of the remaining six has just gone to the sick bay with an injured quad.

"I'll talk to Doc and see if there's something wrong with him or if he's talked himself into an injury," Jason says before going on to explain how in water confidence training they try to induce "the panic mechanism" in the students and then see how they respond.

I ask if that means they'll be seeing those black dots floating in the water (from hypoxia, or lack of oxygen) that I recall from when I almost drowned in big surf off San Diego.

"They'll all see that a few times," he assures me. "A swimming pool environment is a safe place for them to do that. You want to overload them but factor in their level [of training over the sixteen-week course]. If you did week twelve stresses at week two you'd get 75 percent attrition [instead of the 50 percent dropout rate the program averages]. On the other hand, we'd have a 99 percent pass rate if this was all dry PT. People don't know their limits in the water till they find them. Ensley [one of the five students working out today] is a second-generation Coastie, and Charters was on his college swim team. The other three never swam a lap in their lives."

As they head off on their run, I check out the pool. At twenty-five by ten yards it's what real estate agents would call "cozy," plus it belongs to the Supply Center and so has to be given up during family swim time.

After seeing it, the producers of *The Guardian* decided to shoot their Swimmer School training scenes at a larger pool in Shreveport, Louisiana, to make it seem more "realistic." That may have helped inspire Congress to finally fund construction of a new fifty- by 25-meter Olympic-sized pool soon to open.

Building 33's pool area includes climbing ropes and pulleys hanging from the angled roof's rafters and a twelve-foot jump tower with a helicopter cable hoist and rescue basket. I notice some water pistols on a shelf and a plastic bucket reading PAIN AND FEAR GOES HERE. One of the wall banners reads HOME OF COAST GUARD HELICOPTER RESCUE SWIMMER SCHOOL, with a logo of a round bomb on a parachute. This goes back to the early survivalmen who dropped ordnance from biplanes. Today's survival technicians want to change the logo from a bomb to crossed swim fins.

The AST students, Ensley, Moore, Charters, Parsons, and Dobias, return from their run and, after a five-hundred-yard warm-up swim, begin doing laps carrying blue rubber-coated ten-pound bricks. They do half a lap underwater and half a lap holding the brick above the water. Brandon Decardenas returns from the doctor with orders to sit the day out. The two instructors are joined by Senior Chief Jeffrey Danner, who will act as the "pool deck monitor."

The students are pulled out of the water. Jason orders Parsons, a tall, dark, lanky student with a buzz cut, onto the tower.

"He's failed the Drop and Pick Up twice, and you get three chances, so his stress level is going to be way up," Jason explains as we climb the stairs to the platform. Parsons is now seated at the top of the stairs attached to a safety strap as he would be in a helicopter.

"Parsons. You got your head screwed on tight?" Jason inquires as Tim Kessell swims to the center of the pool in a green flight suit.

Jason sets up the scenario. "We have seven minutes of gas on board. Get down with the survivor. Signal what device you want." Parsons unclips his strap, gears up, moves over to sit on the platform edge, and pushes off with his hands, dropping twelve feet into the water. He swims deep underneath Tim to approach him from behind.

"That was the crappiest underwater approach I've ever seen," Jason complains. Parsons tells Tim to calm down and then takes him in a modified rescue hold. Tim acts calm, then "panics" and takes Parsons underwater with him. "Lost control of the swimmer," Jason notes. Parsons regains control.

"He's not doing what we showed him to do. He should dunk him."

Parsons signals for the strop. Jason lowers it on the hoist cable. Tim twists around so they're now facing each other.

"You can't put him in a strop like that," Jason shouts down, his eyes boring holes in the water. Parsons is blinking, looking around wide-eyed. He regains control of Tim, holding him from behind, but has now lost his mask.

"He lost control of the survivor. He's not doing what we showed him to do. Look at his eyes. You can see the fear in his eyes," Jason notes quietly. Tim struggles a little more, and Parson loses control again.

"This is going downhill." Jason shakes his head. "Try to get him underwater," he yells at Parsons. "In real life it sucks to lose your mask," he says. He turns on sprinklers from the tower, adding a light waterfall to the scene as Parsons finally secures the strop and brings Tim up with him. Parsons then tries to hang on to the hook after they disengage on the platform.

"Give me the hook," Jason orders. "Who said you do that? Who? Get off my platform." Parsons slowly, reluctantly drops back into the pool. They order him to retrieve his mask "It's over there on the bottom of the ocean." Tim points to the deep end.

"He didn't do the proper dive, didn't have control. He was panic struck the whole time," Jason notes. Tim agrees.

"He didn't flutter kick, didn't plane you out. It was a crappy signal—don't know if there was any verbal signal."

"He threw his mask away," Tim adds as they climb down and walk around the pool. "Get your gear off, knucklehead. Get in the female head," Jason tells the abashed student while continuing his discussion with Tim. "He didn't want to flutter kick. He was scared."

They go over to the pool deck monitor, who is not a trainer and can therefore be judged a dispassionate observer. "Me and Tim talked it out," Jason begins.

"It's a no-go," Senior Chief Danner replies.

"Me and Tim think he didn't hit his criteria, didn't gain control of the survivor," Jason continues like a dog gnawing on a bone he can't let go of.

Tim goes into the locker room to talk to the dropped student about his future options.

The class is now down from ten to five.

With nothing said, they move on to their next evolution, disentangling from a parachute in the water. They bring a parachute to the edge of the pool and lower a small raft into the pool. Ensley dresses up in a flight suit and helmet and climbs into it. One of the other students turns to Jason. "Is there going to be a raft in the test?"

They use a suspension line to raise the parachute; then Dobias and Moore jump it over the raft into the water. It blossoms above the "pilot" like a dragon's wing before settling on top of him like a wet rag.

Charters is now on the tower in his tee and trunks, black mask, snorkel, fins, and TRI-SAR combination life vest and harness. He jumps off and swims up to the silk-covered raft.

"I'm with the U.S. Coast Guard! I'm here to help you. Are you hurt?" he calls out before pulling the "pilot" out from under the parachute by his lanyard. He swims Ensley around the pool, supporting him on either side of his hip, helping him to remove his chute harness one arm and one leg at a time, shifting his grip, checking his spine, and then going underwater to make sure there are no loose shrouds still entangling him. The harness sinks and settles on the bottom. He swims Ensley to the rescue basket, gets him inside, and signals for it to be hoisted up to the platform.

Moore is next through the evolution, following the same procedure.

"See how he's doing it—flutter kicking on his side, good snorkel management—he has his hip in it," Jason notes. "Stress played a huge role in the [failed] kid not doing so well." Moore is followed by Dobias, who also clears the attachments and backpack harness from the "pilot" after making sure he's uninjured. Ensley goes last, swimming toward a new "pilot."

"Don't grab him across the chute. Go to the closest point to get him," Jason instructs.

A month later I'm in Hawaii talking to Roger Wilson, a rangy, sun-etched forty-year-old AST with an easy smile. "I remember we got this call out of Charleston [South Carolina], the one they dream about," he tells me. "This Marine Corps F-18 Hornet went down, and when we got there the plane was still visible with one wing out of the water and both crewmen in rafts. I could tell the veteran from the rookie. The veteran pilot had cut his parachute lines away. The rookie hadn't and was waving a flare at us. I free-fell in, and the other guy seemed calm, so I decided I'd get the guy who seemed panicked while I was fresh. I swam up and read him the script. 'I'm Roger Wilson, and I'm here to help you. Does anything hurt?'

" 'No, no,' [the rookie said].

"I cleared the chute in the water. I asked him if he had a chest strap on and got that removed, clearing the chute out of the way. I did the spinal tap, got the helo, and came up with him. I free-fell back for the other guy, who was so relaxed I thought he might be injured. I swam up, and he said something kind of light like 'Unbelievable day we're having.'

"I only wish I'd had a video. They could have played it at the school. The training is there for a reason, and you have it ingrained so it kicks in when you need it. When I swam under them the pilots were like 'What were you doing?' I told them, 'What I was trained to do.' "

The next day in Elizabeth City I find the sixth-week students in a classroom disassembling a water pump. They'll also learn how to pack a pump and a parachute and train as emergency medical technicians in Petaluma, California.

The school graduates about forty swimmers a year. Among its alumnae are three active-duty women, including AST Sara Faulkner, who hoisted over fifty people, including four babies, from apartment balconies and a sunken tennis court during Katrina. The last man she hoisted up told her he loved her.

The instructor gives the class a break to talk to me. They're a gangly, downy-cheeked, not very rugged-looking group. Obviously looks can be deceiving.

"I was gonna join the Air Force but decided the Coast Guard is a lifesaving service and it's on the beach. I always liked the water and the ocean," says twenty-one-year-old Brandon Decardenas.

"My dad was in the Coast Guard, and I wasn't the college type," Chris Ensley, also twenty-one, explains. "I don't like guns or killing people, but I like this job and serving my country. I did triathlon to train for this, but I was best at biking and running, not swimming."

"I joined the Coast Guard to be an AST," Keith Charters, twenty-three, volunteers. "I swam in college, and I just like every aspect of it."

"I also joined to be a rescue swimmer," says David Dobias, twenty-one, from Denver. "I saw the movie preview for *The Guardian* and went to the recruiter the next day."

"So what did you think of the movie?"

"It's corny, but it's the truth. Every time you go out you're helping someone."

I ask him where he got the scar that runs along his scalp line. "Rock climbing in Turkey as a kid. My parents were in the Air Force."

Shane Moore is twenty-two and grew up in Long Beach, California. "My dad and brother are in the Army, my brother-in-law in the Marines, and they all said don't join. My sister's in the Coast Guard, and she likes it. So I joined to be a flight mechanic and got in and saw the swimmer program and decided it was the best of the twenty-two jobs [enlisted ratings] available. You get time to work out and stay healthy, and they pay you to swim."

Four of the five of them, it turns out, are from service families. Four of them want to go to Kodiak when they graduate because that's where the action is. Keith Charters wants to go to Cape Cod because that's where his wife is.

I tell them scientists I've talked to say there will be more storm surges, also more Category 4 and 5 hurricanes, because of fossil-fuel-driven climate change. That will mean that in their careers they are likely to see more disasters like Hurricane Katrina.

"That's great!" Chris Ensley exclaims, then gets embarrassed. "I mean, you don't want a hurricane to happen to other people or boats to sink, but you do want to be able to do what you've trained for. I mean, their bad day is our good one."

Not always. Instructor Jason Bunch was an AST in Kodiak for seven years and involved in a famous case with Bob Watson where a small airplane with four people on board crashed into the side of a mountain in the fog. Two died on impact. Jason had to carry a Stokes litter seven hundred feet up a steep slope full of scree and shale and then cut one of two women out of the plane, working his way through sheet metal and wires. "The plane was teeter-tottering as we worked, and we finally got her free and took her [back down the mountain] and hoisted her, but she died."

"So there was one survivor and three deceased?" I ask.

"No, there were two survivors and one of them died," he corrects me with some vehemence. I understand. He'd worked hard to keep her alive, a survivor, not a statistic, and like Kevin Costner said in the movie, you remember the ones you've lost.

Lost in the Glare

You also remember your first and last rescues, according to Lt. Cdr. Jeff Janzen, who actually looks a bit like Kevin Costner. A former rescue swimmer, he's now CO of New York's Maritime Safety and Security Team.

"My first two guys were on a brand-new 22-footer, and the owner had forgotten to put the boat plug in," he recalls. "They pulled the engine and it started sinking. They set off a flare and it explodes in front of our helicopter. So here's a reminder. Don't point your flare at the helicopter that's trying to save you. I did a fifteen-foot jump, and we're twenty-five miles offshore, and we rescued him and his buddy, but he didn't really want to go because he was pissed off his boat was sinking.

"My last rescue was a fishing vessel that was swamped twenty-five miles offshore. These six guys are following me around while I'm trying to set up a pump for them, and I finally say, 'Why are you following me?' They say, 'Well, you're the swimmer. None of us know how to swim.' So we got more dewatering pumps on board, and I got them busy, and we kept it afloat."

Sometimes I feel like I'm interfering with Darwin's selection," AST Dennis Moyer tells me in the swimmer shop at Air Station San Francisco. He was called in during two weeks of rain and flooding in Northern California in December 2005. "Up in Hopland a lady was drunk during the flooding, a chronic alcoholic. She was told to go home and drove down a flooded road and off into a flooded vineyard field.

"We were on our way elsewhere and were flagged down by people on the road. They waved us over, and we saw this car covered up to its roof by water. They put me on a direct [hook]. She was on the driver's side of the car. The water had formed an eddy where she'd opened the door. It was pushing a big volume of water into the vee where the door and frame came together, and she was struggling. I dropped down on an angle and got shoved into this vee, and she's hysterical and I can't lift her. She's saying we're going to die, and she's just barely got her chin above water. So I feel down her side and realize she'd gotten her leg wrapped around the seat belt coming out. So I get my knife out and I cut it free. She was scared, she was convinced we were going to die, but I cut her loose and we got her out of the water."

Dennis's buddy, AST Kelly McCarthy, who's been listening, tells me he decided to join the Coast Guard after watching *Baywatch* one drunken night in college. He's a big guy with green eyes and Prince Valiant–type bangs. He's done a number of SAR cases and rescued a surfer trapped for two days in a cove, but his best story is also a cautionary tale for those who think the life of a rescue swimmer is all tragic heroics and adventurous derring-do.

"This guy got in a fight and then ran from the cops, and they got him up against a cliff [in Pacifica, just south of San Francisco], and he was faking it like he was going to jump and then slipped and fell to the bottom.

"So they put me off to the side of the cliff on the hook. There were all these bushes of poison oak, which I'm super allergic to, and they flew me right through the poison oak. I just put my arms up and hoped my drysuit would keep it off me. The firemen had already reached the guy, and he's bleeding all over the place, and the firemen say he's HIV positive. So now my drysuit is full of poison oak and HIV blood is all over. I'm trying to put a backboard under him, but the cliff's too steep. So this fireman uses his hands as a foothold for me so I can get up there and slip the litter under this guy. The fireman's a paramedic, and I'm an EMT, so we hoist the guy and the fireman to the helicopter. Now I have to climb up the cliff covered in poison oak and HIV blood. When I get to the top the firemen just look at me, shake their heads, and hose me down."

He says his favorite posting was four years at Air Station Detroit, "freshwater and no sharks." San Francisco, of course, is famous for being in the heart of the "Red Triangle" that runs from Monterey out to the Farallon Islands and back to Stinson Beach in Marin County north of the Golden Gate. There are more human-shark "encounters" here than anywhere else on earth, mainly because it's a prime seal breeding area and white sharks sometimes mistake surfers in wetsuits for seals.

"We were doing a [training] recovery off Monterey last week," Kelly reports, "and the swimmer was halfway down the cable, and our pilot saw something bigger than a dolphin messing around with the SpongeBob [dummy], so we canceled. So if we're going to get off the hook [in training], we'll probably do it off Ocean Beach [a San Francisco neighborhood with big shorebreak]. Till now we've been going to the sea buoy that's eighteen miles out, halfway to the Farallones."

Still, sharky waters aren't going to keep him from maintaining his proficiency. After I get the standard briefing on how if our helicopter hits the water it will flip upside down and I should hang on to a point of reference before exiting through a window underwater, I climb into a 65 and take one of the swimmer seats (i.e., cushions) in the back next to Kelly.

The mechanic, Rich Martin, climbs in after removing the wheel chocks.

"Want to take off, sir?"

"Absolutely," Cdr. Wayne Brown assents. "San Francisco Tower . . ."

"Good morning, Coast Guard helo. You can take a Hunters Point departure."

We taxi and lift off, the nose dropping as we lean over, gaining altitude above SFO's United hangers and head out over San Francisco Bay. I watch the two pilots doing their thing. Unlike in fixed-wing aircraft, the lead pilot is seated to the right.

No one is a natural-born helicopter pilot, not when you have to work the cyclic stick between your legs for power and to climb and descend, while handling the collective paddle by your left hip, pitching the blades to take you back and forth and left and right, while also working the foot pedals for hovering, keeping the nose straight, and, as another way to move left and right, directing the tail rotor. Also, since European-built helos like the Dolphin have their rotors spinning in the opposite direction from American copters like the Jayhawk, when you transition from one to the other you have to remember to reverse your foot movements. It can all be mastered, though, and the best helicopter pilots soon get reputations as good "sticks."

Kelly is in his swimmer meditation mode, his legs stretched out atop his SpongeBob dummy, his mask, snorkel, yellow jump helmet, and black fins resting on his lap. We fly over the new spans of the Bay Bridge heading north toward the delta. A few geese briefly join us in formation.

A 41-foot utility boat from Station Vallejo calls on the radio.

"638, good morning. Thanks for coming out today on a short-term request, sir."

"We're just going to do some basket hoists when you're ready."

"Roger that."

"Do you have any wind down there?"

The mech puts a gunner's belt on me so I can stand up and take some pictures.

"Coming left. Visual descent. Stabilize at fifty feet."

"Gonna put our rescue swimmer on the deck,"

"Floats armed—good door speed—doors open," Rich Martin announces. He helps Kelly hook the cable to his TRI-SAR for a direct descent before Kelly swings out the door.

The mech guides the pilot over the 41-foot boat when the pilot can no longer see it from the cockpit.

I look down and see three Coasties, a gal and two guys, standing on the aft deck of the boat under the rotor wash.

Kelly starts dropping down on the cable toward them. I take some shots of his progress while MK Martin runs the show.

"Forward right."

"Forward right fifty."

"Forward right twenty."

"Hold! Swimmer on deck. Swimmer off the hook."

They next go through a couple of evolutions, dropping a trail line and lowering the basket to the deck, then recovering it with the boat stationary and with the boat under way.

"That's awesome how quickly you did that," Commander Brown compliments Rich. "We'll finish and do rescue swimmer evolutions. Pick him up with the hook."

"Go right fifty. Going right thirty and going right twenty. Speed good. Forward. Prepare to take the load . . ."

I take pictures as Kelly comes back up on the hook and is swung inside the cabin.

They fly a short distance away from the 41.

"I'll do a free fall. Vector two evolutions total," Kelly says.

"Deploying Rescue Randy," Rich announces on the ICF.

Rescue Randy, aka SpongeBob, is a red cushion with sewn-on arms and lead-shot-weighted legs so that it floats vertically in the water the way a person would. Rich tosses it unceremoniously out the door.

We circle around after it's away. Kelly then drops out the open door from about eight feet up in his yellow and orange drysuit.

We circle around again. He's on the radio. "I am at your three o'clock, a quarter mile."

"He's gonna be in the glare," Rich warns the pilots. The bay is a diamond-sparkled shimmer.

"I'm at your two o'clock."

It takes me some time to spot a dot in the water not far from the 41-footer. I realize how hard it is to see a person in the water, even on a clear day when you know where he's supposed to be and he's wearing a yellow helmet and carrying a shark's red chew toy.

Flying at night over the Caribbean in a Coast Guard Falcon, we spot a blinking light in the pitch-dark. I figure the highly trained crew will be able to ID it quickly, but after making four passes as low as two hundred feet off the water, using their night-vision goggles and high-tech FLIR (forward-looking infrared) surveillance cameras controlled from the tactical workstation in the back of the jet, the best image they can generate is of some digital circles and squares. They agree there are probably no buoys this far out. They turn on all their lights, including their landing lights, and make another low pass to see if they get a response from below. Nothing. There's also nothing on emergency radio Channel 16. The pilot announces that we're now low on fuel. They report the coordinates of the mysterious blinking light to Key West and leave the scene still not sure what it is we've just seen.

Of course, if you're searching for a target that doesn't want to be found, if it's smugglers, say, that have stopped dead in the water in midocean and thrown a blue tarp over their boat, your odds of finding them are about as good as your odds of winning the lottery.

Which is only to say it's a really big ocean out there. Even the Great Lakes have a great amount of surface area to search that doesn't get any better when it's covered in ice and snow.

Still, after flying with their crews as well as visiting their SAR centers, I'm convinced that if you're lost, in trouble, or making trouble on the water, Coast Guard aviators are the people most likely to find you.

Of course, many of them would demur, which makes me worry that in writing this book my style of loud improvisation is not well suited to their quiet professionalism.

The first few times I talked to Lt. Cdr. Dan Molthen, for example, who was my public affairs contact for my visit to Elizabeth City, the tall, bald, bony pilot didn't think to mention his rescue of twenty-six survivors from a foundering cruise ship in thirty-five-foot seas, his work with Rescue Swimmer Sara Faulkner saving dozens of people in New Orleans, or his involvement in the famous *La Conte* rescue in Alaska.

"Naval aviators are known for their rampant egos," writer George Hall concluded in a 2002 article for *Flying* magazine, "but these guys are so modest and self-effacing that you want to slap them . . . They sound like firemen: glad to be of service, it's just the job, it's what we're trained to do."

To be fair, you could say the same about almost any Coastie. They're generally happy if they're respected by their shipmates, do their jobs well, save some lives, live the Boy Scout and Girl Scout oaths, and catch some awesome rides along the way.

CHAPTER 9

Frontiers

"I asked a friend, 'What's it like here?' She told me, 'It's three thousand miles of fetch [open water that allows waves to build].'"
—Master Chief John Petrie, on Hawaii

"It's wild and the weather is crappy, which gives you the case fodder, so if you want medals and big cases you go to Alaska."
—Senior Chief Lewis Hart, on Alaska

"It's a great deck," Lt. Cdr. Louis Parks assures Ensign Jamie McGinty, his trainee. "Keep forward and down and look at the horizon."

From my rear cabin position behind mechanic Amy Kitmacher, I can see the black radar and com tower of the *Alex Haley* through the pilot's windshield, then big white roll-up hangar doors and *bang!* we hit the flight deck hard. As soon as the talon has locked us on to the swaying deck, we're released and lift off again, sliding away to the left so I can now see down the length of the 282-foot Medium Endurance Cutter we've just landed and launched from.

The *Alex Haley* is stationed out of Kodiak, Alaska, but is now steaming off Hawaii in six- to eight-foot seas from a passing tropical storm. A converted Navy salvage ship, it's been on patrol for months, so its hull is festooned with dripping rust stains and its white paint has taken on a gray salty tinge. I can see the yellow-jacketed landing signal officer and blue-shirted tie-down gang hunkered low on either side of the helicopter hangar bay. We do another approach from the stern as the *Alex Haley* cuts through the ocean at ten knots. I look out the open side door toward the lowering horizon and *bang* we land again, though not quite as jarringly this time. We take off and circle around.

"You've got the proverbial string tied to your ass and the deck," Louis is instructing Jamie, who, as a Direct Commission Officer who transferred from the Army, has never had to land a helicopter on a ship before. "Look out about forty-five degrees at the horizon. Just see the deck with your peripheral vision."

On our next approach, Louis warns, "The winds seem to be buffeting us. You're out of control slightly." We abort and slide left, heeling over so that I can now see the painted circle on the flight deck and the circular steel grate, like a manhole cover, inside of it where the talon is supposed to grab on and pull the helo tight against the deck.

The ship tower radios to say our pitch has increased to about three to five degrees. "You're fine for day landings, but . . ." The transmission goes blurry. The limitations for landing on this ship are seven to eight degrees of pitch and four to five degrees of roll.

For his ship landing qualifications, Jamie needs to do fifteen daytime landings followed by ten night and twelve NVG (night-vision goggle) landings. Louis figures this will take us about three hours, including hot-gassing on the deck (refueling with the engines running).

The cloudy sky is turning an ominous gunmetal gray. Jamie will not be doing his HIFR qualifications tonight. That's a helicopter in-flight refueling, an emergency procedure where the hoist is dropped and a gas line reeled up from the cutter and married to a fuel plug in the door frame. This allows the 65 to stay airborne if the seas have gotten too rough to land, the flight deck is obstructed, or the helicopter is damaged.

I watch Amy, the flight mechanic, use a bar and stick to control the slide and swivel chair she's installed behind the pilots' seats by the open door.

"You have a green deck," the tower announces.

We come in again and drop like a freight elevator to a surprisingly light landing, which fails to please Louis. "You want to hit it hard, like a controlled crash, to get that talon in there," he says. The talon is a small attachment on the belly of the copter that looks like a hydraulic bolt cutter with a downward-facing head.

The Navy has a different approach to landing helicopters on its smaller ships, dropping a cable to a "haul-down" winch that reels them in like a kite. The Coasties prefer to drive their aircraft down to the deck themselves. The Coast Guard's new National Security Cutter will guide them in with an infrared beam to a moving sled that will lock on to a probe on the helicopter's bottom instead of having the talon lock on to the ship.

Earlier I'd mentioned that I'd been on an aircraft carrier observing Navy jet fighter pilots getting their nighttime landing qualifications, having to catch one of four arresting wires on an eight-hundred-foot moving runway with their F-18 Hornets fully cranked in case they "bolted it," sparking the deck with their tailhooks and then having to take off again with their afterburners blazing. Navy pilots say this is the hardest thing you can do in aviation, harder than flying combat missions.

"I'll put landing on a 210 [-foot Coast Guard cutter] in a helicopter at night with the rotor two feet from the infrastructure against those guys trying to catch that third wire," Louis Parks counters.

We do a few more circles and wave-offs as the *Alex Haley* steams hard into the wind. I feel like I'm getting to know all the cutter's rust strips and smudges. We get in close to the boat, hovering over its deck and then *bang*! That one felt more like a controlled crash. "You're consistent now," Louis says approvingly. I can see a blue helmet nod acknowledgment from the right front seat.

"Remember, keep looking at the horizon."

Louis calls the tower asking about their numbers, sounding concerned. We take off, circle again, drop rapidly, and then *bam! whoosh, whoosh*. This is kind of scary in that we hit hard, then seem to bounce up on the tires, the helicopter leaning over right and left, as if it wants to skitter and hop off the deck and would except for that small talon claw. Louis gets back on the radio and asks about tens. One of the blue-suited guys runs a bag out and hands it to Amy. We take off and make a steep turn back toward land.

"That was some crazy, squirrelly shit," Louis declares. "That last one was getting demanding even for me, and I mean this is for training. So we're done. We don't need this." He gets on the radio to the air station. "We're five minutes out and complete."

"You did a good job," he tells Jamie. "The main thing was we got you exposed to it and talking to the boat, but we hit with three sets of tens, and that last one was two tens and they didn't tell us. That cutter has the highest [allowable] limits, and that was still too high."

Climbing out of the 65 back at the air station, Louis reflects on our evolution, "I've done about a thousand ship landings, and that was in the top dozen"—for "squirrelly shit," he means.

The station ops boss, Don Dyer, is in the open hangar dressed down to head home in a T-shirt, shorts, and flip-flops. His ten-year-old son is seated nearby on a mule, a white towing tractor. Louis tells Don the evening was "a little too sporty. There was 10 degrees of pitch. I mean, Jiminy Christmas."

I'm staring at the tall muscular pilot thinking, "Jiminy Christmas? These guys really are Boy Scouts."

As I leave that evening, a few mechanics are still working in the brightly lit hangar with the PA blaring Bob Marley's "Redemption Song" into the warm Hawaiian night.

The Hawaiian island chain is the most isolated archipelago in the world, thousands of miles from anywhere else. Uninterrupted winter waves encountering the islands' steep sides make for world-famous big surf.

The steepness of these tropical islands also reflects their origins as volcanic mountains spawned from the depths of the sea. Hawaii is one of those rare places where you can actually see the land grow. I remember going bodysurfing with my friend Charlie Landon on a black sand beach on the Big Island in 1989. A year later we walked atop the still crunchy Kalapana lava crust past the tops of charred palm trees where the beach had been covered by two-thousand-degree molten lava a few months earlier. A quarter mile farther on, big waves were crashing against a newly created thirty-foot-high coal black cliff. Another two years passed, and we were able to hike that now rock-hard lava field to where the cliff had eroded away to a new black sand beach being caressed by the sea. Soon sprouting coconut seeds would wash ashore.

The Coast Guard's 14th District does its missions on the 12.2 million square miles of Pacific that surrounds Hawaii, an area two and a half times the size of the continental United States.

Air Station Barbers Point on Oahu's South Point embodies Hawaii's sense of isolation even though it's located on the state's most urbanized island.

South Point includes a sprawling, largely abandoned naval air complex and a National Guard base.

To get to the station you have to drive down a lonely two-lane tarmac road through sandy brush, thick with scrub and palms and old ammo bunkers that look like overgrown jungle temples. The road turns and runs along a little-used white sand beach fronting on cobalt blue waters that seem a perfect slice of paradise only twenty degrees hotter. The fenced-in air station includes two large hangars for its four Dolphin helicopters and four big Hercs, Hercules C-130 transports.

The swimmer shop is a long room facing the beachfront road with racks of survival gear, a parachute rigging table, a locker room, a giant movie poster of *The Guardian*, a hanging fiberglass shark, and a wall quiver of eighteen paddleboards and surfboards.

"We've had kite-surfers in trouble right out front here," Roger Wilson, a rangy forty-year-old rescue swimmer who's hanging out in his black swim trunks, tells me. "We've thrown our boards over the fence and paddled out for them and beat the copters. We did that three times so that ops [the air station's operations center] got mad at us. Now we have to call them and tell them if we're going to do that."

I tell him about some of the Coast Guard's windsurfer rescues around San Francisco Bay and also their rescue swimmers' white shark encounter.

"We've moved our training here from where we were chased out of the water by a big tiger shark," he counters.

Tiger sharks aren't the only thing that can rip your flesh in Hawaii. So can what the Hawaiians call "aa," spiny, bristling fields of jagged lava rock that cover tens of thousands of acres across the island chain.

Roger Wilson can't forget an aa helicopter rescue he made on the Big Island in 2004.

"We had this plane crash up in a lava field. I spotted it. There were two people standing in the plane waving to us. It was really just the outline of the plane. It had burned down to the ground. The helicopter couldn't land because it would have blown out all its tires. Plus it's not stable [the aa].

"They lowered me down, and I medically assessed. I had to do it quick because the 65 didn't have much fuel left. Both people had second- and third-degree burns, and the pilot was missing. I got the lady first 'cause I was concerned about her airway [breathing]. The guy was badly burned, too. Neither had shoes on, and they were surrounded by these sharp aa [lava] rocks. I lifted her and put her in the basket. I talked to the guy about the pilot, and he told me which direction she'd gone off in. I then told him I'd have to walk him to the basket. He was a big guy, and I couldn't carry him. It was tough, but I got him there and the helo picked him up.

"Going in I'd seen that there was this huge ravine off to the left and had grabbed chem lights [that give off an eerie green glow when you shake and bend them] and also grabbed an extra flashlight, and after the helo left [while a C-130 remained circling overhead] I listened to see if I could hear anything. I started heading down the cliff [side of the ravine]. It was pitch-black. I had on my boots, TRI-SAR [vest], EMT [medical] pack, regular cliff rescue gear. So I hiked down and left chem lights on high points of the lava field as a trail, and finally after a while I could hear her crying in the distance, 'Don't leave me. Don't leave me.'

"I shouted down in the dark, 'When you see my flashlight, call out,' and then [as he used its beam to search below] she was there. I threw chem lights down to her so I'd know where she was when the flashlight was off and climbed on down [150 feet]. She had second-degree burns and third-degree on her arm, and I knew we couldn't hoist her from there. I told her to rest and we'd have to climb out.

"Her clothes had burned off, and she was cold and sweaty. It was misting and cool. I took off her wet shirt and put my long-sleeved tee on her, and we headed up. I had to carry her partway. She was tiny, like five-three and 110 pounds.

"I pressed her bad arm in toward me so if we hit some rocks it wouldn't be on that side and got her to the top with some breaks because she was tired and dehydrated, and I talked to her. When we were out [of the ravine], I talked to the C-130 on the radio, and they could see the chem light trail, and I told her, 'See, we didn't leave you.'

"I went back to the plane wreck and turned on the strobe and said, 'We'll try to get to the wreckage.' We made it a little more than halfway before the helicopter returned and hoisted her in the basket, and I went back to collect my helmet and other gear and got lifted off on the hook. My boots were completely shredded from the aa."

As he concludes his story, the SAR alarm sounds, two claxons and a PA voice announcing, "Windsurfer on the north shore."

"Looks like you got a good one, Darrell!" He grins at the on-duty swimmer.

"Yeah, if HFD [Honolulu Fire Department] don't get there first," Darrell Leciejewski worries as he gears up.

• • •

In contrast to the remote-seeming Barbers Point Air Station, the Coast Guard station on Sand Island and 14th District Headquarters in the Federal Building on Ala Moana Boulevard occupy the heart of Honolulu's urban waterfront.

The Integrated Support Command on Sand Island is adjacent to the Matson Shipping Terminal and municipal sewage treatment plant and just across the harbor channel from the cruise ship docks. Along with a small boat station, two 378-foot High Endurance Cutters, the *Rush* and the *Jarvis,* are based here, as are two buoy tenders, the *Walnut* and the *Kukui,* a MSST team, and other units, close to a thousand people in all. Additional small boats and cutters are based on Kauai, Maui, and the Big Island.

Local missions include fisheries patrols, port security, escorting military vessels in and out of Pearl Harbor, inspecting cruise ships and cargo vessels, and guarding humpback whales from overeager boat operators getting too close to the sentient giants.

In recent years the Coast Guard has also threatened to arrest environmental protestors, including fifty surfers and kayakers who blocked the 350-foot Hawaii Superferry from making its inaugural landing on Kauai in August 2007. Among the demonstrators' complaints was fear the massive high-speed car ferry would run over humpback whales.

Because of the long distances involved in doing fisheries enforcement, the smaller cutters, the 87s and 110s, form MULEPATs—Multi-Unit Law Enforcement Patrols—with the 225-foot buoy tenders that can supply and refuel them at sea. When I visited Sand Island, one of these patrols had just busted a long-line (multiple hook) tuna fishing boat with bundles of illegal shark fins onboard.

"MULEPATs are more common out here. When we send 110s out with a buoy tender it extends their legs [operational range]," explains Lt. Cdr. Matt Salas, who used to serve on the buoy tender *Walnut*. He's now the District 14 Command Center supervisor.

"Ours is the largest district with the fewest people," he tells me as we wait in the hallway outside the Command Center on the ninth floor of the Federal Building while they sanitize it of classified documents. "Just imagine trying to rescue someone in California with your ambulance in Connecticut."

We enter the long, windowless room with his glassed-in office at one end of it. There are three watch standers on duty by two tiers of consoles facing a six-screen video wall. Off to the left is a TV with CNN playing, and on top of that a black and white security monitor showing the hallway we just left. Paris Hilton saunters across the CNN screen for a news-free moment. Fox News appears on the right quadrant of the media wall squeezing the gray map of the Pacific down to four panels. There are twelve red emblems in the shape of tin cans showing on the map. They are paired off by long connecting lines, like half a dozen extended barbells.

"These are first-pass satellite hits. The first time it hits, the source of the signal can be at either end [of the barbell]," Matt explains. One of the cans changes color from red to yellow off the coast of China. "That hit on a second [satellite] pass [eight hours later] and got a stronger signal," he explains. "The signal indicates an EPIRB—emergency position-indicating radio beacon—off the coast of China. The other end of that signal line is somewhere between Midway and Kwajalein twenty-five hundred miles away. We get a rash of these hits every morning off China. It's the waking giant."

"China generates a lot of signals," the enlisted watch stander behind us agrees.

A week earlier the center's watch floor had been crackling, the bullpen's eight chairs filled and its phones ringing as the staff coordinated the kind of four-thousand-mile long-distance search and rescue case the center is famous for.

In the past the Command Center has diverted an aircraft carrier to pick up a sick fisherman, vectored (directed) ships in to meet an airplane crash-landing in midocean, and dropped a Navy SEAL team by parachute from a Coast Guard C-130 to treat a shark-bite victim in the western Pacific.

This time, July 10, 2007, it was a Panamanian-flagged 420-foot Chinese log carrier, the *Hai Tong No. 7,* with twenty-two on board that went down during a raging typhoon 375 miles northwest of Guam. It was en route from Papua New Guinea to China when it sent out an EPIRB signal that cut off twenty minutes later.

"The EPIRB came in, and we knew there was a storm in the area and had another classified source [the U.S. Navy monitors all sea traffic] saying there was an AIS [ship transponder] in the area, so we let Guam be first responder and we assumed the role of SAR mission coordinator," Chief Warrant Officer Mike Wood explains.

The Coast Guard in Guam issued an immediate broadcast calling on Amver vessels for assistance. Amver, the automated mutual assistance system, is like an Amber Alert for the oceans. Over three thousand commercial ship captains will divert to help sailors in distress, knowing they would do the same for them. The Coast Guard refers to mariners who come to the aid of others as "Good Samaritans."

In this case the container ship *Horizon Falcon,* the bulk carrier *Ikan Bilis,* and four other Good Samaritans responded.

When the *Horizon Falcon* got on scene some forty-eight hours later, it reported an oil slick and rafts of floating logs. The Command Center then dispatched the buoy tender *Sequoia* from Guam, requested air support from the Navy, which launched a P-3 Orion aircraft out of Kadena, Okinawa, and scrambled two of its own C-130s out of Barbers Point.

The P-3 arrived on scene a few hours after the *Horizon Falcon* and spotted three people in orange survival suits floating amid debris. It directed the closest vessels to them and started dropping flares. The *Horizon Falcon* was able to recover two of the survivors out of twenty-foot seas. A three-man crew from the *Falcon* and the first survivor they picked up had to abandon the rescue lifeboat after it was damaged by a breaking wave and climb the ship's pilot ladder to escape. An able-bodied seaman was then harnessed to the ladder and repeatedly submerged by waves before he was able to get a grappling hook onto the second survivor and the two of them were winched clear of the sea. They never reached the third sailor. The *Ikan Bilis* recovered eight more Chinese sailors who'd been tossed around in their survival suits for two days. That left eleven men still unaccounted for.

Lt. JG Lisa Aguirre was one of the Coast Guard pilots from Barbers Point sent to join in the rescue mission.

"Because we're only allowed to fly twelve hours, on the way to Guam we sometimes have to stop at Kwajalein, but the winds were with us, so we got a straight flight to Guam in 11.6 hours," she tells me. "We deadheaded our crew, so we slept in the back [while another crew flew the plane]. Then they refueled us in Guam. We put in maximum fuel [sixty-three hundred pounds]—that took about an hour—and then our crew took over and flew to the search area.

"Once we got there we saw logs and things [oil, floating debris] and Good Samaritan vessels and did a track search about two hundred feet off the water and found six more people, and these big cargo ships recovered them. Three were still alive [after more than three days], but it was too late for the others. We kept searching for four more days but with negative response. We never saw any more people or rafts, just lots of logs."

Still, thirteen lives saved and three bodies recovered out of twenty-two is an impressive accomplishment for a ten-thousand-square-mile search conducted on one of the most remote stretches of our ocean planet.

As far from help as the *Hai Tong No. 7* was that stormy July, that's how far the state of Hawaii will be from help if it gets hit by another major hurricane like Iniki, which devastated the island of Kauai in 1992, or an earthquake, tsunami, or other large-scale disaster. Present emergency response plans include attempts to evacuate tourists and the injured while the rest of the state hunkers down.

"We often talk about what we'll do," says center supervisor Matt Salas. "If things happen here, it won't be like the mainland. We'll have to fend for ourselves. The Department of Defense [with existing military bases in Hawaii] will have to play a major role because we [the Coast Guard] won't be able to surge assets the way we did to New Orleans. We're planning for seventy-two hours or more for Hawaii to be on its own with no airports or functioning harbors."

Kodiak

Alaska doesn't have many airports or functioning harbors unless you count gravel landing strips and fishing docks, but it's huge. If you superimposed a map of the state over a map of the lower forty-eight, its southeast would touch the coast of Georgia, while the end of the Aleutians would reach California. Alaska is four times the size of California but with less than one-fiftieth the population. If caribou could vote, its congressional delegation would have wet noses and antlers.

"It's the most magnificent and terrible place I've ever known," says Rear Adm. Gene Brooks, the Coast Guard's 17th District commander for Alaska. "It has wild vistas that just make your heart hurt to look at them, but also the line between life and death here is very thin."

Along with natural resources including oil, fish, forests, and fresh water, Alaska has one-third of the U.S. coastline, the emptiest, roughest third. Throughout its history as a territory and a state, its coasts and oceans have also been a primary area of responsibility for the U.S. Coast Guard.

As a frontier region, Alaska attracts its share of adventurers, visionaries, and fools: those with big plans, an oversized sense of self-worth, or a willingness to risk all in order to get ahead. Even today commercial fishing remains the most dangerous profession and fishing off Alaska among the riskiest places to practice that profession, a reality reflected in the Discovery Channel TV series *The Most Dangerous Catch*.

Back in 2002, pilot Melissa Rivera was flying an HH-60 Jayhawk out of Cold Bay, Alaska, a forward base, during the red king crab season. She'd just landed after a five-hour patrol when word came that there'd been an explosion on a 160-foot fish-processing vessel named the *Galaxy* and that there were three people in the water.

"It would take two and a half hours to get there, and we were dressed up [in drysuits], so I said, 'We'll take it.' " She and her crew were put on waivers allowing them to fly over six hours, gassed up, and relaunched.

"Halfway there we get word the fire is out of control and there are twenty-six people in the water. So now we have some discussion about what we're going to do, and luckily when we get there, there are three other fishing vessels converging on the scene and a life raft in the water.

"From what we could see there were still six people onboard on the bow and the stern. Also the pilothouse, which was on the stern, was burning. The three people by the pilothouse were standing on stanchions, and the deck was smoking and bubbling around them, and there were twenty-foot seas and there were downed wires and debris around them, so we didn't want to put the basket on the deck.

"We tried to get the basket close to them, but a pyro [explosives] locker blew up just then, so we had to pull back.

"It was a thirty- to forty-foot drop to the water, and we didn't want to ask them to go into the water without survival suits, but we couldn't think of anything else.

"So we put our swimmer, Jason Quinn, in the water. We could see the stern would rise up in these seas where you could see the [propeller] screws, and there was all this oil in the water. The first of them jumped, and the swimmer dragged him into the basket, and we got him up. The cable wrapped around the next survivor after he jumped, but Jason got it off him, and we got all three of them up. One of the three on the bow jumped and was taken up by a fishing boat, and we lifted the next one, and the skipper came up last. He had third-degree burns on his arms where he'd gone into the radio room and made the mayday call on these melting radios and also thrown survival suits to his people. We hoisted another survivor from a Good Samaritan boat who wasn't breathing and did CPR on him all the way to St. Paul. He didn't survive, but twenty-three of the twenty-six survived.

"[Air Station] Kodiak launched two C-130s, and one of them came out to the loran station on St. Paul with a gasbag [large fuel bladder] so we could fly the helo back, but we'd flown nine and a half hours, so we rode back with the C-130 and ended up in Kodiak. We flew again the next day because one of those Good Samaritan crew . . . The storm had gotten worse during the night, and one of them who was wearing a black raincoat fell overboard, and we flew a search for him but never found him."

I'm flying a C-130 Hercules out of Cold Bay in the winter of 2008. The loadmaster has just winched a white Durango SUV onto the plane. It was driven by HH-60 crews during the red crab season and is now being redeployed to St. Paul Island in the middle of the Bering Sea for the opilio, or snow crab, season. Like orcas and eagles, Coast Guard cutters and helicopters follow the fisheries, acting as 911 for "the deadliest catch," while also protecting the resource.

Cold Bay itself is a collection of half a dozen metal airplane hangars and scattered wooden houses on a low rise leading to an open bay facing snow-and-ice-shrouded dragons' teeth of jagged volcanic peaks that mark the end of the five-hundred-mile Alaska peninsula and the beginning of the Aleutian chain.

While there, we dropped off a few Coasties and off-loaded a pallet of supplies including cases of Budweiser for the sixty local residents who maintain the ten-thousand-foot runway that functions as an alternative landing strip for the space shuttle.

When we touched down, a Dolphin helicopter off the cutter *Jarvis* was waiting to meet us with a crewmember on emergency leave. Also waiting is Petty Officer First Class Wil Milam, who will be swapping out with another rescue swimmer. Wil [I forgot to ask if he lost his second *L* on the job] will ride with us to St. Paul, then back to Kodiak and from there head on to Washington, DC, where he's been invited to be one of five armed services representatives at the State of the Union Address thanks to a rescue he pulled off on February 10, 2007.

Wil is a seal-shaped, bullet-headed swimmer with gelled brown hair and lively gray eyes who has worked in Kodiak for the last ten years. At forty-one, he's one of the old men of the nineteen-man Kodiak swimmer shop. Actually it's eighteen men and Jodi Williams, who showed her toughness by reporting back for duty two weeks after giving birth. She'd prepared by doing eight-mile runs while eight months pregnant. Not all Kodiak's swimmers are happy on the job, however.

"I came up here expecting *The Guardian*. I've been here three years and only got wet for the first time last week [hoisting two fishermen]," swimmer Luke Cotturone complains. "Mostly it's medical evacuations. My first SAR case was a woman six months pregnant going into premature labor with vaginal bleeding."

Wil, by contrast, is a happy camper. He's also the station's winter survival camp instructor and an avid hunter and fisherman. He's killed two Kodiak bears, one with an arrow, the other in self-defense.

On the night of his big case the cutter *Mellon,* on which he and his Dolphin 65 crew were deployed, had pulled into Dutch Harbor.

"About 11:45 we get a report of an EPIRB going off forty miles away. It's really snotty out. The wind's blowing sideways, and this storm has knocked out power to Dutch Harbor, and one in the morning we're out there getting buffeted around in thirty- to fifty-knot winds 150 feet off the water and we're getting close. We see a blinking light and a steady light . . . and just then someone yells, 'Flare!' and a flare goes up and glows red in the clouds, and we fly over a raft and I hear the pilot on the ICF [helmet radio line] saying, 'Rescue checklist part one for a swimmer deployment,' and I think, 'Hey, that's me.'

"So we opened the door, and I could see the raft getting tossed around below—like that hurricane scene in *The Guardian*. They lower me [on the hook] and as soon as I get in the water I can't see the raft anymore because of these fifteen- to twenty-foot seas, but you know the helicopter searchlight is lighting it up, and it's twenty degrees off the door, so I swim toward it and pull up onto the raft and instead of survival suits find four Russian guys in street clothes.

"They're speaking broken English, and one of them is already out cold, so I radio up and say, 'I got four guys down here without suits, so deliver the basket as close as possible.' One minute later, the pilot radios, 'We'll send down our aircrew survival suits,' and that sounds like a good idea, so the suits come down on the trail line.

"I'm straddling the raft and go in to pull them down and suddenly feel forty-degree water rushing into my [dry]suit. I figure this plastic T-handle for the zipper must have hung up on the raft ladder, and my [suit] legs are now full of water and I can't lift them, so I get the skipper to help pull me back in. I'm totally soaked and pulling the trail line to the hook where they've attached the drysuits, but two come loose and are floating away, so I jump back in and take off and get them and kick back, and the skipper helps pull me in again, and we finally get the suits on them, and the basket comes down and is jerked away as a wave breaks on it. I get the first [unconscious] guy in it, and now he wakes up and tries to climb out of the basket and gets combative. I push him back down, and up he goes.

"The raft's now floated fifty yards away from me, so I signal for an emergency pickup. I get in the basket, and when they get me in the helicopter I can't get out. They have to pour me out of it, and the suit's so full, there's so much pressure, the water comes gushing out my neck seal. I get on the ICS and tell them I'm soaked.

"They say there's only fifteen minutes of gas left before Bingo [the time they have to leave]. I tell them, 'We can't get those three in the basket on their own, so lower me back down in the basket.' They're like, 'Are you sure, Wil?' because they said my voice was slurred at that point, and I did feel nauseous. So I forced myself to vomit at the door and then went back down and grabbed the first guy to take him in the water and put him in the basket. He wants to sit on the side of it, so I put him down, and he sits up, and I have to punch him in the chest, and then he goes up. I turn and swim ten yards to the raft and signal for the next guy to get into the water, and he's less combative, and we get him up.

"The last guy stands up in the raft and jumps over my head trying to jump into the basket and flips it over 180 degrees in the water. Now the cable is wrapped around the basket. I put him in a cross-chest carry and am trying to untangle the cable from the basket and hook, and a wave breaks over us and he gets lost.

"Then I see him coming back at me, and he jumps me 'cause now he's in full panic mode and I'm just a floating object to climb on, so I do a modified front head hold—I jam the heel of my hand into his chin, then get him in a control cross-chest hold, only I need at least one hand free to work on the cable, and he gets away again. Now he has cable around his neck, and I try to get that free but also have to kick him away. He swims back at me a third time, and I give him another palm to the face and get him under control and in the basket, and up he goes.

"Now I'm supposed to pop the raft [sink it with a knife so it doesn't get spotted again], but forget that. I'm going hypothermic, and I remember the basket coming down, and I think I'm swimming, but the mechanic says I was just sort of pawing the water [he demonstrates fluttering his hands from tucked elbows]. They sort of drug it under me and I dropped into it, and I remember being back in the helicopter and the four fishermen in the back of this small copter and giving them the thumbs-up, and they patted me on the head and gave me the thumbs-up. I don't remember talking to the crew but remember landing and ambulances and fire lights in the rain. Later, in my report, I recalled walking two survivors to the ambulance, and the pilot said, 'No, that was me and the EMT taking you to the ambulance.'

"I remember coming to and not being able to move my arms because I'm wrapped in heated blankets under heat lamps and getting a fourth IV bag of warmed saline solution. What really woke me up was this female voice of a doctor saying, 'Let's get another rectal temperature from Mr. Milam,' and I say, 'No, that's OK.'

" 'How do you feel?' she asked, and I said, 'I need to take a pee,' 'cause I did, and I said, 'I feel wooped.' "

Back on the icy runway in Cold Bay, I talk to the swimmer who's replacing Wil on the *Jarvis*. He's not too impressed. "If it was me it would've been just another SAR case 'cause I wouldn't have broken my zipper."

We take off with Wil and two other passengers, SAR sleds, and the Dodge Durango in the back. I'm standing on the large glassed-in flight deck with five of the Herc's seven crewmembers including pilots Craig Breitung and Steve Axley and navigator David Boschee, who guided a recent C-130 flight over the North Pole to publicize the Coast Guard's increased "Arctic domain awareness," in response to global warming.

"Show me anywhere where you can prove sea level has actually risen or you can say humans had anything to do with it," Steve grouses. I mention that I've been reporting on climate change for fifteen years and the science is pretty robust. Most scientists agree humans are loading the atmosphere with greenhouse gases that heat up the planet.

"Yeah, scientists also say we're related to apes," he responds with an effective conversation stopper.

The big four-engine plane's cargo bay is about the size of a large railroad boxcar with a drop-down ramp in back. It's the Coast Guard's all-purpose aircraft.

Two months earlier, a C-130 dropped a rescue raft right on top of Kodiak fisherman Alan Ryden as he was being tossed about the Gulf of Alaska by twenty-foot seas and fifty-knot winds. His boat had flipped, and he'd been in the water most of the night with only his survival suit and a life ring. After scrambling into the raft, he was later picked up by another fishing boat. It was a "pretty good drop," everyone agrees.

Today's flight is a "log," or logistics mission. We fly out over the Bering Sea above the clouds. Approaching St. Paul in the Pribilof Islands, we can see a towering weather front moving over the small island toward the airstrip. We fly past its snowed-in Aleut town of five hundred, two factory fishing trawlers, and a tall broadcast tower before leaning right toward the runway that looks like a black asterisk in a white cloud bank.

"You're going down to 1,800 feet," Steve announces. "I can see the island popping through . . . ceiling down to 850 feet, 800 feet . . ."

"We're going to do a missed approach," Craig announces as we pull up and veer away before circling back out over the ocean. He spots some ice on his window wiper and asks someone to look back at one of the black dots on the wings to see if they're streaking white, which could indicate icing. They're not.

"You've got about an hour to monkey around up here before Bingo for thirty," Scott Lynch, the bald, walrus-mustached radioman, informs him.

"It's clear here but blowing over the airport," Craig says as we hit some blue sky. "I guarantee I'm not landing with a tailwind," he adds with grim humor I don't get just then. "It's always socked in here," he tells me.

Two days before, an eleven-year-old girl had a sledding accident; she broke her leg and had a head wound that wouldn't stop bleeding. Because the civilian air ambulance couldn't get in, Kodiak sent a C-130 to take her to the hospital in Anchorage.

A hole emerges out of the surrounding clouds. We take another run at the airstrip, landing through blowing white mist onto what's now two inches of runway snow. As we turn and taxi, I ask Craig about a C-130 he commanded that crashed here in July of 2006. Its central wing-box and tail assembly are back at the Kodiak hangar getting ready to be used as replacement parts.

"Typically, landing with a ten-knot tailwind on a sixty-five-hundred-foot runway is not done in the lower forty-eight, and I got some negative feedback, and I'm a little bitter," he says. "Up here in Alaska, people land with thirty-knot tailwinds. It had nothing to do with what happened. Both props on one side malfunctioned, and we controlled it, but the brakes didn't stop us, and rather than have the aircraft go off the runway I put it in reverse and spun to the left."

The nose and underbelly were crunched, and a propeller tore off when a wing hit the ground, but it was still what's called a good crash in that everyone walked away unharmed.

They shut down the plane, and we climb out and watch a mile-high wall of gray cloud front moving across the far side of the field.

Chuck Thompson, a tall chief warrant officer in a tan Carhartt coat, glasses, and a gray cowboy hat that's actually an OSHA-approved hard hat, is waiting by his truck to take me to his loran station while they off-load the Durango. I climb up into the cab, and we drive off across the snowy island toward the 625-foot-tall long-range navigation radio antennae. A technological breakthrough during World War II, these days loran acts as a backup for GPS satellite navigation systems.

Chuck's is one of three isolated Coast Guard loran stations in Alaska. The others are at Port Clarence, near Nome, and on Attu, at the far end of the Aleutians. He tells me he has fifteen people working for him doing one-year tours because it's considered arduous duty. We drive across fields of blowing snow with dead brown puff weeds sticking through the top till we reach the one-story white station downrange from the broadcast tower. He plugs in his truck to an electrical post so the battery doesn't freeze and gives me a twelve-minute tour. They recently added a wing of simple, cleanly appointed rooms for the HH-60 crews to stay in when they forward deploy here. Snow is banked up against the windows. The place reminds me of Palmer Station, Antarctica, where I once spent seven weeks. My favorite touch is the tiki thatch overhangs and beach murals in the recreation room.

We return to the airport in a tracked Ford F350 pickup truck. St. Paul is world famous for its colonies of fur seals, puffins, and reindeer, descendants of the small herd "Hell Roaring" Mike Healy brought back from Siberia in 1891. I wish I could stay a week to see the wildlife. I'd hate to stay a year.

Back on the runway, the Hercules is ready and waiting for me, as the weather is closing in again. We take off into a sudden blowing snowstorm. I can barely make out the landing lights off to our right. Craig starts to accelerate, following his own tire tracks through the snow. "Here we go," he says.

"Nothing like taking off into a bowl of milk," Steve responds.

We lift off and keep climbing till we break out of the clouds at around three thousand feet.

"With snow showers you never know if you'll ice up and get stuck there," Craig says, relaxing.

I ask what determined that we could take off like we just did.

"It was a real scoosh [as in "scoosh powder," not good]," he explains, "but the lights are what, a hundred feet apart?"

"Two hundred," Steve says.

"Right. So you need a quarter-mile visibility to take off, so if you can count eight lights you can take off."

"How many lights could you see?"

"Eight," he deadpans.

"Hey, Craig, it's going in a book." Steve grins. "I'd've said ten."

Two hours later, we land back in Kodiak, taxiing past a few cars waiting by the runway crossing before rolling up to the hangars where big front-grader snowplows are scraping at the ice with their night-lights on. It's 5:00 p.m., slippery and dark.

I'd arrived on the island four days earlier at 8:30 in the morning when it was twelve degrees Fahrenheit and pitch-black. Sunrise was expected by 9:45 and sunset at 4:30, though with winter solstice past, the days were getting longer.

Kodiak is the second-largest island in the United States after Hawaii's Big Island, but unlike the Big Island it's still 98 percent wilderness, with a ruggedly stunning landscape of snow, ice, Sitka spruce forest, white-capped mountain ridges full of wild goats, ocean cliffs striated with frozen waterfalls, and dark sand driftwood beaches, some with good surfing breaks. Fourteen thousand people live here, including some thousand active duty Coast Guard personnel and their two thousand dependents. Three thousand is also the number of Kodiak brown bears [grizzlies] on the island.

Along with the fishing town of Kodiak and the Coast Guard base, there are half a dozen villages with populations of between fifty and two hundred, a winter camp for Navy SEALs, a Star Wars rocket launch site for testing ways of shooting down incoming tax dollars, and cold North Pacific waters brimming with life. The main ways on and off Kodiak are by state ferry and airplane.

A week earlier, a Piper Navajo Chieftain crashed after takeoff from the airport runway, killing six of ten people on board. The nose baggage door had come open just after takeoff, as had happened in two earlier Alaskan crashes involving this same make of aircraft. The pilot, Robin Starrett, was a retired Coast Guard helicopter pilot from the air station.

I head over to the base that sprawls under the white bulk of Old Woman Mountain. At twenty-one thousand acres, it's the largest Coast Guard facility in the United States. About half the property is inside its fence line, including the air station, cutter pier, fish school, housing units, commissary, clinic, gym, pool, and two main roads, one of which crosses the runway/taxiway. Big tractors are blowing snow off the runway as I arrive at the hangars. One huge hangar houses four C-130 Hercules transport planes, the other four Jayhawk and four Dolphin helicopters.

The cargo pier on Womens Bay is homeport to the 225-foot buoy tender *Spar*, the 282-foot cutter *Alex Haley*, and the recently arrived 378-foot High Endurance Cutter *Munro*. On Christmas Eve, eighty-five-knot winds pushed the *Munro* hard into the pier, breaking some stanchions and camels (giant ship bumpers), so the pier and cutter are now undergoing minor repairs.

Lt. Steve Bonn from the air station invites me on an HH-60 flight. Another 60 pilot, Lt. Brian McLaughlin, tells me how he recently rescued three men, a woman, and their small dog after they abandoned a sinking fishing boat between Kodiak and the mainland.

Two weeks before that, he flew to Hinchinbrook Island with some state troopers to recover the body parts of a fisherman who'd fallen off his boat and drowned. When the body came ashore, a bear had eaten it. Hunters found what was left.

The body of one of the fishermen lost in Alaska's famous *La Conte* SAR case had also washed ashore and been eaten by a bear.

We fly out over the fishing harbor, where dozens of boats are getting ready for the local tanner crab season.

Our 60 and a smaller 65 will be doing a flyby past the local high school at the end of this afternoon's memorial service for the dead Piper pilot, Robin Starrett. Some five hundred people from the community are at the service, including a Coast Guard lieutenant who's coordinating the flyby with the station command center by cell phone. He reports it's going to go on a half hour longer than expected.

While waiting, our helicopter practices touch-and-go landings on the gravel airstrip at the small native village of Ouzinkie on Spruce Island. Both Steve Bonn and second pilot Scott Jackson used to fly for the Army's 82nd Airborne aviation brigade. I ask how things are different for them now.

"Different missions, different kinds of flying," Scott says from the right front seat. "We fly in worse weather, but we don't get shot at or fly in sandstorms."

As we take a steep turn above the ocean, I look down and see a fishing boat stacked with crab pots, heading out to sea (on my next flight I'll spot a couple of gray whales). We get word the service will be delayed another half hour.

"Gotta take the boring with the terrifying," Steve notes philosophically.

We fly over Anton Larsen Bay, above a broken trail in its white frozen surface where a 50-foot boat tried to break through the ice a few days ago and holed its bottom. A helicopter put a swimmer down on the ice with a water pump, and they'd managed to keep the boat afloat and get it in to shore. The memorial service is now finishing up.

We circle land's end just north of town and begin parade flying with the 65 one and a half rotor widths behind us and to our right. We fly low past the school, where several hundred mourners have gathered outside the main doors. We circle around for a second flyby before breaking off into "loose screws," regular formation flying about five rotor widths apart.

We head inland over spectacular snow-sheathed spruce forests and deep mountain canyons that give meaning to the term "God's country," then back to the station over the harbor's large commercial fishing fleet.

Keeping the fishing fleet safe and everyone obeying the rules is a big part of what the Coast Guard does on the last frontier, where good fisheries management has helped maintain seemingly healthy stocks of edible marine wildlife including pollock, salmon, halibut, herring, mackerel, and crab. Pollock, however, the largest fishery left in North America, has been in an unexplained decline for several years.

"Fisheries in Alaska is a major part of law enforcement up here. Down in the lower forty-eight it's mostly homeland security, and fish unfortunately are put aside," says Lt. Doug Watson, the executive officer of the North Pacific Regional Fisheries Training Center, the largest of the Coast Guard's five fish schools, located around the third and fourth floors of the commissary building's atrium. Its staff of fourteen trains six hundred to eight hundred students a year on how to do effective boardings and inspections, including boarding of catcher-processor ships—floating fish factories that can turn hundreds of thousands of pounds of living wildlife into frozen fish sticks each day and often stay at sea for years on end, changing out fuel, crews, and product. The day I visit the school, they're finishing a three-day course for a class of fourteen.

Down on the fishing docks, I join Marine Science Technician Third Class Rob Davis and Marine Science Technician Second Class Allie Rogers from the Kodiak Marine Safety Office inspecting a couple of boats about to head out after tanner crab. A few boats not heading out are covered in six inches of ice or fouled with six-foot growths of seaweed.

It's cold and snowing as we climb aboard the *Linnea*, a 58-foot crab boat that's seen better days. We head down a narrow plywood passage and wooden ladder to the engine room, where two mates are working on getting it ready.

"Safety compliance is what we're about," Rob explains. "It includes inspecting fire extinguishers and the life raft to see it's been serviced, is the right size for the crew, and has its hydrostatic [water contact] release up to date. We check for an EPIRB and make sure it's NOAA registered and its battery and hydrostatic releases are good. We check the immersion [survival] suits to make sure they're good, the high-water alarms, and flares, of course."

Capt. Nathan Clark, a slim but grizzled character with a gray beard who's been fishing these waters for twenty-nine years, arrives and leads Rob up a couple of narrow steps from the main deck to the pilothouse. He wonders what good an inspection is if he keeps getting boarded at sea. "I got you guys and Fish and Game and the [state] trooper coming down, and then in Dutch Harbor I get boarded again when I'm pulling my pots."

"We're trying to work it out," Rob sympathizes. "If you have the inspection sticker in the window, even if they board you they shouldn't have to do another inspection."

"Maybe there's just something about me that attracts trouble." Captain Nate grins wryly before going down to the engine room to pull a wire that sets off the high-water alarm and wheelhouse warning light that shows Rob they work.

We retreat to the galley by the open deck, where the stove is turned up red hot and Allie has unrolled and is inspecting the last of four immersion suits. Rob hands the captain his paperwork—two pages, one confirming his voluntary compliance and one a list of contact numbers his wife can call if he goes missing.

Back on the dock the snow's picked up. Another boat, the *New Dawn*, is being inspected by another safety team from their seven-person shop.

The safety inspections are all voluntary. Only the king crab boats are required to have a Coast Guard safety sticker, and that's an Alaska state law, not a federal requirement.

Although commercial fishing is the most dangerous profession in the United States, the industry has resisted mandatory safety standards like those required for cargo ships, cruise ships, and charter boats. As a result of industry pressure, Congress has failed to give the Coast Guard authority to impose new safety rules, at least since 1988, when survival suits, fire extinguishers, and life rafts became mandatory on fishing boats, resulting in hundreds of lives saved. The Coast Guard would like to require that fishing boats also be stable and seaworthy. It recently found a way to get around congressional inaction by reclassifying some large factory trawlers as seafood processors, thus subjecting them to their tougher commercial vessel standards. Unfortunately they had only inspected twelve out of sixty when one of the not-yet-inspected trawlers, the Seattle-based *Alaska Ranger,* suddenly flooded and sank on April 23, 2008, resulting in five more fishermen's deaths.

There are bald eagles on the seawall by the docks as we leave, and one atop a light pole a block away, and more than a dozen hanging out like seagulls on the roof, crane, and big plastic totes of the fish processing plant down the street. I spot one eagle walking around on the ground below a sign reading FISH PARTS ONLY—NO NONFISH PROTEIN OR FOREIGN MATERIAL.

When I start taking pictures, a guy comes out and tells me I'm on private property and have to leave. I know why he's upset.

A few days earlier, someone backed a big truckload of fish guts out of the Ocean Beauty Seafood processing plant without covering it up. Fifty bald eagles swarmed the truck, and twenty drowned in the offal. The remaining slimed birds were flown to Anchorage for cleaning, where most are now recovering.

On the way back to base, I ask Public Affairs Specialist Third Class Richard Brahm, who's giving me a ride, to stop so I can take a picture of a roadside tree with another nine eagles roosting in it. A raven on the other side of the road starts cawing, so I take his picture, too.

Along with SAR and fisheries enforcement, foundering ships is another huge challenge going back to when the revenue cutter *Bear* rescued a storm-tossed whaling fleet off Point Barrow in 1888. Today commercial shipping across the Pacific uses the Great Circle Route through Unimak Pass in the Aleutians.

In July 2006, the giant car carrier *Cougar Ace* lost ballast control and rolled eighty degrees onto its side with 4,700 new 2007 Mazdas on board. The Coast Guard rescued its twenty-three crewmembers, although a salvage worker would later die while righting the vessel. It was then towed to the island of Unalaska and from there to Portland, Oregon.

Earlier, in December 2004, the Malaysian cargo ship *Selendang Ayu* broke up and grounded on Unalaska.

I remember the national news coverage and TV footage showing the ship split in two with close to four hundred thousand gallons of leaking bunker fuel and diesel and millions of pounds of soybeans washing onto the cold rocky shore, killing birds, fish, and otters.

What was not as well reported was how, along with being an ecological disaster, the breakup of the *Selendang Ayu* was also a search and rescue disaster.

I meet former helicopter mechanic turned truck driver Brian Lickfield at Henry's restaurant in downtown Kodiak. After twenty years in the service he's grown a closely trimmed retirement beard that, along with a high, curly mop of reddish hair and full face, gives him a somewhat monkish appearance. We sit down in a booth below a shadow box containing a red king crab roughly five feet across from claw tip to claw tip.

I ask him about some of his service history, and he tells me of the time flying over Lake Erie one winter that his crew watched a guy on a four-wheeler go through the ice.

"There are these ice fishers nearby who decide to help, and we're right there hovering and trying to wave them away, but these guys have to form a chain lying flat on the ice, and then they go through, of course, so now we got four guys to save instead of one. The swimmer went down, and they were all recovered."

He gets a bit edgier when I ask about the *Selendang Ayu* case. The 738-foot cargo ship had lost its engine and drifted for thirteen hours before calling the Coast Guard. A tug had taken it under tow, but then the towline broke and the ship was adrift again. Brian's Jayhawk flew from Cold Bay to Dutch Harbor at 7:00 A.M., where they met another 60 out of Kodiak.

"We didn't get [a full tank of] gas 'cause we wanted to stay light and pick up the crew, but we get out there and they keep us on scene for two hours. This freighter is just not prepared. They'd set anchor, but it was dragging, and they were three or four miles from land when we started hoisting and maybe half that distance when we were done. Crewmen are wandering around with their luggage, and apparently they didn't want them all to leave the ship. We finally pick up nine and take them to the *Alex Haley* in twenty- to thirty-foot seas and follow it into a trough and hoist these nine down in the basket, and the 6021 [the other Jayhawk] picked up another nine. We landed on the beach together and transferred the passengers and took them to Dutch Harbor and thought that was it for us.

"Only a chip light went on in their helicopter that indicated there might be metal in the gear box, so Command Center says we have to go airborne again. We weren't happy, but we sucked it up and took off around 5:30 that night.

"We get back out, and now the freighter is aground and the hull is breached and there's oil in the water and it's sinking on a rocky shoal, and now they want to get off. There's radio communications between the 65 [the cutter-deployed Dolphin] and the *Haley* about getting permission to start hoisting, but we're bigger and can do it in one hoist, so they circle around to watch us and the ship, which is in a precarious position.

"The waves are getting bigger and breaking on the bow, and we're putting the basket on the deck, but they're all huddled in this alcove under the bow and nobody will move to get in the basket with these thirty-foot waves breaking, so Aaron Bean, our swimmer, is sent down to get things moving.

"He went in the basket and walked the first guy over and then the second. Then a big wave broke and washed Aaron down the side of the ship, and I watched him jump back up and get the next guy, and they're now realizing how critical time is. Another wave knocks Aaron down, and it's one wave after another. We got six hoists done, and I saw we were too close to the boom, and I told [pilot] Doug Watson to back out, 'cause I'm his eyes and ears.

"So we back down, and he says, 'Let's finish this up.' We had three hoists left to do, the captain, Aaron, and this crewmember. I have this next crewmember halfway up, and [pilot] Dave Neel, who's flying left [side], spots this big wave coming and says we need to go up. Doug's pulling power, and we got 105, 110 feet above the ship, and I finish the hoist and am pulling this guy in, and Dave is talking about the size of this wave, and I hear this smacking sound as it hits the ship and then, like a blowhole, this water had nowhere to go but up and *whoosh*—it's like a fire hose is hitting me in the cabin. The guys in the 65 said they couldn't see us for three or four seconds. We were totally engulfed in this rogue wave, and I'm screaming, '*Up! Up! Up!*' and hear one engine flame out and could hear it shutting down—we just lost engine one. Over the course of five or six seconds they're trying to fly us out, with alarms and whistles going off, and it got crazy 'cause number one is shut down and the rotor head is slowing down, losing RPMs, and a few seconds later I hear number two shut down, and I'm on the gunner's belt and know what comes next and start to panic as we fall and *bang*, hit the ship. I knew by the bang we'd hit the ship, and I grabbed on to the door handle and hung on, and a second later we fall over and hit the water.

"We rolled, and it was dark and cold, and I never left the door. So now I'm upside down underwater in the dark, and everyone was losing their mind. I tried to swim out two or three times but couldn't and realized I'm tethered to the helicopter, so I reach back and popped the clasp on the gunner's belt, and then I came up and surfaced and I'm in shock, amazed I survived, and the 6020 [his helicopter] is upside down with no tail pylon, it must have gone when we hit the ship, and I can't believe I've lived through a helicopter crash, and it's cold, thirty-eight-degree water, and my hands and face are going numb, though I have on my drysuit and fleece underneath.

"I see the ship, but it's too high to climb with no pilot ladder, and I can see mountaintops in the distance but not the beach because of these big waves, but I know the beach is at least half a mile away. Now suddenly I feel depressed, realizing I'm going to die right here, but I'm at least going to try to make it anyway, so I start swimming. It's harder than it should be, so then I remember to blow up my vest, and it inflates and I'm swimming again but also choking on JPS [jet fuel] and getting pummeled by these waves. Then I see Dave Neel forty to fifty feet away, and out of the corner of my eye I see two other people.

"Then I see the 65 coming in to pick up Dave, and about twelve or fifteen minutes later while I'm still, well, more struggling than swimming, it comes back and puts the basket down next to me, and I get in, and as I'm going up in the basket I look back and see this eight-hundred-foot-long ship on the rocks and the helicopter still floating upside down a few hundred yards away, just beginning to sink now, and I see debris and a couple of people still in the water, and I get inside the cabin and plug in the ICS cord.

"Dave is in back, and Doug Watson comes up next. Dave had gotten out quick, but Doug had gotten hung up on his seat belt and was under for two minutes and had used up his whole air bottle [a small emergency compressed air system strapped to his vest].

"So we'd all survived (the aircrew). The fourth victim had gotten into the bunker oil, and he wouldn't get in the basket but stayed hanging on to it, and so they lifted him that way and got him into the door 150 feet up and realized the cable was twisted around his neck, and he'd been hoisted by his neck!

"I saw [mechanic] Greg Gibbons struggle to free him, and he was covered, head to toe, black with oil, and I put him on his side so if he's still alive he won't swallow the oil. A few minutes later, he starts kicking and screaming. Greg is looking for this other guy lost in the oil, but with the surf conditions he couldn't find him, and I scream at Greg, *"He's alive!"* so they quit the search and head back to Dutch Harbor because this guy is in critical condition.

"The flight back was horrifying because we're flying through this blizzard, these snow squalls, all these big guys in this 65 with this [injured] guy's screaming going on and on, and I think we're going to hit the mountains.

"We land, and they take this guy to the hospital, and his body core temperature is something like seventy-eight degrees and he's covered in oil, but he survived. Funny thing is, at that point no one knew we'd crashed, so they'd left this truck for us, and we drove ourselves to the clinic.

"It took about another hour for the ship to break in half, and Aaron said he asked the captain what would happen and he'd said it would break and then he'd seen it bend and spark and they're off there [floating away] on the bow.

"The 65 refueled [on the *Alex Haley*] and headed back and hoisted them [swimmer Aaron Bean and the ship's captain] from two hundred feet up. Greg said he had orange cable in his hand, which is the last twenty feet of cable. Aaron said the basket came down sideways like a kite it was blowing so hard.

"We thought he was dead and they thought we were dead, and later when we went from the clinic to the hotel there was Aaron, alive, and we gave him a huge hug.

"So that 60 went down and six out of ten people were lost, but we [the flight crew] made it. I can only attribute that to our training, to practicing to where it [escape from a helicopter upside down in cold, dark water] becomes instinctual. Later they estimated that rogue wave was over sixty feet high."

He pauses.

"You know, something like that happening, it changes you." At that moment he reminds me of Joe Ruggiero, who survived the suicide boat attack off Iraq that killed Nate Bruckenthal. He has that same kind of nervous post-traumatic intensity of feeling.

He tells me how he'd recently bought sandwich makings to take home to his wife and left the grocery bags in the back of his truck and went into the video store, and when he came out the ravens had trashed the bags, bread rolls were all over the street, and half a pound of cheese was gone. "I called my wife and was so upset, and she said, 'Brian, listen to yourself. You're shouting at a bunch of birds.' "

I call Public Affairs Specialist Richard Brahm, who offers to pick me up from the restaurant. On the way over, he almost gets into a collision when the car in front of him hits a deer. The deer slides sideways on the icy road, picks itself up, and bounds off into the forest, apparently unharmed.

It's hard not to love a frontier like Alaska. It's also hard to appreciate that even a vast and seemingly pristine frontier like Alaska is vulnerable to human disruption from activities such as industrial overfishing or the 1989 *Exxon Valdez* oil spill that covered Prince William Sound and its coastline in eleven million gallons of crude oil, killing millions of fish, half a million seabirds, thousands of sea otters, hundreds of seals and bald eagles, twenty killer whales, and even a few oil-soaked grizzlies. The marine environment, measured by rates of productivity and reproduction, has never fully recovered, nor have local fishing and Native Alaskan communities. Twenty years later, oil residues can still be found in many shoreline areas simply by digging a foot or two below the surface.

Capt. Andy Berghorn, CO of Kodiak Air Station, was there.

"We did a lot of overflights trying to gain the big picture. It was a frustrating time, and we realized we didn't have the resources to handle something that big. It was hard to see one of the most beautiful places on earth destroyed. You don't think it'll happen in your own backyard and then it does. We weren't prepared."

Today, along with plans for new mineral mining, gas pipelines, and offshore oil drilling, Alaska is facing an even larger threat to terrestrial and marine habitat, coastal regions, and native cultures from fossil-fuel-fired climate change.

Still, the Coast Guard's role as guardian and steward of our public seas is not what it was before the changes wrought by 9/11. Nor, despite claiming a maritime strategy for safety, security, and stewardship, is it clear that the service's historic commitment to environmental protection is going to be fully restored or expanded anytime soon.

CHAPTER 10

Duck Scrubbers

"There's less environmental work. We're energized and challenged by what's most urgent and compelling [homeland security], so some stuff has been pushed back more than we wished."

—Vice Commandant Vivien Crea

"The Exxon Valdez *defined the first ten years of my career, and 9/11 is defining the next ten."*

—Lt. Cdr. Claudia Gelzer, Boston Chief of Port Operations

Oil-covered birds like you've seen on TV look even worse in real life. Not the dead ones so much, except when a gull's ripped a small floating grebe open in the water and is pulling at its toxic guts.

Hong Kong–based shipping executives don't have to use ships that burn heavy bunker fuel, the cancer-causing dregs of the petroleum process, but they do. After you've refined aviation fuel and gasoline and kerosene, diesel and heating oil, you're left with bunker fuel. The only thing you can process after that is roofing tar. Of course, cleaner fuels would prove marginally more expensive, and U.S. consumers might have to pay a penny extra for their tube socks or Chinese-made children's toys.

Besides, with modern navigation charting, radar, Vessel Traffic Systems, trained crews, and experienced pilots, it's not like a large container ship is going to ram into the San Francisco Bay Bridge in the fog and spill fifty-three thousand gallons of that nasty stuff into the water. Which, of course, is exactly what happened on Wednesday morning, November 7, 2007, when the 901-foot *Cosco Busan* hit the base of one of the bridge towers.

Investigators were left shaking their heads in amazement as they tracked the "human error" involved. Coast Guard controllers at the VTS on Yerba Buena Island tried to warn the ship's pilot he was running parallel to the bridge and heading for trouble, but he claimed otherwise. Two minutes later, he took a sharp turn and hit the bridge. Unlike air traffic controllers, the Coast Guard's VTS operators did not have the authority to overrule the pilot or the ship's Chinese captain and order them to change course. A new law has since been proposed to give them that authority.

There's also the question of scale. "Ships are so large now that you don't need an oil tanker for a major spill. Fuel can be a major spill," says Adm. Craig Bone, commander of the 11th District, which includes California. The *Cosco Busan* was carrying twenty-five hundred large shipping containers. There are now ships that carry over ten thousand. Yet giant cargo ships, unlike oil heavy tankers, aren't required to have a tug escort when they enter or leave San Francisco Bay, even on the foggiest of days.

I'm sitting by the dock of the bay—that's what Otis Redding called the Berkeley Municipal Pier in his famous song. Only now it smells like a gas station. On the rock pile below me a surf scoter—a diving duck—is using the bottom of its red bill to preen its oil-blackened feathers. It shakes its head and carefully repeats the process for the half hour I'm there. When I make too sudden a move, it flaps its wings like it's going to flee into the water, where it would likely die of hypothermia, its natural insulation ruined by the oil. I'll see dozens more oiled birds today: scoters, grebes, gulls, a ruddy duck, and cormorants.

The Berkeley marina behind me has a big oily sheen. "Rainbows of oil" is a misnomer. Gasoline leaves rainbow sheens. Bunker fuel leaves green and brown streaks and smudges like marbled meat gone bad. It leaves floating tar balls and disks and globular curlicue pieces and concentrations of hard, asphalt-like toxic chips.

It's been raining throughout the afternoon. The experts aren't sure whether this will help the cleanup efforts. There are nineteen agencies, including the Coast Guard, involved. The oil has spread out through the Golden Gate to Ocean Beach and north to Point Reyes National Seashore. Horseshoe Cove by Surf Station Golden Gate is badly fouled. Angel Island and Alcatraz are a mess.

The western grebe lies exhausted on a rock in the Richmond Marina, where I now live. Stained black, its red eyes seem to burn at me with anger and reproach. I know that's anthropomorphic thinking. As humans we understand that we're killing them, whereas they have no idea what's killing them. The next day they boom off my neighborhood wetland to keep the oil out, though some has already gotten into the salt marsh.

Fifty-three thousand gallons isn't even a large spill compared to dozens of historic disasters like the eight million gallons released in and around the Gulf of Mexico after Hurricane Katrina or the eleven million gallons from the *Exxon Valdez* in 1989 that devastated the pristine waters and wildlife of Alaska's Prince William Sound. Shortly after the *Cosco Busan* spill, the Black Sea and the Korean peninsula are hit by massive oil spills in orders of magnitude larger.

As darkness falls, I encounter a young couple near my home, Amber Kirst and Scott Egan. She's walking below the rocks in the pouring rain with her white pants oil-stained at the ankles, wearing a protective rubber glove and carrying a bag full of oiled litter and dead crabs. "We've got a live crab, too. He was in a Cheetos bag," she tells me, climbing up the rocks to the pathway. "We drove down from Lodi to volunteer, but they said they'd get back to us. It's an hour-and-a-half drive. We needed to do something."

She shows me the little Cheetos crab, with its dark shell. It's still alive. "Should I put it back? Is it too oiled for them to feed on?" She looks at the hundreds of shorebirds hunting in the exposed mudflats and floating just beyond. "It's all so depressing," she concludes before climbing back down to pick up more oiled litter.

We build our homes in floodplains; we move millions of tons of goods and fuel through marine sanctuaries; we continue to burn a product that, used as directed, overheats our planet. Amber and Scott came from Lodi. They needed to do something. We all do.

I'm disappointed that the Coast Guard didn't do more. I believe if it had been a terrorist who had put a gaping hole in the side of that ship, their response would have been much more robust. It turns out that they're over a year behind in their review of response plans for spills from large cargo vessels like this one. They're eighteen years behind on writing final regulations for the Oil Spill Prevention Act of 1990.

On January 11, 2008, outside reviewers commissioned by the Coast Guard publish a 130-page report on the initial response to the spill, detailing what went wrong and what worked. Among the things they find is that a lack of oil-spill training by the first Coast Guard responders contributed to their inability to do an accurate assessment of the spill size. Five of the sector's six marine casualty investigators were not fully qualified, according to a later finding, and the Coast Guard failed to get a state investigator who was qualified out to the damaged ship in a timely manner. The Vessel Traffic System and the Incident Command Center on Yerba Buena Island were also not working together or using the same radio frequencies. The Coast Guard report includes a time line on the response. I have my own time line that reflects the lack of urgency I sensed.

When I heard the news that a ship had hit the Bay Bridge that morning of November 7, I called my public affairs contact to confirm that my interview with Admiral Bone was still on. I was assured the problem was being handled at the sector level and the admiral would be available. At two o'clock I had a two-and-a-half-hour interview with Craig Bone, who before taking over the 11th District had been assistant commandant for prevention (now called assistant commandant for marine safety, security, and stewardship), considered the top regulatory and environmental job in the Coast Guard. At six-one, slim, with silver hair and copper-rimmed glasses, he exudes confidence and authority. I ask about that morning's ship collision with the bridge.

"Helicopters are up. Cutters are on the water. A unified command is operating. This is a perfect example of how the ICS [Incident Command System] works as a way to flow forces and organize everyone to do effective business," he assures me.

Of course, it only works if you have the right information, resources, and trained people on the water. Even as we spoke, the ship was reporting that 140 gallons of fuel had spilled from its 8:30 A.M. collision. The first Coast Guard vessel (from Yerba Buena Island between the bridge's two spans) took forty-three minutes to arrive on scene. Despite mariners' reports of extensive oil on the water, the Coast Guard didn't realize it was actually a 58,000-gallon spill—an estimate later revised down to 53,500—until 4:49 P.M., when they finished testing the fuel tanks. The Captain of the Port, William Uberti, didn't notify the public or city of San Francisco about its actual size until nine that night, having earlier turned away an offer of help from a San Francisco fireboat. With fog and mechanical issues, the first Coast Guard helicopter wasn't airborne and assessing the situation until 4:40 that afternoon.

Admiral Bone points out that maritime accidents like this didn't stop after 9/11. "The port industry didn't stop growing, and every port grew, and demand for offshore resources is growing, and worldwide shipyards are all booked up [building more ships]. Meanwhile we [the Coast Guard] shifted assets to security, and we failed to keep pace on the safety and environmental side. We couldn't provide it at the same level. Also, you have this inability to take people off for advanced training, so our inspection and [maritime accident] investigation expertise has suffered." It's something that deeply troubles him and that he'll speak frankly about during congressional field hearings called by California representatives outraged by the spill response.

The Coast Guard's program for response training in places like San Francisco Bay has been cut back in recent years, as has the state's Oil Spill Prevention and Response staff and the size of the private contractors' standby crews.

On the ship safety side of the equation, much of the U.S. shipyard work that Coast Guard inspectors used to oversee, from the laying of keels to the installation of cables, electrical systems, machinery, fuel tanks, and decking, is now done by private classification societies with the Coast Guard doing general oversight. U.S. ship designs are still run through the Coast Guard's design center, and the Coast Guard still carefully reviews cargoes and safety systems for oil and other hazardous materials coming into U.S. ports, in part because they represent an ongoing security threat.

On September 10, 2002, a Coast Guard boarding team heard noises below the deck of the Liberian-flagged freighter *Palermo Senator* docked in New York. They then measured and got a nuclear hit, a strong radiation signal from the vessel. The ship's manifest, they quickly discovered, included rugs from Pakistan and Afghanistan. The president was due in the city for the first anniversary of 9/11. The ship was immediately ordered offshore, where a NEST—Nuclear Emergency Support Team—from the Department of Energy and a contingent of Navy SEALs joined the Coast Guard. After lots of excitement they figured out that the ship was carrying undeclared pottery and tiles. Ocean water lacks the radioisotopes commonly found in soils and clay, so background radiation, particularly from fired ceramics, will stand out strongly on a vessel. The suspicious noise below deck turned out to be a pipe that had been rolling around.

Two years later, in the summer of 2004, everyone got scared again when the Department of Agriculture received an e-mail saying there was a "biological agent" on the *Rio Puelo,* a container ship bringing Argentine lemons to Canada. The e-mail even gave the number of the containers that the bioagent was allegedly being smuggled in. An Incident Command Center was established for the Coast Guard, DHS, FBI, and others while the ship was held off the coast of New Jersey for nine days. Eventually, after a Coast Guard boarding team was placed on the ship and a battery of biohazard tests conducted, it was escorted into Newark, where its million-pound cargo was fumigated for anthrax and incinerated. Apparently someone figured that if all you have is lemons, make smoke. It's now thought the e-mail may have been sent by one of the grower's Latin American competitors.

Also, of course, right after 9/11 the Captain of the Port of Boston forbade liquefied natural gas ships from entering the harbor for fear they might be used as weapons of mass destruction. "An LNG ship is safer than an aviation gas or ammonia ship," Bone claims. "LNG burns, but it's very hard to make it explode. If I had a handheld rocket, I could think of better targets.

"Also, you look at how the *Sansinena* [a Union Oil tanker] blew up in LA Harbor in 1976 [killing nine people and injuring fifty-six in a huge conflagration that damaged over 250 other ships]. That was a safety incident, not a terrorist incident," he notes. "I am a prevention guy, and we're very passionate about what we do. When a marine inspector leaves a ship, he's willing to place his family members or shipmates aboard knowing that ship can now survive a collision or other event and get people safely off.

"Interventions [Coast Guard safety inspections and corrections] take place every day from dinner-cruise and whale-watching boats to big ferries to cruise ships and LNG ships. More awards should go to people who prevent search and rescues [or oil spill responses] from having to take place."

Still, as Senior Chief Rob Bushie, who used to run the small boat station in Maui, told me, "No one ever got a Gold Lifesaving Medal for designing a safer bilge pump."

By the time my interview with the admiral is over at 4:30, the district's chief of public affairs has gone home for the day. I go home to find my waterfront being posted with oil pollution warning signs.

On Thursday I call the Golden Gate Surf Station to see if I can go out with them. "If you're interested in the oil spill, you don't want to come here," Chief Morgan tells me. "We haven't been given any tasking on that. We're just doing our regular LE [law enforcement] and SAR work."

The same day, fishermen whose crab season opening will be postponed offer to help with the cleanup but are turned down by the Coast Guard and the contractors. The city of San Francisco then hires them to help out.

By Friday the bunker fuel is all over the bay and out the Golden Gate. I talk to the Pacific Strike Team's CO, Cdr. Mike Day, and learn that no skimmers, booms, or other response equipment stored in their big airplane hangar at Novato is being used, though they've assigned people to help organize a command center at Fort Mason. "If they're not satisfied with the contractors, they'll call us in," he tells me. The "they" he's referring to is the Unified Command made up of the contractors working for the Hong Kong shipping company Regal Stone ("the responsible party"), the Coast Guard, and the State of California.

"The strike team's assets cost a lot of money," he'll later explain, "so the responsible party that pays for the cleanup [under the Oil Spill Prevention Act of 1990] would rather not use them. If their Certificate of Financial Responsibility—$61 million liability insurance—is exceeded, then we're called in."

Under this system, the oil and shipping companies responsible for large spills have been paying about three-quarters of the cleanup costs over the last decade, with the federal government picking up the difference, according to a study by the GAO, the Government Accountability Office.

Still, according to that January 2008 report commissioned by the Coast Guard, the contractor did have enough skimmers on the water during the first days of the spill. Unfortunately, the state of cleanup technology is such that their recovering 20 percent of the spilled oil was considered a huge success.

A press conference is called at Rodeo Beach, where they've started cleaning oil that's come ashore. No containment booms have yet been placed by the

Berkeley Marina, at the entry to the lagoon in Bolinas, or by the wetlands where I live in Richmond. Over forty miles of shoreline will eventually be impacted.

I go to the press conference in the Marin Headlands that's taking place between visits of concern by the governor, California's two senators, House Speaker Nancy Pelosi, and Coast Guard Commandant Thad Allen. I pass a coyote and a red-tailed hawk on the way in. This was my late love Nancy Ledansky's favorite local beach. This is where we held her memorial service after she died of breast cancer at the age of forty-three. She'd wondered about environmental factors that may have contributed to her illness.

Now orange plastic fencing and oil spill warning signs block access to the wide cliff-framed strand where fifty-eight contract workers in yellow hazmat suits are removing oil-stained boulders and scraping away contaminated sand with a small front loader called a Bobcat. I've seen real bobcats around here and hope they don't find any dead seabirds to feed on, as toxins tend to bioaccumulate up the food chain.

At the end of the two-lane road is a crowd of park police and rangers, TV satellite trucks, reporters, and State Assemblyman Mark Leno. A Dolphin 65 flies by with city officials on board. A caravan of cars and a van from the Unified Command arrives.

I say hello to Captain Uberti, a bluff bald guy with glasses and a white mustache, who is now the federal official in charge. In 1978, as an OCS student, he sailed on the training ship *Cuyahoga* with half his class. The next week the other half went out and were run down by a large freighter. Four officers and seven crew died. This spill will be the second disaster of his career and will see him replaced as incident commander in less than a week and take early retirement by the end of the month. Right now he's still got his game face on, however.

I ask him about delays in communications, and he dismisses them as not significant. "Everything that needed to be done in terms of response was getting done that morning," he says before striding over to a speaker's podium that's been placed in the road.

"This is the first time in a long time anything like this has occurred," he tells the banked cameras and reporters before letting Barry McFarland, a big hefty guy from the O'Briens Group, the lead contractor, answer their questions. Barry says the response was good and by 11:00 A.M. (two and a half hours after the collision) five skimming vessels were on scene or on the way. He says they've collected eight thousand gallons of oil and oily liquids in two days and have a hundred-plus workers out there today and two hundred more on the way. I ask why the Coast Guard's National Strike Team gear hasn't been used.

"If the Coast Guard is the best tool for us, we'll use it," he claims.

Saturday morning my friend Scott Fielder and I look for oil behind my house and then for bird rescue people to net the several dozen oil-stained birds we spot hauled up on the marina's small beaches. At least five thousand birds will die in the coming days.

The state Fish and Game agency calls informational meetings for volunteers in San Francisco, Berkeley, and Richmond Harbor. When hundreds of people turn out ready to work, they're told to stay away from the beaches, that the oil is toxic and they will be subject to arrest if they try to clean it up. It's a classic case of how in a moment of crisis government's innate fear of the people (and of legal liability) can help make things worse.

The San Francisco Baykeeper, Surfrider Foundation, and other environmental groups organize their own volunteer programs. Some people stage "guerrilla" beach cleanups. One man is handcuffed and cited for refusing orders to stop cleaning up big globs of oil on Muir Beach in Marin County.

In the afternoon I drive to the Incident Command Post, which has moved from Fort Mason to the old Officers Club on Treasure Island next to Yerba Buena Island.

The Incident Command System that's in play here started with the U.S. Forest Service coordinating different agencies fighting western wildfires in the 1970s and was later refined by the Coast Guard strike teams in response to major oil spills.

The main room is divided into distinct groupings.

There's the Situations table with a GIS (geographic information system) unit trying to update incident maps.

The Operations area is made up of eight folding tables pushed together with more than a dozen people and their laptops, sodas, and snacks trying to direct the immediate response. Strike team members are well represented here.

Nearby is the Resource table run by a Strike Team reservist, Chief Gary Burns, trying to keep tabs on where people and stuff are at any given moment.

There's a Planning section trying to estimate where the oil will be tomorrow and what cultural or environmental impacts it will have.

There's also a Logistics and Finance table that's keeping a running count on materials and costs involved.

Up against the far wall is the Environmental table. "We don't have our people there. They're mostly Ph.D.'s and biologists," the strike team's Mike Day tells me. Occupying this table are scientists and resource managers from the National Park Service, the National Oceanic and Atmospheric Administration (NOAA), California Fish and Game, and its Office of Spill Prevention and Response assessing impacts on critical habitats in the bay and along the coast.

There are some two hundred people in and around the command post today and seven hundred in the field. Too many cooks, I think. Mike Day has twenty-eight strike team people working the center and another nine in Southern California going through burned-out neighborhoods identifying hazardous materials in the wake of their big wildfires a few weeks earlier.

The strike team has three rafts they'll be bringing down from their hangar on Sunday for beach damage assessments. I ask if I can go along, and he says they'll make room for me on Monday.

So Sunday I watch more beach cleanups, make calls, and take notes. I run into three citizens trying to capture oiled ducks to send to the Bird Rescue Research Center in Cordelia, where they're being cleaned. Caitlin, Christine, and Julie won't give me their last names for fear Fish and Game might arrest them. That night's TV news has aerial footage of a pod of dolphins swimming through the oil.

Monday morning at 7:00 A.M. I return to the command post. There is now a huge strike team trailer out front with the Coast Guard logo and red racing stripe displayed on its sides for all the world and media to see. I run into Captain Uberti, who tells me about Commandant Allen's visit on Sunday and again doesn't give me a direct answer when I ask about communications problems that first day.

Barry McFarland from the O'Briens Group gives the morning briefing, followed by someone from Fish and Game, the captain, and Admiral Bone, who tells the gathered crowd, "You've turned this around. I did two overflights yesterday. Don't react to the stuff you read. People in this room and in the field are doing a fantastic job, and you can be proud of what you've done. Hopefully at the end of the day the people of San Francisco—they're venting some now—but just stay sensitive and understand it's their homes and issues, though I know for many of you it's also your homes and issues. I'm proud of you."

I join the SCAT—Shoreline Cleanup and Assessment Team—in the parking lot. It's headed by Bruce Joab, a toxicologist from the Office of Spill Prevention and Response, and includes Jacob Henry, an EPA consultant, Bosun's Mate Second Class David Varela, and Bosun's Mate First Class Gary Cohen from the strike team.

Maritime Safety and Security Team members will be driving the rafts, an example of the linked-up Deployable Operations Group in action, if not a particularly striking one. Earlier the DOG sent Pacific Strike Team members to Hawaii to act as extra muscle, fearing a new confrontation with environmental protestors opposed to the interisland Superferry.

We drive over the hill to Yerba Buena and down to the boat basin, where three orange 25-foot Defenders and the three black rafts are waiting. Ours will be heading over to Richardson Bay by Sausalito.

Our recon team pulls out maps of Richardson, a large inlet off the main part of the bay. The MSST teams in their body armor turn and salute the flag as it's raised at 8:00 A.M. This seems odd only because the flagpole is on the other side of a building where we can't see it.

We tie a 15-foot Avon raft with an old two-stroke outboard behind one of the 25s, let out some line, and head off across the bay.

In the middle of the bay, I spot a large sea otter swimming along on its back. They're a rare sight in San Francisco, and normally I'd be thrilled, but now I want to shout, "Dude, get the hell out of here before you get slimed!"

Bosun's Mate David Varela tells me he's worked at the Bodega Bay Surf Station, on the cutter *Boutwell* out of Alameda, at Yerba Buena, and now with the strike team. In other words, he's homesteading the Bay Area, and who can blame him.

Turning into Richardson Bay, we pass a large blue and white skimmer ship, one of three that's been collecting oil offshore. We pass our first injured bird, a western grebe that keeps bending its long, elegant neck to preen its oiled back.

We pull up by the riprap shoreline below a steep cliff next to Bridgeway, the road into Sausalito. Seven of us scramble into the black raft, including two of the MSST guys, Marine Science Technician First Class Burt Wells, a tall fellow I've been out with before, and Port Security Specialist Third Class Sean Fadely.

The team checks its handheld GPS, cameras, and note forms. Bruce says he has Richardson Bay divided into eleven segments to survey and we have four hours to do it in. We begin motoring along the shore and *boom!* The outboard hits a sunken rock. We pull over to a floating dock and lift it up to check the blades. They're OK, so we continue on past the famous Sausalito waterfront and the statue of the seal with a live gull on its back. There's a light sheen of oil on the water here, plus another oiled bird, then some patchy sheens and our first boomed-off beach. It's 9:44 A.M. We go up the channel between Horizons and Scoma's restaurants, then cruise past the ferry dock, which they eye as a place to stage cleanup equipment if they have to.

We enter a few boat marinas and pass some anchor-outs with oiled bottoms. We pull up to the dock at Pelican Harbor, where the harbormaster, Janet Erickson, tells us the oil came in Friday night and hit the anchor-outs and also the cliffs and pylons of waterfront homes across the way in Belvedere. The next harbor entry is boomed off, with some tar balls stuck to the absorbent boom material. We motor past several mega-yachts—*Flipper*, *My Girl*, *Maximus 2*—and a dead floating cormorant.

There are some rafted timbers with a dozen harbor seals, pelicans, and a great blue heron hanging out on top of them, all looking fit enough to eat a fiddler crab.

We enter the houseboat marinas and motor past the seaplane slip and under the Highway 101 bridge into the Sausalito canal and wetlands. We take a long looping look around the shallow lagoon and on our way out are waved over by a fireman who asks if we've seen any oil on this side of the bridge. We tell him we haven't. Going back under the bridge and over to the Strawberry Peninsula, we flush an oiled cormorant, who flaps across the water and then settles back down warbling lovely calls of distress. The water sparkles like diamonds with the cityscape sharp as crystal across the bay.

We pass the Audubon Center in Tiburon. That ends segment seven of eleven. Still, thankfully, the shoreline is largely unsullied.

"Inside or outside of the birds?" Burt asks Bruce as we approach a flock of several hundred floating just offshore.

"This is where we may see oil, so let's head in toward shore even if we flush them," Bruce says.

"It's for their own good," I suggest.

"It's in their interest," he agrees as our raft approaches and they take off in a great squawking and fluttering of wings, flying a lazy few hundred yards before resettling on the water.

We do two more short segments and see some small floating tar balls. "No evidence of shoreline oiling," Bruce notes. A few minutes later approaching the side of Belvedere facing Sausalito, we find two ribbons of oil left from high and higher tide lines running along the pilings of multimillion-dollar waterfront homes and the rocks in between. They remind me of the brown flood line that ran through the streets and neighborhoods of New Orleans after Hurricane Katrina. The ribbons of oil two to four inches thick fade away just below the mansions at the end of the point where our 25-foot ride home is waiting. It's 1:55 P.M.

An HH-60 Jayhawk that's flown up from San Diego passes over the Golden Gate Bridge as we climb back aboard the response boat. The 225-foot black-hulled buoy tender *Aspen* has joined the blue skimmer ship in the middle of the bay where smaller boats with yellow boom lines appear to be circling a slick.

By Tuesday fifteen hundred people are involved in the cleanup, and I'm getting ready to fly off to Bahrain to report on the Coast Guard in Iraq. Before I leave, I head over to my local deli on the other side of the Rosie the Riveter waterfront park. By the dock in front of the deli, a 25-foot Defender and its MSST crew are hanging out, having dropped off a couple of Fish and Game biologists on nearby Baker Island.

"Some woman just came up and gave us a piece of her mind about the oil," one of them tells me. They go into the deli in their wraparound shades, dark blue jumpsuits, body armor, and gunslinger holsters.

"Who are those guys?" another woman asks me.

"Coast Guard."

"Really?" she replies skeptically.

Two weeks later, when I return home from the Persian Gulf, I find twenty mostly Mexican contract workers in hazmat suits cleaning oil off the rocky shore behind my home.

A month later, an oil barge runs into the nearby Richmond Bridge at the north end of the bay, another case of human error. Luckily no oil is spilled this time.

Boston Oil & Gas

If it wanted to, the Coast Guard could make a good case that it's the oldest environmental agency in the United States. After all, the Environmental Protection Agency was only created in 1970 and the Department of the Interior in 1849, while the Revenue Cutter Service got its first resource protection assignment in

1822. That's when Congress directed it to guard stands of live oak trees on public lands along the coast of Florida. Government warships were built using the strong, dense wood of these trees, and by the early nineteenth century timber thieves and "scoundrels" were cutting them down and shipping the lumber north. The arrival of well-armed revenue cutters discouraged the thievery.

By the 1860s, the service was also patrolling fishing and whaling grounds off Alaska and going after seal poachers who threatened to wipe out the fur seal population on the Pribilof Islands. In addition the service provided platforms for the first naturalists and scientists to study and report on the wildlife of Alaska.

Today the Coast Guard regulates and works to prevent oil and chemical pollution, enforces fisheries laws, protects right whales and other endangered species, tries to control the introduction of invasive species like zebra mussels by regulating ballast water exchange in ships entering U.S. ports, and is using its icebreakers as a platform for a new generation of scientists studying the impact of climate change on the Arctic.

Sometimes it also provides platforms of opportunity for marine wildlife rescues. "I was on this 41-footer, and me and my shipmates hoisted this turtle off this fishing boat. It must have been eight feet long and eight hundred pounds. It was huge, and it took four of us to pull it over," recalls Petty Officer Aldomoro Nelson as we're cruising off New Jersey during a search and rescue exercise. "We thought it was dead, then on the way back in I was looking at it and it just like woke up!"

"C'mon, you gave it mouth-to-beak resuscitation," one of his shipmates joshes him.

"Anyway, it looked fine, just kind of angry, so we let it go back into the water."

Despite the importance of the marine stewardship mission, some in the service continue to refer to strike team members and fisheries officers as "duck scrubbers" and "fish kissers," their humor reflecting a certain macho disparagement. After all, no one on the stewardship side refers to members of the Maritime Security Response Team as "gun huggers" or surfmen as "boat tippers," though given their relative contribution to the health of our public seas maybe they should.

The breakup of the supertanker *Torrey Canyon* off the coast of England in 1967 that resulted in thirty million gallons of oil befouling the beaches of France and England alerted the U.S. Coast Guard to the threat posed by large oil tanker spills and the need for a U.S. response plan. Santa Barbara's Union Oil platform spill in 1969 put three million gallons onto the beaches of Southern California and with the battle cry of "Get Oil Out!" helped spark the modern environmental movement. The collision of two oil tankers by the Golden Gate Bridge in 1971 resulted in close to a million-gallon spill. This led to the establishment of directed shipping lanes and creation of the first Coast Guard Vessel Traffic System in San Francisco.

Since Congress established the Clean Water Act of 1972 and the Oil Spill Prevention Act of 1990, the Coast Guard has been responsible for a range of prevention and response activities, including management of the billion-dollar Oil Spill Liability Trust Fund used for emergency cleanups and the investigation of illegal dumping at sea.

While large vessel spills get lots of attention, oily runoff from streets and storm drains and illegal flushing of oily waste by ships puts the equivalent of one and a half *Exxon Valdez* oil spills into America's waters every year. "The amount of oily wastewater being dumped in the ocean every year is just unbelievable," says Tim Collins, deputy director of the Coast Guard Investigative Service.

It's a twenty-degree day in January and I'm with three marine safety inspectors, Lt. JG Chris Herold, Bosun's Mate Colleen Murray, and Marine Science Technician Erik Kallenstaid, doing a port state control (foreign vessel) boarding of the *Romo Maersk*, a 680-foot oil/chemical tanker docked by the tidal mudflats of the Global Petroleum Terminal not far from Boston's Logan Airport.

In 2005, the Maersk shipping company pleaded guilty to providing false documents to the Coast Guard and paid a $500,000 fine after another team of safety inspectors spotted waste oil in an overboard dump pipe on the MV *Jane Maersk*.

That same year MSC, a Hong Kong–based container ship company, was forced to pay a $10.5 million fine for dumping forty tons of sludge from one of its ships, the *MSC Elena*, off the coast of New England using a shipboard constructed "magic pipe" to bypass its oily-waste separator and then lying about it to the Coast Guard.

In the 1990s, Coast Guard investigations led to even larger dumping fines against the cruise ship industry, including a 1999 fine of $18 million against

Royal Caribbean, which admitted to twenty-one felony counts of deliberately dumping waste oil and chemicals from its fleet of cruise ships and then lying about it to the Coast Guard.

The biggest ship pollution fine (to date) was levied against the New York–based tanker company Overseas Shipholding Group, Inc. (OSG), in December 2006. OSG agreed to pay a record $37 million and pleaded guilty to thirty-three felonies relating to the intentional dumping of oil and doctoring of documents on a dozen of its oil tankers. The conviction was the result of a three-and-a-half-year investigation by the Coast Guard Investigative Service and the Justice Department.

In more recent and typical cases, the British-based shipping company PACCSHIP agreed to pay a $1.7 million fine in April 2008 for illegal dumping from two of its ten ships, and that same month the Egyptian shipper National Navigation agreed to pay $7.25 million for nine years of illegal dumping from one of its ships.

Inside Capt. Lars Christiensen's office on the *Romo Maersk*, the inspectors go through the oil record book, garbage management plan, and ballast water management plan and reporting form. They look at his safety equipment certificate and certificate of financial responsibility (spill insurance).

"Captain, your radar is down," Colleen begins, holding another form.

"Yes. The technician is on board. He's fixed it."

"Good. Can I see that report?" she asks. These Coasties in their steel-toed boots and winter-lined hard hats are all business. Erik explains the discharge certificate for slop he's reviewing. Slop is waste from cargo (heating oil in this case); sludge is waste from onboard machinery.

After off-loading its heating oil, the ship will be loading up with ballast water here in Boston Harbor and discharging it in New York Harbor. Ships don't have to report ballast water exchanges within the two-hundred-mile Exclusive Economic Zone, even though this could be another way of spreading invasive species from one port to another.

After a brief visit to the bridge, we head out onto the biting cold deck. "Could you get somebody down there to paint your low line mark [on the hull] so I don't have to write it up?" Erik suggests to the ship's chief.

Looking over the rail, I see a rainbow sheen where water's being flushed from the stern. Soon all three Coasties are leaning half over the rail to investigate.

"It's evaporating," Colleen notes.

"If it keeps coming, we'll put a call in to Waterways [Management Division], as they handle pollution outside the ship," Lt. JG Chris Herold tells me. A few more streams of water jet from the ship, but there are no more oily shimmers. Later they'll note fresh auto lube on the propeller shaft and suspect that as the source.

"We'll check the shaft for any leakage," Ship's Chief Andreas Poulsen promises. He's Danish but from the Faeroe Islands, he says, and yes, as a Faeroe Islander he does hunt whales, "pilot whales you call them."

Erik shows me the topside pump-out connectors for oily waste and sewage discharges. The waste connector has six bolts versus four for the sewage line.

We climb down several decks and ladders into the engine room to visit the oily-waste separator. It's about the size of an oil barrel. The main engine next to it is about the size of a Greyhound bus turned on its side. They point out the separator's discharge valve. If a small digital detector finds more than fifteen parts per million hydrocarbons going through it, it's supposed to set off an alarm. They ask a tall, blond, diffident Danish engineer to test it for them. A buzzer sounds and a red light starts to rotate.

"If you want to do something bad, it's not so hard at all," the engineer tells me. "You could have a bypass [magic pipe] or you could run clean water through the sensor to fool it or you could have a separator without an internal filter—just run and flush it."

Mostly the inspectors are keyed in on the discharge valve, looking for broken paint or fresh paint on the flange or other signs of recent disturbance that could indicate use of a bypass pipe. A lot of the time it's a whistle-blower, a mariner with a conscience, who will set off an oil dumping investigation. Whistle-blowers can also claim a percentage of any fines imposed.

The *Exxon Valdez* defined the first ten years of my career, and 9/11 is defining the next ten," says the inspectors' boss, Lt. Cdr. Claudia Gelzer, chief of port operations and maritime security in Boston. She joined the service in 1991, two years after the oil tanker disaster in Alaska that caught the Coast Guard, and the nation, off guard and resulted in hundreds of new marine safety officer positions being created.

Among her tasks is maintenance of fourteen lighthouses, including Boston Light, the oldest in the United States, other aids to navigation work, port state control inspections (of foreign ships), waterways inspections, hazardous materials investigations, and icebreaking during the winter to maintain maritime mobility.

In 2006, her crew, using forensic "fingerprinting" of oil samples, was able to identify Exxon Mobil and other companies responsible for three spills totaling over thirty thousand gallons that fouled Boston's Chelsea River. Still, their environmental work is eclipsed by Sector Boston's biggest, most resource-intensive task, escorting LNG ships through the harbor.

Natural gas now meets about a quarter of the nation's energy needs. Since it burns cleaner and emits less CO_2 than other fossil fuels, demand is soaring—but for a substance that arrives in the country at 260 degrees below zero, LNG is generating a lot of heat.

An accident or terrorist strike on a liquefied natural gas tanker carrying thirty-three million gallons of highly flammable cargo could potentially generate a fireball a third of a mile across, or at least one hellacious ship and harbor fire, burning at three thousand degrees Fahrenheit, hot enough to melt nearby ship hulls, warehouses, and storage tanks and kill people up to a mile away.

Boston's is the only one of more than half a dozen existing LNG terminals set in an urban port, although there are now proposals for thirty additional sites both on- and offshore, including in urban coastal zones around New York, New Jersey, and California.

The 2005 Energy Act gave the industry-friendly Federal Energy Regulatory Commission (FERC) final say over LNG plant sitings, overruling state authorities, although the Coast Guard can still veto a plan it feels represents a threat to maritime safety.

In late 2007, the Coast Guard blocked a FERC-approved plan for an LNG terminal on the Fall River, Massachusetts, waterfront. Local opposition, feeling stymied by FERC, had come up with a unique plan to block the plant, winning historic landmark protection for an old drawbridge that had been slated for demolition. The narrow width of the drawbridge (ninety-eight feet) and of the gap between it and a nonaligned bridge eleven hundred feet away made navigation by big LNG tankers so risky that the Coast Guard decided it could not approve the siting.

Still, if even a dozen new LNG terminals are approved, which seems to be industry's real aim in proposing several dozen, the added workload for the Coast Guard could prove incredibly burdensome.

In early 2008, the U.S. Government Accountability Office released a study stating that the Coast Guard lacks the funds and training to protect LNG and crude oil tankers from terrorist attacks on a nationwide basis. "Workload demands are likely to rise substantially as new LNG facilities come on line and LNG shipments increase," it reported. "These increased demands could cause the Coast Guard to continue to be unable to meet the standards it has set for keeping U.S. ports secure."

"In the early '90s we'd have maybe five LNG shipments a year. Now it's every five to seven days," says Boston's prevention chief, Tom Miller. "Each time we'll set up a Unified Command Center and have an officer in tactical command [OTC] and a vessel movement officer on the tanker [when it's inbound]. The Tobin Bridge is closed and air traffic held at Logan, at least the runway that could put an aircraft over the tanker. As it transits through metropolitan Boston, we have a security zone one mile ahead and two miles astern and five hundred yards to either side. We have designated ditch sites if we need to ground the vessel and different levels of response tactics [including lethal use of force]. We have a state police helicopter overhead, three 25s, an OTC boat, Mass [achusetts] Environmental, state, and Boston police boats, and police cars hopping down the transit route."

One time an LNG tanker was pulling into its Everett terminal on the Mystic River when a car crusher in the adjacent scrap metal yard got hold of a vehicle that still had fuel in its tank.

"People heard that explosion, and it was like 'game time' for about ten minutes!" Eric Parker recalls excitedly. The normally laid-back twenty-five-year-old African American lieutenant, five-nine and lanky, is the Officer in Tactical Command [OTC] the day I ride along on an outbound escort.

The huge 933-foot black, white, and red LNG tanker *Catalunya Spirit* lets out a billow of steam approaching the high-rises of downtown Boston. From our position to its rear, it looks like a mushroom cloud.

Along with its escort tugs and our 41-foot OTC boat, there's another 41 and a 25, both with lights energized and machine guns manned, as well as a couple of armed Massachusetts and Boston police boats.

A ferry calls on the radio for clearance to pass behind us. I see a police truck and then a patrol car on shore with their blue lights flashing. We follow the tanker out past the airport, the Legal Sea Foods plant, and a shipping dock where another patrol car is sitting, flashing its blue lights. A jet flies overhead but not over the ship.

We continue out past Fort Independence on Castle Island into the shipping channel and past Spectacle Island, where a lot of the fill from Boston's Big Dig ended up. The Boston Harbor ferry calls for clearance to pass behind us. "They just want to make sure they can go through without getting shot," Eric explains.

We're now close to Boston Light. The Unified Command calls on the radio. "We'll wait to hear back from you before we scoot," Eric tells them.

Out past Deer Island, the last tug veers away from the tanker, followed by our security detail.

Back at the North End Coast Guard station, whose headquarters building looks like it's made out of white LEGO blocks (it's supposed to look like a ship's bridge), Chief Warrant Officer Don Tucker shows me his Hawkeye monitors. They're linked to ten powerful cameras spread around Boston Harbor.

"We watched you the whole way out," he says, pointing to a monitor showing the LNG tanker now 7.5 miles beyond Deer Island. You can't quite read its name on the stern but can still identify the unique profile and colors of the big ship.

Six months later, a computer control problem will leave the *Catalunya Spirit* drifting powerless off Cape Cod for five hours with a full load of LNG on board. The Coast Guard gets a tug out to it that then tows it under armed escort to a safe anchorage for repair.

Along with LNG, the Coast Guard is also evaluating the safety of offshore wind farms like ones proposed off Cape Cod and Delaware, as well as other alternative ocean energy systems such as tidal, current, and wave power generators. They've found that the big wind farm turbines create radar blind spots that might make good hideouts for oyster pirates and bad places to do search and rescue. On the other hand, no coastal ecosystem has ever been wiped out by a wind spill.

Busting the Fish Laundry

Besides dealing with oil and gas, the Coast Guard's other big environmental responsibility is protecting living marine resources. A 2003 study in the science journal *Nature* reported that 90 percent of large open-ocean fish, including big tuna, sharks, and billfish, have been wiped out by industrial overfishing since 1950. A 2006 study predicted that if present trends continue, edible species of marine wildlife will be commercially extinct by 2048, a projection confirmed by a 2008 UN report.

In 1976, the Magnuson Fisheries and Conservation Act (now called the Magnuson-Stevens Act) established a two-hundred-mile exclusive fishing zone around the United States and its territories banning foreign fishing vessels. Seven years later, in March 1983, President Ronald Reagan, in one of the most significant but least noted acts of his administration, expanded on this precedent, declaring a two-hundred-mile Exclusive Economic Zone for all marine resources, in effect creating a new wilderness frontier for the United States.

Along with patrolling the EEZ's North Pacific boundary line to keep out Russian factory trawlers, Coast Guard representatives sit on eight regional fisheries councils that establish fishing quotas and regulations on federal waters from three to two hundred miles offshore and also help state fish and game agencies enforce the law within their three-mile state waters.

In Rio Vista, California, deep in the serpentine wetlands and sloughs of the Sacramento delta, I spend a day on a 25-foot RBS (Response Boat Small) with a Coast Guard party and a Fish and Game agent doing joint fisheries and boat safety inspections at the height of the striped bass and sturgeon season. The sturgeon we measure look like scaly relics from the age of the dinosaurs (which they are). We also tow a couple of fishermen whose motor has conked out on them.

More often the Coast Guard does boardings of commercial fishing vessels at sea to make sure rules are followed on how much and what kind of fish or shellfish is taken, how many days at sea are allowed, and what type of gear is used. It also protects the fishermen by making sure they have the right lifesaving equipment onboard.

With many species of commercial fish collapsing, even as prices continue to rise on the global seafood market, tensions on America's fishing grounds can run high. I remember going to a New England Fisheries Council meeting where closures to protect endangered cod in the Gulf of Maine were being discussed, much to the annoyance of the fishermen in attendance.

"If you're going to send armed terrorists aboard my boat, they're going to get an answer, 'cause I'm looking at death through defiance before I go out and put up with this foolishness any longer!" fisherman Dave Marciano warned from the public mike, staring hard at the Coast Guard representative to the council.

"Funny thing is two years ago they saved his ass when his boat broke down," another fishermen later tells me.

"With fishermen it's a love-hate thing," Chief Louis Bevilacqua, the company commander in Cape May, suggests, recalling the time he was on the cutter *Rush* on a fisheries patrol off Alaska during crabbing season. "We rescued this one crew whose boat was sinking, brought them back to Dutch Harbor, and then found out they were illegal immigrants and busted them."

Zeke Grader, executive director of the Pacific Coast Federation of Fishermen's Associations, the largest commercial fishing group on the West Coast, thinks the relationship is good but threatened. "There's a great deal of respect [for the Coast Guard], especially with search and rescue in coastal communities like Fort Bragg and Eureka [California]," he says, "but when you have leaders in Washington, DC, giving orders for them to focus on drug interdiction or this War on Terror, you just have to be sure they don't neglect their traditional roles. If you do it right, if you have a relationship with fishermen, it will help you get your job done, but then you get this strange stuff out of Washington with all the homeland security where it almost becomes fascistic."

The two times you can be sure U.S. fishermen have no complaint with the Coast Guard is when they're doing search and rescue or when they're going after high-seas drift-net pirates.

Probably the most destructive method of fishing ever devised by humans is pelagic (open ocean) drift-net fishing. In the 1980s, a thousand-ship fleet from Japan, Taiwan, and South Korea decimated marine life in the North Pacific with near-invisible plastic monofilament drift nets called "walls of death" that stretched over thirty miles in length and hung thirty-five feet down into the water. While fishing for squid they managed to kill everything else in the water column, including tens of millions of seabirds, seals, sunfish, swordfish, sharks, sea turtles, dolphins, and small whales.

Investigators from the National Oceanic and Atmospheric Administration soon discovered that about 10 percent of the fleet was also targeting high-seas salmon despite a treaty between the United States, Canada, Russia, and Japan that these fish were only to be taken when they returned to their home rivers.

In the winter of 1989, the Coast Guard spotted a Taiwanese fishing vessel drifting in the shipping lanes four hundred miles off the coast of Washington. They towed the fire-scorched derelict into Port Angeles, where it sat dockside for several days with toxic fumes spewing from its interior. Eventually they were able to send a boarding team below deck. What they found there would make a hagfish gag: In the freezer was the eight-month-old rotting corpse of a crewman, his neck broken, his body roped to a mattress. Slimy fish remains filled the rest of the hull. Genetic sampling of the scales and tails showed the fish were U.S. salmon taken at sea. They never were able to determine exactly what happened aboard that drift-net boat or how the man came to die.

That April, the cutter *Jarvis* was patrolling in Arctic fog four hundred miles north of the drift-net squid-fishing boundary when they got a radio call not to "run over our net!"

"Whose net?" they radioed back after identifying themselves. At that point the Taiwanese fishing boat *Cy Yang* cut loose five miles of drift net and fled. When the Taiwanese government finally gave the Coast Guard permission to board the vessel three days later, they'd thrown their catch overboard, though scale samples again showed they'd been taking salmon. Soon the Coast Guard was shooting helicopter video of pirates throwing thirty- and forty-pound salmon overboard while being chased across the ocean.

By then NOAA undercover agents were receiving offers of hundreds of tons of hot salmon in what came to be known as the "fish laundry." Agents negotiated directly with a Taiwanese smuggler for an at-sea delivery of a thousand tons from one of the pirate fleets for $1.3 million. The NOAA agents and the Coast Guard then set up the first high-seas federal sting in history.

In the summer of 1989, a transport ship, the *Red Fin,* sailed out of Dutch Harbor in the Aleutians with undercover agents on board. After two weeks at sea, they rendezvoused with the pirate drift-net fleet. As two of the Taiwanese captains were coming aboard, the High Endurance Cutter *Morgenthau* that had been lying in wait just over the horizon came surging into view, its Klaxon sounding. Then two big C-130s from Kodiak came thundering out of the clouds, adding to the cacophony, dropping smoke bombs around the startled pirates.

The Taiwanese made a run for it. As the *Morgenthau* and *Red Fin* gave chase, the crew of one of the boats threw netting over the side to try to foul their propellers. When that failed they rammed the *Red Fin* amidships. "It was like a Wild West chase on the high seas," one of the *Red Fin*'s crew later recalled. While the *Red Fin* was forced to give up the chase after two and a half days, the *Morgenthau* continued to pursue the pirate ship *Sung Ching* for ten days before finally receiving Taiwanese government permission to board it forty miles off the coast of Taiwan. On board they found 110 metric tons of illegal salmon.

Activists from Earthtrust, Greenpeace, and other environmental groups had spent years complaining about the destruction of the Pacific ecosystem being wrought by drift nets and showing disturbing underwater video of dead sharks, seals, birds, and other creatures entangled in the nets. However, it was the busting of the multimillion-dollar "fish laundry" that lent the force (and monetary motivation) needed by the United States, New Zealand, and others to successfully push for a UN-sanctioned global ban on high-seas drift nets that finally went into effect in 1993.

That global ban also set a precedent that suggests other destructive methods of fishing such as bottom trawling and longlining might yet be banned while there are still wild fish left in the sea. It was certainly a huge victory for ocean stewardship, one that even many Coast Guard fisheries enforcement officers don't know about.

In the years since 1993, the service has continued to chase down drift-net pirates. Recently there's been a small resurgence of this now illegal activity in the western Pacific by mainland Chinese fishermen. The Coast Guard has helped counter this by working in close alliance with the Chinese Fisheries Law Enforcement Command (FLEC) and also has had FLEC observers ride on some of its cutters out of Kodiak.

The cutter *Morgenthau*, which took down the *Sung Ching* drift-net pirates, was first commissioned in 1969 and saw duty off Vietnam, not unlike some of the fathers of Coast Guard personnel serving aboard her today.

By the late 1990s, many of the Coast Guard's older cutters and aircraft were beginning to break down. It was ranked fortieth oldest of the world's forty-two naval fleets, only slightly more up-to-date than the Mexican and Filipino navies. Some cutters and tenders had been under way since World War II.

The leadership of the Coast Guard under Adm. Jim Loy realized that, with the exception of its newest class of buoy tenders, all of its deepwater assets (those that operated more than fifty miles offshore) were going to reach obsolescence around the same time. They thought they might take a common approach to replacing them and hopefully create a streamlined, cost-effective method to provide themselves needed new platforms for the early part of the twenty-first century. More than a decade and several billion dollars later, this has not proved to be the case.

CHAPTER 11

Deepwater

"I may have some protective feeling for Lockheed Martin, but as a board member I'm pretty proud of what we've done."

—Former Coast Guard commandant Admiral James Loy

"I did not want a [Coast Guard] crew to come in harm's way somewhere down the road when I could have done something about it."

—Former Lockheed project engineer Michael Dekort testifying before Congress

It started on YouTube. At least that's where public awareness that there might be major problems with the Coast Guard's twenty-year, $24 billion Deepwater program first surfaced.

In a ten-minute video, a long-faced, uncomfortable-seeming man with a ginger and gray beard sat in front of a file drawer in his bedroom reading a statement about how the newly extended 123-foot Island class cutter that Lockheed

Martin had worked on had faulty security cables, blind spots on its video surveillance, and external infrared cameras that were vulnerable to bad weather.

"Why YouTube?"

"I tried taking it to the *Washington Post* and the Associated Press, but their 'experts' told them I was a nutcase. So I'd heard of YouTube, knew it existed, and I took a shot," says forty-two-year-old Michael DeKort. At six-seven and rail thin, he has an intense topic-focused manner that reminds me of other corporate whistle-blowers I've interviewed.

The YouTube video got a lot of attention at Lockheed and the Coast Guard's Deepwater office. Then the *Navy Times* ran a story, followed by the *Washington Post;* then the 123-foot boats started buckling at sea. Now here we are talking in a hallway outside one of a series of Deepwater congressional hearings taking place in the spring of 2007.

Deepwater's problems have become the focus of a major exposé in the *New York Times,* NBC's "Fleecing of America" has done a segment, *60 Minutes* filmed this hearing for a scathing report they broadcasted, and with the Democrats back in control of the House and Senate, outsourcing of government jobs and private contractor waste, fraud, and abuse have become the focus of congressional oversight hearings for the first time in six years. These range from the $13 billion in cash shipped to Iraq at the beginning of the war that was never accounted for to the Coast Guard's Deepwater program that was managed and run by Lockheed Martin and Northrop Grumman, the same defense contractors who made their money from the aircraft, boats, ships, and electronics they planned, designed, built, and delivered. Deepwater was also a program that deeply divided the Coast Guard against itself, with dissenting voices being ignored in favor of the contractors.

"I saw a meltdown in the organization when all this happened, and I thought, 'We're not taking the eye off the ball [again],'" Coast Guard Commandant Thad Allen later tells me.

How, I wonder, did the 2005 Heroes of Katrina end up having to dig out from a multibillion-dollar acquisitions fiasco two years later, getting pilloried both in the press and by Congress?

I've just arrived at the hearing after running across Capitol Hill from a Coast Guard budget hearing in the Senate Russell Building overseen by Senator Maria Cantwell of Washington state, chair of the Commerce Subcommittee on Oceans, Atmosphere, Fisheries, and Coast Guard.

She and Olympia Snowe of Maine, Ted Stevens of Alaska, Bill Nelson of Florida, and Frank Lautenberg of New Jersey questioned Admiral Allen about the 2008 budget that flatlined for the final year of the Bush administration at $8.4 billion.

"We have to have a budget that is adequate with even more demand in the future," Cantwell says.

"I take no objection to your statement, ma'am," Allen replies. He will come back with a $9.3 billion proposal for '09 that addresses many of the committee's concerns about the need for more ship inspectors and safety officers. Most of their questioning, however, focuses on Deepwater.

Senator Snowe, a longtime champion of the Coast Guard, tells the commandant, "It's difficult to review the budget without recalling the flaws with the Deepwater program . . . So let's make sure the mismanagement of the past is not repeated in the future. The Coast Guard must get back on track, and this announcement [that the Coast Guard will now take direct charge of the program] is an appropriate and long overdue step . . . The spokeswoman for ICGS [Integrated Coast Guard Systems, the management team run by the contractors] said there was not a significant change in this announcement. Is it a major change or not?"

"There is a fundamental change that I discussed with the two CEOs [of Lockheed and Northrop]," Admiral Allen tells her.

"I hope so!"

"That's what I intend, Senator," he says with a nervous barking laugh that suggests how hard it can be when one alpha personality has to defer to another.

"We also want to know what happens with the cutter that's now been jettisoned." She was referring to eight 123-foot boats that were decommissioned after it was found they were at risk of breaking up and sinking in seas over six feet.

"There's no doubt in our mind that the 123 means we have to have recourse to contractual or legal action," he tells her.

"I think this is a travesty."

"I think there was a misestimation," he says and goes into the technical aspects of the Slinky-like hull stresses and deck buckling you get when you stretch a narrow-beamed greyhound of a 110-foot cutter to 123 feet.

"Did you find it shocking?" Snowe wants to know.

"Absolutely," he agrees, "and we are proceeding with our investigation of this."

"I can't see the contractor not taking responsibility. It's unfathomable," she continues, like a leopard seal with a dead penguin, unwilling to let it go.

• • •

The Deepwater hearing on the House side is being held in Room 2167 of the labyrinth-like Rayburn Office Building by the Coast Guard and Maritime Transportation Subcommittee of the House Transportation and Infrastructure Committee, overseen by Rep. Elijah Cummings of Maryland. It has been going on since 2:00 P.M. and will continue past midnight with some twenty-five members of Congress coming and going.

They want to find out why the 123 failed, why communications cables were not properly sheathed to prevent eavesdropping or properly fireproofed, why the composite hull design for a Fast Response Cutter was too slow and heavy, why the first big National Security Cutters are not being built to meet their projected thirty-year life span yet nearly doubled in price, and why much of this information has been withheld from Congress.

Cummings is questioning DeKort, the whistle-blower, about his early concerns with the 123 program.

"How high did you take your concerns?"

"I took the matter to the CEO and board [of Lockheed] on at least two occasions. I was told my allegations were baseless."

"Did you ever contact the Coast Guard directly?"

"I contacted the group commander of boats in Key West, also a lieutenant commander on the commandant's staff [Commandant Thomas Collins, 2002–6]. I was told 'thank you,' that was the response I got . . . I was lead system engineer for the 123s' C4ISR [command, control, communications, computers, intelligence, surveillance, and reconnaissance]. When I came on board everything was pretty much locked in . . . I was told, 'We have a design of record.' "

"What were your major concerns?"

"Putting equipment on a Coast Guard vessel that won't survive the elements, that can be eavesdropped on, that can burn, that creates blind spots. Had these [first eight] boats not cracked, all forty-nine boats [contracted for] would have been delivered [in that condition]."

Later I ask DeKort about the nonwaterproof radios Lockheed had planned to put on the cutter's rigid inflatable boats. Like $600 toilet seats on military aircraft, this is the kind of small detail in a larger contract screwup that everyone can understand.

"With the radios, even the vendor said, 'Don't use my radio,' but they thought they'd use a radio the Coast Guard liked—and the Coast Guard did.

They liked them on the bridge of a 378-foot cutter, not the exposed deck of an open boat."

"I can't believe how overblown the whole congressional hearing thing is," Troy Scully, the tall, young, handsome spokesman for Lockheed Martin, tells me outside another oversight hearing. "The 110s [that became 123s] were shitty boats to begin with!"

This is not what I hear from the Coast Guard men and women serving on the 110s I visit.

Months later Mr. Scully will point out that of the $96 million the Coast Guard wants back from the 123 contract, only $3 million involves Lockheed's topside work, implying the rest is Northrop's fault.

The Product Line

On April 17, 2007, Admiral Allen announced his decision to decommission the eight 123-foot patrol boats that had been delivered to the Coast Guard and begin seeking redress from the contractors.

"Let me state this tactfully," he later tells me. "In the past we never raised [contract] issues to the CEO level, and that can be daunting sometimes with these people in the private sector . . . What they didn't understand is that the 123s became a leadership issue for us. It tests the credibility of the senior [Coast Guard] leadership with the deck plate [enlisted rates, chiefs, and junior officers]. If I can't get shafts in alignment [one of the reasons the boats buckled], it becomes a referendum on me."

Admiral Allen and the CEOs of Lockheed and Northrop began holding quarterly meetings to sort out their differences. "He doesn't blame me," Lockheed CEO Bob Stevens later told the *Wall Street Journal*, "but he sure as hell holds me accountable."

A March 6, 2008, story by reporter August Cole went on to explain that with all the congressional attention on Deepwater, the big defense contractors worried that "Deepwater's troubles will tarnish far bigger military programs," which is why the two CEOs now regularly update "one of their smallest government customers."

The original plan for Deepwater called for the delivery of three classes of cutters, along with new and upgraded aircraft and lots of state-of-the-art technologies, including robot helicopters, sensors, surveillance gear, and Department of Defense security-compatible communications systems.

Aviation elements included the upgrading of the Dolphin helicopter to the

C model, an easy fix given that they'd long needed the more powerful Turbomeca engines they were originally designed for. Jayhawk helicopters got new avionics packages. C-130 Hercules transport planes were also upgraded, and a long-range search version, the HC-130J, was put into service.

Replacing the aging fleet of Falcon jets are twin-engine Spanish-built CASA aircraft. With their glassy flight decks and rear cargo ramps, they look like sporty, flat-backed Mini Hercs. Still, I wondered why prop planes were selected to replace jets.

"We had an integrator [the ICGS contractor] that was supposed to pull this all together with a cap on how much to spend. Would it have been the same if [Coast Guard] Aviation made the decision? Maybe, maybe not," the service's aviation chief, Capt. Mike Moore, tells me in the spring of 2007. "What I tell the aviators is the decision has been made, and if that's the decision let's move forward."

On February 20, 2008, a CASA aircraft, now called an Ocean Sentry, performed its first search and rescue mission. Two Air Force F-15 fighter jets collided over the Gulf of Mexico off the Florida panhandle, and both pilots managed to bail out. The Ocean Sentry was diverted from a training flight out of Mobile, Alabama, to become the on-scene coordinator.

The first Coast Guard aircraft with AIS (ship transponder tracking) on board, the Sentry was able to identify and communicate with civilian vessels in the area, including a Good Samaritan fishing vessel, the *Nina*, that was directed to recover one of the pilots the aircrew had spotted. Unlike the Falcon jet, the Sentry's bubble observation windows let the aircrew look straight down while conducting their search, and its communications suite allowed it to coordinate with an Air Force tanker and two other Air Force F-15s, the fishing boat, and other civilians on the water, as well as Coast Guard helicopters, Falcons, and a 41-foot utility boat that rushed to the scene. A Coast Guard helicopter lifted one of the injured pilots off the fishing boat while another recovered the second pilot in the water. The first pilot survived the collision; the second did not.

Along with Sentry aircrews another sixty-nine sets of eyes that were supposed to take flight with Deepwater were Eagle Eye unmanned aerial vehicle (UAV) robot helicopters from Bell Helicopter. After five years of development under ICGS, the Coast Guard shut down the program in late 2007. It's now looking at existing alternatives, including the Navy's Fire Scout UAV, for at-sea operations. For cutter operations closer to shore, it's looking at shared use of Department of Homeland Security Predator drones.

Along with C4ISR [command, control, communications, computers, intelligence, surveillance, and reconnaissance, in case you've forgotten], ship construction makes up the biggest slice of the Deepwater pie.

The stretching out of the 110s to 123s was supposed to act as a bridge to hold the service over until the introduction of a 140-foot Fast Response Cutter (FRC). This was to be built in the same time frame as the 418-foot National Security Cutter (NSC), the Coast Guard's largest, most powerful vessel, to be followed shortly thereafter by a 360-foot Offshore Patrol Cutter (OPC).

While converting the 110s, ICGS had a radical new idea for the Fast Response Cutter. Instead of a steel hull, they would build it with a composite hull, a kind of supertough fiberglass.

Northrop had built a $68 million composite hull assembly line at its Mississippi shipyard hoping to sell the Navy on the idea for its new class of Littoral Combat Ship (LCS), designed for close-to-shore (also known as littoral) combat against mine-laying vessels, submarines, and gunboats.

After the Navy said no, Northrop announced it would be using the hull for the Coast Guard's fifty-eight Fast Response Cutters.

"It was a pure business decision," a former Northrop executive who didn't want to be named told the *New York Times*, "and it was the wrong one."

"They had a desire to see what was possible after losing that [LCS] contract. The Coast Guard became their test bed," Admiral Allen later noted.

Many Coast Guard engineers were skeptical about the plan from the beginning, saying the composite boat was going to be too slow and heavy, calling it a "brick." Northrop backhandedly acknowledged this when it added two engines to the two in its original design.

"Even a brick, if you put enough horsepower on it, you could make it plane on the water," retired Coast Guard engineer Capt. Kevin Jarvis told *60 Minutes*.

After investing three years and $38 million, the Coast Guard pulled the plug on the Fast Response Cutter deal with ICGS in March 2007. It then put the contract out for competitive bidding. In September 2008 it chose Bollinger Shipyards of Louisiana to construct thirty-four large 153-foot "Sentinel Class" FRCs. The new patrol boat is based on an existing, water-proven Dutch-built vessel, the Damen Stan 4708.

The largest of the Deepwater vessels and pride of the fleet is the 418-foot National Security Cutter, eight of which are being or will be built by Northrop Grumman at its shipyard in Pascagoula, Mississippi.

The National Security Cutter has also had its share of problems, including structural flaws first identified by Coast Guard engineers that could shorten its thirty-year lifespan. As a result of these design flaws, the first two Legend-class ships, the *Bertholf* and the *Waesche*, will go to sea for a year and then go into dry dock for up to a year of structural retrofitting at an estimated cost of $70 million. The third will need about $15 million of retrofitting work, and the fourth through eighth will have the problem corrected in their design phase.

The *Bertholf*, the first of the National Security Cutters (named after the Coast Guard's first commandant), was also found to have many of the same problems with electronic shielding that plagued the 123s. Crewmembers named one of its new radars "Helen Keller" because of its inability to see what it was supposed to. Even after the ship's 2008 handover to the Coast Guard, continued testing, retrofitting, and shakedown cruises mean it won't be fully operational until 2010.

With the first ship costing around $640 million and the full run of eight totaling around $4 billion, the contractors and Coast Guard had to come up with a way to replace twelve Vietnam-era High Endurance Cutters with eight high-priced National Security Cutters. They did this by rotating four crews for every three ships in order to keep them at sea longer.

A number of sailors and ships' COs I spoke with were skeptical of this scheme, worrying that their future shipmates' "pride of ownership" might be lost among the rotating crews. The skipper of the *Bertholf* thinks that after the first three ships are brought online the whole rotating crew idea may have to be revisited.

While the first National Security Cutters are about two years behind schedule, the next Deepwater asset, the 360-foot Offshore Patrol Cutter, has fallen even further behind. Its design phase is now set to begin in 2010.

So, as I wondered earlier, how did the Heroes of Katrina 2005 end up with the Deepwater Fiasco of 2007? The answer is both complex and fascinating and goes back a lot further than two years.

From Governors Island to ICGS

I'm visiting Governors Island on a cold winter day, and everywhere I look is a scenic wonder—the two-hundred-year-old stone battlements of Fort Jay and Castle Williams, the tree-lined historic district where British governors, Civil War generals, and future Coast Guard commandants lived. The views of lower Manhattan, a seven-minute ferry ride away, or toward the Statue of Liberty are breathtaking. Even the views of the high-rises on the Jersey waterfront and the shipping terminal at Red Hook in Brooklyn just across Buttermilk Channel make one want to pause and enjoy the moment. For years the Army generals in charge of the island complained about the loud buoy bell in Buttermilk Channel, and the Coast Guard apologetically explained that it was essential for navigation. Within months of the Coast Guard taking over the island, the bell was gone.

From 1966 to 1996, this was the heart of the Coast Guard, its largest base and island community, with over five thousand people living an idyllic small-town life in the heart of America's greatest harbor. This was the service's most prestigious and visible symbol, home to its white-hulled fleet and its Atlantic Command. Growing up in New York, all I knew about the Coast Guard was that they were on Governors Island.

Then in 1996 they left, relocating bits and pieces of commands to Staten Island and New Jersey and the tidewaters of Virginia and North Carolina. By doing so, they explained, they would save $54 million a year, less than half of what the Navy spends each year maintaining a single aircraft carrier. By the time they moved, however, the Coast Guard felt there was little choice.

That same year, the service launched its Deepwater acquisitions program. The loss of Governors Island and the eventual scandal and restructuring of Deepwater are not unrelated. You just have to follow the money, or lack thereof.

By the 1990s, the Coast Guard was facing a downward spiral of budgetary cutbacks and aging assets, including aircraft, patrol boats, and deepwater cutters, that were becoming dangerously vulnerable to accidents and breakdowns. In December 1989, the grounding and eventual scuttling of the *Mesquite*, a World War II buoy tender, on Lake Superior sparked a Coast Guard effort to replace twenty-six of its aging tenders, most of them more than fifty years old, at a proposed cost of $1 billion. In 1992, Congress authorized replacement of just eleven for $200 million. The Coast Guard had a lot of real needs but didn't seem to have the congressional influence to get those needs met. Nor did it have much support within its own cabinet department.

President Lyndon Johnson created the Department of Transportation (DOT) in 1966 and pushed the transfer of the Coast Guard from the Department of the Treasury to give his new creation more ballast in terms of numbers of employees, but within DOT the cause of the Coast Guard would never gain much traction. Next to the Federal Highway Administration or Federal Aviation Administration, with their close links to the politically influential oil, auto, cement, and airlines industries, the Coast Guard, with its small surfboat contracts and surplus Navy ships, had about as much clout as Amtrak.

In the early 1980s, the Reagan administration's Lt. Col. Oliver North (who'd later gain infamy for his role in the Iran-Contra scandal) championed and defended the Coast Guard against plans by Office of Management and Budget (OMB) chief David Stockman to outsource and privatize it.

In 1994, the Clinton administration called for a "streamlining" of the federal government and asked agencies to propose ways they could operate with a 10 percent reduction in force. While other agencies in the Department of Transportation and across the government used bureaucratic delay and obfuscation to avoid the cuts, the Coast Guard voluntarily reduced its personnel by 12 percent, laying off four thousand people. This inspired some service wags to suggest that if they could do more with less, they should be able to do everything with nothing. Many well-qualified midcareer officers, seeing the handwriting on the pilothouse wall, also began to leave the service in search of more stable employment.

By the time the Coast Guard left Governors Island as a cost-saving measure, its High Endurance Cutters, many built in the late 1960s, were experiencing a 25 percent loss of function due to unscheduled maintenance, as were their older patrol boats. Coast Guard helicopter in-flight engine power losses were occurring at a rate of 329 mishaps per 100,000 flying hours. The Federal Aviation Administration considers helicopters experiencing more than 1 mishap per 100,000 hours unsafe and unreliable. Still, no one suggested the Coast Guard reduce its search and rescue missions to protect its own people.

Rather, the Clinton administration's Office of Management and Budget wanted to know if there was really a need for the Coast Guard, if its functions couldn't be carried out by other agencies of government or (as had been suggested by the Reagan White House) handed off to the private sector.

While the Coast Guard didn't want to see its missions privatized, it began thinking it might need to see its lobbying efforts privatized.

Its deepwater ships and aircraft, which operated more than fifty miles offshore, were all approaching bloc obsolescence, facing the end of their useful lives at around the same time. So were many of its other assets, but much of the senior leadership was made up of blue-water cuttermen, and that became their immediate focus.

"When it was clear everything that went [more than] fifty miles offshore was aging at the same rate, we went through some strategic planning and did a roles-and-mission study with all our federal customers . . . all sitting around the table and talking about what they'd want twenty-five years down the road," former Coast Guard commandant James Loy recalls. Loy, a decorated Vietnam veteran, now works for the Cohen Group, the Washington, DC, lobbying firm founded by former secretary of defense William Cohen.

During his time as commandant (1998 to 2002), the Coast Guard decided that rather than contract for individual assets like patrol boats and Medium and High Endurance Cutters as it had in the past, the service would go with a "system of systems" approach asking competing industry teams to offer a single management plan and design for a whole package of deepwater assets—cutters, aircraft, sensors, communications, and logistics.

The original competing teams were led by Lockheed, Avondale Shipyard, and Science Applications International Corporation (SAIC).

These three consortiums were given their own offices on the top floor of Coast Guard headquarters. "I remember being asked, 'Are you read into Deepwater?' " says Adm. Gary Blore, now head of Coast Guard Acquisitions. "For the different consortiums you had to [read and] sign a nondisclosure clause, and they had their own security badges and locked doors. The fifth floor became this neighborhood of exclusivity."

In 2002, the Deepwater contract was awarded to ICGS, Integrated Coast Guard Systems, a joint venture of Lockheed Martin and Northrop Grumman. Its initial projected cost was $12 billion to $15 billion, though with post-9/11 contract revisions to make ships impervious to nuclear, biological, and chemical attack, with Hurricane Katrina damage to the National Security Cutter's Mississippi shipyard, and with ICGS doing the math, that number soon ballooned to $24 billion.

"We needed to sell the integrated system approach to acquisitions to the Office of Federal Procurement Policy at OMB," Admiral Loy recalls, "and I had many conversations about recognizing the shortfalls in terms of our [the Coast Guard's] lack of acquisitions and oversight expertise. That was one reason we were so open to industry expertise," he tells me, and I wonder if I've just missed something.

If you don't have enough farmers to build and guard your integrated system of henhouses and chicken runs, the normal reaction is not to be more open to the fox's expertise.

A clearer explanation of the Coast Guard's integrated "system of systems" approach can be found in a 2004 master's thesis written by Boston businessman and consultant Vikram Mansharamani.

Vikram tells me that while working on his PhD thesis at MIT's Sloan School of Management he met Admiral Allen, who was there getting his MBA. After some conversations, Vikram decided to do an independent study on Deepwater (that became one of his two master's) because it struck him as so absurd from a business point of view.

"I was shocked by this systems approach, looking at this idea that you give over management to the supplier and they tell you what you need and deliver it. You know, 'You need a marble Jacuzzi for this house I'm building you.' 'I do?' 'Sure everyone wants to look at their plasma TV from their marble Jacuzzi.' But everything happens for a reason, and I saw how this worked at a political level as interest groups met their needs."

Titled "The Deepwater Program: A Case Study in Organizational Transformation Inspired by the Parallel Interaction of Internal and External Core Groups" (like I said, it's a thesis) and based in part on interviews he conducted with key members of Coast Guard senior management between 1996 and 2003 before Deepwater became controversial, it highlights the unease that existed on the part of Coast Guard leadership about their ability to find the money needed to modernize their fleet.

Vikram puts it in terms of push and pull funding. Push funding is when agencies try to get appropriations based on their needs by lobbying (or "educating," since the armed services don't officially "lobby") on their own behalf, arguing in terms of the common good they provide the public. This is what the Coast Guard did to get new buoy tenders, but with very limited success, despite the obvious benefits that well-maintained aids to navigation provide for the nation's maritime commerce and twenty million recreational boaters.

Pull funding, by contrast, is when third parties (lobbyists) represent an agency or department's interests on Capitol Hill. Examples include the oil, auto, and asphalt industries lobbying for the Department of Transportation's pork-heavy highway bill or Tier 1 defense contractors wrangling congressional votes when the Department of Defense has some multibillion-dollar weapons system climbing in a gravity-defying cost spiral.

"The Coast Guard was underresourced, competing with submarines and $3 billion to $5 billion aircraft carriers and $1 billion destroyers. They came up on the short end against huge, well-heeled constituencies that know how to work Congress," Democratic Rep. Gene Taylor of Mississippi, one of only three Coast Guard veterans in Congress, tells me.

For the Coast Guard to modernize its deepwater assets would require Congress to approve up to a billion dollars a year in targeted acquisitions, something the modern Coast Guard had never attempted—although basic sausage making for the defense establishment.

To spark the interest of Tier 1 defense contractors and make the Coast Guard's requirements attractive to them, headquarters decided to bundle more than fifteen major projects into one "system of systems" package. They even created a manufacturer's incentive for future overseas sales, as the Air Force does with jet fighters.

"A partnership with a Tier 1 supplier affords one the opportunity to leverage their network, influence, and political savvy in terms of funding obtainment," Adm. Patrick Stillman, the Coast Guard's first Deepwater executive officer, told Vikram in 2003.

Future commandant Thad Allen, then chief of staff, concurred. When asked why the integrated systems approach was used to increase the scope of the Deepwater program, he stated that "it was the price of admission to the game."

"They have armies of lobbyists, they can help get dollars to get the job done. The White House and Congress listen to big industrial concerns" is how retired Coast Guard budget officer Capt. Jim McEntire later explained it to *New York Times* reporter Eric Lipton.

In 2002, the year their ICGS joint venture took charge of Deepwater, Lockheed and Northrop spent close to $10 million lobbying the federal government and another $4 million in campaign contributions to Washington politicians. Between 2000 and 2007, Lockheed alone spent $33 million on lobbying and $6 million on campaign donations.

Unfortunately, Coast Guard leadership, with what would prove to be a costly case of political naivety, looked at these big defense contractors, saw they were large and gray and had fins on their backs, and thought, "Cool, now we're swimming with the dolphins."

"We did have this idea that we would have these innovative ideas, that industry was so smart we'd slap our face in amazement," Admiral Blore, head of Coast Guard Acquisitions, tells me. "In the end it was pretty traditional looking. 'Let's have a large, medium, and baby platform; let's have a rotary wing and a propeller plane.' It was really nothing we wouldn't have thought of ourselves."

By the Short Hairs

While Admiral Loy could be said to be the architect of Deepwater, it was his successor, Commandant Thomas Collins, who would award the contract to ICGS to upgrade and replace ninety-one ships and 261 aircraft and make offshore communications secure and interoperable, at least among Deepwater assets and the Navy if not with other parts of the Coast Guard (the contract hadn't specified that). In 2005, Loy, now with the Cohen Group, joined the board of directors of Lockheed Martin. In the previous year, Lockheed-Martin had paid the Cohen Group half a million dollars in consulting fees. Loy was placed on the board's ethics and corporate responsibility committee.

Loy believes the major problem with ICGS was that it was set up as an equal partnership between Lockheed and Northrop. "The governing structure was doomed to, I won't say failure, but doomed to be a problem when it was split fifty-fifty. I mean, someone has to be in charge. I may have some protective feeling for Lockheed-Martin, but as a board member I'm pretty proud of what we've done."

"I was unpleasantly surprised how much contention there was between these two competing business interests. There was a lot of immaturity evident," notes an executive from a subcontracting company that developed classified software for Deepwater and asked that he and his company not be named.

The problems that grew to plague Deepwater involved more than sibling rivalry, however.

"I talked to the guy who built the RIB (rigid inflatable boat) for the 123 for $125,000 and turned it over to Lockheed, which billed the Coast Guard something in the neighborhood of $500,000, explaining that the difference was their lobbying fee to work Congress," Representative Taylor tells me.

It's stories like this that inspired the Justice Department to open an ongoing criminal investigation into the Deepwater 123 project.

Key Deepwater problems that I'm not the first to identify included these:

- not enough oversight/authority by the Coast Guard
- failure of the Coast Guard to seek out project expertise it lacked from the U.S. Navy early in the process
- contract language that was vague and included incentives that rewarded

the contractor in the present while delaying proof of product into the future when the whole "system of systems" was delivered

- competition and blame-shifting between the two ICGS partners
- attempts to push new technologies that benefited the contractor rather than the customer
- attempts to go with naval warfare systems and "off-the-shelf" products that already existed but didn't necessarily meet the Coast Guard's needs
- Coast Guard Aviation excluded from product decisions
- Coast Guard surface operators excluded from product decisions
- Coast Guard engineers and naval architects excluded from product design and decisions
- lack of strong congressional oversight until the program began imploding in public sight

All that was still to come, however. Having outsourced its management responsibility to the new "systems integrator," the Coast Guard set up a new Deepwater office in its boxy blue headquarters building at Buzzards Point by the confluence of the less than pure Potomac and Anacostia rivers. The office included roughly seventy-five Coasties and seventy-five contractors. Their first job was to sell the deal internally, which they did with lots of slick PR materials provided by ICGS.

"I had just come back from [duty with] the inspector general's office in the Department of Commerce investigating waste, fraud, and abuse," recalls Jon Sall, special agent in charge of the Coast Guard Investigative Service in Miami. "Suddenly I'm looking at these Deepwater full-color brochures with CDs enclosed that went out to everyone in every part of the Coast Guard. They're touting how 'this is a new kind of contract and a partnership with industry,' and I'm thinking, 'These guys are gonna fleece the Coast Guard. These beltway bandits have us by the short hairs.' "

Chief Chris Smith, in charge of electronics and IT for Coast Guard forces deployed in Bahrain, had a similar feeling. "When I was an [enlisted] E-5, this lieutenant came to sell Deepwater to us. I remember asking, 'Where's the oversight?' and he said I needed more of a corporate mentality. He may have been from Deepwater, but he didn't have this." He taps the cutterman's patch on his chest. "I didn't trust their loyalty. I wouldn't want them on a [vessel] boarding team with me. Anyone above 06 [captain] level who didn't speak out on this needs to be fired."

Unfortunately, those who did speak out, including Rear Adm. Errol Brown, the Coast Guard's chief engineer (and first black admiral), and Capt. Kevin Jarvis, who ran the Engineering Logistics Center at the Coast Guard shipyard in Baltimore, were ignored or told that they were out of line criticizing a "world-class shipbuilder" like Northrop.

Capt. Mathew Bliven is a ship driver, naval architect, and engineer who was on Coast Guard inspection teams during the construction of the 110-foot cutters in the 1980s and 175- and 225-foot buoy tenders in the 1990s. "My experience with acquisitions is you get what you inspect for," he says. "We had fifty to sixty people in the shipyard [Marinette Marine, in Wisconsin] with the 175s and 225s holding the contractor accountable. With the Deepwater plan there was very little on-site oversight."

I first met Adm. Gary Blore in the spring of 2007, when he was executive officer in charge of the Deepwater office, which had moved around the corner from the service's boxy blue headquarters to the Jemal Building, a boxy brown one that had previously housed the FBI's D.C. field office. Even though he's a big guy who scowls easily, I still thought the loyalty question was a legitimate one and so asked if, working as closely as they did with the contractors, Coast Guard officers in the Deepwater office had "gone native."

"It started as esprit de corps, and I wouldn't be as strong as you're saying, 'going native,' but you work with industry and you get all this criticism from other parts of the organization [the Coast Guard] and you seek solace and share a sense of common cause [with industry]," he admits. Just then his aide interrupts to say that Admiral Allen is now on CNN talking about Deepwater.

We take a break to join half a dozen staffers seated in front of a flat-screen TV. It's midafternoon. Before the commandant gets to speak, the cable news channel has an updated report on a pair of stray whales that have wandered into the Sacramento delta in California. Coast Guard crews from Station Rio Vista are helping herd them back toward the ocean.

CNN's Kyra Phillips then interviews Admiral Allen for about ten minutes. She's breezy and lovely. He's stolid and spit-shined.

She talks about Deepwater and asks about millions of tax dollars wasted on the 123s and structural problems on the National Security Cutter. He assures her, "Our National Security Cutters will be the most capable cutters we've ever produced for the Coast Guard."

She tells him she's been on these cutters "going through Antarctica and cutting through the ice and getting to the South Pole. They're—it's an incredible ship." She's talking about a Coast Guard icebreaker. He's talking about the next-generation Coast Guard multimission ship, the first of which is still under construction in Mississippi.

He explains the added costs of making them "more survivable in a chemical, nuclear, biological attack . . . Everything was directed at the new requirements and the new threat environment we found ourselves in after 9/11." He continues to talk on about maritime domain awareness, the need for persistent surveillance in the marine environment, and how to detect "anomalous activity" and intercept it.

"We look forward to seeing solutions to those problems," she responds convincingly. "Admiral Thad Allen, head of the U.S. Coast Guard, I appreciate your time today, sir."

"Thank you, Kyra."

There's an immediate discussion in the Deepwater office of how they thought he did.

I'm thinking, if the Coast Guard helps save the whales they're heroes. If the whales die they're the guys who can't even float a boat. Eventually the whales will head back out to sea through the Golden Gate, but on their own schedule, at night, so that the paparazzi are unable to catch their departure.

My next conversation with Admiral Blore is in 2008 after the Coast Guard has taken charge of Deepwater management and promoted him to head of their new Acquisitions Directorate. The latest catch phrase is "The Coast Guard is the system of systems." Dozens of civilian contract management employees are being hired on, and, in the interim, Navy experts from the Naval Sea Systems Command and Naval Air Systems Command have been contracted (at government rate) to provide third-party review and expertise on cost estimates, design review, and other oversight issues.

"That relationship works great 'cause the Navy knows how to speak Coast Guard and to a large degree you substitute the Navy for ICGS," Admiral Blore explains, which makes me wonder why this wasn't thought of six years earlier.

Blore seems less combative now, more assured that things are finally on the right track. Still, he takes exception to the "foxes guarding the henhouse" metaphor.

"Industry was not just out for itself or it could have been eating chickens every night," he claims, pointing to some outside contracts that were awarded by Lockheed and Northrop, including the potential billion-dollar Eagle Eye contract to Bell Helicopter.

Yet without adequate oversight or direction from the customer (the Coast

Guard), Deepwater failed to deliver on many of its promises, including timely production of fully functioning vessels.

Deep Steam

This wasn't the first time that the service got it wrong on a major acquisition program and untried technologies even while making a necessary transition from one historic era to another.

In the 1840s, recognizing that the age of sail was coming to a close, the Revenue Service built eight steam-powered vessels, some with bell-shaped hulls that used horizontal underwater paddlewheels for propulsion rather than sidewheels. It also purchased cutters that used the new largely untried Ericsson screw propeller. Early in their testing, major problems emerged with the cutters' performance or lack thereof.

In 1845, Capt. William Howard, an early advocate turned critic of the horizontal Hunter wheel, was upbraided for trying to convert one of the ships into a more seaworthy sidewheel steamer.

Construction delays, noncompetitive bidding, and cost overruns continued through the Mexican-American War, during which the new cutters proved to be a greater danger to their crews than to the enemy.

By 1849, all eight steamships—including one originally estimated to cost less than $50,000 whose final price tag ran over $220,000—had been converted to lightships, sold off to private investors, or transferred to the U.S. Coast Survey. They had sailed under the Revenue Service for about three years. The entire program that was supposed to cost under $400,000 ended up costing the government over $2 million. After that, the Treasury Department and its Revenue Service were not allowed to build or purchase any new ships without congressional authorization.

Today legislation that echoes Congress's displeasure more than 150 years ago requires that the Coast Guard maintain firm control over its Deepwater program, have open and competitive bidding for new assets, and periodically report progress on its acquisitions to congressional oversight committees in the House and Senate.

Oversight

Elijah Cummings is a big man with a creased melon of a head and a slow, deliberate manner that can make him seem like an immovable object to any self-styled irresistible force. As chair of the Coast Guard and Maritime Transportation Subcommittee of the House Committee on Transportation and Infrastructure, the six-term congressman oversees all aspects of the service.

In the middle of a series of innocuous questions to a witness during that marathon Deepwater hearing in 2007 he asked, "And who awarded $4 million out of a possible $4.6 million [contract] bonus when we got boats that aren't even floating?"

When the inspector general for the Department of Homeland Security, who'd been frustrated in his own investigations of Deepwater, told Cummings the contracts were based on attitude and effort rather than outcome, the congressman cut to the chase. "Would you be for pulling the plug?" he asked.

"He's got a very matter-of-fact manner about him, an everyman approach that can catch witnesses off guard," says Steve Ellis, an ex–Coast Guard lieutenant jg who, as vice president of the nonprofit Taxpayers for Common Sense, has followed the Baltimore Democrat's career. "He's got that Columbo [TV detective] approach that can lull them into overconfidence. Whenever he starts a question with 'Maybe I just don't get this . . .' you know he gets it exactly."

I meet with the congressman at his office off a marble hallway in Rayburn 2235. All the House and Senate offices have paired U.S. and state flags on either side of their doors, so you have to read the numbers carefully to find your way.

Cummings's small reception area includes an office manager's desk, blue carpet, a two-person green couch, and framed photos on the wall including Cummings with Bill Clinton when he was president, Bill Cosby, House Speaker Nancy Pelosi, South Africa's Nelson Mandela, and the University of Maryland's Juan Dixon the year he led the Terrapins to their first NCAA basketball title. In his inner office Cummings has a meeting table in front of his desk below a large black-and-white lithograph of African American cowboys in the Old West [he represents West Baltimore].

"I didn't want it [the Coast Guard subcommittee chairmanship]. I can't swim, and I get sick on small boats," the former head of the Congressional Black Caucus admits in his carefully measured baritone. "I wanted Appropriations or Ways and Means, and at first when the Speaker [Pelosi] asked me to take this [in 2006] I didn't pay attention to it. I was mourning what could've been, but that's changed now . . . I recently turned down an offer to go on the Commerce Committee and decided to stay here and have an influence where I can affect every American. I'm committed to and enjoy it and want to help these men and women do things that will have an effect . . . I've been all over the place to talk with Coast Guard people. I do want them to know they're appreciated by the American people and by Congress."

An aide tells him a floor vote is coming on a resolution he's introduced. He asks her to see if he's the floor manager for it. She leaves, returns, tells him he's not.

I ask him how he views Deepwater a year after his hearings and with oversight legislation he and Senator Cantwell have introduced coming into effect.

"We're out of deep water but still almost over our heads. It was an embarrassment not just to the Coast Guard but to the nation . . . The Coast Guard has to be honest with itself and needs a 'Come to Jesus' meeting to say what they'll now do and do well in terms of personnel and inspections."

"Yet they don't have much of a constituency in Congress, not like the Department of Defense," I point out.

"I am thoroughly convinced in my fifty-seven years of life that one person can take on an issue and direct their energy to make a situation better. One train of thought is they're our Thin Blue Line at sea and need to be thickened, but some members [of Congress] don't see it that way—it's like Army, Navy, Marines, Air Force, but there's a reluctance to understand the Coast Guard's jobs. After 9/11 their responsibilities increased, and we as Congress haven't kept up, and so it's like a rubber band stretched to the nth degree, and while I don't see it breaking I can see weak spots forming in the band. Right now it's symbolic of what could become a culture of mediocrity. Something's got to give. Congress has to increase its size, and my goal is at least ten thousand more (service members) over the next seven years.

"I think the public has high expectations of the Coast Guard when things like Katrina happen, but [at the same time] they almost can take it for granted. Of those thirty three thousand they saved, over twenty thousand would have died in New Orleans if not for the Coast Guard. That's taken for granted.

"Like the theologian Swindoll said"—he then spells out the radio evangelist's name to make sure I use the quote—"The best things you do are unseen, unnoticed, unappreciated, and unapplauded."

His aide is now anxiously waiting on him. He slowly gets up to leave, offering to answer any other questions I might have at another time.

In the reception area, there's a TV tuned to closed-circuit coverage from the House floor, where his floor manager explains that Representative Cummings has unfortunately been delayed and so he'd like permission to enter his statement in the record. They then pass Cummings's resolution honoring pre–Civil War abolitionist and Underground Railroad conductor Harriet Tubman of Maryland, another American hero who has been too little noticed, appreciated, or applauded.

Senator Cantwell's caught the flu, "or some infection," flying back from a fact-finding trip to Asia, so our meeting at her office is canceled. After a number of attempts to reschedule, we finally talk on the phone.

After my chat with Cummings, I ask her if she wanted to be chair of the Senate Commerce Subcommittee on Oceans, Atmosphere, Fisheries, and Coast Guard.

"We see everyday impacts of the Coast Guard on fisheries, drug interdiction, keeping our [Puget Sound] ferry fleet safe, so it was obvious to me that this was important."

"So you wanted the chairmanship?"

"Yes."

She goes on to explain the connection between the oceans and the Coast Guard. "There's a larger discussion on the health of the oceans and climate debate and ocean acidification [from carbon dioxide], but they're not a central element. The Coast Guard is enforcement but doesn't do policy. When you have changes like are now taking place in the Arctic, the first persons you think of, the first day job, is going to be the Coast Guard's, but for larger policy questions about how to deal with resource development and climate, that will take place elsewhere."

I ask if the Coast Guard has a constituency in the Senate beyond herself and Senator Snowe of Maine. She says there are some other interested senators, including John Kerry, who used to chair her subcommittee, and Frank Lautenberg of New Jersey. So I figure that's at least four out of one hundred.

While it's now in the Department of Homeland Security, Senator Cantwell believes that because of its multiple roles the Coast Guard could be in several other places. Even so, she isn't thinking about moving them, "at this time."

She recognizes that the Coast Guard has to grow significantly, "to keep pace with its traditional and emerging missions, but right now I'm more focused on the Deepwater program and making sure the resources get delivered and the taxpayer is protected. We're not out of the woods yet. This problem got way out of hand, so there are still changes that need to take place and outside agencies [the Navy, the GAO, the Congressional Budget Office] that have a role to play.

"I think Admiral Allen did a great job with Hurricane Katrina . . . but this acquisitions disaster is bigger than he is. He's well intended, but like most people would, he just wants to be free of it as soon as possible, but it's not that simple. There's going to be continued oversight."

Out to Sea

I'm talking with the first CO of a National Security Cutter, Capt. Patrick Stadt, a smart, low-key CO with cool gray eyes, a long, lined face, and lanky six-foot frame, at his office on Coast Guard Island in Alameda, California. The *Bertholf* is supposed to be docked outside, but due to program delays there's just him and some eighty-five crewmembers who have been training here without a ship for eight months. They're getting ready to depart for Pascagoula, Mississippi, where they'll spend an additional five months living in a hotel near the Northrop shipyard during the cutter's builder and acceptance trials.

I ask if he's excited about getting command of a state-of-the-art vessel like *Bertholf*.

"I wouldn't call it state-of-the-art. Requirements [in the contract] were good but not thorough," he explains with a frankness that impresses me. "It might be a different ship if we [the Coast Guard] built it from the bottom up. We certainly had people challenging it from the bottom up. Still, it's better than anything we've ever had before."

General Quarters—all hands man battle stations throughout the ship," the pipe announces with a familiar double ah-oogah alarm just after 8:00 A.M. I'm on board the *Bertholf* for a weeklong run from Miami to Baltimore in June 2008 before it heads home to Alameda for the first time via Cancún, the Panama Canal, and Puerto Vallarta.

Captain Stadt is seated in his command chair in the chilly CIC—Combat Information Center—one deck below the wide, glassy bridge. His seat faces a large flat screen on the forward bulkhead showing a FLIR (forward-looking infrared) video image of the main gun mount. Also in front of him are half a dozen puddle-shaped dual-terminal workstations that look like something out of an early *Star Trek* episode. Because of the classified electronics' tendency to drip condensation when the room gets above fifty degrees, the people manning these stations are wearing blue winter peacoats. From his Captain Kirk–like chair, Pat Stadt calls the shots for today's gunnery exercise.

We're in Giant Killer, a Navy live-fire range off Virginia that still has its share of fishing boats and freighters that the *Bertholf* has asked to stand at least fifteen miles off. On the aft helicopter flight deck, a dozen crewmembers are inflating a "Giant Killer Tomato" [no relation to the range]. This is a ten-foot by seven-foot floating orange balloon with silver Mylar panels that makes it look like a cartoon pilothouse. When it's ready, they lift it over their heads and toss it over the side.

Soon the 57 mm Bofors gun on the foc'sle, the first of its kind on a U.S. warship, starts firing two-, four-, and then twenty-round bursts at the killer tomato three thousand yards out. After ninety rounds, the video display on the bridge shows a close-up of the target slowly deflating and sinking. The gun crew goes forward and starts tossing empty copper shell casings over the side. Later the Navy contract people riding aboard tell me it was a very successful shoot, which makes me hope the homeland is never attacked by an armada of giant orange balloons.

Next it's time to test-fire the CIWS (pronounced "Sea Whiz") Close-In Weapons System, a 4,500-rounds-per-minute domed Gatling gun located toward the rear of the ship above the helicopter control shack. This is the first Coast Guard CIWS that can not only shoot at incoming aircraft and missiles but also be used for warning and disabling fire aimed at surface targets. It fires six bursts of a hundred rounds each. From forward on the bridge its rippling fire sounds like an industrial sewing machine, if one that stitches only funeral shrouds. The fifth and sixth bursts pockmark a newly inflated "tomato" with 20 mm shell holes.

Then they fire chaff and rockets from launcher tubes just off the bridge's wings. The chaff rounds boom like mortars and (except for a few dud canisters that splash into the sea) burst overhead in smoky white fireworks, releasing spiraling clouds of silver foil designed to distract the radar on an incoming missile. The rockets roar more loudly, leaving smoke trails and puffs of chaff that create additional false radar targets.

Along with its armaments, the *Bertholf* has numerous other innovative aspects. Chief among them is simply the fact that it's a large, modern ship, which is a cultural sea change for a service more used to patching up and making do with thirty- and forty-year-old cutters that would look more at home in maritime museums than on the open sea.

At 418 feet in length and a beamy 54 feet wide, the *Bertholf* has a smooth, quiet ride, at least in the low seas we pass through. They're hoping to take it into the Bering Sea off Alaska soon for a test drive in big gnarly waters. It's a crew-friendly ship with wide passageways, a large galley, a gym, and staterooms that include flat-screen TVs and computers. Most officers and chiefs share two-bunk staterooms. Unlike the service's High Endurance Cutters that often crowd crews into twelve- and sixteen-person berthing areas, no stateroom on the *Bertholf* has more than six racks stacked two high (as opposed to narrow triple bunks). Being a highly automated ship, the *Bertholf* also has a downsized crew of 113 rather than the 165 or so normally found on 378-foot cutters.

"With people holed up in their rooms, it can get kind of like a creepy movie at night with its empty passageways," says Electronics Chief Warrant Officer Matt Boyle, whom I stumble upon alone in the wardroom. This might appeal to the stolid, brushy-haired Boyle, who, having done most of his *Bertholf* tour ashore, is soon slated to run the isolated loran station in Port Clarence, Alaska, where dead walruses wash up on the empty beach.

On visits to the computerized engine control room (ECR) and main engine rooms, I get to check out the ship's two near pristine 10,000 hp diesels and 30,000 hp GE jet gas turbine that can be controlled by touch screens from here or the bridge. The ship's unique cross-connect gear allows a single diesel engine to run both propellers at up to eighteen knots or go to twenty-eight knots in CONDEC, combined diesel and gas turbine mode. With five modes of operation and greatly increased fuel efficiency, the *Bertholf* can easily match the twelve-thousand-mile range of smaller, lighter 378s, according to "fuel, oil, and water king" Machinery Technician First Class Jason Hoppenrath.

I board the *Bertholf* on a Friday evening in Miami at the tail end of a reception being held on its large flight deck. With its sleek and stealthy white silhouette, the ship blends well with the city's ultramodern skyline. The reception's white party tents, once the ship is operational, will double as shade and shelter for undocumented migrants taken aboard during at-sea interdictions.

On arrival, I'm suffering from a flu-like headache and hacking cough. Sick bay corpsman Chief Rocky Gipson checks my lungs and ears before giving me some cough drops and decongestants. I then settle in to my below-deck stateroom shared with three Naval Sea Systems contractors.

We get under way the next morning, sailing out of the Port of Miami until we're in deep cobalt blue water. On the bridge I meet the salty and taciturn Master Chief Bob Montague.

"Morning," I say.

"Glad you didn't put 'Good' before that, because it hasn't been for me," he complains, hankering for a cigarette. Bob has spent eleven years at sea out of twenty-three in the service. The Chief's Mess, which is billeted for fifteen but sailing with 19 chiefs, has over 120 years of sea time and 300 years of service between them.

Engineering Chief Warrant Officer Richard "Sam" Sambenedetto has ten years at sea out of his eighteen in the Coast Guard. The beta testers for this new ship, I quickly realize, are among the saltiest in the service. Sam is a big guy with colorful nautical tattoos covering his forearms, including rope braids, a sailing ship, flags, his kids' names, and an American eagle. Grandfathered in before the service's new, more restrictive rules on tats, his eight knuckles read SHIP MATE.

Up on the bridge, executive officer Capt. Kelly Hatfield and operations chief Cdr. Joe LeCato are going at it as they have been for the past two years. Five-nine and five-seven, both bald, mustached, smart, and rotund, they could be brothers and act like they are. In a few days, Kelly will be leaving for a shore assignment and Joe will replace him as XO.

"You should write a side chapter on how incompetents gain leadership," Kelly suggests to me, nodding toward his replacement.

"You could write it today," Joe shoots back.

I head down ladders and through several airlocks designed to protect the core of the ship against chemical or biological attack till I reach the sturdy drop-down "Rescue door" on the starboard side of the ship. Common on cruise ships, this water-level access door and the watertight compartment behind it are new to the Coast Guard.

At the moment they're using them to disembark visitors from Miami's District 7, including its commander Adm. Steve Branham.

Bosun's Mate 1 Jordan Baptiste off-loads the visitors from his 33-foot Special Purpose Craft (SPC) onto a 110-foot cutter standing by, then returns for the captain, the XO, and myself. I climb aboard the red jet-drive boat, straddling one of its saddle seats next to Jordan, and we do a quick loop around the ship as it's under way, inspecting some less than satisfactory paintwork from the shipyard.

We then take up position behind the stern notch ramp with its sliding doors, overhead lifting cranes, and deck cradles designed so that the *Bertholf* can quickly launch and recover two rigid-hull inflatables. A third small boat deploys from a davit on the right side of the ship.

The *Bertholf* is cruising at twelve knots. "Hang on," Jordan warns before he guns the jet drive and we ride up the rubber-lined ramp with a clacking thump and jerk as a net line stretched between hydraulic arms captures our bow horn. It feels like a wooden roller coaster hitting the brakes too hard. We're now towed up the notch as the big stern doors close behind us. Jordan thinks they're too slow and bulky and should be replaced by lighter gull-wing doors that lift up and out. The CO adds this to his list of needed changes.

I soon fall into a shipboard routine, waking up with the 6:30 reveille pipe. After breakfast I head up to the bridge, then wander the ship doing interviews with the crew and outside evaluators, undogging and redogging (opening and closing) latches on multiple watertight doors in order to get around, and also catch some deck time in the warmth outside the skin of the ship. I watch the occasional flying fish, turtles, and a sunset pod of dolphins first spotted on the Spook Nine weapons radar. Captain Stadt has a standing order to be called to the bridge when marine life is spotted. In the evenings after transcribing my notes, I usually join some of the officers or crew watching a movie. Often it's a war movie: *Kelly's Heroes*, *The Kingdom*, *300*, *Black Hawk Down*. Lights Out is at 2200 hours (10:00 P.M.).

Saturday afternoon they announce "Steel Beach" and "Fish Call." Young Coasties head out on the flight deck in their bathing suits with beach towels to catch some sun on the rough gray nonskid or bring out a few rods and try to catch a fish without much luck (someone caught a four- to five-foot dorado when they were transiting the Gulf of Mexico). A soft football gets tossed around. The helicopter crash netting is lowered and becomes passable nylon hammocks. Below on the boat deck, the smokers are tossing their cigarette butts over the side.

Each afternoon there's Crew Quarters called on the flight deck. At one XO Kelly Hatfield tells them he's been called to his new job early and will be leaving them in Baltimore.

"The last couple of days have been sad for me. I didn't have time to prepare to move on. This is my sixth ship and the best crew I ever had, so consider that special." He begins to choke up. Sam and one of the chiefs step forward, bracket him, and pat him on the back. I try to imagine an Army warrant officer and sergeant stepping forward to comfort a colonel while he's addressing the troops. Some Coast Guard things just don't translate.

"The point is your work's not done just because I'm leaving, so stay focused," Hatfield continues firmly. "Take respites where you can but don't lose your momentum. In the next few days the commandant, the secretary of homeland security, and about ten other admirals are coming aboard because this ship is so important, so stay focused."

Two weeks earlier, the *Bertholf* had landed a big HH-60 Jayhawk on its flight deck, something no other cutter has tried in over a decade. Now, as we enter Chesapeake Bay, a smaller HH-65C Dolphin from Florida's HITRON antidrug squad approaches. They've installed a new tracked trolley system on the flight deck to guide and secure helicopters as they land. This automated trolley system was designed to eliminate the need for a tie-down crew on deck in rough seas.

No Coast Guard helicopter has yet had a probe attached to lock with the robot sled's griper claw, however. The second deck hangar was built for a pair of unmanned aerial vehicles, but use of the Navy's Fire Scout is likely years away even if—with maritime radar added—it proves practical for Coast Guard missions.

Meanwhile Captain Stadt wants the *Bertholf* to do its first operational deployment with a pair of Dolphins or a Jayhawk on its flight deck to extend the ship's tactical reach.

I watch the 65's approach from inside the helicopter shack above the flight deck (the icebreaker *Healy* is the only other Coast Guard vessel to have one). Helicopter control officer Lt. Krystyn Pecora is just over five feet tall and has to stand on an upside-down plastic milk crate to do her work. "6518 . . . This is Tower, you are cleared to land," she instructs the approaching orange chopper. From inside the shack, she can also hit an emergency button to spray nine hundred gallons per minute of fire-suppressing foam, eliminating the need for a fire crew on the flight deck.

"Green deck! All stations Green deck!" she announces. The ship will now hold its course and speed steady till the 65 lands or is waved off by the yellow-shirted Landing Signal Officer standing below us.

The pilot lands it gently, and four blue-shirted tie-down crewmembers run out under the still-turning rotor blades to secure the orange helicopter to the deck with safety straps. I head down to talk to the crew and check out their machine gun and sniper rifle, used to warn and then disable drug-running go-fast boats.

On Thursday night we anchor three miles off Annapolis, and a long gray utility boat from the U.S. Naval Academy shuttles us ashore for a "Cinderella liberty" (everyone has to be back on board by midnight).

The crew are all scrubbing, sanding, painting, and polishing the ship as we approach Baltimore the next day. The CO spots someone's touch-up paint job that was poorly executed. "They have a future with Northrop Grumann," he notes dryly.

Visitors have been shuttling aboard all day. Coast Guard Commandant Thad Allen arrives on the service's new rugged-looking 45-foot RBM (Response Boat Medium), along with Master Chief Skip Bowen.

They talk to the crew and are soon joined by the secretary of homeland security, a passel of admirals, and other VIPs.

Entering Baltimore Harbor, we're greeted by a water-spraying fireboat, a dockside crowd of reporters and camera crews, black-clad security agents, Rep. Elijah Cummings, and dozens of curious tourists behind metal police barricades at the Broadway Pier in the popular Fells Point waterfront district.

"I'm glad you came up to my neighborhood," Cummings tells the commandant.

"Purely coincidental, Congressman," Thad Allen quips.

"I'll take that," Cummings replies, grinning.

There will be a Coast Guard Foundation reception that evening and two days of public tours and congressional visitors up from DC before they sail again.

There are still eight shipboard problem areas to be resolved between the contractor and the Coast Guard, plus the dry-dock time that will be needed to reshape the ship's hull in order to extend its life (Northrop Grumann claims this is unnecessary; the Navy and Coast Guard disagree).

"We'll spend three to four years getting it up to Coast Guard standards," Kelly Hatfield predicts.

Captain Stadt agrees but still believes it's a fine ship.

While the *Bertholf* may be a fine ship and an impressive addition to the Coast Guard, it's also clear that, in the wake of the Deepwater contracting fiasco, it will be a long time before National Security Cutters replace the service's twelve aging High Endurance Cutters, and longer still before there's a truly twenty-first-century deepwater fleet.

In the interim, to paraphrase a discredited former secretary of defense, the Coast Guard won't be operating with the fleet they'd like. Instead, as Thad Allen told the crew, "We have to manage with the fleet we've got."

CHAPTER 12

Red, White, and Black

"Sea duty is not punishment. To think of it that way is to dishonor every sailor who has ever walked the decks of a Coast Guard or Revenue cutter."
—CDR. WAYNE PARENT

"When the crew gets seasick they keep working—they stay on watch with a plastic bag and keep working. The bags get incinerated. We call them puke burns."
—CAPT. CRAIG "BARK" LLOYD, COAST GUARD CUTTER *MUNRO*

Black Hull

"Kelly just got hammered," Lt. Meredith Phillips notes from the high glassed-in bridge of the *Aspen*. We've just passed under the shadow of the Golden Gate Bridge, and already twelve-foot seas are breaking over the buoy tender's bow. The soaking-wet rigger, Shannon Kelly, climbs down from the fo'c'sle and tosses her cup of "bug juice," now half saltwater, over the side as she squishes past two seventeen-foot-high, eight-thousand-pound green buoys secured to the rolling deck.

"Let's slow down," Lt. Cdr. Steve Wittrock, the *Aspen*'s CO orders.

Commissioned in 2001, the 225-foot black-hulled *Aspen* is, though seven years older than the *Bertholf*, still one of the Coast Guard's newest vessels. Along with red-hulled icebreakers and white-hulled Medium and High Endurance Cutters, black-hulled seagoing buoy tenders are part of the service's deepwater fleet, which regularly operates more than fifty miles offshore. These sixty-five large vessels form the leading edge of the Coast Guard when it comes to counternarcotics and migrant interdiction, securing sea lanes from threats of piracy and terrorism, providing for science at the poles, and maintaining vital aids to navigation that global trade depends on. They also make port calls around the world, training and carrying out professional exchanges with local coast guards from China to West Africa, presenting a positive image of non-U.S. gunboat diplomacy.

The *Aspen*, based at Yerba Buena Island, does most of its work on San Francisco Bay and along the West Coast from Baja to the Oregon border. Designed to service and maintain buoys and other aids to navigation, it also does law enforcement work, including fisheries and counterdrug patrols. It normally doesn't do buoy servicing in February, but with four Northern California buoys reported missing, damaged, or displaced by recent winter storms, Steve is hoping to sneak through a weather window between the low-pressure fronts that have been hammering the coast. Unfortunately the twenty-four-hour forecast is now calling for twelve-foot seas and high winds. That's enough to convince the National Oceanographic and Atmospheric Administration to pull its technician off the boat and delay a repair on one of its big offshore weather buoys. Steve is hoping the twenty-knot winds will die down soon and the swells ease overnight. For safety's sake he gets on the ship's pipe and announces a weather deck. For the next thirty hours, the decks and ladders outside the ship's skin will be off-limits to the crew of fifty, who will have to get around using internal stairwell ladders.

"Look at that." Steve, medium height, with light brown hair and an easygoing manner, nods toward a rainbow arching over Point Bonito.

The radio reports a sailboat demasted and drifting off Monterey, and there's some discussion on the bridge over whether the *Aspen* will now be ordered to turn left instead of right. Sector decides to send the *Pike*, an 87-foot patrol boat, instead. It will be pushing its limits, with a hard ride south and difficult tow back, but this will permit the *Aspen* to continue on its mission 250 miles north to Eureka, where a channel buoy has broken loose and gone missing and another is reported out of position. On the way back down south, they'll replace a damaged buoy at the Noyo River mouth by Fort Bragg, where a fourth buoy is also said to be out of position, or "discrep," as the crew calls it, referring to "discrepancies" when the buoys are not where they're supposed to be. The Coast Guard is committed to making sure 99.8 percent of America's 6,500 major navigational buoys are "nondiscrepant," that is, fully operational, well maintained, and where they belong. Until recently I was among the tens of millions of Americans who had no idea this is one of the Coast Guard's missions.

Yet whenever I sail out of a U.S. harbor or port, I always look to spot the green daymarkers, or buoys, to the right of the harbor channel and the red ones to the left, to be sure we're in safe water. "Red, right, returning" is the way to remember where to look for the red buoys when coming back into port. Along with radar, GPS and loran, Coast Guard lighthouses, light buoys, and sea buoys help recreational boaters and commercial mariners navigate in and out of our great ports, rivers, and bays, while NOAA weather buoys, which the Coast Guard also maintains and repairs, help determine when it's even safe to be at sea.

By lunch, the boat has begun pitching and rolling, a chief has spilled his chicken soup on a stairwell deck, and the seas have turned jade, the skies an ominous gray, and Lieutenant Phillips, along with a number of her shipmates, a distinctive greenish tinge.

This is in marked contrast to the calm blue day months earlier when the Discovery Channel's *Dirty Jobs* filmed on the *Aspen*, making it the most famous buoy tender in the Coast Guard fleet.

The deck crew tells how they spent two weeks pulling and dropping buoys till they found a really crusty fouled one for the show's host, Mike Rowe, to help clean. They'd used their big forty-thousand-pound marine crane and cross-deck winches to lift the barnacle-, mussel- and kelp-encrusted buoy onto the deck, then handed him a long-handled scraper blade. "Did anyone have any idea barnacles smell so bad?" Mike Rowe says in the TV segment, grinning as he scrapes the big, meaty yellow crustaceans off the underside of the buoy. He describes their runny chunks as "some sort of maritime omelet." Buoy deck supervisor Josh Peelman then has Mike "shoot the tube," climbing up inside the forced-air chamber that rings the buoy bell whenever waves start creating suction and pressure. Anything obstructing the tube will reduce the sound, so Mike has to go inside with a small handheld camera and begin scraping it clean. "I'm pulling hunks of this stuff as I go," he explains in a claustrophobic close-up shot. "Blockage coming down," he calls out on reaching the top of the tube. "Tool coming down. Host coming down." He then helps "heat and beat" an anchor chain rivet pin with a torch and sledgehammer before the buoy goes back in the water.

While the segment makes it seem like cool (if dirty) work, it lacks the added three-dimensional drama of tossing seas and gusting winds. Also, they'd just aired an earlier episode in which Mike goes fishing for slime eels off New England, and no job, no matter how dirty, can match the pure disgust factor of handling blind, mucus-spewing deep-ocean flesh borers. It was enough to make a hagfish gag.

Rough seas or not, our first day out is also Super Bowl Sunday, February 3, 2008, with the unbeaten New England Patriots facing off against the New York Giants. Folks are viewing the game in the officers' wardroom and on the enlisted mess deck below, except for those on watch or hunkered down in their racks trying not to get sick. The cooks have prepared hot wings, ranch dip, and other game treats for those feeling up to it.

Early in the game I'm gnawing a small poultry leg at one of the floor-bolted mess tables when Bosun's Mate Second Class Patrick "Paddy" White joins me. The newest deck supervisor, Paddy is short and rotund, wears glasses, and has a fierce commitment to his job. He explains that when the work gets under way I'll be seeing green hard hats ("break-ins" learning the job), blue hats (qualified riggers), yellow hats (buoy supervisors acting as riggers), and white hats (buoy deck supervisors). One of the *Aspen's* four chiefs will be running the crane while the others watch over the work from the fo'c'sle (forward) deck and the captain and officers from the bridge. I'm not convinced I'll get to see any of this, however, as the seas are continuing to build. Every half hour or so the TV screens go black as we're hit by a big wave that throws the satellite receiver off kilter.

Back in the wardroom, five officers are watching the game, including Steve and his XO, Lt. Stephanie Morrison, one of three sisters from upstate New York now serving in the Coast Guard.

"Maybe those NOAA guys knew something we didn't," Steve jokes halfheartedly as we slam-bang through fifteen- to twenty-foot seas. "People slow down as they get beat up by rising seas. Everyone gets tired. It takes a lot of energy just to stay upright."

Chief Warrant Officer Pat Barron, a former Marine who reminds me of a younger, fitter Rodney Dangerfield, demonstrates by getting up and letting his body sway back and forth in a forty-degree arc with the movement of the ship. Actually he's standing upright. It's the ship that's swaying.

Lt. JG Justin Erdman, a tall, gangly academy grad, tells me he still loves working buoy tenders. "Law enforcement is a lot of waiting around. There you're reacting—here you're doing."

"It's that feeling of instantaneous gratification," agrees Stephanie, the XO. "You look back at a channel you've worked and there are all those buoys you put in. It's very hands-on, very tangible work."

"I did four years at a shore-based ANT [Aids to Navigation Team] in Georgetown, South Carolina, and it was the best job of my military career," Pat Barron adds to the amen chorus. ANT use trucks and small utility boats to maintain lighthouses, channel markers, and river buoys. "We had three hundred ATONs [aides to navigation they were responsible for], and there were inspections and maintenance, and hurricanes would come along, and it was just boom, boom, boom. It just never stopped happening." He smiles fondly.

Late in the final quarter of the seesawing football game, the ship's hit broadside by a big wave and the TV screens go black for almost two minutes with only two minutes forty seconds left on the clock. The signal returns as Eli Manning passes long to David Tyree for an unbelievable off-the-helmet catch. This is followed by a final touchdown with thirty-five seconds left in the game as the Giants break the Patriots' perfect season to win the 2008 Super Bowl. There's a big cheer from the mess deck below; no surprise to me the Coasties are rooting for the underdogs.

I go up on the bridge and watch the ship's bow dropping into the troughs followed by torrents of white water cascading over the bow as we rise into the next wave. The wind-carried spray splashes the windows in front of us even though we're seventy-six feet up, over seven and a half stories off the water.

The bridge at night is kept dark except for the low glow of the radars and some spooky red lights that don't affect night vision. You want that extra sensory edge to be able to spot the unexpected, especially on a black and stormy night like this one. Unable to take notes, I listen to the murmured conversation of the half-dozen junior officers and seamen on watch that soon blends into the white noise of the ocean as they keep a steady course heading into the building seas that will keep us pitching but reduce our side-to-side roll.

I'm beginning to feel that same headache and vertigo I've felt during storms in the North Atlantic and the Southern Ocean off Cape Horn, so I stagger down three decks to the cabin one of the chiefs has offered to share with me, bang my elbows trying to brush my teeth at the aluminum sink, then climb into my upper fold-down rack, where I spend the next eleven hours sleeping intermittently as the seas grow to twenty feet with forty-knot winds. For Coast Guard cutters in Alaska's Bering Sea, this would be considered mild winter weather.

Rough seas are a Coast Guard cutterman's fate. While the Navy values speed and lethality in their ships, the Coast Guard's missions require endurance and seaworthiness.

My friend retired Navy Capt. Phil Renaud once worked at the Naval Pacific Meteorology and Oceanography Center in Pearl Harbor issuing heavy-weather advisories to try to keep ships out of harm's way.

"Frequently we would issue a 'divert' recommendation to a Coast Guard cutter on fisheries patrol in the Aleutian Island chain of Alaska due to an impending 'bomb'—a rapidly deepening low-pressure system. Often, the Coast Guard captain would politely thank us and then state that mission requirements precluded them from following our recommendation," he recalls.

"On one occasion we received a weather observation from the middle of an eastern Pacific hurricane. The hurricane was well forecast, and we issued many 'remain in port' advisories. One of the watch officers just about jumped out of his chair when he received this observation from a Coast Guard cutter under way off the Mexican coast reporting seventy kilometers of sustained winds with seas building above twenty-five feet. Of course we immediately sent an advisory message in an attempt to route the ship safely out of the hurricane's path. With style and grace, the captain thanked us for our support and stated that pursuit of a drug smuggler took higher priority. I guess that old adage of the postal service equally applies to the Coast Guard: 'Neither rain, nor sleet, nor hurricanes will stop the Coast Guard from pursuit of the bad guys.' "

The next morning I climb back up to the *Aspen*'s bridge. The seas have settled a bit. There's a twelve- to fourteen-foot northwest swell coming at twelve-second intervals with two feet of wind waves atop it. "It's sporty," Steve notes.

A crewman with his hoodie up is watching the radar screen.

"Did you sleep, sir?" he asks the captain.

"Yes," Steve tells him.

"I can't in these conditions. I was awake in my rack for eight hours waiting for my watch."

Steve says they found the missing four-ton buoy on a beach north of Eureka last night. He goes below to map things out with his officers.

By noon the offshore swells are down to ten feet and we can get back out on the buoy deck. It's a brisk cloudy day. In the distance the snow-capped coastal range of Northern California looks as wild and rugged as when Sir Francis Drake first sailed these waters in the sixteenth century. A pair of albatrosses circle around the ship—a good omen.

Buoy Deck Supervisor Paddy White has two guys, Bosun's Mates Dan Mendez and Liston Jackson, up atop one of the buoys in climbing harnesses. They're installing a green warning light, retro (reflective tape), batteries, a solar panel with metal legs, coils, and plastic bird spikes—ineffectively designed to keep birds from standing or pooping on the solar panel. The whole Rube Goldberg contraption looks like it could be knocked off with a Super Soaker water gun.

Paddy shows me the next generation of buoy illumination—a small Canadian-made solar cube with superefficient LED lights and internal batteries that can be easily bolted on and off the buoy. Unfortunately, they only have one on board for the two buoys they'll be dropping on this trip.

Through much of the twentieth century, Coasties installed old 12-volt car batteries to power buoys and when they ran out of juice tossed them over the side. By the 1990s, they were sending divers down to retrieve piles of these old batteries that they'd since identified as hazardous waste.

I examine big coils of thick chain and the four- and six-ton square concrete "sinkers," or "rocks," that will anchor these two buoys.

"The last storm dragged a [12,700-pound] rock and broke the chain and sent the seventy-eight-hundred-pound buoy drifting off, so this time we'll add more chain," Paddy explains. "A hundred and fifty-five feet of chain is about an extra two thousand pounds."

They begin moving the chains around with big metal hooks.

"What do you call the hooks?" I ask.

"They're called chain hooks." Bosun's Mate Second Class Paul Vanacore grins.

I ask Paddy if he joined the Coast Guard with buoy tending in mind.

"When I came in I didn't even know we had a black [hull] fleet," he admits, "but I like it. It's more hands-on. There's more seamanship involved."

Five miles out from Humboldt Bay, we hit a line in the water where the ocean turns from deep blue to mud brown. It looks like the mouth of the Amazon, this vast outflow of storm sediment stretching up and down the coast. The last time I saw a phenomenon like this was during the El Niño winter storms of 1983. The bridge goes quiet as we enter the choppy brown cauldron. Steve and Stephanie scan the harbor channel with binoculars. Big fifteen-foot waves are rolling through.

"Right ten degrees rudder," Steve instructs.

"Rudders right ten degrees."

"Aye."

They stop to test the ship's dynamic positioning thrusters to see if the cutter will stick in one place or drift. Then we turn away from the coast, pounding back out to sea. The captain looks pensive.

"Any thoughts at this point?" I ask.

"The North Pacific is no fun in early February . . . We're going to try to anchor in Trinidad Harbor. Hopefully we can tuck in there with some leeward protection so people can get some sleep tonight."

He leaves the bridge in the hands of Lt. Meredith Phillips and two other women. As we approach Trinidad Lighthouse three hours later, twelve-foot breakers can be seen rolling around the point, making the harbor better for surfing than anchoring. It's decided we'll stay offshore steaming slowly into the swells till midnight, then turn around.

When I wake up at 7:30 we're back at the mouth of Humboldt Bay, where the seas have dropped to eight feet under cloudy skies. Half a dozen fishing boats are heading out on the iron gray sea after having been stuck in port for several days.

A 47-foot surfboat from the Humboldt Boat Station comes out to drop off two bar pilots who will help determine where to locate the new replacement buoy.

We enter the harbor channel inside the seawall. I talk to Bosun's Mate Second Class Joshua Peelman, the big redheaded deck supervisor who starred in that *Dirty Jobs* segment. He's been onboard the *Aspen* for three years, longer than anyone else. His father served in the Coast Guard for twenty-two years. "I'm the son of the son of a sailor, like in the Jimmy Buffett song," he tells me, putting on his white hard hat.

The bow thruster starts rumbling to life below our feet, the dynamic positioning fixing us in place. He orders his crew to turn off the deck radio as it's time to get to work. The big chain drum (inhaul winch) sits on the buoy deck below the glassed-in control booth for the spar marine crane with its two hooks. A second cross-deck winch used for side balance sits to its left. Josh's crew hauls a length of chain across the deck and hangs it over an iron block. There they use a propane torch to heat up a rivet pin inserted into a shackle that will extend the chain's length. When its head is white-hot, Paddy and another crewman beat the pin down with sledgehammers; then a third crewmember comes in with a smaller hammer to flatten the head flush with the shackle.

They move to new positions, and Josh begins giving hand signals. The crane operator, Chief Ken Miller, watches Josh's thumb and first two fingers as a hook and sling are secured to a big concrete sinker and they open the low starboard gate. Two fingers go up, and the six-ton "rock" slides across the green deck as the drum pulls chain. Two fingers go down, and it hops and slides again before swinging out over the side, where it hangs suspended. Josh works the chain into a roller slot on the edge of the cutter.

The plan is to now have one of the *Aspen*'s small boats go out and check the water depth. A sixteenth-century drop line with a lead weight attached to it is still a more accurate measuring device than electronic depth finders, I'm told. A moment later, a tugboat comes by and offers to do the sounding for them so they don't have to launch the boat.

Josh's crew includes Paddy, rigger Shannon Kelly, Mendez and Jackson, and two cooks, Robert Longsworth Jr. and Jen Wright. I'm warned not to step over the chain lying on the deck, a golden safety rule. They lower the 12,700-pound sinker down the side of the ship into the water, leaving some attached chain on deck.

They then use pneumatic drills to undo the "gripes" or chocks, that secure the far green buoy to the deck. They drag the sinker's chain end across the deck, getting ready to marry it up to the buoy's dual suspension chains.

"Break outboard and inward gripes," Josh directs. "You're forward," he tells Rob. "You're with me, Dave," he directs me. "Chief, we're gonna break in and out and then shackle it up."

"Nice surf, long rides," Paddy notes as a wave rolls by.

"Too cold for me," Josh says.

If a large wave were to roll out from under the buoy or sinker as they were going over the side, it could create a "shock load" that might rip the crane from the deck (it's happened before).

"We're going live!" Josh announces as they connect the chain to the buoy.

"Swells coming," Paddy warns, and they wait out the next set.

One of the crew breaks the last outboard gripe. The cross-deck snatch block (the balancing drum) starts pulling the buoy sideways as the main boom lifts it up off the deck. This creates tension that leans the buoy over forty-five degrees and prevents it from swinging loose.

This big clanging industrial choreography reminds me of the drill decks of offshore oil rigs I've been on but with more sea movement.

"Get slack," Josh directs one of the riggers. The boat is turning as Josh gives a thumbs-up with his left hand, two fingers down with his right hand held underneath the left, then thrusts his left arm out as the buoy moves across the deck toward the open gate, dragging its chains, which are connected to a pair of swing arms that can drop below the surface. Two riggers follow behind with two small tag lines attached.

"Ready cross deck!" Josh calls out. As the big buoy goes over the side and hits the water, the boom hook is removed. The heavy chain rushes off the deck, dropping into the water. There are just two ropes still connected to it as the buoy floats upright. They release the pelican hook and then the cage line. The cage (a Rube Goldberg–like structure) is now bobbing even with the deck as the green navigation buoy begins to drift away. It's 10:10 A.M. The deck radio is turned back on. Bob Seger's singing " 'bout that old-time rock and roll."

The original plan had been to dock back in the city tonight, but that's not going to happen, and I have a plane to catch, so I gather my bags from the wardroom and join crewmember Electronics Technician First Class Dan Piccola, who's also due back, along with the bar pilots. The 47-foot surfboat pulls up to the side of the *Aspen*. We climb down a short rope ladder, step aboard, and wave good-bye, heading over to the Humboldt Bay Surf Station.

This surf station has been active since 1856. Its white and red main building and boathouse date back to 1936. Its communications center is located in its rooftop cupola. Along with three active boats, it has a fully restored World War II–era motor rescue boat on a launch rail. We spend a few hours admiring the station's rich history, wild dunes, wind-sculpted trees, and shorebirds before catching a van ride five hours south to San Francisco.

Red Hull

It's hard to say where the soul of the Coast Guard lies: in its shore-based lifesaving stations, dangling on the cables of its rescue helicopters, or bounding across wild seas on its blue-water cutters. Perhaps it's in the heart of every Coastie who's ever had to head out on rough water, be it sweet, brackish, or salty.

Bosun's Mate Second Class Paul Vanacore recalls serving on the High Endurance Cutter *Sherman* when it did a round-the-world tour.

"We left Alaméda and went to Hawaii, Guam, Singapore, Japan, the Persian Gulf, the Seychelles, Madagascar, Cape Town [in] South Africa—where we helped rescue a car carrier that was dead in the water and listing badly in fifteen-foot swells—then on to Cape Verde, Barbados, Aruba, through the Panama Canal to San Diego and home, where we were greeted like returning heroes with roses dropping from the Golden Gate Bridge and a band waiting at the pier."

In 2005, the Coast Guard's largest ship, the 420-foot red-hulled icebreaker/research vessel *Healy*, sailed from Seattle to the North Pole and on over the top of the world to Norway. The scientists on board wanted to keep stopping to do ice-core sampling, but the autumn ice was hardening fast, and the captain, fearing they would get stuck and be forced to winter over, told them that wasn't going to happen.

From Tromsö, Norway, they headed toward Dublin but on the way hit a huge storm that raged for days, building to forty-foot seas and seventy-knot winds—until the night it got worse.

Chief Wayne Kidd, a salty old fireplug of a sailor who looks like British actor Bob Hoskins, was standing watch on the bridge at 3:00 A.M. when the rogue wave hit. "I remember we could feel it (the sixteen-thousand-ton ship) just climbing and climbing and climbing this one wave, and as we came down the back side into the trough the next one must have been twice as big, and it just broke on us. Blue water was up to the bridge window [over sixty feet up], and it ripped the cab off the forward crane and lifted it onto the elevated deck. It snapped a fourteen-thousand-pound anchor shaft and flooded the forward berthing in four feet of water. You have these gooseneck air vents to prevent water from getting in, but they were underwater themselves."

After making repairs, they sailed on from Dublin to the Azores, to St. Maarten in the Caribbean, through the Panama Canal to Cabo San Lucas, Mexico, and then home to Seattle.

Today's departure from Seattle's Pier 36 is a little more low-key. The *Healy* is off on a six-month scientific deployment north of the Aleutians, though I'll be leaving her in Edmonds, Washington, after they've done a few hours field-testing their acoustic Doppler current profiler. This is one of a suite of sensors onboard for the 2008 Bering Sea Ecological Study that will examine the impact of climate change on that productive marine habitat. "This time our only port calls will be at Dutch [Harbor, Alaska]," Chief Kidd tells me.

On the eighty-two-foot-wide bridge, Capt. Ted Lindstrom is pacing, occasionally stepping outside to check the lines and escort tug. Six-two and north of 250 pounds with a husky voice, white hair, and a clipped white mustache, he reminds me of a bull walrus, which seems appropriate given that part of the *Healy's* work will involve helicopter surveillance and tagging of walruses.

They test the different pipes (bleats and buzzes) for Man Overboard, Flight Crash, and Ship's Whistle.

The bow thruster rumbles to life.

One of the cranes "breaks the brow," lifting the gangplank aboard as it had earlier lifted several "science vans," shipping containers outfitted as marine labs.

"Permission to get under way?" Ensign Zack Bender, one of the junior officers running the bridge under the supervision of more experienced mariners, asks the captain.

"Let's do it," he replies.

The ship's horn lets off one long and three short blasts.

The ISC (Integrated Support Command) stevedores ashore toss all the ship's lines at once.

"They want those parking spaces." The captain grins, looking down at the *Healy*'s pier with its thirty-five now empty spots.

I look across the Coast Guard station toward the snow-covered mass of Mt. Rainier rising majestically behind the clock tower of the Starbucks Center. We slowly pull out of the channel, moving into Puget Sound through the Port of Seattle, coming about and heading north past the Space Needle and a couple of green and white passenger ferries on the Bainbridge Island run.

Along with the *Healy*, the Coast Guard operates two other red-hulled seagoing icebreakers, the *Polar Sea* and the *Polar Star*, also docked at Pier 36. It also operates a smaller icebreaker, the *Mackinaw*, on the Great Lakes.

"All ahead sixty shaft turns," Ensign Bender instructs.

"All ahead sixty shaft turns, aye," the seaman on the throttle responds.

The *Healy*'s six diesel electric engines can generate 30,000 hp and break 4.5 feet of ice at three knots or eight feet backing off and ramming the ice.

The older "heavy icebreakers," the *Polar Star*, which was commissioned in 1976, and its sister ship the *Polar Sea*, commissioned in '78, can generate 75,000 hp with diesels and jet turbines and break six feet of ice at three knots or twenty-one feet backing and ramming, making them nearly as powerful as the largest nuclear-powered Russian icebreakers. With their rounded steel bows, the *Polars* ride up on the ice and crush it beneath their thirteen thousand tons of dead weight. Taking their time, they can crack and crush up to forty feet of certain types of ice.

For forty years, until 2005, the Coast Guard ran the nation's icebreaker program that managed these ships. Then the White House Office of Science and Technology handed the program—worth more than $60 million—over to the National Science Foundation (NSF) figuring that, as the icebreakers' major client, it ought to run the program.

In 2006, as one of its first actions, the NSF ordered the *Polar Star* tied up to its dock in "caretaker" status, essentially mothballing it. The NSF takeover also marked the end of the Coast Guard's Polar Operations helicopter wing, which included four HH-65s that specialized in extreme polar flying. The NSF prefers to lease commercial helicopters.

A tour through the 399-foot *Polar Sea* gives me a sense of why the NSF doesn't want to use the Coast Guard's older icebreakers on its science missions. The 1970s lab and library spaces are barely adequate for modern oceanography, the deployment area for the cage-like CTD—conductivity, temperature, and depth—rosette (a basic tool for ocean sampling) is cramped, and acoustic mapping and sensing work is near impossible when the loud and vibrating ship is under way or breaking ice.

On the other hand, the *Polars* have been as far north and south as it's possible to sail on our ocean planet and spent over a quarter century clearing and grooming channels through the ice to maintain supply routes for the NSF's big McMurdo Station in Antarctica. When the NSF tried to use a Russian icebreaker for Operation Deep Freeze in 2006, the Russian broke a blade and the *Polar Star* had to rush down from Seattle to stand by while repairs were made.

In 2007, the *Polar Sea* cleared the twenty-mile channel to McMurdo along with an NSF-leased Swedish icebreaker. It was the *Polar Sea*'s eighteenth deployment to Antarctica. It's also been to the Arctic eighteen times.

The newer, larger Coast Guard Cutter *Healy* was built as a research support vessel with a computer lab, a dry lab, a wet lab, a biochemical lab, a dive locker, a science freezer, climate control chambers, and a conference room. Besides its helicopter hangar it also has two A-frames, five cranes, and a large staging area for deploying equipment, along with berthing for up to fifty scientists (the *Polars* can take up to thirty-five). The *Healy* can also control its radiated noise to allow for underwater acoustic work. In addition, it can carry up to eight science vans, and its crew of eighty-five includes half a dozen marine science technicians.

"We cater to the scientists, put their gear in the water and collect the mud and water and stuff so they can sample it in the warm and dry [labs]," explains Marine Science Technician First Class Eric Rocklage as he tours me around the aft deck. Along with rosettes, nets, and sediment core samplers, they've deployed a large ROV robot submarine off the rear A-frame to collect vampire squid and other exotica and dropped a seventy-foot-long jumbo piston core to collect bottom strata.

He shows me the "man-basket" that a crane will lower over the side to put scientists on the ice, along with their Coast Guard escort of lifeguards and bear gunners. On their last deployment, as they were heading north they passed a skinny polar bear floating south on a small ice floe. Even though polar bears can swim long distances, this one's situation looked fairly hopeless in the increasingly open waters of the Arctic.

The *Healy*'s official brochure describes its 1997 sideways launch at the Avondale shipyard in New Orleans as "spectacular," which has a nicer ring to it than "disastrous." What happened is the backsplash from the thirty-five-million-pound ship sent timbers, mud, sand, concrete, and torrents of water over the crowd of a thousand gathered for the launch. About half a dozen people were injured. "Hell Roaring" Mike Healy, the cutter's hero namesake and a man little inclined to swoon at the sight of mud and blood, would have likely found some measure of mirth in the mishap.

The front third of the *Healy* is called the "hotel." This is where the crew and scientists stay and also houses various amenities like a gym and laundry. The midsection of the ship houses its engines and power plant, and the aft section with its labs and work decks is given over to science.

In a hallway outside the common dining mess (shared by officers, chiefs, and enlisted), I find a wooden plaque with photo inlays of Lt. Jessica Hill and Bosun's Mate Second Class Steven Duque, two divers who died below the ice on August 17, 2006, at longitude 77-12.965 N. latitude 177-38.400 W.

"Your spirit will endure always and you will never be forgotten," reads their shipmates' inscription.

It was during an "ice liberty" on four-foot-thick pack ice almost five hundred miles north of Barrow, Alaska, that they decided to do a training dive without a real trainer on hand. At the time, diving was considered a "collateral" duty on the icebreakers. Having cut a hole in the ice by the ship's bow, their plan was to do two twenty-foot-deep dives for twenty minutes each. A third diver who was to go with them had to climb out when his drysuit sprang a leak in the twenty-nine-degree water. He returned to the ship as crewmen and scientists continued to play football, drink beer, and do "polar bear" cannonballs into the below-freezing saltwater.

Hill, thirty-one, and Duque, twenty-two, loaded up with more than sixty pounds of weights, gave brief instructions to their volunteer line handlers, and dropped below. The handlers felt the lines play out rapidly and thought the scuba divers were swimming under the ice's surface. When the third diver returned later and saw that over two hundred feet had been let out, he ordered the two divers pulled back up. They showed no signs of life when they were hauled out, nor did an hour of CPR revive them. In the immediate aftermath of the fatal accident, the cutter's CO, Capt. Douglas Russell, was relieved of duty (and subsequently replaced by Ted Lindstrom).

A Coast Guard investigation later determined that the divers carried excessive weight that dragged them down to 187 and 220 feet, where they quickly ran out of air and died. Their dive plan and experience were inadequate for the situation, the report concluded. In addition, the scuba equipment in the ship's dive locker had not been inspected in five years, and there was not an experienced dive master onboard nor a diver standing by at the surface as there should have been. In fact, at the time of their deaths there was not a certified Master Diver in the entire Coast Guard. As a result of this tragedy, the service revamped its dive program.

Today the Deployable Operations Group has taken charge of the training and standardization of the program, establishing two permanent dive lockers with thirty-six divers each in California and Virginia. These dedicated divers are made available for specific missions on icebreakers and for port security and other purposes. In addition, the Guam-based buoy tender *Sequoia* continues to maintain its own dive team for aides to navigation work around shallow coral reefs in the Pacific.

Whether breaking ice, diving or doing science or search and rescue, the role of the Coast Guard in the Arctic is a rapidly changing one.

Throughout the forty-five years of the Cold War, much of the Coast Guard's icebreaking mission in the Arctic was done in support of the Navy's nuclear submarines and their underice warfare activities. If a nuclear war were to break out, the plan was to have U.S. ballistic missile subs, or "boomers," break through the surface of the ice and rain mass death onto the cities and peoples of the Soviet Union. This was part of a larger plan that went by the acronym MAD—Mutually Assured Destruction.

That apocalypse never happened. Today's is a slower-moving one if no less frightening. It's been in process since the beginning of the Industrial Revolution but only positively identified in the 1950s as the ongoing alteration of the planet's climate through the addition of anthropogenic (human-sourced) pollutants, including carbon dioxide. Fossil-fuel-fired climate change has, among other impacts, replaced the Cold War with a "Cold Rush."

So I'm not surprised to find a pirate flag on the wall of the *Healy*'s computer lab. This was the hub of activity during their 2007 sea floor mapping expedition sponsored by the State Department at the same time Russia was planting a titanium flag on the seabed beneath the North Pole and Canada was war-gaming armed interdictions in the Northwest Passage. All are part of a frenzied rush by the Arctic powers—Russia, Canada, Norway, Denmark, and the United States—to seize new riches including oil, minerals, fish and trade routes.

Under provisions of the UN's Law of the Sea Treaty, countries can claim extensions of their two-hundred-mile Exclusive Economic Zones if they can document subsurface extensions of their continental shelves. Russia is one of the claimants of the Lomonosov Ridge that runs under the North Pole. The United States is looking to claim a submarine plateau called the Chukchi Cap that could extend the U.S. EEZ a hundred nautical miles into oil-rich waters.

While ownership of vast parts of the Arctic remain in dispute, it's clear that along our northern coast the United States is far from ready to deal with increased resource extraction, shipping, and tourism.

"I have to be prepared to do everything we do in Los Angeles and be able to do it on this new frontier, this 'fifth coast,' but you can't do that with normal ships," warns Rear Adm. Gene Brooks, the 17th District commander of Coast Guard forces in Alaska.

"When I got here in summer 2006, I traveled around and thought [that] by 2020, 2030 we're gonna have to start working," he tells me. "Only my first year convinced me climate change is already here."

"Global warming makes us more viable to the nation," the *Polar Sea*'s CO, Capt. Carl Uchytil, argues without irony. We're standing in his icebreaker's loft con, its small black crow's nest 105 feet up. "From here we can see out to where the ice ain't," he explains. "That way you sometimes find a route [through the ice] that's less direct but easier."

Among the changes an ice-free Arctic is expected to bring is a dramatic shift in shipping routes between Asia and Europe, with commercial fleets of container ships, bulk carriers, and ice-hardened oil tankers using either the Northern Sea Route above Russia or moving through the Northwest Passage that Canada considers domestic waters but the United States and other countries claim is an international strait. In 1985, the *Polar Sea* crossed the icebound Northwest Passage without permission from Canada.

"They protested when we did that," Carl Uchytil recalls. "They flew Cessnas [small aircraft] over and dropped pamphlets asking us to respect Canadian sovereignty."

One of the legal requirements for declaring an international strait is its historic—and unchallenged—use by foreign vessels. These days the United States always "informs" Canada when it's transiting the passage but doesn't consider this a "request." Canada considers it a request but never denies permission.

Among surprises during the ice-free summer of 2007 was the transiting of three cruise ships through the Northwest Passage and the unannounced arrival of a shipload of four hundred German-speaking tourists on the beach in the Arctic town of Barrow, Alaska. A number of fishing boats were also seen moving from the Bering Sea into the Arctic Circle, following a shift of edible fish species north.

The summer of 2008 became a test bed for the Coast Guard to assess its needs if maritime services are to be extended from southern and central Alaska to the fast-melting west and north. There were biweekly surveillance flights by C-130 aircraft over the Chukchi and Beaufort seas and the Arctic Ocean, the establishment of a two-week lifesaving station with helicopters and small boats on the beach in Barrow, and a security operation with small boats at the oil facility in Prudhoe Bay.

The *Polar Sea* also went on a multimission cruise that included fisheries law enforcement and community outreach to Shishmaref and Kivalina, two Native Alaskan towns among more than half a dozen on the Chukchi Sea considering evacuation as a result of coastal storm erosion linked to the loss of protective sea ice.

As human activity increases in the Arctic region, the need for U.S. icebreakers will also increase. As Captain Uchytil points out, "As long as the earth is tilted twenty-three degrees from the sun there's always going to be some ice at the poles."

A 2006 study by the National Research Council titled *Polar Icebreakers in a Changing World: An Assessment of U.S. Needs* recommended the construction of two new icebreakers that might cost up to a billion dollars each but could, along with the *Healy*, provide the United States the beginnings of an effective icebreaking fleet. In the interim the report calls for the continued use of the *Polar Sea* and continued standby status for the *Polar Star*.

Admiral Brooks in Alaska thinks that he'll soon need three or four new icebreakers and seven to nine ice-hardened patrol ships, "for a start."

Riding the *Healy* just before sunset, we encounter light showers and a double rainbow breaking over the Mukilteo Lighthouse at Point Elliot. A Washington State Ferry drifts through the color bands on the water.

Two hours later we're standing on the cutter's darkened bridge getting a boat briefing from Bosun's Mate First Class Billy Glenzer. He and Bosun's Mate Third Class Andrew Yeckley will be taking me, a contractor, and a senior chief ashore. We'll be riding a 22-foot rigid-hull inflatable. The air temperature is fifty-two, the water temperature forty-eight with light winds and a one- to two-foot chop. We'll be wearing Mustang survival suits and crash helmets.

After the briefing, we assemble on the open deck by the orange RHI's starboard side cradle. When the boat's ready, we climb aboard and sit up front with our backs against its inflated tubes. The winch release starts with a jerk as we're clackity-clacked forty feet down the side of the ship into the water. As we begin to back off its forklift-like cradle, Yeckley reports the jet drive's throttle is stuck in reverse. The winch hook is reattached and we're cranked back up the side of the icebreaker. We walk over to the port side, where the ship's second RHI is readied. Chief Kidd mans its winch control console. We're again lowered into the water.

This time all goes well, and we peel off toward the flickering lights of shore. Billy Glenzer makes his way to the bow with a handheld floodlight and scans the dark water ahead of us for floating debris as we thump along at thirty knots. Ten minutes later, we slow down and enter the Edmonds Marina, pulling in just past the fuel dock. We return our gear to the two Coasties and walk up a ramp to a parking lot, where my friends will soon meet me. The *Healy*, heading off into a northern ocean wilderness, won't be back in these waters for over half a year.

White Hull

The Coast Guard's forty Medium and High Endurance Cutters are the flagships of its deepwater fleet. Depending on their size they can deploy for six to eight weeks or three to six months. All but two of its twelve High Endurance Cutters are located on the West Coast and Hawaii. All but three of the Medium Endurance Cutters are stationed on the Atlantic Ocean, where distances and sea states tend to be less extreme. Of course, there's always the exception.

In his book *The Perfect Storm,* author Sebastian Junger describes a harrowing SAR mission carried out during a historic New England blow on October 30, 1991, by the 205-foot Medium Endurance Cutter *Tamaroa,* a retrofitted World War II salvage tug. The "*Tam*" almost lost three crewmen putting a small boat over the side in an attempt to save three other people on a foundering sailboat. All six were later rescued by a Coast Guard helicopter.

The *Tam* then steamed four hours to the site of a downed Air National Guard helicopter. The *Tam*'s captain decided to send his people out on the deck in thirty- to forty-foot seas. Crouched on the slick, wind-battered deck that was seesawing 110 degrees and periodically being buried by breaking waves, they were able to use flares, ropes, and cargo nets draped over the side to recover four of the five airmen, hauling them out of the nighttime sea like billfish on a gaff. "I certainly hope that was the high point of my career," the CO later joked, meaning it.

Among the large cutters I've visited are two stationed in Kodiak, Alaska: the 378-foot High Endurance Cutter *Munro* and a onetime Navy salvage ship, the 282-foot Medium Endurance Cutter *Alex Haley*. All other Medium Endurance Cutters are either 210 or 270 feet long. The 210s, built in the 1960s and upgraded in the 1980s and '90s, tend to be top-heavy, to leak oil, and to require lots of maintenance, not unlike the 378s, which are also corroding and breaking down after more than three decades of service.

"Only the Coast Guard would take a forty-year old ship, call it new, and expect to run it through 2015," Cdr. Kevin Jones, CO of the *Alex Haley*, jokes about his hand-me-down ship with the slightly perverse pride of his service.

The cutter is named after the Coast Guard's first chief journalist, Alex Haley, who, as an African American, had to start his career as a "mess boy" in 1939. After twenty years of service that spanned World War II and the Korean

War, he went on to global fame as collaborator on *The Autobiography of Malcolm X* and author of the Pulitzer Prize–winning novel of slavery and family survival *Roots,* which later became a TV miniseries viewed by 130 million people.

The ship that bears his name is also unique and distinctive. I notice how beamy it is as soon as I climb aboard. There's room to walk past other folks in the passageways. The workspaces, mess, and berthing areas are wide and spacious enough to delight its crew of 105. The flight deck is one of the biggest in the service, though it didn't feel that way when we were landing on it in those rolling seas off Hawaii.

Launched in 1968 and later commissioned as the USS *Edenton,* it was handed over to the Coast Guard in 1997, given a $20 million makeover, rechristened *Alex Haley,* and sent to Alaska.

Weighing three thousand gross tons, it's just three hundred tons light of a High Endurance Cutter, and with a beam of fifty feet it's actually seven feet wider. "She's a fat-bottomed gal." The CO Kevin Jones grins. "We're lower and wider and slower. We're a turtle, but we ride through the storms."

We're sitting in the officers' wardroom having a two-entrée meal of egg rolls and chipped beef, classic sailor's grub that, when served on toast, is known as SOS (look it up). The talk turns to their recent hunt on Adak Island returning from their last cruise. They killed five caribou and had the carcasses, heads and all, curing on the fantail when Executive Officer Tony Williams reminded them to take the dead critters down before coming into port. It was December, and he worried his four-year-old daughter would think they'd killed Santa's reindeer. It sounds like they had an exciting cruise even before the cariboucide.

"We had a deep-fat fire under way with flames on the ceiling, and it flashed over, and the fire party took a half hour to put it out," Kevin recounts. I'm actually not surprised they had a grease fire, as I discreetly slip one of the egg rolls off to the side of my plate. "One of the helicopters was launching, and since they'd gotten through the preflight [checklist] we decided to launch him as we fought the fire," he continues. "Afterward the whole ship smelled like McDonald's for a week, all the way up to the bridge."

If that wasn't enough, they then hit one of the Bering Sea's infamous low-pressure systems with thirty-foot seas and 105 mph winds.

"They're really just like unnamed hurricanes, and you know you'll damage the ship, lose a mast, have portholes leak, but just pray no one's hurt," Kevin says. "So we're icing up, and we try to find the lee side of an island [for protection—to cut down on the wind and wave size]. We get on the lee side of St. George, but it's a small island only about one mile wide, so for three or four days we're steaming back and forth for a mile. Then we got chased around by the next low."

That's when they got a SAR call about a fishing boat in trouble and launched their HH-65 Dolphin helicopter off to Cold Bay.

Kevin, a brushy-haired midcareer officer with a slightly hangdog look, shows me pictures from this second storm with an ice-covered flight deck and the ship's bow buried in eighteen-foot seas.

"We were directed toward Dutch Harbor, and the helicopter had [at some point during the SAR evolution] damaged a strut. So on December tenth we had to do a lily-pad HIFR under way." That's the emergency helicopter in-flight refueling procedure, in which the 65 mechanic lowers the hoist cable to the deck of the rolling ship and a gas line is reeled back up and connected to a fuel plug in the door frame of the helicopter. "It was a hop, skip, and a jump where they flew from Cold Bay to us and on to Kodiak," he explains before taking me on a tour of the bridge.

Whereas the buoy tender *Aspen* and icebreaker *Healy* have advanced computerized steering systems on their bridges, the bridge of the *Alex Haley* would make a World War II cutter captain feel right at home. While it has the modern radar, digital charts, satellite communications, and other essentials for today's multimission work, it also has a hard-to-miss bronze steering wheel and a leaning board that sailors—standing upright—brace against while driving the ship.

With no automatic steering or course correction, Kevin, the CO, has his deck crew switch out every fifteen to twenty minutes, one of them at the wheel battling to keep a steady course through bone-jarring seas while the others stand lookout on the bridge wings through the violence of Arctic rain, sleet, snow, and spray, perhaps comforting themselves with the thought that others have seen worse.

One day in a typhoon we did a sixty-three-degree roll in fifty-foot seas with seventy to eighty sustained knots [of wind]. She creaked and moaned, but she kept us safe. It was quite an adventure," Chief Greg Papineau recalls. We're sitting in the wardroom of the High Endurance Cutter *Munro,* but he's not talking about the *Munro,* named after the Medal of Honor winner. He's talking about another World War II combatant, this one a survivor called the *Storis* (derived from the Scandinavian name for "great ice") that he served on before transferring to the *Munro* in 2007. Chief Papineau himself is a well-salted forty-five-year-old Bosun's Mate, thickset with a respectable beer belly, reddish mustache, and rolling gait.

"*Storis* was round bottomed so she could go over eighty-five or ninety degrees and come back up," he recalls. "She bobbed like a cork. We had more than a few people fly out of their racks [wake up in midair out of their bunks after a wave hit the ship], but no one was hurt too bad."

Decommissioned in 2007 after sixty-four years of service, most of it in Alaska, the 230-foot *Storis* saved over 250 lives (and twenty-five boats) in Alaskan waters, busted Soviet, Japanese, and other foreign fishing vessels poaching in U.S. waters, and provided needed services to a hundred thousand people in remote and otherwise inaccessible parts of the state.

"I remember we'd go to different villages with a Russian Orthodox chaplain. We had a Christmas service on St. George Island, and it was the first service they'd had with a priest in nine years," Chief Papineau says.

"Another trip, to Adak, the kids all came around 'cause we were the new excitement in town. There's a kid on this ship who joined the Coast Guard because of that visit we made in 1996. So did his sister. Up on St. Lawrence [Island] we brought medical doctors and dentists; this was back before they had contract doctors. The elders have these oral histories of the villages, and the *Storis* is in the Native elders' stories because of our visits. She had a magic about her," he recalls, describing the decommissioning ceremony in Kodiak. "We had this tough kid onboard, his father was an Army Ranger and he'd smoke a cigarette and chew tobacco at the same time, and drink two Budweisers, and the day he left he looked like Niagara Falls. Everyone was crying, like."

The chief is one of five *Storis* crewmembers who volunteered to transfer to the *Munro* after it came north from California to replace the World War II cutter. Like Chief Papineau, the *Munro*'s CO, Capt. Craig "Bark" Lloyd, a towering, square-jawed veteran, is familiar with Alaska's waters and their unique challenges, having once commanded the *Alex Haley*.

"We had a guy with a halibut hook in his eye," Captain Lloyd recalls from the *Munro*'s bridge. "The [fishing boat's] master gets on the radio and says, 'Maybe I can push it through,' and we're gagging and making choking noises, and finally I have to say, 'Quiet!' so the doc can talk to him and tell him, 'Put a mug over his face and tape it in place with all the gaffer's tape you can find and we'll come get him,' and the corpsman says, 'We'll need a helicopter' . . .

[Later] the pilot's talking to the master of the vessel, who says, 'I don't think you can do this. I got a gantry and antennas [acting as obstructions], and its rocking and it's nighttime and not nice weather, and the master's complaining it can't be done, but they do the safety brief for him and lower the basket, and as we're flying back with the injured guy the master's on the radio saying, 'That's amazing. I didn't know you people could do that kind of thing.' We brought the guy back to the ship and ran toward St. Paul for eight hours till we were close enough for the helicopter to get him ashore and treated."

"It was a big hook?" I ask.

"A huge hook."

"Did they save his eye?"

"You know, with SAR cases a lot of times you just don't hear what the final outcome is."

The Coast Guard's big cutters remind me of the warships of my youth that blockaded Cuba and fired at phantoms in the Gulf of Tonkin, which makes sense since they're the same vintage, only painted white. The Navy keeps its gray ships for about fifteen years, then has Congress buy them new ones. The average age of the perennially underfunded Coast Guard fleet is thirty-five years.

The 378-foot-long *Munro* was commissioned in 1971 and has a crew of 175. Below its bridge is the captain's quarters, officers' berthing, and an electronics shop; another deck down is a navigation office and a small conference room with ripped furniture, scarred bulkheads, a faded porthole curtain, and pullout metal drawers from the days of disco.

It has five departments when under way—operations, engineering, supply, aviation, and weapons. Its weaponry includes a 76 mm deck gun and an aft-mounted CIWS antiaircraft and missile system that can fire forty-five hundred rounds per minute. At the forward gun control station, I'm shown the big cylinder they use for hand-loading the 76 mm shells. Only one of the dozen 378s still has a functioning ammo hoist from its below-deck magazines.

The weapons department also runs the deck crews that launch and recover the small boats and helicopter, handle the external hoists, and paint and scrape the ship.

The aviation department is run by the chief pilot of the helicopter that deploys with the *Munro* from Kodiak Air Station.

The operations department runs navigation, intelligence, communications, and selection and approach to targets from the ship's Combat Information Center three levels below the main deck. It also oversees the radio room and top-secret electronic servers and sensors.

The supply division covers all the ship's requisitions and housekeeping from stocking the galley—whose food service handlers might purchase $90,000 of groceries for a single deployment—to maintaining the gym, laundry, paint, lines, chains, and anchors.

While the captain, XO, and department heads get their own single staterooms, most junior officers and chiefs live in two- and four-rack staterooms. Most of the enlisted live in sixteen- to twenty-rack berthing areas that include two heads and two showers. Since the cutter pitches a lot in heavy seas, it's easy to hit your head on the lower half of these narrow double-stacked bunks. Bumps and lacerations are the common currency of the cutter's sick bay.

Captain Lloyd recalls that on a recent fisheries operation he was in his stateroom and "we were hit by a big wave on the beam, and my [lounge] chair took a roll to port and the chair and I went over and the [dining] table and all the chairs from the table rolled to port and back again, and the phone rings. I had my radio clipped to me and say, 'Whoever's calling, I can't get to the phone right now 'cause I'm under this chair!' They radio back and say, 'Sir, we just want to inform you that we had a nineteen-degree roll to port.' " Since their staterooms tend to be higher up and forward in the vessel, closer to the bridge, where movement is magnified, it's not unusual to find the officers trying to get some sleep in their wardroom when the weather gets rough.

The engineering department includes propulsion, generators, boilers, damage control, freshwater evaporators, wiring, and plumbing. Down in the engine room I'm shown the two diesel engines that can generate 3,500 hp each and the Pratt & Whitney gas turbines that can generate 18,000 hp each. They switch from one to the other when they want to kick in the afterburners and chase after bad guys. This allows them to surge from about eighteen to twenty-eight knots. Cruising on the diesels at twelve knots they burn about 210 gallons of diesel an hour; going all out on turbines, 2,897 gallons per hour. In the tropics the *Munro*'s engine room can reach 130 degrees, but in Alaska it rarely gets above 100.

Captain Lloyd, who is about to head off to a meeting of 378 captains to discuss how to keep their aging vessels operational through the next decade, tells me the *Munro* was sent north to Alaska because it was in the best condition of the four High Endurance Cutters in Alameda (he doesn't mention another reason—ex-Senator Ted Stevens of Alaska had long been demanding a 378 for his state). "Actually it's in the best condition of the eight on the West Coast," Captain Lloyd claims (there are also two in Hawaii and two in South Carolina).

There's no question the *Munro* is in better shape than the *Rush, Morgenthau, Chase,* or *Hamilton.* In 2008, the *Rush* had to abort a SAR mission in the Bering Sea when water began seeping through a two-foot corrosion crack that opened up, basically a hole in its hull. It docked in Dutch Harbor while another cutter, the *Jarvis,* took over the rescue mission. In recent years, the *Morgenthau* and *Chase* have also experienced corrosion failures. The *Hamilton,* the oldest of the 378s, was commissioned in 1967 and will likely be the first of its class to retire, but not before 2011 at the earliest.

Two months later, I'm visiting the cutter *Sherman* in California. *Sherman* recently returned from a counternarcotics patrol in the eastern Pacific, where it seized and sank two drug boats. Unable to access the hidden compartments in one of them, it rammed the 60-foot fishing boat, breaking it open like a piñata, releasing six tons of baled cocaine that floated to the surface for collection by the cutter's small boats. Under differing bilateral treaties, fourteen of the seventeen drug runners arrested were returned to their home countries of Ecuador and Costa Rica for trial, while three Colombians were sent to Florida to stand trial in the United States.

Touring the *Sherman,* I get to see lots of rust spots and corrosion along with some earnest efforts at upkeep. It's Good Friday, and Capt. Mathew Bliven has just received an e-mail message from the *Munro*'s Bark Lloyd, who's out on patrol.

"First day of spring," Captain Lloyd writes. "Here in the Bering, the current dry bulb temp is 6 degrees. Wind chill is 39 below. Just recovered the helo. Thankfully the ice edge keeps the seas down . . . Port calls for this patrol: Dutch, Dutch, and Dutch. And I'm happy. Lookouts are scanning for the Easter Walrus."

Two days later, at 2:50 A.M. Easter Sunday 2008, the captain of a 203-foot factory trawler radios, "Mayday, mayday! This is the *Alaska Ranger* . . . We are flooding, taking on water in our rudder room." He tells the Coast Guard they are 120 miles west of Dutch Harbor in twenty-foot seas with thirty-knot winds and abandoning ship. The *Munro* steams toward the scene. Once it gets within eighty miles it launches its Dolphin helicopter in high winds. A forward-deployed HH-60 Jayhawk also takes off from St. Paul Island and a C-130 from Kodiak.

The Jayhawk is the first to get on scene two and a half hours later. Its pilots are Lts. Steve Bonn and Brian McLaughlin, whom I met and flew with in Kodiak. Brian describes what they encountered.

"As we approached we saw three strobe lights and figured those were the rafts. A little closer and there was a fourth light, fifth, sixth, and the numbers just kept growing. The first strobe we flew over was a pair of survivors in Gumby suits waving at us.

"[Climbing higher] we did a quick 'big picture' scan and saw the ocean flashing at us over about a mile-long stretch, yet no *Alaska Ranger* that we could see. The scene was very grim."

The *Ranger* had sunk within fifteen minutes of its mayday call. Of its forty-seven survivors floating on the waves, many had not made it to life rafts, though they all had survival suits on.

The Jayhawk put its rescue swimmer, Aviation Survival Technician Second Class O'Brien Hollow, in the water and began hoisting crewmen amid big rolling waves and swirling snow squalls. Having filled their cabin with what they believed to be thirteen fishermen, they flew to the *Munro* and lowered them by basket to waiting crewmembers on the cutter's pitching deck (the cutter crew would only count twelve).

The *Munro* then refueled the large helicopter in the air, using HIFR. Before it could finish, the cutter's 65 returned from its rescue mission, landing another five survivors. They'd also lost a *Ranger* crewman whose survival suit had filled with water and who had fallen forty-five feet from their rescue basket. Short of room the Dolphin had to leave their swimmer, Aviation Survival Technician Third Class Abram Heller, behind along with a helicopter raft that he climbed into with three fishermen from the sunken trawler.

By now the *Ranger*'s sister ship, the *Alaska Warrior*, had arrived on scene and recovered more people from life rafts. The Jayhawk went back and recovered five more, including the Dolphin's rescue swimmer, and returned them to the *Munro*.

Four senior *Alaska Ranger* crewmembers, including the man who'd fallen from the rescue basket, didn't survive. Capt. Eric Jacobsen and these others had been floating in the frigid water for some six hours before they died of hypothermia. They were called heroes, having sacrificed themselves to make sure the rest of the crew made it. A fifth *Ranger* crewman was lost at sea. It took several hours before the Coast Guard realized that twelve rather than thirteen survivors had been off-loaded from the first helicopter recovery and that someone was still missing. The *Munro* spent the night searching for the man, Satashi Konno, a Japanese national and the ship's fish master, without success.

Meanwhile the *Munro*'s mess deck had been converted to a medical ward with heaters, sleeping bags, blankets, hot drinks, and IVs of warm saline solution for the rescued, this operation overseen by the ship's corpsman. At one point Captain Lloyd spotted a recovering fisherman huddled by himself sketching out a tattoo design: an anchor with the words RANGER SURVIVOR.

"I ask all my new crew what their moms and dads do," Lloyd told me earlier, "and a really common answer I get from about 10 percent of them is their mom's a nurse. So you have this rescue personality—people whose mothers were nurturing for a living, and they want a life like that, but with more adventure."

Shortly after the rescue, the Coast Guard opened an investigation into why the Seattle-based *Alaska Ranger,* a onetime oil service ship in the Gulf of Mexico, sank. It also began to examine what went wrong with its own efforts. Of course, far more went right than wrong when you consider the conditions in which forty-two out of forty-seven souls were saved.

From prepositioning to decisive action in incredibly confusing and dangerous circumstances, the *Alaska Ranger* case, despite its tragic losses, is still a thing of wonder, an example of how the Coast Guard can do a lot with a little, saving lives in places near and far, both fiery and frigid, any day of the year.

Even so, if the Coast Guard were a private corporation, it would probably have filed for Chapter 11 by now. As many of its cutters rust out from beneath it, funding lags, and delivery of new assets is delayed, its mission requirements continue to skyrocket.

In an era of expanding global trade, the world's fleet of large commercial ships will soon grow from eighty thousand to over one hundred thousand. The United States' port activity and maritime trade is also projected to increase in the next decade. Also expected to grow are the number of Category 4 and 5 hurricanes and intensity of El Niño storms linked to climate change. Droughts, coastal flooding, political instability, and the world's expanding population will also have a direct impact on illegal migration by sea, while food security is threatened by the collapse of the ocean's wild fisheries and pollution of the sea. As living resources decline, the tendency to cheat will likely see some fishermen turn to piracy, and some pirates link up with drug cartels and terrorists on the high seas. Terrorism will continue to threaten ninety-five thousand miles of U.S. shoreline, as will the collapse of aging bridges, piers, and other infrastructure. Additional threats include invasive species like Asian mussels that can sink navigation buoys with their cumulative weight, harmful algal blooms that can sicken people, and toxic and deadly accidents and oil spills on our waterways.

At the same time, the Coast Guard is being asked to take on new regulatory and security roles for LNG terminals, greater oversight for twenty million recreational vessels, and responsibility for our emerging open-water fifth coast in the Arctic.

How can the Coast Guard find ways to grow and bring others along on these new and expanded missions during an economic recession and waning trillion-dollar war? How can it deliver to the public when the public isn't even aware of all the services it now provides, or else has different priorities and expectations? The next few years will tell. The challenges for its leadership are immense and immediate.

CHAPTER 13

The Next Surge

"I really don't know why it is that all of us are so committed to the sea, except I think it's because in addition to the fact that the sea changes, and the light changes, and ships change, it's because we all came from the sea."
—President John F. Kennedy

"Past successes don't guarantee future performance."
—Coast Guard Commandant Thad Allen on the state of the U.S. Coast Guard

Leadership counts. While secretaries of the navy and chiefs of naval operations (the Navy's top military position) tend to come and go with little change to the fleet, the Coast Guard is such a small, multifaceted organization that its leadership can have a profound impact on its direction. Its founding commandant, Ellsworth Bertholf, and its longest-serving commandant, World War II's Russell Waesche, both came to shape and personify the service they led.

Being an institutional orphan in Washington whose neglectful foster parents have included the Treasury Department, Navy Department, Department of Transportation, and Department of Homeland Security, the Coast Guard is also more reliant on its commandants to provide guidance over time. Unfortunately, this can sometimes lead to erratic course corrections, such as the shift from the militarizing mission of Adm. Paul Yost (1986–90) to the environmental and corporate management ethos of his successor, Adm. William Kime (1990–94).

Strong personalities also compete to leave their imprint on the institution. A recent example is the competing visions of Commandants Jim Loy (1998–2002) and Thad Allen (2006–2010) with Admiral Thomas Collins serving in between.

Jim Loy, who was at the helm on 9/11, was a staunch defender of the organization during a time of shrinking budgets, the initiator of Deepwater fleet expansion, and the first commandant to go on to greater recognition as head of the Transportation Security Administration and number two at the Department of Homeland Security before becoming a lobbyist.

Thad Allen, by contrast, won his fame while still Admiral Collins's chief of staff cleaning up other people's messes as head of federal response after Hurricane Katrina.

When he became the boss, Admiral Allen issued ten Commandant Intent Action Orders (or CIAOs, pronounced "chows"). Taken as a whole they represent his attempt at a radical transformation of the Coast Guard as it enters its third century.

In lieu of the Atlantic and Pacific area commands, he initiated the transition to a single operational command and numbered headquarters staff system like the Pentagon's. This consolidation is supposed to reflect the global nature of the maritime domain the Coast Guard now works in while also marking an end to the historic M&O (Marine Safety and Operations) division of the service, though lack of funding and training for marine safety still hobbles many of its missions.

Admiral Allen also created a single Acquisitions Directorate to oversee fleet and asset growth so that the service never needs to "outsource" its future to private contractors again, as occurred under Deepwater.

He also created the Deployable Operations Group (DOG) as part of his newly perceived triad of Coast Guard assets: cutter forces, shore forces, and deployable forces.

Another of his CIAOs adopts the integrated logistics model pioneered by the aviation wing of the Coast Guard and takes it servicewide so that everything from clothing to National Security Cutters will now have standardized lines of supply and life cycles.

His directives also encourage greater "interoperability" between the Coast Guard, the Department of Homeland Security, and other marine stakeholders.

Finally, Admiral Allen got the service to commit to regular scenario planning to prepare for future maritime challenges, be they intentional (terrorism), industrial (accidents), or environmental (disasters).

As a result of this kind of outside-the-hull thinking, *U.S. News and World Report* named Thad Allen one of "America's 20 Best Leaders."

On the Road

We meet at 5:00 A.M. in FAA Hangar 6 at Reagan National Airport. There's Allen's assistant Mike "Batch" Batchelder, a strapping, shaven-headed thirty-something engineer. There's Adm. Dave Pekoske, assistant commandant for operations, who'll use the plane ride as a chance to debrief the boss; there's his public affairs guy, Cdr. Brendan McPherson, and the low-key, gray-haired Paul Dahl, one of his CGIS security detail. Some large local Coasties and his aircraft's four-man crew complete the posse.

Out on the tarmac sits one of the Dolphin helicopters used for the Capitol air defense mission, a flying billboard to warn off potentially hostile aircraft, as well as the service's Gulfstream jet and the Citation 604 we'll be riding in.

I pass my bag to a crewman and climb aboard the executive jet. Inside, the fog of air-conditioning vapor venting at floor level reminds me of disco smoke as I check out the passenger compartment's dozen posh leather seats, shiny reflective wood finish, and mirrored rear wall.

"The Boss," Admiral Allen, climbs aboard. He's just over six feet and 235 pounds, a stocky hard charger with a gruff foghorn baritone that he's now using to effect, complaining to his press aide, Brendan, about a Minneapolis newspaper headline that reads "Coast Guard May Scrap Two Cutters." It was a follow-up story on congressional testimony he'd given the day before, in which he'd told a congressman that not in the farthest reaches of his mind could he see such a thing happening.

Brendan points out that the story was accurate, just not the headline.

We take off fast and smooth. This is a two-day trip. The commandant is on the road at least two days a week. Yesterday was a typical stay-at-home day during which he rode his bike fifteen miles into work with a couple of CGIS agents, had a staff brief on operations at 8:00 A.M., then testified at that congressional hearing of the Coast Guard and Maritime Transportation Subcommittee at 11:00. In the afternoon he had a White House meeting with the secretary of homeland security and more staff briefings back at the office.

On his return, he'll be preparing for a trip to St. Petersburg, Russia, for a meeting of the North Pacific Coast Guard Forum made up of the coast guards of Russia, China, Japan, South Korea, Canada, and the United States. On my next visit to DC, he'll be off meeting his counterparts in El Salvador, Ecuador, and Colombia.

About halfway through the flight, when he's finished talking with Dave Pekoske, I'm invited to take a chair opposite the admiral, who gives me his biography. Some of the highlights are already known, at least within the service, including the fact that he's the son of an enlisted chief petty officer and grew up on and around various Coast Guard bases.

"My dad retired in '65, and with our moving to Arizona everyone says I'm from there, but I grew up mostly in Alaska, Washington, California. It was natural to consider the Coast Guard Academy [after high school], but the reason I went is I thought I was too small for Division one football and so I was accepted to Annapolis and Cal Berkeley on a ROTC scholarship."

"You could have gone to Berkeley in 1967?"

"Yeah, and seen my program burned down, but I chose the academy because in division three I got to play four years of football."

I ask about Objee, the mascot.

"There was a bear keeper, but I never wrestled with the bear, and it probably wasn't a good quality of life for the animal. Of course, cadets will do anything."

Brendan, who's been listening in from across the aisle, mentions he saw a YouTube video of a cadet trying to ride a floor buffer.

After graduating, Allen served on a World War II surplus cutter doing ocean observing and weather station patrols out of Miami. In 1972, he was on the second helicopter to respond to the crash of an L1011 jetliner in the Everglades. It was his first exposure to a catastrophic event and got him thinking about how best to respond.

He then went to Puerto Rico to run a SAR center, grew a beard, and had a bachelor pad on the beach. "It was a Pirates of the Caribbean scene," he says, almost cracking a smile.

He'd wanted to go to Vietnam even though the war was by then winding down. His detailer (a kind of in-service career counselor but with more say) told him there was an opening to run a loran station in Thailand. His CO,

Roger Rufe, said there was no such thing as a bad command, so in the fall of 1974, as a lieutenant junior grade, he got his first command. At the time, there were two loran stations in Thailand and two in Vietnam that the Coast Guard had turned over to contractors.

Within a year of arriving, he had to oversee the evacuation of the loran stations in Vietnam during the 1975 Communist spring offensive while keeping his own running through the fall of Saigon and subsequent *Mayaguez* incident off the coast of Cambodia. That involved the seizure of a U.S. merchant ship by the Khmer Rouge and a bloody rescue mission by the Marines, who didn't know the sailors had already been released.

Allen had been promised an at-sea assignment after his Southeast Asian tour, and when that didn't come through he considered leaving the service. He was getting ready to marry Pam (now his wife of more than thirty years) and apply for a job with the Drug Enforcement Administration when he got a call from a disgusted detailer telling him he could have the job he wanted as an operations officer on a cutter. After two years at sea he went on to a liaison job with the DEA, where he "learned a lot of interagency stuff." Although he was still only a lieutenant, his next assignment was as a group commander running four SAR stations in New Jersey.

From there he worked his way into command of the *Citrus*, a buoy tender turned cutter that he ran out of Coos Bay, Oregon, doing fisheries patrols up and down the coast.

He went on to a series of staff jobs and picked up a master's in public administration from George Washington University and an SM in Management from the Sloan School at MIT, all the while fighting with his detailers, his own unique strategy for advancing through the ranks.

In 1995, the Bath Iron Works in Maine was suing the Coast Guard for $60 million, and Todd Shipyards in Seattle, which had earlier filed for Chapter 11, was working on Coast Guard High Endurance Cutters. Allen spent two years renegotiating and stabilizing the contracts. This would put him in good stead later on as commandant to confront the CEOs of Lockheed and Northrop over the Deepwater management fiasco.

Among his other career assignments, Allen was commander of the ever frenetic District 7 in Miami from 1999 to 2001.

On 9/11 he was in charge of the Coast Guard Atlantic Area, a command he's subsequently abolished. He then became chief of staff under Commandant Collins.

Eight days after Katrina made landfall, he was asked to become deputy primary federal official (DPFO) to FEMA head Mike Brown. He was in Baton Rouge that night and New Orleans the next morning. Three days later, half an hour before a press conference, he was told he'd be relieving Brown as PFO.

Allen, who based himself off the helicopter assault ship *Iwo Jima* in New Orleans, is credited with doing an exceptional job pulling various agencies, volunteer groups, and suspicious citizens together to help get posthurricane reconstruction under way. He mostly left his Coast Guard people alone, recognizing they were already doing the right thing.

While in the Gulf area he was told he was being considered for commandant and ended up writing his proposal for how he'd transform the organization hunched over a laptop in a Baton Rouge hotel room while still working sixteen-hour days on hurricane recovery.

We land at the old Quonset Point Naval Air Station in Rhode Island, where we're greeted by three Navy officers and local CGIS agents with a dark blue Chevy Tahoe that Admiral Allen climbs into. Brendan and I join Agent Dan Bradford in a black Ford follow-up vehicle. As we're driving over the high bridge to Newport, a pickup truck slips between the SUV and us. Dan hits the dash-mounted siren and blue lights, and the guy gets out of the way quick.

We pull up at the conference center inside the gates of the Naval War College, where the commandant is scheduled to be part of a symposium titled "Toward a New Maritime Strategy." There's a state trooper standing by the governor of Rhode Island, and a new bunch of guys with earpieces and suits show up with the chief of naval operations and the commandant of the Marine Corps.

There are about a thousand people, uniformed and civilian, inside the clamshell-shaped auditorium for the opening panel that includes Allen, Chief of Naval Operations Mike Mullen (soon to be named Chairman of the Joint Chiefs of Staff) and Gen. Jim Conway, head of the Marine Corps. Things get going at 8:15 A.M.

I'm struck by the contrast between Mullen and Conway's purely military perspective on "maritime strategy," and that of the Coast Guard commandant's.

Mullen uses a lot of military shorthand, talking about his "desire to solve things together," and says, "Our mission set is expanding. There is the high end threat [let's say China, which he doesn't], the terrorist threat, but also disaster assistance and assuring the smooth flow of commerce . . . That's why the taxpayers give us $115 billion a year." (That's fourteen times what the Coast Guard gets.)

In lieu of a joke, Conway starts with a quote about how "Marines have to make sacrifices, and not the least of these hardships is to serve with sailors," before going on to tell the audience that "the Marine Corps is unique, being the smallest of the services." The Coast Guard commandant, seated next to him, maintains a look of blank equanimity. There are 185,000 Marines, 42,000 active-duty Coast Guard.

Conway talks about how Marines are turning things around in Iraq and also Afghanistan and says these are not wars but the first battles of the Long War on Terror. His worry is that they're not preparing enough for future amphibious operations. That seems to be his major maritime strategy concern, how ready they are to assault a beach.

Allen then gives a clear and engaging talk, opening with an Arthur C. Clarke quote saying, in effect, that from space you'd look back and call it Planet Ocean.

"There are no hard lines on the map like on the land, we have bands, not bright lines . . . We don't track ocean traffic like we track aircraft for safety, but we may need this capability . . . We [the Coast Guard] are both military and regulatory. We deal with all hazards, all threats, all the time. So it's a fair question to ask what constitutes adequate maritime security for the home team. Operating under Title 10 and Title 14, we're bureaucratically multilingual. We can talk to first responders—to police chiefs and firemen—and then turn around and talk with Navy SEALs. We also take a different approach [from the other armed forces], believing that transparency breeds security—we need partnerships based on trust in order to exchange information and feel comfortable contacting and working with each other."

Allen cites examples of strategic concerns including the placement of LNG facilities on the U.S. coastline and a small boat conference he's convened to reduce the risk of improvised small boat explosive devices like the one used against the USS *Cole* and the one that killed Nate Bruckenthal and two Navy sailors off Iraq. He talks about Arctic policy as melting ice from global warming opens up new shipping lanes and even mentions invasive species in ballast water and how they found cholera in the ballast water of a ship in Mobile, Alabama, "so you can see the implications."

"We're looking at a broader, richer mosaic of safety, security, and stewardship. This stuff marries up perfectly across the three sea services," he claims.

My own impression is that while he's talking about varied asymmetrical threats on the global commons, the audience is thinking counterinsurgency and maybe Iranian submarines.

After the panel, the three service leaders hold a brief press conference attended mostly by military and defense industry reporters. I ask about changing conditions in the Arctic, and Mullen hands it off to Allen, referring to him as "my icebreaker guy."

Somewhere backstage Allen has changed into new ODU (Operational Dress Uniform) work clothes: a blue jacket and bill cap. We climb back into our vehicles and drive to a rundown section of waterfront at the old Navy Yard where three Coast Guard buoy tenders, the *Ida Lewis*, the *Juniper*, and the *Willow*, are berthed.

Here he gets a briefing on pier repairs from a tall civilian, who explains the pier was built back in 1956. In the next two to three years the buoy tenders won't be able to stay unless it's fixed. It will take $16 million to $18 million in funding to renovate it; $10 million has been earmarked.

"OK got ya." The Commandant, who's read the briefing paper, nods impatiently.

They need to shift the funding to the other side of the pier, though.

"Got ya."

They need to renovate the pier. Senator Jack Reed approved the funding but is open to moving the project a few hundred feet over.

"Here?"

"No, the other side. We have ten thousand pilings."

"Got ya."

"And Senator Reed approved it."

"I gotcha, I gotcha." He knows everything he's being told, but the man feels compelled to finish his presentation then asks if the admiral has any questions.

"No, that's it. Tell Senator Reed I touched Jesus' wound here," he says, then walks down the money-hungry pier and up the *Willow*'s gangway to be with his people.

He enters the wardroom, where the buoy tender's CO, Lt. Cdr. Jeff Dow, briefs him on their recent "underway," a law enforcement cruise in the Florida Straits where they detained a number of migrants and the small boat they put over the side was rammed by a smuggler on a Jet-Ski who didn't want to give up. At one point they had 122 Cubans under a shade canopy on their buoy deck, including four pregnant women and twenty children.

"Where do you want to go next?" Allen asks the thirty-something CO.

"I'd like to stay on the *Willow*," he replies.

"Where's your family? What's your wife do?"

"We're here. She does hairdressing and cosmetics. I think she'd also like to stay in the area."

"You're sucking up to the right people." The admiral grins, something he rarely does except on deck with the working Coast Guard.

Months later, in early 2008, Dow would be relieved of command while charges he'd had an "inappropriate relationship" with a subordinate were investigated. Subsequently he was found to have committed conduct unbecoming an officer and gentleman, received a written reprimand, and had some of his pay forfeited.

The crew holds an All Hands on the buoy deck, forming a rectangle with Allen, Adm. Tim Sullivan from the 1st District, and the hefty, sun-reddened CO making up the fourth side below the *Willow*'s high white bridge. A 41-foot utility boat and an armed 25-foot RBS are standing by on the outside of the ship across the channel from an old aircraft carrier. Allen gives out awards for their recent three-week operation that "sheltered and processed" 353 Cuban migrants and nine smugglers.

After the awards he calls the crew closer in and shows them the new ODU he's wearing, pointing out that it's untucked at the waist and roomy at the hips. He passes out a swatch of fabric explaining how they can't just throw out $10 million worth of old uniforms, so initially the new ODU will be optional for purchase, but as the old uniforms wear out they'll make the switch. He talks about how PPEs—Personal Protective Equipment, meaning sidearms—may go to thigh holsters or even shoulder holsters to deal with the untucked shirt.

He wants an integrated system for everything they wear and segues this into his talk about simplifying logistics and supply chains, "like the aviation folks do. Curtis Bay [Baltimore, the Coast Guard shipyard] will become the product line source for all 225s [large buoy tenders] like Elizabeth City is for aviation—but you'll have to trust the system and not squirrel away extra parts. We can no longer have one-boat stations with two boats, the second functioning as an engine holder." The mechanic next to me grins at that.

"I would never talk down to the deck people," Allen later tells me, "but I want to explain the parts of the reforms that impact how they work day to day."

He asks if they have any questions. They do. One is about privatizing ATON, the aids to navigation mission that is the *Willow*'s bread and butter.

He claims Hurricanes Katrina and Rita proved that recovery of maritime commerce works best as a government job. "There were rivers with altered bottoms and debris and all their navigation buoys gone, and no private contractor would do the job or could get insurance to do it, but the Coast Guard did, marking the best water."

Along with proposals to privatize Coast Guard missions like ATON and icebreaking, Congress has periodically proposed charging money for search and rescue. The Coast Guard has always resisted this idea, believing that if people think it's going to cost them money they will delay calling for help until the risks become so great that more lives, including the lives of their rescuers, are lost.

"You're in a high-risk environment," Allen tells his people. "Take care of each other. Watch your backs, and not just on the job, but when you're out *there* don't let your buddy do something stupid. I couldn't be prouder of you guys."

He's given a *Willow* T-shirt and bill cap. "If anyone wants a picture with—"

"I want a picture with you, sir," one of the crew shouts out, to the amusement of his shipmates. The digital and video cameras are pulled out as the crew of hardworking men and women pose with their boss in groups of one, two, and four.

We then climb onto the 41-footer. Chief Warrant Officer Kevin Galvin, an old friend of the commandant's, is driving. We head across the gray choppy waters of Narragansett Bay to Station Castle Rock, escorted by the machine-gun-mounted 25. Galvin offers Allen the wheel. The crew feed him coordinates and distance. "Fourteen hundred yards left on this course." We pass the Rose Island Lighthouse, Fort Adams, Castle Hill Light, and the stunning old-money "cottages" of Newport.

We slow and enter a narrow channel that takes us to the red-roofed white shingle Castle Rock Station that still has the old rail ramp the Life-Saving Service used for sliding their wooden boats into the water.

At the top of a forested hill they've set up a white tent and a barbecue station offering hot dogs and burgers. There are about a hundred Coasties here from Sector SE New England. After everyone starts eating and they give recognition to a chief on his fiftieth birthday, Admiral Allen does a variation on what he calls his "spiel," including the fashion show. "It's untucked, with pockets here and here, and very pleasing for us in petite sizes," he jokes. He talks about the Deployable Operations Group, streamlining logistics, and other challenges such as fixing the inland Coast Guard's shore facilities.

He's asked if people can take pictures with him. "If the camera can tolerate it," he replies, not for the first time. I notice the stewards of our public seas don't recycle their cans and plastic bottles, which all go into a single garbage can with the BBQ trash.

The commandant next climbs aboard an HH-60 that will fly him and a few officers to the Chatham Surf Station on Cape Cod on his way to Boston. I catch a ride with one of the CGIS vans to the waterfront hotel in Boston where we'll be staying.

That evening I'm invited to a dinner at Admiral Sullivan's house in Beverly, north of Boston. The spacious Hospital Point Coast Guard residence with its adjoining lighthouse overlooking scenic Salem Harbor is elegant and impressive, even if it was once the site of a smallpox hospital.

Cars are shuttled around and CGIS radios chatter until the commandant and his escort, including an unmarked state police car, arrive. Unlike most states, Massachusetts always gives him a trooper escort. I later figure out why when he tells me his children are Yankees fans.

There are a dozen people at the party and a dinner buffet including oysters, clam chowder, crab cakes, and crab claws. Admiral Allen is dressed casually in tan slacks and an understated blue and brown aloha shirt. He tells a couple of people about how he went into the Margaritaville Café in New Orleans after Katrina to show his support and wrote a note on a napkin and Jimmy Buffett called back months later, thrilling his office manager. Among his ambitions, he says, is to get the popular NPR radio program *Prairie Home Companion* to do a show at the Coast Guard Academy.

I go into the kitchen and meet the house manager, Food Service Specialist First Class Brittney Gonzales, and her dinner crew, which includes her husband, Machinery Technician First Class Raul Gonzales, whom she's wrangled into helping out, and Food Service Specialists Second Class Melissa Olson and Michael King. The enlisted ratings with the most at-sea time are not coxswains, gunners, or mechanics but cooks. The commandant comes in to greet them, and after dinner they're introduced to the party guests.

Gonzales, who used to cook on a Medium Endurance Cutter, is one of a handful of house managers working at admirals' residences. They each do a stint at the commandant's house before their assignments. "So they're working where I'm living and I'm living in their workplace" is how the commandant explains it. Later he will instruct Raul Gonzales on the proper way to chill a glass for a Manhattan.

On the Road, Day 2

Thursday starts early with a fast-moving caravan of four vehicles pulling up at a cable news station. The commandant enters with an entourage of eight plus me. Waiting in the greenroom, he begins to read a newspaper, then checks his Palm for other news and e-mails. Next week he'll fly to New York to do a boating safety spot for the *Today* show. He's led into the studio and seated across from Karen, the attractive morning hostess, while the soundman mikes him. Before they go on air, Karen tells him she lived in Slidell, Louisiana, during Hurricane Katrina and was with the CBS affiliate in New Orleans and thanks him for all he did down there.

When they go live she asks, "How prepared are we in New England for a major storm?" He says that people need to prepare to get along on their own for seventy-two hours before counting on the government to respond to a crisis. He talks about safety, security, and stewardship of our oceans, and their five minutes are up. They cut to the weatherman, who also reminds the viewers of the need for hurricane preparedness.

On the way out, I suggest the admiral do public service announcements on hurricane preparedness. His press aide, Brendan, worries the head of FEMA might take offense.

Heading back to Boston, we hit morning rush hour. The state trooper hits his lights and siren, and the caravan cuts across three lanes of traffic and rolls onto the shoulder moving fast.

Back at the hotel's concrete wharf, we board a machine-gun-equipped 41-footer and head out into the harbor. There are fourteen people on board, including a couple of enlisted Coasties modeling CBRN (chemical, biological, radiological, and nuclear) ODUs in green and blue that also function as floatation suits with hoods. If they put on their protective gloves and air masks and a death-spewing witches' brew comes along, leaving the rest of us dead or writhing on the deck with foam and spittle on our lips, they'd still be comfy enough to take over the boat's helm and machine gun. One of the two types of CBRN suits is used by British forces, the other by U.S. Special Forces. The question is which is better suited for the Coast Guard's marine environmental demands. Recently retired Coast Guard Strike Team member Dave Dugery is evaluating the two for SAIC, a Coast Guard contractor.

"You're the systems integrator. You don't have a vested interest in any of the suits?" the commandant asks.

"No, we don't," Dave assures him.

That's what newspaper editors call "the nut graph," the key bit that holds a story together. With the Deepwater program, the systems integrator had a $24 billion vested interest in the boats.

We pull up by the old red and white Coast Guard lightship *Nantucket*, moored in the middle of the harbor. We're welcomed aboard by Bill, a Boston lawyer who purchased it on eBay, then spent $5 million converting it into a palatial floating home and conference center that he charters out in the summer. We're toured through the mahogany-, brass-, and marble-laden rooms as he shows the admiral how the mast light still works, a light he claims "immigrants once saw as a beacon of hope, welcome, and warning."

Bill's wife is ready to move back to the land, though, and "as a steward of this national treasure," Bill would be willing to sell it to the Coast Guard Foundation for the $5 million he put into it, rather than his $7.5 million asking price.

The Commandant thanks him for his stewardship. Bill tells him his ninety-four-year-old dad is still in the Coast Guard Auxiliary.

We get back on the 41-footer and head up Chelsea Creek close by the LNG terminal, the Tobin Bridge, and the Chelsea Bridge, which has been scheduled for replacement since 1992 and is, according to Coast Guard Bridge Program manager Gary Kassof, "a disaster waiting to happen."

Cruising past the *King Edwin,* a huge blue-hulled fuel tanker flagged in the Marshall Islands, I understand what he means. The gap at the Chelsea Street Bridge is ninety-six feet wide. The tanker is ninety feet wide by some six hundred feet long. We pull over by the Conoco-Phillips tank farm to watch four tugboats gingerly playing the *King Edwin* through the slot, one of them at the ship's rear acting as a counterweight. It's a delicate maritime ballet, always at risk of a stumble. There are some six or eight collisions with this bridge every year, none catastrophic to date.

We're then dropped off at the Boston Coast Guard station in the North End, where, after posing for pictures with the crew, the commandant meets with top district officers.

Afterward there's a retirement ceremony for Chief Warrant Officer Dan Parker, who served with Thad Allen in Thailand. There are about 125 people attending. The slim gray-haired Coastie talks about some of his career highlights as an engineer and safety inspector sent to Antarctica, Thailand, and various oil rigs off the coast of Africa.

After the ceremony is completed with an officer reading him out of the service ("Shipmate—this watch stands relieved"), there's a reception and roast for Parker with valiant attempts at humor. Thad Allen skips the humor part and tells of their time in Thailand when the loran needed an emergency repair and "we had Dan upside down with a torch and the fuel line packed with ice and everyone else backed off except for three [guys] who were standing by with fire extinguishers."

The admiral's next stop is at the *Boston Globe* for a sit-down with two of its editorial page writers, Don and Larry. There are old campaign posters of LBJ, Nixon, and Kennedy adorning the conference room walls. They start out by asking him about a quote that morning from the secretary of defense saying force can't solve all problems. He responds with a rapid-fire unrelated answer. Whenever he gets a question he doesn't like, he talks faster.

They finally find an area of mutual interest discussing proposed new LNG sites off Massachusetts and on Long Island Sound. There are over forty applications for new LNG terminals in the United States, and the Coast Guard has to approve each plan for safety and security. On the eastern seaboard, the liquefied natural gas will come from gasification plants in Trinidad and Algeria.

"I went to Trinidad and took a tour, and its LNG is spotless and secure. Those are conditions of their bank loan and insurance, which is something to look into," he suggests. "We are satisfied with Algeria," he adds, without mentioning a 2004 accidental explosion that killed twenty-seven workers, injured eighty, and caused over a billion dollars of damage to the port.

Other topics discussed for possible future editorials include shipping container security (a Customs job), wind turbines off Cape Cod (the Coasties pull out the maps on this one), and ship strikes of endangered northern right whales, of whom there are only some three hundred left. Because of their tendency to loll at the surface, these great oil-rich cetaceans became the "right" (easy) whale to kill for New England's early whalers. Today this same tendency leaves the last right whales vulnerable to being struck and killed by container ships, tankers, and other vessels plying the shipping lanes off New England. The Coast Guard has taken modest steps to try to reduce these fatal collisions, including shifting one shipping lane out of a feeding area.

From the *Globe* the caravan heads to Logan Airport, where we are waved through the North Security Gate and driven up to the commandant's jet waiting for him on the tarmac.

After we take off, I ask him what the Coast Guard of the future will look like, and he gives me the Thad Allen doctrine.

"We can't predict the future. We need an organization that can adapt to change, that can fluidly respond to whatever the environment requires—and that's no small thing. Change is hard, [especially] trying to deal just with the rush of business, the tyranny of the present. My legacy isn't the CIAOs. I told my flag corps [admirals] I'm a transition commandant. We are an organization that is changecentric, asymmetrical, and very flat [accessible and driven from all levels of command]. Of course, they can tell me to go to hell," he concludes, "but if they don't adapt, it's not going to be my failure of imagination."

He's constantly in campaign mode, and what's interesting is how much of that is focused internally on the Coast Guard itself. He's trying to sell his vision to the next generation of leaders from the deck plate to the chief's mess to junior officers in the field as well as the captains and admirals at headquarters. He plans to talk to all fifty thousand active-duty and reserve members by the time his term is up in 2010. In his first year he met with seventeen thousand.

He also met with a hundred members of Congress, recognizing, as few before him have, that just doing the right thing does not get you the resources you need in Washington.

"The Coast Guard doesn't do politics and policy," says former Coast Guard Academy professor and now Council on Foreign Relations fellow Scott Borgerson. "We can save people off rooftops after a Category 5 hurricane, but we can't understand a high school graph about how a bill becomes law."

Thad Allen seems to understands politics and policy and has begun working hard to make friends among congressional majority Democrats, to eradicate their identification of him as a Bush administration figure. "We don't always see eye to eye, but I respect the commandant. The man has integrity," says House Coast Guard Subcommittee chair Elijah Cummings.

Allen has also become a strong policy advocate for a cogent U.S. response to the Arctic meltdown, the rapid loss of sea ice due to fossil-fuel-fired climate change. "I'm agnostic on climate change, science and everything else," he'll later claim in a press conference. "All I know is there's water where there didn't used to be, and I have statutory responsibilities to operate there."

I understand his reluctance to challenge the commander in chief (George W. Bush at the time), but to me that sounds a bit like "I'm agnostic on what caused the damage at Pearl Harbor; all I know is we have to refloat those ships and get them operating again."

"I'm unconstrained to do the right thing," the admiral claims, taking a Jack Daniel's from one of the crew. "My three kids are all grown; my wife is the assistant dean at George Mason [University]. I can put in the twelve- to eighteen-hour days. I'm fairly passionate. I wear people down."

"He doesn't play golf. Work is his hobby" is how Batch, his assistant, explains it.

He's also a believer in applying social network theory to organizational change. Social network theory analogizes complex systems such as cellular biology, power grids, the spread of diseases, and the Internet with social networks to study the ways in which groups of people organize themselves, identifying key nodes, or hubs, be they neurons in the brain or a SAR coordinator at a surf station, that can facilitate and accelerate growth and communication but are also highly vulnerable to disruption and sabotage.

In this context, Thad Allen's saying his organization is "asymmetrical" was more likely a reference to its simultaneous formal and informal networks of communications, rather than the military definition of asymmetrical I'd taken it to be: an imbalance of forces leading to the use of compensatory tactics and strategies by the nominally weaker side. Either way, the Coast Guard fits the bill.

The admiral recommends I read two books on social network theory, *Linked*, by Albert-Laszlo Barabasi, and *Nexus*, by Mark Buchanan. I ask him what book he's reading now and he says *Guns, Germs, and Steel*, by Jared Diamond, which is a different type of social theory, one using a scientific view of history to demonstrate that geography and environment, not race or culture, were key to the development of the technologies and immunities that gave "Western civilization" its edge in global hegemony, at least through the early part of the twenty-first century.

So how, in a world of accelerating socioecological change, unrestrained markets, nongovernmental players, and ubiquitous information, does one institutionalize reform in a 220-year-old organization, I wonder.

"In 1998, [then Commandant] Bob Kramek put Jim Loy on staff with a high-level plan, the Long View Project," Allen explains. "It was to take five or six strategic drivers—globalization, energy, population . . . and we came out with twenty-five future scenarios, and senior leadership looked at these and got a core five or six futures and described these worlds. We'd build twenty-five-year strategies and then bring them back together and look across these five or six futures, and we had some commonalities, we had two or three keepers, and one was Maritime Domain Awareness."

This is the somewhat Orwellian concept of a close to real-time observation system of the global maritime domain and anything happening on or in the sea that could impact U.S. safety or security, the economy, or the environment. It includes layered defense, and a simple example of its implementation was when Thad Allen, as Atlantic Commander, was able to divert Coast Guard cutters at sea into U.S. ports within twenty-four hours of the September 11, 2001, attacks, cinching a security belt tight around the continental homeland.

"In looking at 9/11 you can see it worked. Another plan was to create a single command [structure for the Coast Guard]," he says, "but you had to put M&O [Maritime Safety and Operations] into one organization and people said it was 'too hard' and we didn't trust ourselves enough [until he did it].

"In the summer of 2002 I came in as chief of staff, and in 2003 we did the Long View again, only we called it the Evergreen Project. The payoff was, the Evergreen [plan] became the [2005 federal] National Maritime Strategy. So I propose we do this every four years, during the first year of each commandant's tenure. My chief of staff is starting the next set of scenarios, so we're institutionalizing this, institutionalizing change with Evergreen [which to me sounds more like Everblue]."

Perhaps the most agreeable part of Thad Allen's Coast Guard, at least from a journalist's perspective, is his focus on transparency and diversity. He has a unique way of taking what many would see as democratic or moral imperatives and giving them a steely sheen of operational necessity, arguing, for example, that transparency is essential to both "self-correcting behavior" within the service and building trust with its outside partners.

When asked why diversity is a necessity, he points to the Coast Guard's need for more Spanish speakers for migrant interdiction but also to a wider operational need to reflect the makeup of the public it works with every day. "What makes us different from the other services is we deploy where we work and live. We're the ultimate in community-based policing."

We land back at National Airport and he gives me a military coin on his way out, the armed services' version of a baseball trading card.

Second in Command

Before her decision to retire in 2009, it was uncertain if Vice Commandant Vivien Crea was going to be the next admiral to head the U.S. Coast Guard, but it would have made sense. Like Thad Allen she's whip smart, but she also had a more collaborative style of leadership that will be needed if the service is to institutionalize the dramatic changes he began. Plus, as the first woman to head one of the U.S. armed services, she would have commanded the kind of public attention (and hopefully respect) that is needed if the organization's leadership wants to cultivate the internal and external constituencies needed to expand the Coast Guard.

Whether in her headquarters office overlooking the Anacostia River in DC, decorated with photographs of aircraft she's piloted and paintings from the Coast Guard Art Program, talking to a stream of officers, contractors, and officials at a National Press Club event, or meeting her people aboard the

Bertholf, Vivien Crea radiates a kind of self-assured confidence that makes her seem both formidable and approachable. She has an impressive ability to grasp and retain detail and draw the best out of those around her, while also maintaining a navigator's sense of focus except when it comes to tracking her reading glasses. About five-nine with sharp gray eyes and today's reading glasses pushed high onto her feathery helmet of gray-brown hair, she recounts how she came to be where she is.

"As an Army brat fresh out of college, I was interested in environmental protection and looked into NOAA and the EPA before deciding on the Coast Guard. I joined the second class of women to go through Officer Candidate School [winning her commission in 1973]. It was a lot of fun with a couple of barriers. They didn't know what to do with us. We couldn't [were not allowed to] go on cutters or to flight school if it meant landing on cutters, so I went to headquarters," she recalls.

Eventually she did become a pilot, the Coast Guard's first female aircraft commander, flying C-130 Hercules, a Gulfstream 11 executive jet, and HH-65 Dolphin helicopters. She was also the first woman to command an air station.

"Because Officer Candidate School was a few years ahead of the academy [in accepting women] and they had four years more [schooling] till they got into the fleet, we had a six- or seven-year jump on them, so the female flag officers [admirals] we have now are all OCS," she explains.

Until her husband retired from the Coast Guard with the rank of captain a few years ago, she also worked to balance her schedule with his so that they might find a few days a month of common ground while pursuing their careers protecting America's waters.

In addition to her other duties, Crea is the Department of Homeland Security's principal federal official in charge of government response in case of a pandemic influenza outbreak.

"We have to be adaptive," she explains. "The only certainty of the ocean is it's very unpredictable, so that encourages flexible on-scene initiative [within the Coast Guard]. We train with common terminology, equipment, and processes. We do a few things that are fundamental: trust each other, have that common training, a bias for action, on-scene initiative, core values, and stewardship of the public trust.

"The bigger you get, the harder it is to keep these things integrated. So there's an advantage to being lean and hungry."

"Even though they keep giving you new jobs to do?"

"Our common definition of what we do is, we do everything wet . . . It's serious business," she adds as I grin, glancing at an oil-stained life ring on the wall.

Later, looking around her office, I see that the old oil-stained ring is from the *Blackthorn*, a Coast Guard buoy tender that collided with a tanker in Tampa Bay on January 28, 1980. Twenty-three of its crew were lost that night.

She's quick to admit that presently more is required of the Coast Guard than it can deliver on a sustained basis. "We don't have enough bench strength," she says. "We're *this* thick [holding two of her fingers a fraction of an inch apart], but we go in first!"

That's how I've come to see the Coast Guard, as a maritime multimission version of the U.S. Marines who "go in first," only with one-fifth the people and one-tenth the equipment.

Fortunately the Coast Guard has created a force multiplier in its commitment to on-scene initiative and the trust it places in its enlisted ranks to make command decisions and run many of its operating assets like surf stations, swimmer shops, patrol boats, and river tenders.

Chief Ross Fowle, the CO of the harbor tug *Line* in New York, served three years in the Army before joining the Coast Guard.

"As an E-4, I'd have to ask four people and get signatures to take a Humvee out to pick up a FedEx box. In the Coast Guard as an enlisted E-4, I would take out a 47 [-foot surfboat] without calling anyone. There's that much difference in bureaucracy, or at least in trust."

"The enlisted in the Coast Guard are a lot more empowered than in other services," agrees Senior Chief Lewis Hart, an ex-Marine turned Coastie who helps oversee the Rescue Swimmer School in Elizabeth City. "In the Marines, you don't move till you're told to. Here they expect you to figure it out—and go get it done. Lots of prior-service guys will first wait for an order and then realize it's not coming. They [the Coast Guard leadership] expect you to be a self-starter. They have faith in their people. What's so cool is we have this latitude to initiate commonsense action, and if what you do is based on good order and discipline, no one flips out when you do it."

While the Coast Guard is officially keen on how FEMA, Customs Enforcement, and other Department of Homeland Security agencies can now share their burden, history and experience suggest it will still be Coasties doing most of the grunt work the next time a major disaster confronts the nation along our ninety-five thousand miles of coastline, on our Great Lakes and rivers, or on our vast ocean frontier.

At present the Coast Guard's $9 billion annual operating budget is equal to what three weeks of U.S. military operations in Iraq cost during 2008.

"So our problem is capacity," says Commandant Allen. "We have authorities. We have capabilities. We have competencies. The issue is capacity."

Rep. Elijah Cummings has been told that the Coast Guard has the ability to grow by around ten thousand over the next seven years. However, given the rate of change in the maritime environment in terms of offshore activity, climate disruption, coastal sprawl, piracy, terrorism, and the collapse of living resources, it may actually need to double in the coming decade and double again in the following to make this smallest of armed services closer in size to the U.S. Marine Corps than to the New York City Police Department.

"It would take a radical recalibration of Coast Guard leadership to deal with the level of growth that may be required," says Scott Borgerson, the former director of the Coast Guard Academy's Institute of Leadership. "There are many admirable qualities in the Coast Guard, but without question there's also a junior varsity attitude where they're not ready to go to this next level," he claims.

Ready or not, as we all learned on 9/11, after the invasion of Iraq, and again with Hurricane Katrina, history tends to force the issues.

While politicians, like sharks, tend to be hardwired to a few simple stimuli, in their case money and votes, Deepwater taught the Coast Guard that Rescue Warriors are not genetically predisposed to run with big-money contractors and lobbyists if it means cutting corners. What the Coast Guard needs more than anything else is a political constituency of engaged citizens willing to demand that America's forgotten armed service get the resources necessary to fulfill its missions.

Certainly the Coast Guard's fifty thousand active-duty and reserve members as well as their families, civilian employees, and twenty-eight-thousand-strong volunteer auxiliary need to keep building a base of support in the areas where they operate, not only on our coasts but on the Great Lakes and along the inland rivers of America.

Conversely, the public needs to be fully informed about what's happening to their Coast Guard, including the degree to which its work has reoriented since 9/11. Today the thirteen Maritime Safety and Security Teams each spend about $1.5 million a year for their port security operations, about the same amount as the twelve High Endurance Cutters spend to carry out their offshore missions.

Few among the public are aware of the Coast Guard's Airborne Use of

Force doctrine or know that Coast Guard helicopters are armed with machine guns and sniper rifles.

The Coast Guard has long bragged that unlike other armed services in times of peace (which some of us can recall), the Coast Guard is operational every day of the year and not just training for the next war. Now, though, hundreds of members of the Maritime Security Response Team do nothing but train for a potential armed confrontation with terrorists and their superiors are looking to establish at least four more teams across the nation.

The widespread reaction to live weapons training on the Great Lakes in 2006 reflected the public's ambiguity about the Coast Guard's changed role in the Department of Homeland Security. They want the security missions to keep them safe from terrorists, criminals, and nut jobs, but they also want assurance that traditional Coast Guard missions like search and rescue, marine safety, and environmental stewardship are not being neglected.

Also, while the Coast Guard's leadership is delighted at having gone from being a victim of benign neglect in the Department of Transportation to a big fish in the murky pond of DHS, that doesn't necessarily mean this is where they can best serve the public interest as a multimission maritime agency.

The Department of the Ocean?

"They need to get out of DHS. I voted for it [establishing the Department of Homeland Security] after 9/11, but they are always a stepchild. I would at a minimum put them back under the secretary of transportation or maybe create a secretary of the Coast Guard," Rep. Gene Taylor, the Coast Guard veteran from Mississippi, tells me. "When the Deepwater program was having all those problems, who in DHS stepped forward to assume responsibility?" he asks. "We only heard from Admiral Allen. As far as [then Secretary of Homeland Security] Michael Chertoff is concerned, it was not that important. No one staked their reputation or career on this. If you don't want that responsibility or are not willing to step up, maybe give it to someone who *does* think it's important."

The United States is and always has been an oceanic society. It owes much of its wealth, bounty, and heritage to the sea around us. The ocean provides us with the oxygen we breathe, is a driver of climate and weather, brings rain to our farmers and food to our tables. It offers us recreation, transportation, protein, medicine, energy, security, and a sense of awe and wonder from sea to shining sea.

Forty years ago, in 1969, the Stratton Commission, a White House–appointed blue ribbon panel on oceans, published a report titled *Our Nation and the Sea,* which helped spawn major policy reforms, including the Coastal Zone Management Act, the Marine Mammal Protection Act, the Marine Sanctuary Act, and the Clean Water Act. However, its key recommendation, the creation of an independent U.S. ocean agency built around the Coast Guard, never came to pass.

Part of the reason was timing. President Lyndon Johnson had just created the Department of Transportation and had transferred the Coast Guard from the Treasury Department to DOT to give it more heft. As a result, instead of assigning oversight of our oceans to the "Guardians of the Sea," the next President, Richard Nixon, went on to create the National Oceanographic and Atmospheric Administration out of the Bureau of Commercial Fisheries, the Weather Bureau, and some other marine offices before sinking it in the trade-driven Department of Commerce, then run by his campaign fund-raiser and future Watergate bagman Maurice Stans.

It would be another generation before new commissions were established to look at the state of America's coasts and oceans. Much had changed in the interim.

Although the Census Bureau declared the western frontier closed in 1890, on March 10, 1983, President Ronald Reagan, in one of the most significant and least-noted acts of his administration, established the U.S. Exclusive Economic Zone that extends two hundred miles out to sea from America's shore, in effect creating a vast new blue frontier six times the size of the Louisiana Purchase. At 3.4 million square nautical miles, our EEZ is 30 percent larger than the continental land base of the United States. It is a wilder, more challenging frontier than any known to past generations of Americans, one that is also part of a larger global ocean that constitutes 71 percent of our planet's surface area and over 95 percent of its living habitat. This is the territory on which the U.S. Coast Guard operates every day.

In 2000, with a majority of Americans living in our coastal zones, 97 percent of our trade coming through our ports, hurricane damage taking a precipitous upswing, and coastal habitats, water quality, and wildlife in steep decline, two new ocean panels were created. The eighteen-member Pew Oceans Commission was established by the Pew Charitable Trusts, which had grown tired of waiting for Congress to take action on the oceans. Pew's action inspired a congressional reaction, and within months a sixteen-member U.S. Commission on Ocean Policy had been named by President George W. Bush.

The Pew Commission was made up of scientists, fishermen, environmentalists, and elected officials including the governor of New York and had as its primary focus America's living marine resources. Its chair, Leon Panetta, was a former congressman, lifelong Democrat, and chief of staff in the Clinton White House.

The U.S. Commission included representatives from the offshore oil industry, ports, Navy admirals, academics, and *Titanic* explorer Bob Ballard and had a broader mandate to look at all aspects of the sea including commerce and defense. Its chair, Adm. Jim Watkins, was a former chief of naval operations, a lifelong Republican and secretary of energy under the first President Bush.

After several years of public hearings around the country, they put out reports in 2003 and 2004. Given their very different makeups, their findings were remarkably similar. Both commissions concluded that the physical and ecological degradation of America's coasts and oceans had reached a critical stage that now threatened the nation's economy, security, and environment. They proposed a range of solutions aimed at boosting our ability to maintain our ocean-dependent economy while restoring healthy and abundant seas and preventing natural disasters like Hurricane Katrina from turning into human catastrophes as a result of bad policy choices.

Inside the Pew Commission, retired Coast Guard Adm. Roger Rufe, who headed the Ocean Conservancy, lobbied hard for the old Stratton Commission proposal that a new ocean agency be created, this time with the Coast Guard and NOAA at its heart. While Leon Panetta worried this would be a hard sell in Washington, they eventually agreed to move forward on the idea.

Then, thirty-five years after the Coast Guard got shunted off to the Department of Transportation, the post–9/11 Bush administration, for political reasons, established the Department of Homeland Security and made the Coast Guard a part of it.

The Pew Commission went ahead and proposed "an independent agency outside the Department of Commerce to address the national interest in the oceans and atmosphere," presumably now to be made up of a reinvigorated NOAA.

Before his retirement Senator Fritz Hollings of South Carolina, a longtime ocean champion on the Hill, called members of the U.S. Commission on Ocean Policy "sissies" for not making a similar recommendation for an independent Department of the Oceans.

U.S. Commission members told me they did not believe an independent agency was "politically feasible" at the time, especially after Congress had just done a major government reorganization with the creation of the Department of Homeland Security.

I think of all the places it's ever been, the Department of Homeland Security is the best place for the Coast Guard unless they had a Department of the Oceans," Roger Rufe now tells me.

Roger left the Ocean Conservancy in 2006 to become director of operations for DHS, where he's working to develop adaptive capabilities packages along the lines of the Coast Guard's Deployable Operations Group.

Unlike many of the political appointees in DHS, Roger's background as both a Coastie and a conservationist allows him to recognize that the homeland is threatened by more than just jihadi terrorists and that while we may or may not ever see a dirty bomb go off in America there will always be another hurricane season. Which is another reason he isn't willing to give up the Coast Guard.

"I just can't imagine a new government reorganization taking place now," he tells me. "I'd say it's nigh impossible in the absence of something like 9/11."

Senator Cantwell of Washington isn't so sure. "The jury is still out on Homeland Security," she says. "When you have these asymmetrical threats to our country, is a centralized linear bureaucracy the best response? When we had these drills in Puget Sound for protecting our ferries, people said the Department of Homeland Security wasn't there but the Coast Guard was. They see the Coast Guard as something that's unique and also local."

Of course, 9/11 wasn't the first time there was a historic shift in the Coast Guard's direction and priorities. There were huge shifts as a result of Prohibition in the 1920s, World War II, the Drug Wars of the 1980s, and the *Exxon Valdez* oil spill.

The trick is not to track the distortions but to find a balance, recognizing that while certain security threats are not going away, others are just as rapidly emerging. It doesn't take particular insight to see that beyond the threat of terrorism, climate change is going to require a huge shift in priorities and resources. Not only will increased response to extreme weather events such as hurricanes and flooding be required, but more attention will have to be given to America's increasingly ice-free fifth coast on the Arctic and to the maritime migration routes from poorer impacted nations like Haiti, where food riots broke out in the spring of 2008, followed two weeks later by the drowning death of more than twenty Haitians trying to flee by boat to the United States.

There's no question that the Coast Guard could take on a much more central and robust role in fulfilling its historic mandate as America's "Guardians of the Sea."

A Department of the Ocean incorporating the Coast Guard, NOAA, and some marine policy offices from the State Department and elsewhere might serve the nation well in protecting, exploring, and restoring our last great wilderness frontier. Plus, who better to confront environmental lawbreakers and pirates than Coasties with 57 mm deck guns? Of course, I'm not talking about what's politically feasible in today's Washington; I'm talking about what would best serve the public interest.

In any case, and wherever they might settle over time, America's Rescue Warriors need the capacity to meet the growing challenges of our new millennium, a capacity in terms of people and dollars they don't presently have, a capacity we as a nation need to give them.

Much about the Coast Guard is still missing from this book. There are the lighthouses, those sentinels of the sea they continue to operate and maintain after 220 years; there are the two Coast Guard astronauts, Bruce Melnick and Dan Burbank, who looked down from space to see their area of responsibility as the entire blue part of our blue planet.

There's the Inland Coast Guard that gets little notice until there's flooding and tornadoes in the Midwest or a highway bridge collapses. There's the honor guard on parade, the Field Intelligence Support Teams on the docks, the Baltimore shipyard, the Maritime Law Enforcement Academy, international trainers, and attachés from the Green Zone of Iraq to the Gulf of Guinea, not to mention Officer Snook, the anti-water-pollution fish mascot. There are civilian tool makers like Darnell Chamblee at the Aircraft Repair and Supply Center fabricating jewelry like three-piece universal joints that would take twenty-four months to order from the manufacturer, and the thousands of Coast Guard Auxiliary volunteers with their force-multiplying boats and airplanes such as Linda Vetter in San Francisco and Dan Charter in New Jersey. The Coast Guard has its own art program, museum, and foundation, along with an operational language and nomenclature for getting "into the game." It has, in anthropological terms, all the trappings of a culture except for a rejection of "the other." Instead, theirs is a culture based on a willingness to sacrifice, "so that others may live."

Two miles off New Jersey's Cape May Lighthouse, we put on our helmets and take off our rings and watches to avoid degloving injuries in which the flesh could be stripped away. The first Dolphin 65 approaches from the north. We fold down the black whip antennae on the side of the 47-foot surf-boat, though there are still plenty of mast obstructions to foul a line as we beat against a light chop. The helo's mechanic stands in the open door of the 65 and lowers the rescue basket to the two crewmen on the aft deck. They ground it with a short-handled baton so that the static electricity that can build up in the cable doesn't shock them, then snag it and bring it aboard. It's about the size of a shopping cart, and I'm amazed one or even two large fishermen can fit inside it, provided their survival instincts have kicked in. The copter pulls up the basket and makes another practice run, this time coming up on our wake with a weighted trail line. After the crew snags it, the mechanic attaches the basket and puts it on the winch line. The 65's swimmer has now squeezed in next to him, sitting in the small open door thirty feet above us.

We next stop dead in the water. They fly away and return to repeat the evolution. With the rolling of the boat in the two- to three-foot seas and the battering downdraft from the helicopter, it's actually harder doing the recovery stopped than under way.

The wild lily-pad ripples look like natural art, though I suppose I'd find their symmetrical patterns less pleasing if I were in the water getting blasted by the cyclonic prop wash, trying to breathe through blinding pellets of salt spray.

The boat crew gives the thumbs-up with arms spread, and the mechanic, now twenty-five feet above us, reels in the cable and basket through his gloved hand before they roar off. A second 65 approaches from Atlantic City, and we go through another training evolution with them.

After they leave, we take off. Lt. Cdr. Steve Love of the Cape May Boat Station (where they once searched for my friend David Guggenheim's missing dad) lets me take the controls. I hand them back before we approach the Lewes Ferry Terminal and head up a marshy channel. They inspect some pier pilings jutting into the canal as a possible hazard to navigation. A monarch butterfly flits past us. Steve tells me how three days earlier they picked up some people from a marine mammal stranding center and helped them recover a seal that was entangled with fishing line and unable to eat because the filament had tied up around its mouth. "He still tried to bite us, though."

Back offshore we pass a whale-watching boat, and the tourists all wave to us. "We pulled two people off a capsized sailboat here two weeks ago," Steve says, then grins. "We rescue people, too."

Then he points to a spot near the 150-year-old Coast Guard lighthouse, his expression changing. "This tour boat, they lost a Boy Scout overboard about a year and a half ago. We recovered the body about a month later. We kept looking, thinking that that might help the family. You think about losing a child like that, that's the hard part of our job."

The sun is shining brightly, though the air has cooled. The water is that deep blue cobalt color of the open sea and I realize how, when I'm done writing this book, I'm going to miss these honorable guys and gals.

If honor, respect, and devotion to duty can still resonate as a calling for tens of thousands of young people going in harm's way on our ocean frontier to keep us safe, I'd say that makes a pretty good case for the U.S. Coast Guard being the blue in our red, white, and blue.

SELECT BIBLIOGRAPHY

Adamson, Hans Christian. *Keepers of the Lights*. New York: Greenberg, 1955.

Barry, John M. *Rising Tide: The Great Mississippi Flood of 1927 and How It Changed America*. New York: Touchstone, 1998.

Beard, Barrett Thomas. *Wonderful Flying Machines: A History of U.S. Coast Guard Helicopters*. Annapolis, MD: Naval Institute Press, 1996.

Beard, Tom, José Hanson, and Paul C. Scotti, eds. *The Coast Guard*. Seattle: Foundation for Coast Guard History/Hugh Lauter Levin Assoc., 2004.

Bell, Kensil. *Always Ready! The Story of the United States Coast Guard*. New York: Dodd, Mead, 1943.

Berry, Erick. *You Have to Go Out!* New York: David McKay, 1964.

Bonner, Kit, and Carolyn Bonner. *Always Ready: Today's U.S. Coast Guard*. St. Paul, MN: MBI Publishing, 2004.

Brinkley, Douglas. *The Great Deluge*. New York: William Morrow, 2006.

Calonius, Erik. *The Wanderer: The Last American Slave Ship and the Conspiracy That Set Its Sails*. New York: St. Martin's Press, 2006.

Capelotti, P. J. *Rogue Wave: The U.S. Coast Guard On and After 9/11*. Washington: Department of Homeland Security/U.S. Coast Guard, 2005.

Carse, Robert. *Rum Row*. New York: Rinehart, 1959; rpt. Mystic, CT: Flat Hammock Press, 2007.

Chernow, Ron. *Alexander Hamilton*. New York: Penguin, 2005.

Clifford, Mary Louise, and J. Candace Clifford. *Women Who Kept the Lights*. Alexandria, VA: Cypress Communications, 2000.

Dana, Richard Henry, Jr. *Two Years Before the Mast*. 1840. New York: Barnes & Noble Classics, 2007.

DeWire, Elinor. *Lighthouses: Sentinels of the American Coast*. Portland, OR: Graphic Arts Center, 2003.

Drumm, Russell. *The Barque of Saviors*. Boston: Houghton Mifflin, 2001.

Faircount Media Group. *The Shield of Freedom: A Guide to the United States Coast Guard, 2007*. Tampa: Faircount, 2008.

Flynn, Stephen. *America the Vulnerable*. New York: HarperCollins, 2004.

———. *The Edge of Disaster*. New York: Random House, 2007.

Foley, George F., Jr. *Sinbad of the Coast Guard*. New York: Dodd, Mead, 1945. New ed. with introduction by Michael Walling. Mystic, CT: Flat Hammock Press, 2005.

Fuss, Charles M., Jr. *Sea of Grass: The Maritime Drug War, 1970–1990*. Annapolis, MD: Naval Institute Press, 1996.

Glen, Susan L. *Images of America: Governors Island*. Charleston, SC: Arcadia Publishing, 2006.

Helvarg, David. *Blue Frontier: Dispatches from America's Ocean Wilderness*. San Francisco: Sierra Club Books, 2006.

Holland, Francis Ross, Jr. *America's Lighthouses*. Brattleboro, VT: Stephen Greene Press, 1972.

Intergovernmental Panel on Climate Change. *Climate Change 2007: The Physical Science Basis–Summary for Policymakers*. Contribution of Working Group 1 to the Fourth Assessment Report. Geneva: IPCC Secretariat, 2007.

Jeffers, H. Paul. *Burning Cold*. St. Paul, MN: Zenith Press, 2006.

Johnson, Robert Erwin. *Guardians of the Sea*. Annapolis, MD: Naval Institute Press, 1987.

Judd, Ralph. *The Coast Guard in Film*. Victoria, BC: Trafford Publishing, 2006.

Junger, Sebastian. *The Perfect Storm*. New York: Norton, 1997.

Kaplan, H .R., and James F. Hunt. *This Is the Coast Guard*. Cambridge, MD: Cornell Maritime Press, 1972.

King, Irving H. *The Coast Guard Under Sail*. Annapolis, MD: Naval Institute Press, 1989.

Krietemeyer, George E. *The Coast Guardsman's Manual*. 9th ed. Annapolis, MD: Naval Institute Press, 2000.

Kroll, C. Douglas. *Commodore Ellsworth P. Bertholf*. Annapolis, MD: Naval Institute Press, 2002.

Labaree, Benjamin, William Fowler Jr., John Hattendorf, Jeffrey Safford, Edward Sloan, and Andrew German. *America and the Sea: A Maritime History*. Mystic, CT: Mystic Seaport Museum, 1998.

LaGuardia-Kotite, Martha J. *So Others May Live*. Guilford, CT: Lyons Press, 2006.

Langewiesche, William. *The Outlaw Sea*. New York: North Point Press, 2004.

Larzelere, Alex. *The Coast Guard at War: Vietnam, 1965–1975*. Annapolis, MD: Naval Institute Press, 1997.

Lewan, Todd. *The Last Run*. New York: HarperCollins, 2004.

Magee, Mike, ed. *All Available Boats: The Evacuation of Manhattan Island on September 11, 2001*. New York: Spencer Books, 2002.

Mansharamani, Vikram. "The Deepwater Program: A Case Study in Organizational Transformation Inspired by the Parallel Interaction of Internal and External Core Groups." M.S. thesis, Massachusetts Institute of Technology, 2004.

National Research Council of the National Academies. Committee on the Assessment of U.S. Coast Guard Polar Icebreaker Roles and Future Needs. *Polar Icebreakers in a Changing World*. Washington: National Academies Press, 2007.

Noble, Dennis L. *Rescued by the U.S. Coast Guard*. Annapolis, MD: Naval Institute Press, 2005.

———. *That Others Might Live*. Annapolis, MD: Naval Institute Press, 1994.

———. *The Rescue of the Gale Runner*. Gainesville: University Press of Florida, 2002.

O'Toole, James M. *Passing for White: Race, Religion, and the Healy Family, 1820–1920*. Amherst: University of Massachusetts Press, 2002.

Ostrom, Thomas P. *USCG: 1790 to the Present*. Oakland, OR: Red Anvil Press, 2004.

Pearcy, Arthur. *U.S. Coast Guard Aircraft Since 1916*. Annapolis, MD: Naval Institute Press, 1991.

Pew Oceans Commission. *America's Living Oceans: Charting a Course for Sea Change*. Arlington, VA: Pew Oceans Commission, 2003.

Philbrick, Nathaniel. *Sea of Glory*. New York: Penguin, 2003.

Phillips, Donald T., and James M. Loy. *Character in Action*. Annapolis, MD: Naval Institute Press, 2003.

Schreiner, Samuel A., Jr. *Mayday! Mayday!* New York: Donald I. Fine, 1990.

Shanks, Ralph, and Wick York; Lisa Woo Shanks, ed. *The U.S. Life-Saving Service*. Novato, CA: Costaño Books, 2004.

Shannon, Terry. *Sentinels of Our Shores*. San Carlos, CA: Golden Gate Junior Books, 1969.

Skoma, Lenore. *The Keeper of Lime Rock: The Remarkable True Story of Ida Lewis, America's Most Celebrated Lighthouse Keeper*. Philadelphia: Running Press, 2003.

U.S. Coast Guard Office of Budget and Programs. *U.S. Coast Guard Posture Statement*. CG-82, Feb. 2008.

U.S. Coast Guard. *U.S. Coast Guard: America's Maritime Guardian*. Coast Guard Publication 1. Washington: U.S. Department of Transportation/U.S. Coast Guard, 2002.

———. *U.S. Coast Guard Incident Management Handbook*. COMDTPUB P3120.17. Washington: GPO, 2001.

U.S. Commission on Ocean Policy. *An Ocean Blueprint for the 21st Century*. Washington: U.S. Commission on Ocean Policy, 2004.

U.S. Congress. House. Select Bipartisan Committee to Investigate the Preparation for and Response to Hurricane Katrina. *A Failure of Initiative*. Washington: GPO, 2006.

U.S. Department of Homeland Security. Office of Inspector General. *Acquisition of the National Security Cutter, U.S. Coast Guard*. OIG-07-23, Jan. 2007.

———. *Improvements Needed in the U.S. Coast Guard's Acquisition and Implementation of Deepwater Information Technology Systems*. OIG-06-55, Aug. 2006.

———. *110'/123' Maritime Patrol Boat Modernization Project*. OIG-07-27, Feb. 2007.

U.S. General Accounting Office. *Coast Guard: Deepwater Program Acquisition Schedule Update Needed*. GAO-04-695, June 2004.

———. *Coast Guard: Progress Being Made on Deepwater Project, but Risks Remain*. GAO-01-564, May 2001.

———. *Coast Guard's Acquisition Management: Deepwater Program: Justification and Affordability Need to Be Addressed More Thoroughly*. GAO/RCED-99-6, Oct. 1998.

——— Office. *Contract Management: Coast Guard's Deepwater Program Needs Increased Attention to Management and Contractor Oversight*. GAO-04-380, March 2004.

U.S. Government Accountability Office. *Coast Guard: Changes to Deepwater Plan Appear Sound, and Program Management Has Improved, but Continued Monitoring Is Warranted*. GAO-06-546, April 2006.

———. *Coast Guard: Observations on the Preparation, Response, and Recovery Missions Related to Hurricane Katrina*. GAO-06-903, July 2006.

———. *Coast Guard: Observations on the Fiscal Year 2009 Budget, Recent Performance, and Related Challenges*. GAO-08-494T, March 2008.

———. *Maritime Transportation: Major Oil Spills Occur Infrequently, but Risks Remain*. GAO-08-357T, Dec. 2007.

———. *Preliminary Observations on the Condition of Deepwater Legacy Assets and Acquisition Management Challenges*. GAO-05-651T, June 2005.

Walling, Michael G. *Bloodstained Sea: The U.S. Coast Guard in the Battle of the Atlantic, 1941–1944*. Camden, ME: International Marine/McGraw-Hill, 2004.

Wells, William R., II. *Shots That Hit*. Washington: Department of Transportation/U.S. Coast Guard, 1993.

Willoughby, Malcolm F. *Rum War at Sea*. Washington: Treasury Department/U.S. Coast Guard, 1964.

Wright, David, and David Zoby. *Fire on the Beach: Recovering the Lost Story of Richard Etheridge and the Pea Island Lifesavers*. New York: Oxford University Press, 2002.

INDEX